PRINCIPLES OF
ROMAN ARCHITECTURE

PRINCIPLES OF ROMAN ARCHITECTURE

MARK WILSON JONES

YALE UNIVERSITY PRESS   NEW HAVEN AND LONDON

Published with the assistance of
THE LEVERHULME TRUST
THE GRAHAM FOUNDATION
THE SAMUEL H. KRESS FOUNDATION

Designed by Gillian Malpass and Mark Wilson Jones

Printed in Singapore

Library of Congress Cataloging-in-Publication Data

Wilson Jones, Mark
    Principles of Roman architecture / Mark Wilson Jones.
        p.   cm.
    Includes bibliographical references and index.
    ISBN 0-300-08138-3 (alk. paper)
    1. Architecture, Roman.   2. Architecture–Rome.   I. Title.
NA310.W55   2000
722′.7 – dc21   99-14920
                                                                    CIP

A catalogue record for this book is available from
The British Library

FRONTISPIECE   The interior of the Temple of Bacchus,
Baalbek, Lebanon (mid-2nd century AD),
looking from the adyton back towards the entrance.

ENDPAPERS   The Temple of Artemis, Gerasa (Jordan),
detail of exterior columns.

For Donatella and Georgia,
always on my mind

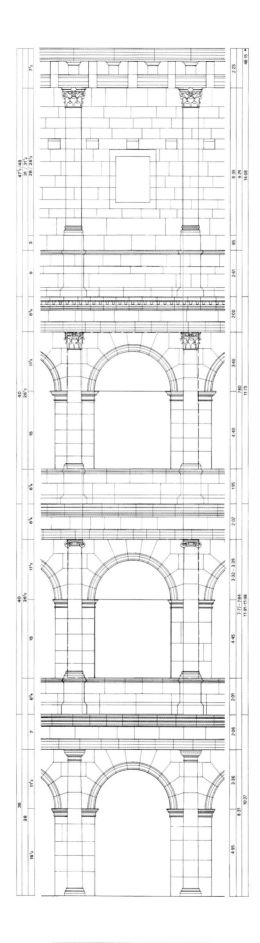

CONTENTS

NOTE TO THE READER

MODERN PLACE NAMES ARE PREFERRED over their ancient equivalents (e.g. Baalbek rather than Heliopolis, Turin rather than Augusta Taurinorum), unless the former are relatively obscure by the standards of general usage.

The bibliography aims to be representative rather than comprehensive, and is biased towards recent publications and ones that are relatively easily accessible in specialist libraries. It is arranged in sections according to chapters and sub-themes. Each section is identified by the abbreviation S. in square brackets, e.g. [S.2A] or [S. 7E]. There is also a general section at the beginning of the bibliography which is abbreviated S.G, so the reference 'Lanciani 1897 [S.GA]' shows that the full citation appears in the general section, part A. The absence of such an abbreviation after author-date references in the notes means that the citation can be found in the section relating to the current chapter. References to Vitruvius are generally given in the text, the translations being those of William Hickey Morgan's edition.

Selected measurements relating to buildings discussed in the text are listed in Appendix A, and grouped according to the appropriate chapter, while those relating to Corinthian columns are listed in Appendix B. Again, these do not pretend to be comprehensive, and for more detail the reader should consult the source publications cited, or other works included in the bibliography. Unless otherwise stated, all measurements in the 'imperial' system (feet, inches and so on) refer to ancient units, usually based on the Roman foot of around 296 mm rather than its modern Anglo-American equivalent of 304.8 mm.

The main research for this book was concluded in 1997, but I have endeavoured to take account of later publications whenever feasible.

ACKNOWLEDGEMENTS

THIS BOOK IS NOT JUST a funnel for my own research, but a funnel too for the ideas and efforts of all those who have collaborated or exchanged ideas with me over the past few years. I have been supported by many institutions in many ways, and in human terms too by gifts of friendship and unselfishness for which I am boundlessly grateful. I wish here to express my heartfelt thanks: to Amanda Claridge, Lucos Cozza, John Onians and Patrizio Pensabene for helping me to believe enough in the project in the first place; to Paul Davies, David Hemsoll and David Jacobson, with whom I had the pleasure of writing articles that underpin parts of this work; to the late Heinrich Bauer, Malcolm Bell, Deborah Brown, Arnaldo Bruschi, Joseph Connors, Jim Coulton, Ippolita d'Ayala Valva, Janet DeLaine, John Dobbins, Clayton Fant, Lisa Fentress, Eric Fernie, Herman Geertman, Pierre Gros, Gilbert Hallier, Lothar Haselberger, Thomas Howe, John Humphrey, Susan Kane, Michael Koortbojian, Ann Kuttner, Lynne Lancaster, Roy Lewis, Manolis Korres, Rowland Mainstone, Martin Maischberger, Indra McEwen, Dieter Mertens, Andrew Morrogh, Frank Newby, Giorgio Ortolani, James Packer, Clementina Panella, Gianni Ponti, Friedrich Rakob, Peter Rockwell, Rolff Rottländer, Ingrid Rowland, Joseph Rykwert, Frank Salmon, Richard Schofield, Frank Sear, Florian Seiler, John Stamper, Peter Stewart, Robert Tavernor, Susan Walker, Katharine Welch, Bill Westfall and Fausto Zevi for sharing their own work and for freely giving much welcome advice and criticism; to the Soprintendenza Archeologica di Roma, and in particular Giangiacomo Martines along with Alessandra Capodiferro, Cinzia Conti, Maria Grazia Filetici, Irene Iacopi, Piero Meogrossi and Rosella Rea not just for access to monuments in Rome, but also for sharing their knowledge of them; to the Soprintendenza Beni Architettonici e Ambientali and in particular Mario Lolli Ghetti and Giovanni Bellardi, for repeated access to the Pantheon, where Piero Cardone was always ready to be of assistance; to the Commune di Roma and in particular Eugenio La Rocca, Roberto Meneghini and Lucrezia Ungaro, again for their scholarship quite apart from matters of an administrative nature; to the foreign academies in Rome for the use not just of their facilities but also for acting as the forum for so many invaluable scholarly encounters, chiefly the American Academy at Rome and the German Archaeological Institute, but above all the British School – my springboard for getting to know the city during two unforgettable years as the resident Rome Scholar in Architecture – and in particular Maria Pia Malvezzi, Valerie Scott and Andrew Wallace Hadrill, as well as others connected with the School back in Britain, including Robert Adam, John Lloyd, Geoffrey Rickman and John Tarn; to the libraries and staff of the Warburg Institute and the Institute of Classical Studies in London, for the use of their facilities and valuable guidance; to Nuşin Asgari, Dominique Darde, Naïde Ferchiou, Moshe Fischer for expert hospitality during study tours outside Italy; to Marc Belderbos, Fulvia Bianchi, Matthias Bruno, Donatella Cavezzali, Prue Chiles, Gabriella Greco, Philip Jacks, Matthias Bruno, Micheal McCarthy, John Moreland, Hugh Petter, along with Ben Bolgar and Carmine Carapella and other past students on the Rome Programme of the University of Notre Dame School of Architecture in Indiana, for help with the recording and drawing of surveys; to John Burge, Marco Pelletti of Cooperativa Modus, Tommaso Semeraro and Christine Simonis for their excellent drawings; to the following institutions for the financial support without which this project could not have flourished: the Leverhulme Trust for a research grant in the early stages; the Graham Foundation for a research grant in the concluding stages; the British Academy for supporting smaller projects which led to the present one; the Samuel H. Kress Foundation for a contribution towards the cost of reproductions; to the London office of Yale University Press, especially Elizabeth McWilliams and Abby Waldman, for somehow maintaining a judicious equilibrium between patience and efficiency, to Ruth Thackeray for her copyediting, and most of all to Gillian Malpass for being a model editor; and last but not least to my family for unfailing patience and for sustaining me through good times and bad.

Having divided people up according to the above categories, I remain conscious that the desire to avoid repetition has prevented repeated thanks to those deserving of mention in each of them.

PREFACE

AFTER TWO MILLENNIA Greek and Roman architecture still exerts an extraordinary influence, having made an indelible imprint on the collective psyche of western culture. Ancient buildings set standards of quality and rigour that continue to pervade ideas of what constitutes good design. Architects working in the classical tradition have always considered the study of the monuments as essential training, but even an iconoclast like Le Corbusier confessed to finding inspiration in the same source. Indeed, few travellers to Mediterranean countries resist the power of ruins poignantly to evoke humanity's quest for order, beauty and permanence. Their battered carcasses still induce a sense of wonder, provoking question after question in the mind of expert and non-expert alike. How did they first appear? What were they used for? How were they constructed? How were the materials obtained and transported? The question of how they were designed – the subject of this book – is potentially the most intriguing of all, for it embraces a range of such issues while leading directly to the heart of ancient architects' creative work.

This book is the fruit of the conviction that the answers are relevant to architects and designers as well as students of history. The Romans achieved a remarkably robust and yet subtle grasp of how to reconcile the potentially conflicting demands of theory, beauty, content and practicality. There is much still to learn from this unique capacity for synthesis even if today's perceptions and requirements are so radically different. As the inventor Buckminster Fuller (1895–1983) remarked, 'hope for the future is rooted in the memory of the past'.

My first sustained contact with Roman buildings came during tenure of the Rome Scholarship in Architecture at the British School. I went there primarily to explore the work of Renaissance architects, and one of the aims on my agenda was to gauge the degree to which it was informed by an appreciation of ancient practice. But using the existing literature to find out how 'the ancients' had designed in the first place

proved surprisingly difficult, in part because the study of ancient architecture has suffered from the tendency to view it as the domain of archaeology. However laudable they might otherwise be, archaeological publications often proffer an unexacting standard of architectural discussion, generally limiting themselves to issues of chronology, function and constructional technique. I came to see the need for a fresh look at Roman architecture from an architect's standpoint.

This study therefore concentrates on those aspects of Roman architecture that are expressly architectural in nature: design, composition, proportion and geometry – vital ingredients of the glue binding together everything from the overall concept for a project to its details. Scholarly convention has it that the way in which mathematics enters into design is usually considered under the heading of proportion, which is both off-putting and misleading, for proportion is of course a subset of design and not the other way round. But whatever the name chosen for this subject, it is undoubtedly one that is long due for re-appraisal, just as Peter Kidson notes in his entry on architectural proportion in the *Dictionary of Art*:

> It is possible to read magisterial studies of ancient and medieval buildings without ever encountering the notion that their designs might have been based on principles of proportion; and the very existence of such studies implies that even if proportions were present, their contribution to the proper understanding of the design was minimal. This is in marked contrast to the treatment of proportion in Renaissance and Baroque architecture, where its central importance has always been recognized.[1]

So, Kidson concludes that 'There is an overwhelming case for placing proportion once more high on the agenda', and one of the aims of this book is to fill the lacuna he identifies for the Roman age. Moreover, although the prime focus here is on the imperial period, some of the lessons learnt may be more widely applicable, for I believe that right from classical antiquity down to the Middle Ages there is greater continuity than is conveyed by most textbooks, preoccupied as they are with the important task of charting change and influence in the flow of human creativity.

The design of buildings is not only the architect's prerogative: it emerges out of a liaison with patrons and builders too, but the issues which are not necessarily the province of the architect – whether political, iconographical or decorative – are those which receive less emphasis here. Nor, as just intimated, are questions of chronology a priority; in the present context it is important not so much when a particular building was designed, but *why* it was designed as it was, and *how*? Since some modes of design remain in essence unchanged for centuries, the first task is to identify them, and only where there is a definite shift of intentions is it necessary to pin down when this occurred. In many areas there is frankly more work to be done before it is possible to get this far.

Most of Rome's chief ancient monuments were shrouded in scaffolding at some point during the 1980s and early 1990s, a unique circumstance that allowed me to scrutinize them at first hand and to make my own surveys. The prevailing view about ancient design method stresses its empirical component and the absence of any normative patterns, but on the contrary, the more I studied the monuments the more I saw signs of patterns, of shared principles – albeit not necessarily those promoted by Vitruvius and his Renaissance followers. The emphasis so often accorded to Vitruvius' three prerequisites of architecture – firmness, commodity and delight (*firmitas*, *utilitas* and *venustas*) – conspires to convey too great a stress on the practical and hedonistic aspects of Roman practice, obscuring a profound concern for abstract and subtle issues. A large part of this book is aimed at investigating and describing the principles that I understand to be paramount,

and its scope has therefore been adapted to suit this purpose. The vast spread of Roman culture over time and space, and the sheer quantity of construction left behind, has led many scholars to filter buildings according to functional types: temples, baths, amphitheatres, villas, aqueducts and so on. A typological format is an obvious candidate for the study of design procedures too, but one that brings with it the danger of losing sight of the prime goal – precisely those general principles that transcend such divisions. So leaving for the future the possibility of a second volume structured by type, this book is organized around a series of thematic chapters (Part I) and the detailed analyses of individual buildings (Part II) which allow us to see how principles bend to specific circumstances.

With this aim in mind, Part II takes as its point of departure phenomena that elude neat interpretations, ones that are in some way odd, enigmatic, illogical. While such things might blandly be assimilated within the overall picture as exceptions that prove the rule, resorting to such an easy truth minimizes opportunities to deepen an appreciation of how ancient architects worked. Indeed, the most puzzling buildings are those that demand particularly intense scrutiny, for if a model of Roman practice can be formulated which embraces not only the normal but also the abnormal, this is when it starts to take on real authority. For this purpose the chosen subjects of study are Trajan's Column (chapter 8) and the Pantheon (chapters 9 and 10), since they are not only exceptionally well preserved but also singularly curious. The latter constitutes probably the most debated problem of Roman architectural history, and as such its resolution makes a natural secondary goal of my research. Each of the chapters that precede those dedicated to this extraordinary structure are in fact in some sense preparatory steps towards this end.

INTRODUCTION

THE PROBLEM OF INTERPRETATION

THE PAUCITY OF KNOWLEDGE about ancient architects, combined with the limitations of the surviving literary sources, make the monuments themselves the primary source for understanding Roman architectural design. This brings into prominence the problem of how they should be interpreted, for the mute stones speak in different tongues to different people. After much soul-searching, art historical discourse is now acutely aware of its subjective nature, and the extent to which it mirrors both personal conviction and the prevailing intellectual climate,[1] an idea powerfully conveyed by Sigfried Giedion in his influential book *Space, Time and Architecture*:

> History is not simply the repository of unchanging facts, but a process, a pattern of living and changing attitudes and interpretations. . . . The backward look transforms the object; every spectator at every period – at every moment, indeed – inevitably transforms the past according to his own nature. . . . History cannot be touched without changing it.[2]

Take the famous sculptural group of the death of Laocoön and his sons in the Vatican Museums; the same pieces of marble could represent calm grandeur for Johann Winckelmann and an 'apotheosis of tortured expressionism . . . a terrible symbol of Hellenistic civilization at its last gasp' for Peter Green.[3] Emotion and taste might seem to weigh less in the interpretation of architecture than that of painting or sculpture, but their influence is only better disguised. Moreover, the nature of the archaeological record is such that it is often

0.1   Reconstruction of the elevation of the Forum Romanum, looking towards the so-called Tabularium, by Constant Moyaux (1866). This is one of the highly accomplished studies produced by prize-winning architects (*pensionnaires*) at the French Academy in Rome. The principal building which does not appear in figure 0.2 is the Temple of Concord, just behind the Arch of Septimius Severus.

0.2 (*above*) Forum Romanum seen through the portico of the Temple of Antoninus and Faustina (ca. AD 150). In the distance Palazzo Senatori rises out of substructures formed by the building known as the Tabularium (but also identified as the Atrium Libertatis). Against this background may be seen, from right to left, the Arch of Septimius Severus (fig. 6.26), the Temple of Vespasian, the Column of Focas and the Temple of Saturn.

0.3   City gate at Turin known as Porta Palatina (Augustan period), compared elevations: (a) based on survey of its actual state; (b) according to Giuliano da Sangallo (ca. 1495). Note the way he 'corrects' the composition by aligning the tiers of orders.

necessary to fill in lacunae in the evidence, a process in which personal preferences are bound to come to the fore. Suffice a brief glance at the Forum Romanum in its actual state (fig. 0.2) and any of the more comprehensive reconstructions available (fig. 0.1) to see how much latitude there is for judgement. Paper restorations of ancient buildings are in fact notoriously subjective, and plenty of them have been made to conform with ideas about how they *ought* to have looked in spite of contrary evidence. Renaissance survey drawings, for example, frequently 'correct' misalignments, lapses of symmetry and anything else felt to be out of place.[4] A case in point is Giuliano da Sangallo's 'improvement' of the Augustan gateway at Turin

(fig. 0.3),[5] while the Pantheon was a repeated victim of this practice, as shown in chapters 9 and 10. So the Renaissance conception of antiquity was a self-fulfilling myth: theory was projected onto the ancient ruins, which in turn were used as evidence to justify the theory.

Despite the quantitative basis of metrical and proportional studies, and the quasi-scientific manner in which they are sometimes presented, there is even in this field a remarkable span of opinion. The trouble here is that the lacunae to be filled in are not so much physical as virtual, for the aim of such endeavour is to reconstruct the mental processes that went into the creation of a building. What is more, it is all too evident that analysis does not necessarily improve with time, but that doctrines come and go as much on account of fashion as for their intrinsic validity, as Rudolf Wittkower has masterfully shown in his essay 'The Changing Concept of Proportion'.[6] *Mutatis mutandis*, there are three chief schools of thought on the subject of mathematics and architectural design. The first upholds the importance of simple arithmetical relationships, the second that of geometrical relationships, while the third regards both to be subordinate to other issues, whether artistic judgement on the one hand or the means of production on the other. While each of these positions goes back to antiquity (appearing to differing degrees in Vitruvius' treatise), the striking thing is the way they predominate in distinct historical periods.

The Renaissance is inextricably bound up with arithmetical proportion. This is a time when mathematical harmony was considered an axiom of good design. In part due to the influence of Neo-Platonism, microcosm and macrocosm were held to relate by number, a way of thinking that favoured whole number or commensurable arithmetical ratios over the geometrical and incommensurable ratios which are generally associated with medieval practice. Wittkower may have exaggerated in singling out commensurability 'as the nodal point of Renaissance aesthetics',[7] but his assertion remains substantially valid, as so many of the contemporary codifications of the orders illustrate (figs 0.4 and 0.5).

The bridge between beauty and mathematics came under sustained attack in the eighteenth century; Wittkower saw the turning-point as Edmund Burke's *Enquiry into the Origin of our Ideas of the Sublime and the Beautiful* (1757), with its refutation that beauty had anything to do with calculation, as well as the work of David Hume, which in effect launched a philosophical system supporting the notion that beauty is in the

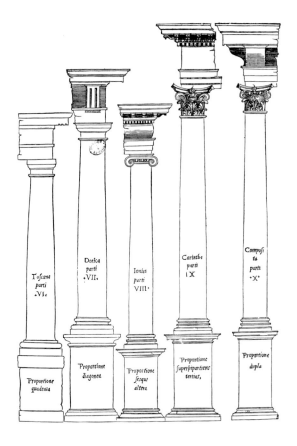

0.4 (*above left*) The five orders according to Serlio (1537), with from left to right Tuscan, Doric, Ionic, Corinthian and Composite. Note the annotated proportional ratios in roman numerals, with the slenderness ratios of the columns progressing from 6 to 10.

0.5 (*above right*) The five orders according to Claude Perrault (1683), with slenderness ratios ranging from $7\frac{1}{3}$ to 10.

0.6 (*right*) A plate from Antoine Desgodets' *Les édifices antiques de Rome* (1682) showing the order of the Temple of Saturn (AD 360–380, incorporating recycled elements from earlier buildings). Measurements are recorded in terms of the French foot (*pied du Roi*) of 325 mm and in minutes, 60 of which equal the lower diameter of the column. Desgodets' surveys provided the raw data for Perrault's analysis of ancient proportions.

eye of the beholder.[8] The Romantic movement fostered an increasing preoccupation with the irrational, the imaginative, the visionary, but for many geometry was yet compatible with such things in as much as it involved drawing and therefore art. During the nineteenth century a great variety of geometrical theories

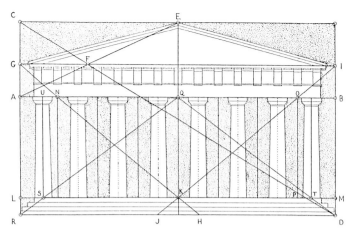

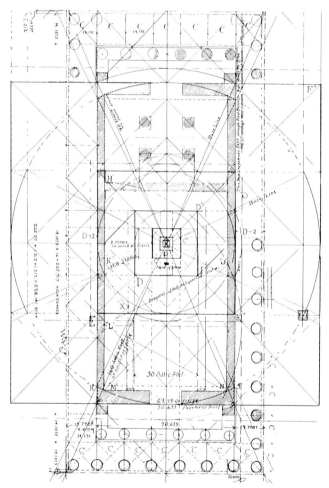

0.7 (*top*) Design analysis of the front of the Parthenon, Athens, according to Jay Hambidge (1924).

0.8 Design analysis of the Parthenon, according to Robert Gardner (1925).

became increasingly popular, and in the first decades of the twentieth such speculations became epidemic, typified by Jay Hambidge's seductive notion of 'Dynamic Symmetry' (fig. 0.7).[9] The aura surrounding the ratio known as the golden section inspired Le Corbusier and like-minded artists to set up a group called after it, Le Section d'Or. A related phenomenon is probably best understood in psychological terms, namely the need to unify the architecture of different periods via a single underlying theme or force. Various scholars have sought to show how everything from Egyptian temples to Gothic cathedrals answer to a single type of geometrical conception, whether the golden section,[10] the equilateral triangle,[11] the 'Sacred Cut' and so on.[12] These geometries continue to attract support (see pp. 101–6, 126–7), if not to such a wide-ranging extent as they did a few decades ago.

No doubt a backlash was inevitable. Sir Theodore Cook, whose work on organic growth patterns had inspired in part the notion of Dynamic Symmetry, published in 1922 an attack on interpretations of this kind with the crushing title 'A New Disease in Architecture'.[13] William Bell Dinsmoor, the leading inter-war expert on Greek archaeology, poured scorn on attempts to derive the Parthenon and other Greek temples 'from more of less intricate geometrical diagrams such as interrelated concentric circles and squares, pentagons or pentagrams, hexagons and hexagrams, octagons, decagons, "whirling squares" or the "golden section"'.[14] Figure 0.8, taken from Robert Gardner's book of 1925, *The Parthenon: Its Science of Forms*, is representative of the sort of thing that Dinsmoor had in mind.[15] Of course it almost goes without saying that scholars are still a long way from agreeing how the Parthenon was created, witness the often discordant interpretations assembled in the publication of the *ParthenonKongress* of 1982.[16] At best, it seems that buildings are problematic subjects for a mathematical postmortem, with so many limits (axes, edges, mouldings etc.) that could potentially have been important to the original designer. At worst, enterprises of this sort are misguided humbug deserving of parody, witness Umberto Eco's fictional analysis of a lottery kiosk in *Foucault's Pendulum*:

go and measure that kiosk. You will see that the length of the shelf is 149 centimetres, that is to say one hundred-billionth of the distance Earth-Sun. The height at the back divided by the width of the window makes 176/56 = 3.14 (i.e. π). The height at the front is 19 centimetres and so equal to the Greek lunar cycle. The sum of the heights of the two frontal projections and the two rear projections makes 190 × 2 + 176 × 2 = 732, or the date of the victory at Poitiers. The thickness of the shelf is 3.1 centimetres and the width of the cornice of the window is 8.8 centimetres. Substituting the numbers with the corresponding letters of the alphabet we have $C_{10}H_8$, the formula of naphthalene.[17]

There are dangers in squeezing the chequered history of ideas into too tight a historical framework, and there are, of course, plenty of instances that buck the trend. Cesare Cesariano's geometrical analysis of Milan Cathedral, for example, is a strange inclusion in any edition of Vitruvius, let alone one of the early sixteenth century. When discussing proportions at the end of the next century François Blondel confined himself, as might be expected, to simple arithmetical relationships, but turning to the Pantheon he convinced himself of the merits of geometry instead (fig. 0.9), thus explaining perhaps its unique character.[18] Then again the eighteenth-century belief in the importance of perception was anticipated by a current of fifteenth-century opinion that Leon Battista Alberti denounced,[19] not to mention Michelangelo's famous remark that 'all the reasoning of geometry and arithmetic, and all the proofs of perspective are of no use to a man without an eye'.[20]

Such cases aside, a broad spectrum of ideas about architectural design can be directly related to the backcloth just described. Changing attitudes towards the design of the orders makes a particularly good barometer. In the Renaissance period, columns and their components were habitually defined by canons of proportion; dozens of variations presented a sequence from Tuscan through to Composite graded by ornament and slenderness (figs 0.4 and 0.5). The ratios involved were almost invariably simple, so Serlio's column heights, for example, progressed in rational fashion from 6, 7, 8, 9 to 10 diameters tall, thus beginning and ending with the two numbers that Vitruvius (III, 1) held to be perfect.

Interestingly enough in the present context, the development of ideas about proportion has repeatedly been influenced by the study of ancient architecture.

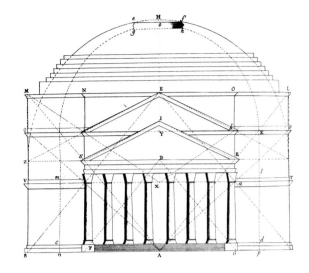

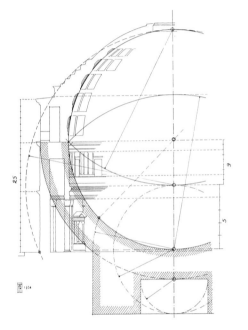

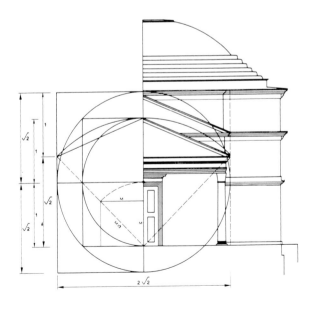

0.9 (*top*) Design analysis of the front of the Pantheon, Rome, according to François Blondel (1698). The actual proportions have been subtly modified to suit the proposal.

0.10 (*centre and bottom right*) Design analyses of the Pantheon: (a) sectional elevation of rotunda according to André Texier (1934); (b) elevation of exterior, according to Herman Geertman (1980).

It is true that Serlio, like so many before and after, was guilty of extensive numerical tidying, but the previous generation of architects in Rome had already begun to bring to the art of surveying the same spirit of attentive observation that Leonardo da Vinci brought to anatomical dissection. Dimensions, calculations and analytical notes on the survey drawings of Antonio da Sangallo the Younger and Baldassare Peruzzi bear witness to a nascent archaeological approach,[21] and it was this that sowed the seeds of dissent that ultimately fractured the cosy vision of neat patterns. Peruzzi's lost comparative study of the orders apparently showed him that Vitruvius had fixed on only a few possibilities, which were not among the most beautiful.[22] Although the issue of proportion continued to excite debate,[23] significant progress was not made until the newly formed Académie Royale de l'Architecture (1671) set out to resolve the question by commissioning Antoine Desgodets to make a comparative survey of Rome's most prominent antiquities.[24] The outcome was a milestone in its field (even if Desgodets' team sometimes faked accuracy for details that were inaccessible); for the first time it was possible to compare a series of detailed surveys drawn and annotated in the same way (fig. 0.6). Their evaluation was entrusted to Claude Perrault, the respected physicist-physician and dilettante architect, who produced a series of tables that seemed to demonstrate irrefutably that the ancients did not adhere to mathematical rules after all.[25]

In part as a result of Perrault's arguments, by the eighteenth century the mathematics of the orders had slipped down the agenda, and it is similarly typical of nineteenth-century academic method that J.-N.-L. Durand, the guiding light at the Ecole Polytechnique, should reduce composition to one of the simplest of all geometrical concepts, the grid.[26] Square grids supplemented by diagonal axes and arcs of a circle were used to organize both plan and elevation, a matrix in which the orders were obliged to fit as best they could. The same may be said of the geometrical schemes produced by scholars in the twentieth century to explain the design of whole structures such as the Pantheon (fig. 1.16), for again the size of the order depends on the diagram rather than the other way around.[27] And André Texier's study of the Library of Hadrian (fig. 1.16) illustrates how geometry could be applied to detailed design too. The orders, it seems, escaped the tyranny of arithmetic only to succumb to the tyranny of geometry instead.

By and large, however, contemporary scholarship has but extended Perrault's thesis, this time often rejecting geometrical as well as arithmetical method. Excavations from all around the Mediterranean continue to document the Greeks' and the Romans' taste for variety. What is more, some proportions change with time, a fact that also sits ill with the existence of fixed rules.[28] Recent textbooks state the case plainly, as in the words of Pierre Gros:

> The empirical character of Roman architecture, and the almost total absence of a normative system, is soon clear to anyone who studies it, whatever the type of building and whatever the period considered.[29]

Meanwhile, William MacDonald affirms that

> the orders were viewed undogmatically and were freely set about: the results resemble neither Vitruvius' putative norms nor the work of his Renaissance interpreters.[30]

So today's reader can be forgiven for agreeing with Sir John Summerson's dismissal of past thinking about proportions as 'a vast amount of pretentious nonsense', and refusing, as he did, to tackle the subject.[31] But to do so is to bypass a cornerstone of Roman practice. Besides, statements of this kind leave an uncomfortable vacuum, suggesting how the Romans did *not* design, rather than how they actually did.

TOWARDS A NEW SENSIBILITY

Against this background any new interpretation inevitably invites criticism. Must it not just be a late twentieth-century re-reading of history in its own image? Why should it be any better than the preceding ones it hopes to supersede? But while the answer to the first question must be yes – and there is nothing wrong with that – the second invites some brief introductory comments.

A mainstay of any modern appraisal of the built evidence is the comparative study of numerous exempla, the aim being not so much to ape statistical method as to combat the all too human tendency to select material that fits one's argument. It is true that comparison of like with like was already the basis of the work of Desgodets and Perrault in the 1680s, but there are important reasons why today this tool is potentially a much more effective one. Firstly there is the sheer weight of documentation, for whereas their data was culled almost exclusively from monuments in Rome itself, a great deal of information is now available from a range of ancient sites, from Morocco to Syria, from Egypt to Britain. Secondly (long after the point was apparent to connoisseurs in sixteenth-century Rome[32]), there is now a general recognition of the need to take into account the units of measurement used in antiquity, that is to say the Roman foot (or other local units subject to geographical location). This simple insight can lead to results that go far beyond the strict limits of metrology, a case in point being the theory advanced in chapter 10 to explain the form of the Pantheon portico.

The onus on modern scholarship is to distinguish the historically probable from the historically improbable. The prime arbiter in this endeavour is archaeological evidence of a technical nature, which must be taken into account even if it goes against accepted wisdom. It is salutary to recall the controversy over the reconstruction of the interior frieze from the Temple of Apollo at Bassae (fig. 7.3) which arose due to its component blocks being shipped off to London in 1812 without any record of their *in situ* position. For over a century the problem of the original sequence vexed a series of scholars, who proposed different 'definitive' solutions at intervals, each justified by a critique of the artistic, narrative and iconographic ideas behind the composition. Then Dinsmoor initiated something of a revolution in terms of methodology, for he put to one side the sculptural content and focused instead on the concealed edges of the blocks, in particular the cuttings for the metal dowels that tied the blocks to the wall. By matching the cuttings to the housings on the standing temple a layout emerged that resembled none of the previous proposals argued on art-historical grounds. While it must be admitted that Dinsmoor's specific proposal has been repeatedly challenged, no one disputes the fundamental value of his method; indeed the prime motor behind subsequent revisions has been the discovery of additional information of this kind.[33] So are we ever to trust complex reconstructions made on the purported understanding of the content of ancient sculpture?

Issues of technique relating to the production, erection and finishing of stone can in fact tell a great deal about design. Virtually neglected until the post-war researches of John Ward-Perkins was the system which supplied the Roman building machine with stone and marble, but thankfully there is now a thriving body of scholars dedicated to this area of research. Explorations at numerous Greek and Roman quarries have unearthed hoards of unfinished architectural blocks yielding invaluable clues about the procedures used to create them. For example, the extended speculations about the possible meaning of the Vitruvian term *scamilli impares* has finally been resolved by the discovery of real ones – that is to say circular countersinkings of varying depth – confirming that they

served in the calibration of the upward curvature of Greek temple platforms.[34] 'Hard' evidence relating to earlier phases of architectural design is relatively rare, and consists mainly of architects' working drawings and masons' marks. All but ignored until the 1970s, these have since come under intense scrutiny. More and more have come to light, and each divulges some precious insight into ancient architects' methods (chapter 3).

There are now known several sets of masons' marks relating to fluting, namely guidelines scored on to the otherwise complete surface of column shafts (figs 0.11 and 0.12). The initial step was to establish regular intervals near the top and bottom of column shafts. This involved the successive use of dividers, which were first used to identify the main quadrants and then to set out the individual fillets. Thereafter the relative width of fillet and flute was guided by ratios like 1:3 and 3:10, lines were scribed to define their edges, and circles added for the scalloped ends of each flute before cutting them (fig. 0.14).[35] What is interesting to note here is that each set of marks is slightly different from its cousins. So architects and/or masons did not resort to rote, but rather worked loosely around an agreed framework. As may be seen time and again in

0.11 Column shafts from the Central Baths, Pompeii, showing different states of working in hand when Vesuvius erupted in AD 79. Note the incised preparatory lines defining the orthogonal axes of the shaft and the setting out of the fluting.

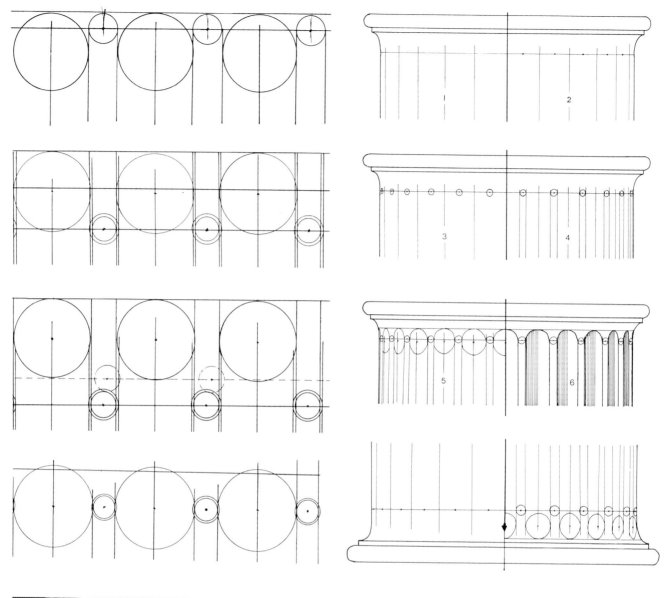

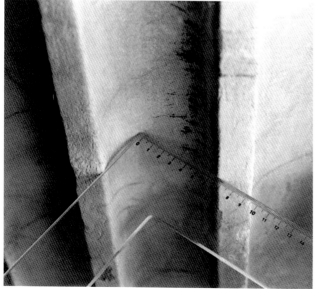

0.12 (*above left*) Masons' marks for setting out fluting inscribed on the circumference of column shafts in Rome: (a) Forum of Augustus (15–2 BC); (b) Temple of Vespasian (AD ca. 90); (c) Forum of Trajan (AD 105–112); (d) Temple of Hadrian (AD 140).

0.14 (*above*) Fabrication sequence for the creation of fluting typically used for Ionic, Corinthian and Composite shafts in the late republican and imperial periods.

0.13 (*left*) Demonstration of the applicability of the set-square method described by Vitruvius for gauging the shape of fluting, using the example of the columns of the tholos by the Tiber (mid- to late 2nd century BC). The desired profile – a perfect semicircle – is obtained when a set square rotates freely between the arrises of the fillets, as indeed occurs in this instance.

a range of contexts, the Romans' attitude to design was flexible; it was a matter of applying principles rather than fixed rules or recipes.

Despite the criticism that may be directed at Renaissance architects' habit of making surveys fit their own agenda, it is well to remember that the evidence sometimes supports their theories at the expense of more recent ones. A case in point is the means of calibrating entasis, the subtle swelling typically given to column shafts, as attested by ancient working drawings discovered at Aphrodisias, Pergamon and Didyma. In fact the first of these (fig. 6.31) bears an uncanny resemblance to Alberti's solution (fig. 0.15a), thus vindicating his claim to have derived it from the 'careful and studious observation of the works of the best (ancient) architects'.[36] Meanwhile Serlio's method (fig. 0.15b) corresponds closely with that used at Didyma (fig. 6.29).[37] Evidently ancient architects had no desire to complicate matters by using the parabolas and hyperbolas advocated by the champions of geometrical wizardry who published on the subject in the nineteenth and early twentieth centuries (p. 128).

At other times Renaissance architects' sympathy with antiquity comes out not explicitly in their publications, but implicitly via their buildings. To Baldassare Peruzzi goes the credit for intuiting a principle that was as fundamental to ancient architecture as it is absent from modern textbooks on the subject. Every set of doors in Palazzo Massimo (fig. 0.16) takes the same overall proportions based on a double-square opening, yet each set of mouldings is a unicum, a studied essay on how to avoid monotony. Here is a remarkable grasp of the dialogue between rule and variety that is more than anything the 'secret' of the antique approach to design.[38] Peruzzi appreciated that Roman architects succeeded in capturing the human condition: that we are all the same and yet unique.

Peruzzi's sensibility serves as an antidote to the often overly narrow vision of modern specialists, who while they might admit that the Romans used proportion, see it as just a tool for pragmatic ends. For example, the occurrence of round dimensions in disparate facets of building, from brick production to town planning, is associated with convenience and organizational efficiency. Likewise where simple columnar ratios are recognized, they tend to be regarded as mere rules of thumb, and therefore symptomatic of an essentially mechanical approach. But why impoverish the appreciation of architecture by imposing a rigid line of interpretation, be it excessively theoretical or excessively pragmatic? After all, the phenomenon of Roman architecture is the output of generation upon

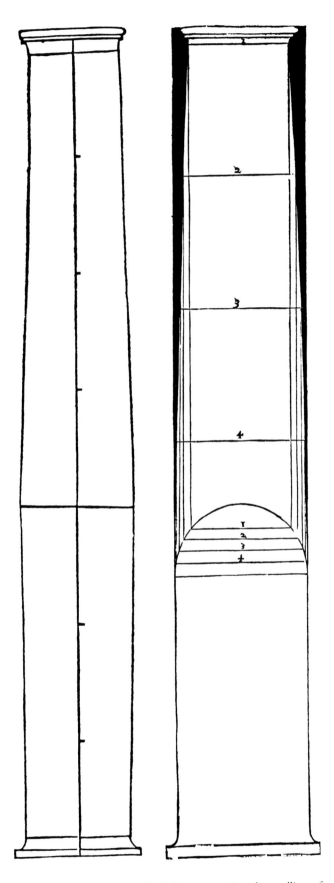

0.15 Two Renaissance methods for constructing the swelling of column shafts known as entasis: (a) according to Leon Battista Alberti (ca. 1450); (b) according to Sebastiano Serlio (1537).

0.16 The doors of Palazzo Massimo, Rome (1531–6) by Baldassare Peruzzi, arranged in ascending size 1:75 and 1:25. Each set of architraves and cornices displays a unique sequence of mouldings, yet key proportions are constant (all openings have a height-to-width ratio of 2:1, and the total height of each door case relates to that of the opening as 4:3).

generation of practitioners, each with their own particular concerns. It goes without saying that individuals must have held diverging views. Just consider, for example, the world of difference between the notion of Doric as it appears in the ultra-conventional propylon in Athens (fig. 2.7) as opposed to the playful solutions adopted at the Palazzo delle Colonne (fig. 2.8), the Hall of Doric pilasters at Hadrian's Villa (fig. 2.9) and other buildings illustrated in chapter 6.

It is also important to realize that goals of contrasting character need not be mutually exclusive. It is a commonplace to hear ideals and practicalities opposed as if the one negates the other, but this book aims to go beyond such simplistic oppositions and to grasp the dynamic and even paradoxical equilibrium between the ideal and the contingent, between rule and variety, that was the true goal of Roman architects. Design,

after all, is a multi-faceted activity that often eludes the logic of linear and exclusive argumentation.

To the ancient mind design was the art of reconciling harmoniously various types of input. In this regard it is worth dwelling for a moment on the words of two quite different writers. First are those of Plato, in a passage in which he sought to distinguish between absolute and relative beauty:

I do not mean by beauty of form such beauty as that of animals or pictures . . . but straight lines and circles and the plain and solid figures that are formed out of them by turning-lathes and rulers and measures of angles; for these I affirm to be not only relatively beautiful like other things, but they are eternally and absolutely beautiful.[39]

Second are those of the Roman surveyor Hyginus Gromaticus, describing the practice of land parcellation known as centuriation:

it has its origin in the heavens and its legacy is timeless; it is an easy-to-use system for surveyors which includes a certain width for straight-line boundaries; the appearance of the maps is beautiful and the marking out of the fields themselves is attractive.[40]

So here then is the sacred, the practical and the beautiful all rolled into one seamless, indivisible continuity. To make the same point in the realm of detailed design, it is well to return to the issue of fluting to look this time at the way theoretical, practical and aesthetic issues interact to determine the profile of the flutes themselves. Doric and Tuscan aside, Roman architects displayed a marked preference for semicircular profiles. Exceptions there were, of course (pilasters, for example, often have more shallow flutes because the revetment was too thin for the full depth given to columns), but the semicircle probably accounted for two-thirds or more of all imperial production. Why was this? From a theoretical standpoint the semicircle partakes of the mathematical perfection of the circle, while it is at the same time singularly appropriate given the circularity of columns. But a semicircular flute was also eminently practical, for this shape could be achieved by the method Vitruvius described (III, 5, 14), that is to say by progressively cutting away the stone between adjacent fillets until a set square placed between them rotates freely (fig. 0.13).[41] The great advantage of this method was that having laid out the sides of the flutes (figs 0.11 and 0.12) there was no need at all for any further measurement. And, unlike methods that relied on templates, column diminution implied no extra effort: the depth of the flutes was bound to reduce in proportion with the distance between the fillets. So it is clear that the most elementary technique imaginable produced the purest geometrical form: an irresistible combination for Roman architects. At the same time it goes without saying that the result had to be beautiful; for fluting is after all a decorative device *par excellence*. It contributes to the sense of verticality, like pin stripes on a pair of trousers or suit, while enhancing the roundness of shafts by creating a *chiaroscuro* effect. But then again, the very existence of fluting has a practical aspect. In the Roman period it is normally present only in shafts made up of drums, where it served to minimize the impact of jointing by creating lines of shadow in the other direction. By contrast, monolithic shafts were normally not fluted since there were no joints to hide, and furthermore a smooth surface best exploited the natural beauty of decorative stone.[42]

So it is this harmonious synchronism of principles, practicality and beauty that explains the longevity of the standard form of fluting. Here then in microcosm is a paradigm of Roman practice: only an interpretation which keeps these forces in balance has a chance of offering a meaningful insight into the architecture of the time.

WHEN THINGS WENT WRONG

Not everything by any means can be resolved so sweetly. Architects know only too well that in real life buildings do not always turn out as they initially had in mind. Compromise, changes of direction and imperfect execution are the normal stuff of building. For my own part, I have yet to see one of my own projects built without undergoing some sort of modification with respect to the original intentions. With luck, changes may be beneficial, but often they are not. Many designers will at some stage in their career have had cause to identify with Augustus Pugin when he complained – with characteristic melodrama – 'I have passed my life thinking of fine things, studying fine things, designing fine things and realising very poor ones. . . . I can truly say that I have been compelled to commit absolute suicide with every building in which I have been engaged.'[43]

Unwanted results may be attributed to a variety of causes, perhaps the fault of the builder, perhaps the result of circumstances that no one could have foreseen, perhaps a change of mind on the part of the client, perhaps the fault of the architect too. First of all, however, flaws or compromises must be *identified* for what they are. Problems of this nature are hardly ever broached in the context of Roman architecture. One obstacle is the near total loss of sketches, specifications and other preparatory material, a fact that has understandably led archaeologists to approach the subject as a *fait accompli* rather than a process (chapter 3). Another is the tendency to view the works of ancient builders through rose-tinted spectacles, as though they must be perfect almost by definition.

To give the lie to such a notion it is enough to conclude this introduction with a selection of more or less obvious mishaps. It is hardly surprising that long tunnels cut from both ends could fail occasionally to meet in the middle, a disaster that occurred at Saldae (Algeria), but that was put to rights – as the inscription he commissioned proudly records – by one Nonius Datus, an expert surveyor attached to the military.[44] Straightforward errors of workmanship are easy to recognize. A delightful example is an Ionic capital belonging to the synagogue at Gamla in Israel (fig. 0.17). The rule, of course, is for the volutes to mirror one another, just like horns of a ram: they should begin at the abacus and converge in a spiral, clock-wise on the right, anti-clockwise on the left. The mason must have been either a novice or very, very distracted: he made *both* volutes anti-clockwise, with the right hand one – unique in the

0.17 Ionic capital from the synagogue at Gamla, Israel (4th or 5th century AD). Contrary to accepted practice everywhere, the right hand volute winds in the wrong direction.

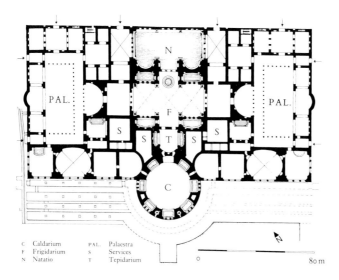

C   Caldarium   PAL. Palaestra
F   Frigidarium   S   Services
N   Natatio   T   Tepidarium
0   80 m

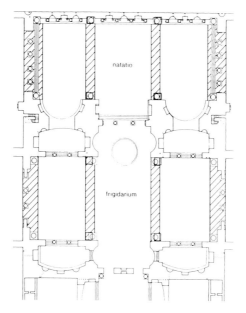

history of the Ionic capital – meeting the shaft at the neck.

Builders' errors occur even in Rome's most exalted monuments, as in the *natatio* of the Baths of Caracalla. This space was surely supposed to be perfectly symmetrical, in harmony with the plan as a whole, but the left-hand bay is appreciably wider than its mirror image on the right (figs 0.18 and 0.19). The discrepancy originated in the displacement by some 3 ft of a section of the foundations with respect to the correct position. This fault was only rectified at the level of the seating, resulting in an asymmetrical crescent shape for the bench contained within the left-hand apse.[45] One also wonders whether the crescent shapes on the upper level of the amphitheatre at Nîmes (fig. 0.20) were a similar making-do. These result from the use of different centres for different arches, a solution not uncommon in substructures, but one that was certainly unusual in such a prominent location, besides being notably absent from the 'twin' amphitheatre at Arles (fig. 6.22b). The error or compromise at Nîmes, if that is what it is, probably derives from a conflict between the composition of the façade and the demands of the circulation system immediately behind.[46] Amphitheatres were in fact one of the most onerous building types in the Romans' repertoire, since the oval shape raised technical difficulties in terms of layout and specification. In part for this reason, and in part because of errors or short-cuts made when converting measurements from standard Roman feet to their equivalents in the local unit, the facade of the amphitheatre at El Jem is one of the most ragged ever put up by ancient builders (fig. 0.23).[47]

The effect of corner details has to be anticipated whenever an architect wishes to achieve regular rhythms in elevation, a problem that famously afflicts the Doric order (p. 110). The Corinthian cornice, with its regular modillions, presented analogous problems, albeit less obtrusive given that they are so much smaller than triglyphs. Achieving a consistent modillion rhythm in a simple rectangular building was a straightforward matter, but series of setbacks and projections introduced complexities which often argued against perfect regularity (pp. 29–30). At the Temple of Venus

0.18 (*centre left*) Plan of the Baths of Caracalla, Rome (AD 212–216), 1 : 2500.

0.19 (*left*) Plan of the *natatio* of the Baths of Caracalla. The bay towards the right (south-east) was set out incorrectly at foundation level, being wider than its supposed mirror image towards the north-west (left). The error was rectified at ground level, resulting in a bench shaped like a crescent moon in the exedra.

0.20 Upper level of the facade of the amphitheatre at Nîmes, France (AD ca. 90). Note the unusual horseshoe shape of the reveal between the transverse vaults and the arches on the front face of the building (cf. fig. 6.22).

Genetrix the cornice over one of the re-entrant corners at the rear got completely out of control (fig. 0.21). There was no space available for the intended square corner coffer, forcing the modillion on one side to shrink to a blunt stub. The masons were at a loss to know how to carve such a thing, so they left it blank, and the typical rhythms of dentils and egg and dart had to be abandoned too.[48]

At this point it should be remembered that Greek buildings are hardly free of imperfections. The shrunken triglyphs and the squashed metopes over the pronaos of the second Temple of Hera at Paestum (fig. 0.22), for example, came about because the architect and/or builder failed to realize the effect of replicating the order of the peristyle in the pronaos at the same time as raising it up on a step. It appears that the incompatibility of this solution with the desired flat

0.21 Marble cornice block from the Temple of Venus Genetrix in the Forum of Caesar, Rome, re-erected in the Trajanic period (dedicated AD 113). Note the awkward arrangement of the various elements of the mouldings as they turn the corner, and in particular the transformation of the modillion into an undecorated stub.

0.22 Detail of the second Temple of Hera or so-called basilica at Paestum (ca. 470 BC), showing the contrasting proportions of the triglyph and metope friezes relating to the main facade and the pronaos. The frieze over the pronaos is the consequence of error or misunderstanding rather than a deliberate departure from normal practice.

ceiling did not come to light until the architrave was in place, at which point the only option available was to reduce the frieze height. In more general terms the likely root of such difficulties was the lack of familiarity with drawing in the archaic and early classical periods, depriving architects of a valuable tool for visualizing spatial relationships. By contrast, Hellenistic and Roman architects were readily conversant with drawings and models. Faults in their work are more likely to lie with the sheer complexity, size and speed of construction. Whereas Greek and Hellenistic projects are not particularly noted for speed, in the Roman world this was one way by which the emperors and potentates showed off their power. Ancient authors note with admiration the rapidity with which the Colosseum and the Baths of Titus were built, for example.[49] An inscription on the tomb of Gaius Cestius claims it was erected in just 330 days.[50] Precise start and finish dates are often difficult to determine, but there are occasions when literary sources, inscriptions and brickstamps furnish a reasonably secure picture. The Hadrianeum, a medium-to-large peripteral temple with thirty-eight or more columns 50 ft tall took less than six years from conception to completion.[51] The giant bath complexes of Trajan and Caracalla took only five. Hard as it may be to believe, the brick and concrete superstructure of the latter was put up in just three.[52] This is an incredible statistic for a building technology based on the 'wet' trades and labour intensive operations, and in this context a relatively minor error such as that affecting its *natatio* (discussed earlier) is only to be expected.

Speculative as they are, the preceding observations serve to stimulate a critical approach to looking at ancient monuments. Seeking to explain atypical or puzzling features encourages ways of seeing that may be more valuable than the conclusions themselves, forcing us to tackle some of the least charted aspects of Roman practice. This in turn offers opportunities for a more vital appreciation of what was indeed a most vital form of human expression.

0.23 (*facing page*) Perimeter of the amphitheatre at El Jem, Tunisia (AD 230–238).

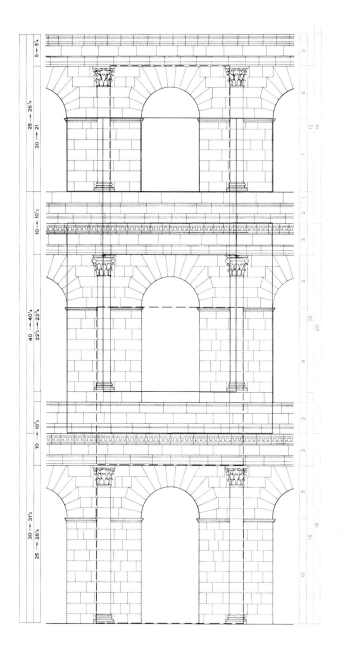

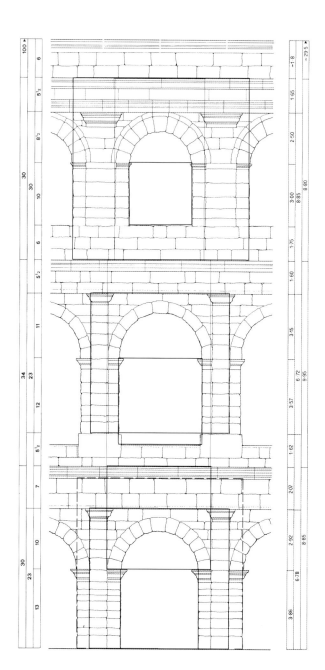

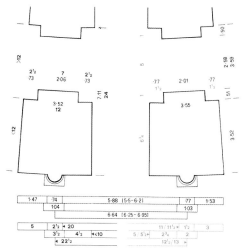

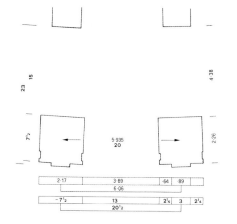

PART I

Elevations of typical bays of the amphitheatres at El Jem (*left*) and Verona (*right*).
1 : 1 relationships are highlighted by red squares,
and 1 : 2 relationships by blue double squares.
Measurements are in Roman feet (red) and Punic cubits (blue).

I

QUESTIONS OF IDENTITY

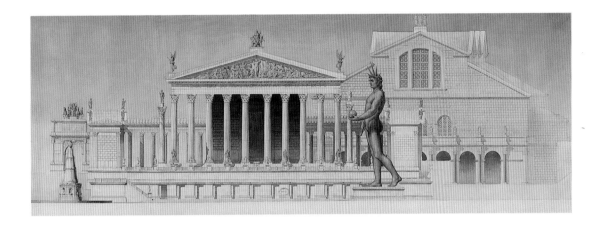

STUDIES OF CREATIVE PROCESSES in art or architecture tend to focus on individual protagonists, it being undeniable that the personalities of such figures as Michelangelo, Borromini, Gaudi or Frank Lloyd Wright fundamentally affected their output. But Roman architects are unsung heroes, shrouded by anonymity. While it may be possible to have a good idea about the original appearance of their buildings, including perhaps fittings and statuary, as well as the sort of activities that went on inside them (figs 1.1 and 1.2), the people responsible remain elusive. Precious little of precision may be said about the built work of even the two best known names on the Roman architectural stage, Vitruvius and the emperor Hadrian. Fascinating as it would be to compare Vitruvius' treatise with his practice, the 'father' of architecture has left not a single construction that is known today. By contrast, great tracts of building are linked to Hadrian, one of the greatest patrons of any period, but in his case it is tricky to know how much of it, if any, he actually designed.

Less is known about Roman architects than their Greek forerunners, who were frequently mentioned in inscriptions recording specifications, contracts or accounts relating to building.[1] Since it ceased to be normal practice to carve them in stone, virtually no comparable Roman texts survive, and those that do fail to indicate the architects involved.[2] The main written source on Roman architecture, Vitruvius' treatise (the subject of the next chapter), understandably provides no information about practitioners of the imperial period, which was only just dawning. Nor does it yield much about those of the republican period, for Vitruvius did not consider them on the same level as their Greek counterparts, some of whom had by his day attained an almost mythical status. In the preface to his second book, for example, he recounts at length the story of how the planner of Alexandria, Dinocrates, originally attracted his patron Alexander the Great's attention by dressing up as Hercules and proposing a hair-brained scheme for shaping Mount Athos into human form (fig. 1.3).

1.1 Perspective reconstruction of the main block of the Baths of Diocletian, Rome (AD ca. 298–306), by Edmond Paulin (1880) (detail). The sectional cut runs through the *frigidarium* and associated subordinated spaces.

1.2 Temple of Venus and Rome, Rome, first built AD ca. 130 and reconstructed by Maxentius. Reconstruction of the east elevation by Ernest-Georges Coquart (1863), with the *Meta Sudans* and the Arch of Titus (left) and the Basilica of Maxentius (right).

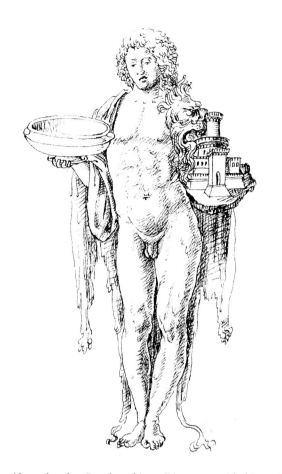

1.3 Alexander the Great's architect Dinocrates with his project for re-shaping Mount Athos, as visualized by Francesco di Giorgio on the basis of Vitruvius' description.

Lists of Roman architects' names have been compiled from other sources, including inscriptions on their tombs and passing references in letters and general histories; signatory inscriptions can also be found on some buildings, but they are too few and far between to constitute a reliable corpus.[3] It is ironic that potentially the most significant example, the name Vitruvius Cerdo inscribed on the Arch of the Gavi at Verona, has been primarily a source of confusion. For a long time this was identified with *the* Vitruvius, but in reality the two men lived decades apart, although they may have been related. The name Vitruvius actually occurs in a considerable number of inscriptions from around the Roman world, but none can be attributed with surety to the treatise writer. His cognomen is often cited as Pollio, but in reality this is no more certain than is his first name, variously Gaius, Lucius or Marcus according to different manuscript traditions.[4]

The cryptic character of Roman inscriptions is in fact a perennial source of difficulties. These are exemplified by the famous one on the front of the Pantheon, which identifies the great general Agrippa as the founder (fig. 10.2), even though it was erected well over a century after his death (pp. 200–02). And it so happens that hardly much less controversy surrounds the dedicatory inscription for Trajan's Column (see chapter 8). It is also instructive to reflect on the quality of the documentation relating to the so-called Tabularium, the massive backdrop to the Forum Romanum that is one of the most important monuments of the late republic (figs 0.1 and 0.2). In the fifteenth century an inscription was found in its substructures that cited Quintus Lutatius Catulus as the patron of a record office or *tabularium*, hence the name traditionally given to the whole building, the presumed repository of Rome's state archives. This also points towards the designer, by virtue of another inscription recording one L. Cornelius as Catulus' *praefectus fabrum* (chief surveyor or architect). But the idea that the ancient city ever had such an enormous record office now seems something of a mirage, and it is more likely that the *tabularium* in question was only a suite of rooms. Then there is the problem of knowing whether the Catulus mentioned in both inscriptions was really the same person. In short both the complex as a whole and its architect remain as good as anonymous.[5]

The most critical problem is the absence of plural well-preserved buildings reliably connected with the same architect, making it impossible to gauge how a particular individual reacted in different circumstances, and thus removing a basic staple of art historical analysis. To judge by the texts, one of the most important architects of the late republican period was a Greek immigrant from Salamis, a certain Hermodoros. He had the distinction of being mentioned by Cicero and Pliny the Elder as well as Vitruvius,[6] who assign him a series of important buildings including three major temples in the southern Campus Martius, that of Jupiter Stator, the first in Rome to be constructed of solid marble, one of Mars and another of Neptune. But all are lost save for some vestiges under the church of San Salvatore in Campo which perhaps belonged to Mars' temple.[7] A better chance to appreciate the nature of Hermodoros' work is potentially presented by one of Rome's better preserved monuments, the round temple or tholos by the Tiber (figs 4.7 and 4.13). This has been attributed to him on the grounds that it was built in the second half of the second century BC, around the time of his other temples, and that it was likewise made of Greek marble, and in part by Greek craftsmen too.[8] These are all quite reasonable pointers, but they are hardly enough to clinch the issue.[9]

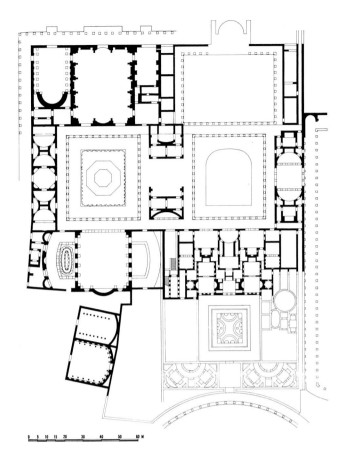

1.4 Plan of the Flavian palace on the Palatine, Rome, designed by Rabirius (inaugurated AD 92), 1 : 2000.

1.5 (*above right*) Detail of a cornice block from the Flavian palace, Rome. Note the lack of vertical alignment between the different types of moulding and the presence of small rings of tracery between the dentils, a characteristic that has sometimes been interpreted as the 'signature' of Rabirius, but one that is more likely to be the trademark of a particular workshop.

Nor is there much definite evidence for the careers of leading architects of the imperial period such as Severus and Rabirius. It may be that Severus directed the rebuilding of large areas of Rome destroyed by the great fire of AD 64, but the literature specifically assigns him only Nero's Golden House and the Avernus-Tiber canal. Moreover, the mention of the Golden House is a conundrum in itself, for nobody quite knows its full extent. Then again, of Domitian's grandiose projects possibly designed by Rabirius, only the Flavian palace on the Palatine is certainly his (figs 1.4 and 1.5).[10] No doubt both Severus and Rabirius were consummate architects, but this is not the point; it is impossible to know the confines of what they did, or how to distinguish their hands from those of their colleagues.

APOLLODORUS

Only a single Roman architect may be securely linked to more than one existing building of note: Apollodorus, Trajan's *praefectus fabrum*, or minister of works.[11] In addition, he was probably the author of a treatise on siege engines, of which part survives, and the only member of his profession to be the subject of an extended passage by a writer other than Vitruvius. To begin with his constructions, ancient sources credit him with what was evidently a magnificent bridge over the Danube, and in Rome an unidentified concert hall, Trajan's Baths and Trajan's Forum, the latter complex being widely considered to be the city's greatest architectural achievement. Although the ruins of the baths are substantial, they are isolated from one another and hard to take in; none the less the plan can be reliably reconstructed on paper. Trajan's Forum too is a shadow of its former glory (fig. 8.1), but the numerous columns visible on the site together with new evidence emerging from current excavations continue to provoke new reconstructions (fig. 8.2). The most imposing and most complete remnant of the forum is of course Trajan's Column, a masterpiece in its own right, and one that presumably came under Apollodorus' umbrella.

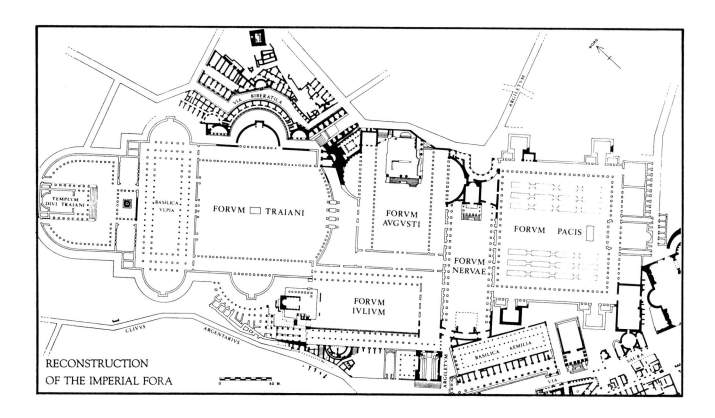

RECONSTRUCTION
OF THE IMPERIAL FORA

1.6   Plan of the imperial fora, Rome.

Apollodorus has also been linked to a variety of other structures built under Trajan's patronage in Rome and elsewhere,[12] of which the most important is Trajan's Markets (figs 1.7 and 1.18). There is even some reason to think that Apollodorus could have designed the Pantheon, and according to one view it was precisely his expertise as an engineer that lay behind its audacious span.[13] This particular attribution raises issues that are too complex to be tackled satisfactorily here, and are considered instead in the concluding chapters; in any case the difficulties of assessing authorship are well illustrated by Trajan's Markets. The idea that Apollodorus designed them is really based only on their proximity to the same emperor's forum, combined with the fact that he was his principal architect. Essentially the argument condenses to a question: why would Trajan have chosen someone else?[14] But even if an inscription discovered in 1992 does imply that the markets were regarded as part of Trajan's Forum, at least by the turn of the third century,[15] this need not necessarily mean they constituted a unified urban plan, let alone the work of the same person. Indeed it is possible to mount a diametrically opposed argument based on the contrasting character of the two projects. The

forum has a perfectly symmetrical and level plan, while its formal language relied on marble columns and trabeation. The markets weld themselves to a hilly, asymmetrical site, and are built throughout of brick-lined concrete walls and vaulting, with marble used merely as applied ornament. The blind barrier wall that separates the two could suggest that the forum turned its back on the markets, as it were, and one scholar even sees it as a gesture of hostility between Apollodorus and a rival architect, evoking the famous antipathy between Bernini and Borromini in the seventeenth century.[16] But this barrier in reality performed the same function as the huge boundary wall that protected the Forum of Augustus and its magnificent Temple of Mars Ultor from fire in the residential district beyond (figs 1.6 and 1.7), a device which had unquestionably proved its worth in the conflagration of 64. As for the many contrasts in character, they could less reflect the work of different personalities than differences in terms of site, programme and budget. It should also be noted that Apollodorus' Baths of Trajan contain materials typical of the forum (monolithic granite shafts and coloured marble facing), as well as those typical of Trajan's Markets. There is arguably more than just a passing resemblance between the concave hemicycle (fig. 1.18) and, seen from the exterior, the great convex exedra of the baths precinct: here in both cases is a brick wall pierced by arched openings, with projecting balconies sustained by chunky travertine brackets.[17] But questions of attribution cannot be resolved by such arguments, as it is not known how many other architects – including Apollodorus' collaborators – might have reacted in similar ways. Perhaps it is better to speak of an Apollodorus school or circle of influence (a notion pursued in chapter 9), although there does remain a sporting chance that Apollodorus himself was indeed the creator of Trajan's Markets; I would guess that the odds are better than 50:50, but not much so.

As for the treatise on siege engines, it has been argued that this is the work of at least two authors, and that neither was necessarily the same as the man responsible for Trajan's projects in Rome.[18] Since Apollodorus was quite a popular name at the time, the buildings, the bridge and the military treatise could have been split among different individuals. Did the one source that cites Apollodorus 'of Damascus' as the author of the Danube bridge do so in order to distinguish him from a namesake?[19] Yet it still remains a real possibility that all these strands were indeed pulled together in a man of many-sided genius, a living testimony to the polymath ideal invoked more than a century earlier by Vitruvius (pp. 39–40). One could argue back and forth *ad infinitum*, but the point is simply that ideas about Apollodorus, single or plural, rest on shifting sands. The fact that he is the best-known imperial architect underlines how little is known about the rest. While it is only human to try and personalize the vast archaeological heritage wherever possible, taken too far this can muddy appreciation as much as stimulate it.

The famous story of his quarrel with Trajan's successor Hadrian gives glimpses of Apollodorus' character: exacting, principled and abrasive. This was described in the eighty-volume history of Rome by Dio Cassius, himself twice consul under the emperor Septimius Severus. Some volumes survive intact and others were abridged by Byzantine scholars; the following passage comes unfortunately from the latter group, but it is still worth quoting extensively since it contains interesting material on almost every line:

> [Hadrian] first banished and later put to death Apollodorus, the architect who had built the various creations of Trajan in Rome – the forum, the odeon and the baths. The reason assigned was that he had been guilty of some misdemeanour, but the true reason was that once when Trajan was consulting him on some point he had said to Hadrian, who had interrupted him with some remark: 'Be off and draw your pumpkins. You don't

1.7 Axonometric view of the Markets of Trajan, Rome (AD ca. 105), school of Apollodorus?

understand any of these matters' – it chanced that Hadrian at the time was pluming himself upon some such drawing. When he became emperor, therefore, he remembered this slight and would not endure the man's freedom of speech. He sent him the design of the Temple of Venus and Rome by way of showing him that a great work could be accomplished without his aid, and asked Apollodorus whether the proposed design was satisfactory. The architect in his reply stated first, in regard to the temple, that it ought to have been built on high ground ... so that it might have stood out more conspicuously on the Sacred Way. . . . Secondly, in regard to the statues, he said that they had been made too tall for the height of the cella. 'For now,' he said, 'if the goddesses wish to get up and go out, they will be unable to do so.' When he wrote this so bluntly to Hadrian, the emperor . . . restrained neither his anger nor his grief, but slew the man. Indeed, his nature was such that he was jealous not only of the living, but also of the dead.[20]

All this is if anything more problematic than the attributions: a fascinating mix of fact and fiction. The disparaging reference to pumpkins or gourds was most likely an allusion to the scalloped vaults that were used to such effect at the future emperor's Villa at Tivoli, for there is an uncanny similarity between their profile and the curved segments of this vegetable; a scalloped or umbrella dome takes the shape that would be created if a giant half-pumpkin were used as the formwork (fig. 5.15).[21] The comments about the Temple of Venus and Rome are more dubious, as discussed in chapter 10, but the most striking part of the whole episode, Apollodorus' execution, was certainly invented as a slur on Hadrian, in keeping with Dio Cassius' efforts to portray him in a bad light.[22] Another source that defamed Hadrian on various occasions, the *Historia Augusta*, would surely have repeated the charge had there been any substance to it, but instead it links both men without a hint of friction.[23]

THE EMPEROR-ARCHITECT?

The theory that Hadrian sometimes took charge of design himself is an intriguing one, since it could account for the unique character of some of his projects, including the Villa at Tivoli (fig. 5.14) and, so some say, the Pantheon.[24] Hadrian was a man of undoubted intellectual and artistic brilliance; according to the author of the *Historia Augusta*, he was 'greatly interested in poetry and letters' and 'very expert in arithmetic, geometry and painting'.[25] It may seem unlikely that the emperor did more than dabble in architecture amidst his myriad duties and cultural pursuits, yet Thomas Jefferson, President of the United States for two terms, Governor of Virginia and founder of its university, still managed to find the time to create buildings and landscapes of lasting quality. He had a scaled-down Pantheon built as the focus for the university (fig. 10.13), so could not Hadrian have designed the prototype?

The problem with the Jefferson parallel is twofold. On the one hand his main projects date to either before or after his major appointments, whereas Hadrian's were built during his reign, of which more than half was spent far from Rome. On the other, it is less likely that in antiquity a passion for architecture was regarded to be as fitting for the educated landowner as it was in the eighteenth century. Architecture was too closely wedded to the manual trades to be a traditional pastime of the Roman aristocracy. The correct interpretation is probably that implied by the phrase in his biography which said Hadrian built 'with the aid of' the architects Decrianus and Apollodorus.[26] The emperor may be thought of as an architect in the broad sense of the term, as someone with the capacity for conceiving space and manipulating form; but if and when he did launch a specific design, its elaboration would have been the province of professionals. His creative output was most probably confined to briefing his architects to develop his obsessions (notably the scalloped vaulting to which Dio alludes), and pushing them in directions he approved of. In the fifteenth century Antonio Filarete acknowledged the patron's input with his analogy for the genesis of a building, likening the patron to its father, and the architect to its mother.[27] The father-patron seminates an idea in the mind of the mother-architect, who, after a period of gestation, delivers a project. In these terms, then, Hadrian was an unusually participatory and domineering father. At a time when Rome's political and economic power was at its zenith, Hadrian's position allowed him to instigate new buildings continuously, 'collecting them as other men collect sculpture or gems'.[28] He was no doubt the guiding spirit behind his extraordinary Villa; his personal plaything and architectural laboratory, it is the legacy of an inspired guru who guided his acolytes by force of a will stronger than theirs.

Hadrian must also have expected to have set the tone for the more important urban programmes in Rome and other cities. As mentioned above, Dio credited him with the design of the Temple of Venus and Rome, and it may well have been he who insisted on the low stylobate, the long proportions and the all-enveloping colonnade that were normal characteristics of Greek rather than Roman temples. These characteristics echo those of the Olympieion in Athens (fig. 2.11), a building that Hadrian himself brought to completion.[29] This is just the sort of thing to be expected from a patron with noted philhellenic leanings. And it may have been Hadrian too who conceived of the unique plan with the pair of back-to-back cellae (fig. 1.8). It rings of an intellectual conceit consistent with Hadrian's mind, one that could have been attracted by a sort of architectural palindrome. If Venus is equated with love (*amor*) then here is ROMA:AMOR whichever way you read, front to back or back to front, in sympathy with the mirror symmetry of the groundplan.[30]

In briefly considering the profession as a whole, it is first of all essential to understand the depth of imperial architects' debt to the Greek world, and especially the Hellenistic age, the period defined by modern scholarship as beginning in 323 BC with the death of Alexander the Great and ending in 31 BC, with the effective eclipse of the dynasties founded by his commanders following the defeat of Cleopatra at Actium. In these three centuries the practice of architecture became a profession. Up until that time the term *architekton* had referred to any expert in charge of a team of craftsmen; a 'career' in architecture might involve just one or two major projects, so few people earned their living by designing buildings alone. The demands of the Periclean building programme no doubt encouraged specialization, a trend that was to accelerate with the explosion of commissions in the wake of Alexander's conquests. The expanding cities of Asia Minor called for not just temples, stoas, theatres and fortifications, but also town halls, commemorative monuments, gymnasia, palaces, warehouses and harbour facilities. To cope with this demand, civic authorities began to employ architects on a permanent basis.[31] All manner of advances made at this time became fundamental to Roman practice, whether in the field of theory, draughting techniques, construction, water management, the manipulation of heavy weights, and so on. In short the Romans inherited not just their lexicon of architecture – building types, orders and ornament – but much more besides.

The accumulated Greek heritage filtered down via a number of routes, including the publication of treatises (pp. 37, 39). Conquest gave the Romans the physical possession of Greek territory. Following the victories, *inter alia*, at Syracuse in 212, Taranto in 209, Cynoscephalae in 197, Magnesia in 188 and Corinth in 146, untold quantities of loot were carted off to Rome for public display and private profit.[32] Sometimes this included parts of buildings, as when Sulla had columns from the Olympieion in Athens re-erected on the Capitoline (p. 152). Entrepreneurs set up ventures in Greece and Asia Minor to supply an insatiable demand for architectural elements and luxury fittings like those recovered from the spectacular shipwreck at Mahdia.[33] But equally important was the traffic in human resources, with substantial numbers of Greek-speaking artisans and architects arriving in Rome. Of the numerous architects whom Cicero cited, most still had Greek names (although this does not necessarily mean they were first generation immigrants). Their education gave

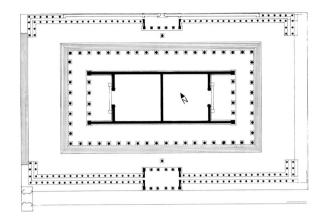

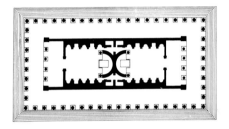

1.8 Temple of Venus and Rome: (a) diagrammatic reconstruction of the original Hadrianic plan, 1 : 2000; (b) the plan as transformed by Maxentius (AD ca. 310), 1 : 2000.

them the edge over the native stock, of whom many were illiterate, having risen through the building trades.[34] A further sign of the inroads made by Greek architects is the snide comment made by the same author when writing from Rome to his friend Atticus after he had moved to Athens: 'A fellow "countryman" of yours [i.e. an architect] is enlarging the city [Rome], which he had not seen but two years ago, and which he thinks is too small for him, even though in the past it was big enough for the master himself [i.e. Caesar]'.[35]

There were occasional movements against the flow. Cossutius went to Athens to work on the Olympieion in the 170s BC, to be followed by several of his relatives; Agrippa seems to have brought architects from Rome for the transformation of the Odeon, again in Athens; Herod may have done the same for some of his projects in Palestine, but these are very much the exceptions that prove the rule.[36] As Trajan's Governor of Bithnya (northern Turkey), Pliny the Younger requested that an architect be sent from Rome to resolve an intractable dispute over public buildings at Claudiopolis, but the emperor objected that it was more usual for architects to travel in the opposite direction – a remark that underlines Rome's continued debt to the east.[37]

Generalizations about architects' place in society require substantial qualification, since the range of possibilities was so extreme. At the top end of the scale stood Hadrian, emperor and dilettante, a freakish example, but one that finds parallels in more remote times. Gudea, a Mesopotamian ruler of about 2200 BC, had himself portrayed as an architect in a series of seated statues; in one he sits with a blank drawing-board on his lap, ruler and compasses at the ready, in another the board displays a finished plan (figs 1.9 and 1.10). The position of Apollodorus, a man who could stand his ground in the face of his sovereign, must also have been exceptional. Vitruvius himself probably belonged to the *apparitores*, officials who bridged the divide between the uppermost echelons of society and the populace at large, and his position must have been near the top end of the architect's social world.[38] The funerary relief of the architect-surveyor T. Statilius Aper (fig. 1.12) represents perhaps a median level in terms of social status.[39] While he could evidently afford a capable sculptor and a large piece of marble, it is also significant that the symbols of his trade chosen to accompany him include a roll or tube of drawings on the front of his monument, and a case of pens, measuring instruments and an abacus on the side. These invoke both education and a non-manual occupation, unlike the plumb-bobs and other practical tools that frequently appear on tombs belonging to builders or architects of humbler fortune (figs 1.11 and 1.13).[40] Freed slaves or their sons (no female architect is known from antiquity) were often among their number; and according to a doubtless inflated source, Crassus was

1.9 (*below left*) Statue of Gudea, the ruler of Lagash (ca. 2200 BC), seated with a drawing-board and plan on his lap. This is one of a series of statues of Gudea made of black diorite or granite on display at the Louvre, Paris.

1.10 (*below right*) Detail of plan on Gudea's lap.

reputed to have kept no fewer than 500 slaves who were architects, builders or both.[41]

In antiquity architects and engineers were practically indistinguishable, while the fact that Cicero troubled to spell out the distinction between *architectari* and *fabricari* (builders) confirms that in the late republican period they too commonly overlapped.[42] Of course the title builder also takes in a vast compass, from the jobbing handyman to the head of a large construction business. Cossutius, the reputed designer of the Olympieion in Athens (fig. 2.11) and one of the few Roman architects named by Vitruvius (VII, Pref., 15–17), belonged to a wealthy family whose interests included the extraction and supply of marble.[43] Presumably this Cossutius, or an immediate relative, was also one of the principal contractors. Vitruvius (X, Pref., 1–2) also relates how the city of Ephesos once had a

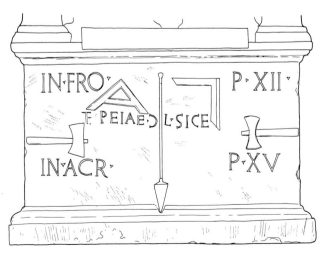

1.11 (*above left*) Tombstone of an architect or builder belonging to the *gens Aebutia*, Capitoline Museums, Rome. The owner's livelihood is symbolized by setting out instruments including plummet or plumb bob (*perpendiculum*), A-frame and bob (*libella cum perpendiculo*), set square, foot rule and a pair of dividers.

1.12 (*above right*) Funerary altar of the architect-surveyor (*mensor aedificior*) T. Statilius Aper, early 2nd century AD, Capitoline Museums, Rome; Luna marble slab, 1.89 metres high. With his wife Orcivia Anthis portrayed in the pediment above, Statilius Aper is accompanied by a child (Thanatos?), a boar, a document case (*capsa*) and on top of that either a roll of parchment(s) or a tube for protecting them.

1.13 (*right*) Base of a funeral monument belonging to a builder, with representations of setting out instruments and inscriptions recording the overall dimensions of the plot, 12 × 15 ft (IN·FRO[NTE]·P[EDES]·XII − IN·ACR[O]·P[EDES]·XV).

1.14 Scene from a Roman construction site at the port of Terracina, south of Rome. A high-ranking official (possibly Agrippa) sits while giving instructions. The architect, who is identified by a scroll of drawings or specifications in one hand, appears three times: to the right of his patron, by the A-frame jib, and by the group of workmen on the left.

law that compelled architects to pay for any overspend exceeding 25 per cent of the budget, which presupposes that architects enjoyed considerable personal wealth. Part of a sculptural relief found at Terracina presents a rare insight into the world of a successful architect-contractor (fig. 1.14). Unlike the static representations of funerary portraits, this shows an architect in action at the town port, as indicated by the tip of a trireme just visible at the right-hand edge of the block. The fact that this was a major operation is conveyed by the presence of a high-ranking official seated on a *sella curulis*, possibly Agrippa. Meanwhile the architect is represented no fewer than three times, each time with a *volumen* or roll of drawings in one hand. In chronological sequence he appears first by his master's side, and subsequently to both the right and left of the A-frame lifting device in the act of directing the workforce. The quality of the relief, the fact he was shown thrice and his close relationship with such a senior figure all suggest that this architect was a man of elevated social status, perhaps the main contractor (*redemptor*) for the whole project.[44]

In the imperial period the output of the private sector eventually came to be dwarfed by both the military and the civil arms of the state. Skills were rationalized along with the manufacture and supply of materials. Frontinus' manual on Rome's water supply mentions some two dozen grades of administrators and technicians, architects and engineers among them, in the municipal water department, or *statio aquarum*. Some sort of apprenticeship training would be a prerequisite for such a system, but virtually nothing is known of this. In late antiquity at any rate, the emperor Constantine issued an edict that encouraged the recruitment in the African provinces of potential architectural students/ apprentices 'who are about eighteen years old and have

had a taste of the liberal arts', with inducements including a salary and exemption from certain civic obligations.[45] A degree of specialization may have been encouraged in the interest of raising technical standards: an inscription tells of a hydraulic specialist stationed at the legionary headquarters of Lambaesis (in modern-day Algeria); not far away at El Jem (Tunisia) the peculiarities of the amphitheatre suggest that it was designed by an amphitheatre expert from Rome who did not stay long enough to supervise works on site.[46] According to one writer Hadrian organized his building programme like a military campaign, enrolling 'by cohorts and centuries, on the model of the legions, builders, geometers, architects, and every sort of expert in construction and decoration'.[47] A reference to the deployment of 100 gangs of 100 men in the construction of Santa Sofia in Constantinople may be apocryphal, but it still evokes something of the military spirit of the imperial organization that Justinian inherited.[48]

In this context individual architects did not stand out against the ranks unless they were closely linked to an emperor – as were Vitruvius, Severus, Rabirius and Apollodorus. Works of art by such names as Apelles, Myron, Polykleitos or Praxiteles commanded fabulous sums, but the owner of a building gained little by vaunting the name of its architect. When Roman society did invest buildings with human interest, it was through the statues they might contain and the identity of their patrons. The name of the famous republican general and Caesar's rival, Pompey, lived on at his palace on the Esquiline hill; it was still called the Domus Pompeiana even when inhabited by the emperor Gordian I three centuries later.[49] Today we speak of Nero's Golden House, not Severus', and Trajan's Forum, not Apollodorus'. Patrons' names were of course perpetuated in prominent inscriptions, while with few exceptions,[50] those of architects appeared in smaller letters in some less important location, if at all.

Architects were not the only people who shaped space. In many ancient societies the basic form of cult buildings was imposed by religious authorities, and under an extreme view the architect-mother (to return to Filarete's image) carried out an essentially executive function, administering building contracts and resolving technical issues. In the secular realm, the proprietorial feelings of patrons were primarily extensions of their financial investments and control of real estate. With Hadrian as the conspicuous exception, it seems that most emperors and their delegates were concerned to dictate constructional strategy only when it had political repercussions. Sometimes, but only sometimes, this had an impact on architectural style.

1.15 Detail of the exterior of the amphitheatre at Verona (cf. p. 16).

Claudius channelled imperial funds into infrastructure; he drained the Fucine Lake, built a harbour complex at Ostia and Rome's most impressive aqueducts, the Aqua Claudia and the Aqua Anio Novus. Evidently it was thought appropriate that the appearance of such projects should speak of their origin or function, so the classicizing look of Augustan projects (figs 2.3, 2.4 and 3.30), which had more or less continued during Tiberius' reign, made way for a contrived rustic honesty, as at Claudius' harbour warehousing at Portus, the Porta Maggiore (fig. 6.17) or the amphitheatre at Verona (fig. 1.15).[51] Usually, however, those in power were content to be seen to be in command, just as was the magistrate in the Terracina relief. Trajan, in replying to Pliny the Younger's anxieties over the projects in Bithnya, never offered concrete advice unless the issues at stake were financial, legal or religious. Otherwise he recommended Pliny to decide for himself or appoint a suitably qualified architect/engineer.[52]

Builders and craftsmen too had a hand in design, their influence being seen primarily at the level of detail. While a degree of disjunction between planning and style is only to be expected – since one may reflect practical requirements, the other taste and fashion – it may sometimes mark a division of responsibility between architects and craftsmen. Thus the architect of the Maison Carrée (figs 3.29–3.31) could adapt the plan of the Temple of Apollo Sosianus – or that of some common ancestor – without mimicking it stylistically. Conversely, the decoration of the coeval temples of the Castori and of Concord in the Forum Romanum are similar enough as to have been executed by the same workshop, yet their plans are markedly different, the latter having an unusual transverse cella like the Temple of the Castori (Castor and Pollux) *in circo* (fig. 3.3).[53] In the middle and later imperial periods some quarries exported nearly finished items all around the Mediterranean, the style of which was outside the control of local architects, except when they took the trouble of sending full-scale prototypes to the quarries.[54] Then there were itinerant workshops who moved from one site to another, leaving behind their trademarks, as it were, in the form of recurrent decorative motifs and carving techniques, along with the occasional actual signature.[55] I would guess that the curious inter-dentil 'eyelets' that occur in some Flavian entablatures (fig. 1.5) are not, as sometimes suggested, the 'signature' of the architect Rabirius, but rather the sort of thing that workshops would adopt as part of their house style.

Architectural drawings furnish further clues as to where to place the boundary between architect and artisan. Significantly, Hellenistic and Roman examples were not as a rule concerned with the rhythm of decorative motifs like dentils or egg and dart.[56] This suggests that only the scansion of relatively large elements like triglyphs or modillions, the brackets belonging to the Corinthian cornice, were normally taken into consideration due to their relatively great visual impact (figs 3.16 and 10.15). Otherwise smaller details were left for craftsmen to resolve as construction progressed. Since the essential thing was to achieve a satisfactory corner condition for each band of mouldings, it was common to start with the corners and then work away from them. This approach meant that it was normal for there to be no sustained pattern of vertical relationships between separate bands, as in the case of the cornice illustrated in figure 1.5. On the other hand, considerable care was sometimes taken to subdivide the modillion spacing into exact numbers of eggs or dentils, which might well represent an architect's as opposed to

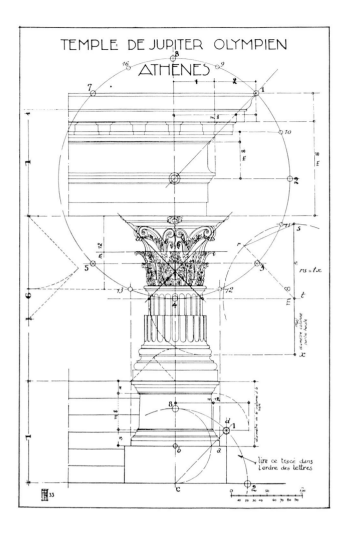

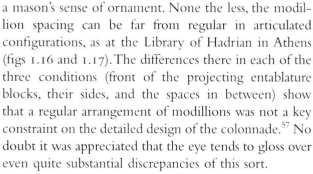

1.16   Design analysis of the main order of the Library of Hadrian, Athens (AD ca. 130), according to André Texier (1934).

1.17 (*right*)   The façade of the Library of Hadrian: view of the part to the left side of the entrance.

a mason's sense of ornament. None the less, the modillion spacing can be far from regular in articulated configurations, as at the Library of Hadrian in Athens (figs 1.16 and 1.17). The differences there in each of the three conditions (front of the projecting entablature blocks, their sides, and the spaces in between) show that a regular arrangement of modillions was not a key constraint on the detailed design of the colonnade.[57] No doubt it was appreciated that the eye tends to gloss over even quite substantial discrepancies of this sort.

So not only is the identity of Roman architects frustratingly indistinct, but it is difficult to define their sphere of responsibility *vis-à-vis* patrons and craftsmen. This state of affairs represents no great obstacle to the present enquiry, however, its being concerned not so

much with authorship as with *how* and *why* design proceeded as it did. Ultimately it is the buildings themselves that constitute the chief source of evidence. The one human figure to whom constant reference needs to be made is Vitruvius, whose voice represents the only authentic and sustained insight into the workings of a Roman architect's mind.

1.18   Detail of the hemicycle of the Markets of Trajan, Rome (AD 105), school of Apollodorus? The bays with monopitch pediments, which lack mirror symmetry in themselves, are arranged into symmetrical split-pediment groups centred on either the main transverse axis or the two diagonal axes.

II

VITRUVIUS AND THEORY

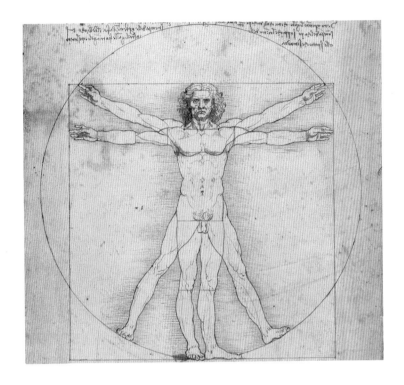

As the only surviving ancient treatise on architecture, Vitruvius' *De architectura* is an essential companion in any enquiry about Roman design, being a mine of information, anecdote and personal reflection without parallel. It presents a panoramic view of ancient practice, turning from urban planning to acoustics, from design theory to stucco technique, from chronometry to military engineering. The contents of the ten books, in outline, develop as follows:

   I: Education; theory; siting and layout of cities
  II: The origin of dwelling; building materials
 III: Theory; modes of temple design; Ionic order
 IV: Doric, Corinthian and Tuscan; more on temples
  V: Various types of civic building
 VI: Domestic architecture in town and country
 VII: Finishes: floors, vaults, stucco and painting
VIII: Water: detection, quality, transport and storage
 IX: Astronomy, astrology, clocks and sundials
  X: Military engines; mechanical and surveying devices

In fact, so all-embracing is Vitruvius' scope, that it is more instructive to focus on what he did *not* cover. He says nothing about amphitheatres (the only building type the Romans invented) and little about monu-

2.1 Fantastical architectural decoration known as '4th style', from the so-called House of Castor and Pollux, Pompeii. Despite Vitruvius' criticism, this form of painting was very popular.

2.2 (*above*) Leonardo da Vinci's interpretation of the ideal male human body, following the spirit if not the letter of Vitruvius' account.

33

mental baths (those totems of the imperial city), the Corinthian order (the Romans' preference over Doric and Ionic), the use of concrete (the quintessential Roman building material) or the coloured imported marbles with which it was commonly dressed (fig. 5.1). These omissions can in part be explained because Vitruvius wrote before consolidation in each of these areas. The precise date of *De architectura* remains elusive, however, with scholars dividing either side of the watershed of 27 BC, when Octavian received the title Augustus – for it was to Augustus (fig. 2.3) that Vitruvius dedicated his opus. Supporters of a later date link the very existence of his treatise to the ensuing programme of cultural and urban renewal. Supporters of an earlier date reckon it explains his silence on the architectural developments just cited, as well as references to buildings that burnt down before 27 BC.[1] But there are objections to both arguments, creating an impasse which some have sought to get around with the idea that Vitruvius started his treatise in the mid-30s BC, but took almost twenty years to complete it.[2] The answer need not be so convoluted once it is borne in mind that Vitruvius wrote as an old man, his looks being 'marred by age', to quote his own expression (II, Pref., 4). The paradox resolves itself if he wrote the bulk of his treatise between 28 and 23 BC, while relying in large part on ideas and experience acquired earlier in life, during the 40s and 50s. It seems that he clung almost pathetically to what he had learnt from his teachers in his youth.[3]

2.3   Statue of Augustus from the Villa of Livia at Prima Porta, now in the Vatican Museums, Braccio Nuovo (Tiberian copy AD ca. 15 of Augustan original ca. 20 BC).

2.4   Perspective reconstruction of the Temple of Mars Ultor and the Forum of Augustus. For a probable ancient representation of the façade, see fig. 3.8.

VITRUVIUS IN CONTEXT

Vitruvius' reverence for the past is manifest not only in what he chose to leave out, but also in his sanction of a number of more or less glaring anachronisms. He makes the corner columns of peristyles slightly fatter that the rest, a refinement that is practically unknown after the classical period. His Corinthian capital is what Pierre Gros has termed a 'télescopage' of elements from the fourth and first centuries BC (p. 145). His Doric capital is in many ways consistent with ones from the third and second centuries BC,[4] while his 'Ionic' base goes back to an archaic type used at Ephesos.[5] His temple plans too have more in common with Greek models than the norm in Rome. With such a track record it is understandable that scholars can react almost with surprise when buildings are found to match Vitruvian schemes reasonably well, his Latin theatre (fig. 2.5) being a case in point.[6]

The failings of the ten books do not end here. Their structure and sequence lack clarity of purpose, and several passages, especially those on theory, are confusing or in direct contradiction with one another;[7] pieces of information required to complete a chain of instructions are frequently missing;[8] inaccuracies of historical detail are common; the level of technical and scientific knowledge is unremarkable.[9] Hence the dual fortune of Vitruvius' endeavour, with negative criticism casting a shadow over the tradition of homage that gathered strength progressively from the time when Einhard, Charlemagne's biographer and chancellor, encouraged scholars to pay Vitruvius due attention.[10] This paradox is a leitmotif of the first full-blooded 'modern' treatise of architecture, Leon Battista Alberti's *De re aedificatoria*. Countless paraphrases and allusions betray Alberti's debt; yet at the same time he complained about Vitruvius' opaque prose, saying he 'writes neither Greek nor Latin and as far as we are concerned he need not have written at all since we cannot understand that kind of writing'.[11] Antonio da Sangallo vented his frustration over trying to make sense of the ancient writer's recommendations by scribbling over one of his drawings '*Vitruvio e goffo*', stupid or inept.[12] A current of twentieth-century criticism has served but to flesh out this view, relegating him to the ranks of 'minor' writers: mediocre, dull and thick-witted.[13] Poor Vitruvius!

But there is a real danger of getting carried away in an orgy of recrimination. It may be true that Vitruvius is mentioned by just five ancient authors (Pliny the Elder, Frontinus, Faventius, Servius and Sidonius Apollinaris), but he was respected all the same. When Faventius compiled his much shorter manual on building some three centuries later, Vitruvius was still his prime source.[14] Significant too are the passing comments of the non-architect Apollinaris (Bishop of Laodiceia in Syria about 360), when praising Mamertus for a recently published book of his:

> here [is] a learning peerless and unique, able to hold its own with distinction in many fields . . . not declining to hold the quill with Orpheus, the staff with Aesculapius [Asklepius], the rod with Archimedes, the horoscope with Euphrates, the compass with Perdix, the plummet with Vitruvius.[15]

So here is Vitruvius' name in exalted company indeed: Orpheus, Archimedes and Asklepius, a god no less! Proof that this was not just a quirk of that particular letter is found in a chatty passage in another letter in which Apollinaris asks a friend for news:

> What are you doing these days? . . . Do you hunt? do you build? do you live the life of a countryman? . . . As

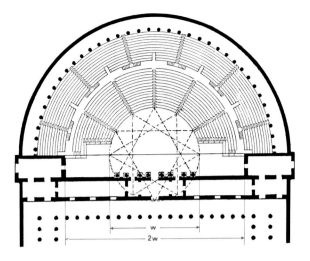

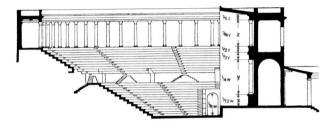

2.5 Vitruvius' prescription for the outline design of the generic Latin theatre. Note that while the plan is based on a geometrical organization, the elevation conforms to a series of simple arithmetical ratios.

regards Vitruvius or Columella, whether you are a devotee of one of them, or both together, you are acting splendidly – for you are competent to follow each of them like one of their best disciples, I mean as an agriculturist or an architect of the first rank.[16]

Recent scholarship has in fact done much to accommodate the roller-coaster fortune of Vitruvius in the light of his historical context. First of all there is his background to consider. He served as a military engineer under Julius Caesar during the Gallic Wars (58–50 BC), and his mature career coincided with the period of unrest and internecine wars that lasted from his master's assassination in 44 BC to Octavian's triumphant return to Rome in 29 BC. Most of Vitruvius' professional output must inevitably have been taken up with producing and repairing military hardware (I, Pref., 2). The competence in matters relating to hydraulic engineering displayed in Book VIII has led to speculation that he held a senior position in Agrippa's programme of improvements to Rome's water supply.[17] In any event, the fact that he claimed responsibility for only one building (V,1,6), the Basilica at Fanum (fig. 2.17),

2.6 Wall decoration from the House of Augustus on the Palatine, Rome.

confirms that his principal expertise was engineering. It is ironic that the 'father of architecture' may not have had much experience in civic building. At any rate it is clear that Vitruvius was *not* responsible for the foremost projects of his day, such as the theatres of Pompey and Marcellus, Augustus' Forum (fig. 2.4) and Agrippa's Pantheon. These and other grand public works transformed Rome under his very eyes, yet to all of this he

2.7 Propylon to the Roman agora, Athens (dedicated last decade of 1st century BC), an unusually literal reinterpretation of Doric prototypes of the classical period.

was an outsider.[18] This helps explain the recurrent tone of resignation – almost an inferiority complex – that characterizes personal reflections such as the following:

> I have never been eager to make money by my art, but have gone on the principle that slender means and a good reputation are preferable to wealth and disrepute. For this reason, only a little celebrity has followed; but still, my hope is that, with the publication of these books, I shall become known even to posterity. And it is not to be wondered at that I am so generally unknown. Other architects go about and ask for opportunities to practise their profession; but I have been taught by my instructors that it is the proper thing to undertake a charge only after being asked, and not to ask for it (VI, Pref., 5; cf. III, Pref., 3).

It is not uncommon for frustrated professionals to adopt a reactionary pose in the face of the new trends which pass them by, just as does Vitruvius on repeated occasions; here are his views on wall-painting:

> A picture is a representation of a thing which really exists or which can exist: for example, a man, a house, a ship . . . mythological episodes, the battles of Troy, or the wanderings of Ulysses, with landscape backgrounds. . . . But those subjects . . . are scorned in these days of bad taste. We now have paintings of monstrosities, rather than truthful representations of definite things. For instance, reeds are put in the place of columns, fluted appendages with curly leaves and volutes instead of pediments. . . . Such things do not exist and cannot exist and never have existed. Yet when people see these frauds, they find no fault with them but on the contrary are delighted. Their understanding is darkened by decadent critical principles (VII, 5, 1–4).

The possibility that the idiom of fresco painting then in vogue, which now goes by the name of '2nd style' (fig. 2.6), was based on architectural stage-sets rather than real buildings could help explain its exotic character,[19] but in any case Vitruvius seems blind to the delights of illusionism, abstraction and make-believe. It is difficult to imagine what on earth he would have said of the more fantastical '4th style' (fig. 2.1). He was never so forthright about specific buildings, but various remarks give away his likes and dislikes. All four temples that he judged in 'a class of their own' (VII, Pref., 16–17) were notable for their great size, marble construction and the regularity of their plans; two of these, the Hellenistic temples at Didyma and Ephesos, were particularly huge, while the Olympieion at Athens (figs 2.11 and 2.19) was almost in the same league. At a humbler scale he would certainly have pre-

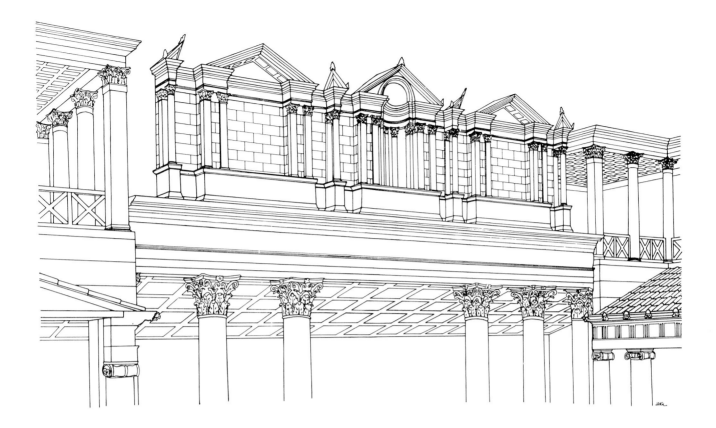

ferred the thoroughly orthodox propylon of the Roman agora in Athens (fig. 2.7) to the hybrid Doric porticoes that he would have seen in the house of his patron Augustus and elsewhere in Rome,[20] not to mention the travesty of academic principles represented by a building like the so-called Palazzo delle Colonne at Ptolemais (fig. 2.8). The same could be said of later examples of Doric, to mention just the uncommonly slim, rectangular, pilasters that give their name to a courtyard at Hadrian's Villa (fig. 2.9) besides others illustrated in chapter 6. Indeed Vitruvius' conservatism is a crucial factor which helps explain the lack of depth on up-and-coming subjects like the amphitheatre, the Corinthian order or concrete.

The shortcomings of Vitruvius' treatise are also related to the particular difficulties associated with such an extraordinarily ambitious enterprise, for he was after all the first author ever to attempt a comprehensive treatise on architecture. He drew on an encyclopedic range of material, whether philosophical, technological or architectural; and his cause was not helped by having to rely on translated digests of Greek sources in encyclopedias and technical handbooks, or what Silvio Ferri has called *manualetti*.[21] His background, as mentioned above, was thoroughly practical, and with a respectable but not brilliant education it is understandable that literary skills could sometimes fail him

2.8 (*top*) Reconstruction of the upper order of the north side of the peristyle court of the Palazzo delle Colonne, Ptolemais, Libya (1st century BC?). Note the mixed orders, the extreme shift of scale between them, and the absence of alignment between the vertical elements of the upper and lower levels.

2.9 Peristyle of the so-called Hall of Doric pilasters, Hadrian's Villa (AD ca. 130). Note the rectangular cross-section of the pilasters and their extreme slenderness seen from the front.

37

– as indeed he himself was conscious (I,I,I7). It is evident that linguistic predicaments often caused the discontinuities and contradictions that hamper the reader's progress. One difficulty was that of presenting technical material to a wider public, and another – which lay at the root of Alberti's disapproval – was that of knowing when to translate Greek terms, and when to keep them where Latin was inadequate.[22] It should be remembered that Vitruvius' generation was the first to grapple seriously with this problem, and that Latin is a language relatively ill-equipped for rendering abstractions (as opposed to, say, description). Even a writer of Cicero's calibre resorted to using various Latin equivalents for a single Greek word in the hope of converging on its meaning. The problem had evidently not gone away even by the time of the emperor Tiberius; in his effort to rid Greek from official communications he on one occasion demanded that the word εμβλεμα (emblem) be substituted by a native term in a decree of the senate, or 'if one could not be found, that the idea be expressed by several words, if necessary, and by periphrasis'.[23]

It is also important to remember Vitruvius' objectives. He was writing less a manual for his fellow colleagues than a work that expounded the virtues of architecture to patrons and other non-specialists – from Augustus to Apollinaris – who were yet concerned with putting buildings up.[24] Vitruvius' preoccupation with defining rules and standards was in part to guide such an audience in their judgement, and in part to raise the status of architects and the tone of architectural discourse.[25] Just like his Renaissance followers, Vitruvius underlined the role of mathematics so as to convince his readers that architecture was an art based on science and reason, not empiricism. From this viewpoint, the details of the design process were less important; many of his recipes were no doubt included to illustrate *the sort of thing* an architect should do when confronted with such and such a subject. Likewise it is for purely didactic purposes that Vitruvius described idealized models that no contemporary architect would dream of using; it is for this reason that one can search practically in vain for his radial city, his 'Greek' house,[26] or his corner solution for the Doric frieze.[27] A similar approach characterizes the geographical studies of his near contemporary Strabo, who might pay less attention to a thriving Roman colony than an extinct Greek city that was connected with some appealing legend or anecdote.[28] And who criticizes Virgil should his *Georgics* paint an inaccurate picture of agricultural practice? Vitruvius too aims at poetry, though of not such a literary kind.

So it is clear that consulting Vitruvius' text demands a certain care. Sometimes what he says seems to correspond simply and directly to archaeological evidence, while sometimes it may be anything from unhelpful to downright misleading. Everything depends on the background to the topic in question. Are there, then, any Vitruvian principles that are generally valid? Paradoxically, it seems that the more abstract the topic, the more chance there is of an echo in actual practice. In his view the work of any architect worthy of the title must address objectives of a theoretical nature, and other sources confirm that his conviction was not unrepresentative, but rather prevailed throughout Graeco-Roman antiquity. His treatment of theory therefore warrants a more detailed examination, not least because during the course of this book it will provide valuable insights into the preoccupations of his fellow architects.

VITRUVIAN THEORY

It must first of all be emphasized that placing this discussion before the chapters devoted to actual buildings is not meant to imply that theory necessarily anticipated practice. On the contrary, architecture was an important stimulus for ancient intellectual activity. So it is, for example, that we find orthogonal city plans (as at Selinunte, Megara Hyblaea or Olynthos) before the birth of its supposed inventor, Hippodamos. As for Vitruvius, it is surely significant that he declared architecture to be born *ex fabrica et ratiocinatione*, or from practice first and theory second (I,I,I).

Vitruvius' treatise is by far the most important surviving source of ancient – that is is to say predominantly Greek – architectural theory. The very concepts to which he introduces his readers in the opening chapters of Book I are Greek. Book III, the one with the most sustained theoretical content, is precisely that which leans most heavily on Greek sources, in particular the writings of Hermogenes.[29] Vitruvius himself made no attempt to disguise his debt; indeed, after citing numerous earlier writers on related topics, he explained how:

> From their commentaries I have gathered what I saw was useful for the present subject, and formed it into one complete treatise, and this principally because I saw that many books in this field had been published by the Greeks, but very few indeed by our countrymen (VII, Pref., I4).

Vitruvius was hardly guilty of exaggeration. The main rival native work was Varro's rapid-fire coverage of architecture in one of nine books of a lost treatise on the liberal arts.[30] By contrast, specialist texts were not uncommon in Greece as early as the fifth century BC, to judge by Socrates' sarcastic reproof of a fellow philosopher for his hobby of collecting treatises – was he thinking of becoming an architect?[31] Production seems to have reached a peak between the fourth and second centuries; at any rate the bulk of the works that Vitruvius lists date from this time, including those by Pytheos and Hermogenes, on which he relied most. Their buildings appealed to him by virtue of simple proportions, the crisp marble details and the limpid clarity of their plans (fig. 2.10). A commentary on individual projects such as these was a typical format for treatises, otherwise related topics included theory, perspective, the design and proportions of the orders, and innovations in the field of construction and mechanics, such as Chersiphron's device for transporting column drums of colossal dimensions.[32] In the preface to Book VII, Vitruvius cites no fewer than forty Greek treatises on such subjects, while lamenting the lack of any writings by Cossutius, the one Roman architect to have done something really great, the Olympieion (figs 2.11 and 2.19). His whole undertaking, then, is symptomatic of the quest to raise Rome to the level of Hellenic culture. There can be no better symbol of this endeavour than his insistence on the title *architectus* – a word derived from the Greek *architekton* – as opposed to *faber* or *redemptor*, the Latin terms which hitherto had also embraced building contractors.[33]

While Vitruvius' treatment of practical subjects is largely self-explanatory, that of theory is more problematic. With his background as a military architect-engineer, he was less well prepared for dealing with abstractions. None the less his whole programme demanded a prominent place for theory, for it distinguished architecture from mere building, and besides, Vitruvius evidently enjoyed his speculative forays.

The education of the architect (I,1)

Vitruvius' most sustained treatment of theory occupies the first three chapters of Book I, beginning with the declaration that 'The architect should be equipped with knowledge of many branches of study and varied kinds of learning, for it is by his judgement that the other arts are put to the test.' Accordingly, Vitruvius proceeded with a lengthy homily on education. The architect should not only be skilled in drawing, but also have a working grasp of a range of subjects: geometry

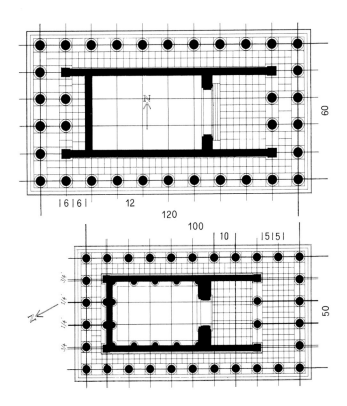

2.10 Plans of Hellenistic Ionic temples based on a gridded organization, 1 : 500. In each case the presumed module equals the width of the plinth of the column, or half the width of one bay.
(a) Temple of Athena Polias at Priene by Pytheos, ca. 340 BC. The module equals 6 Attic feet, making the column spacing 12 ft and the interaxial length of the peristyle 120 ft.
(b) Temple of Leto at the Letöon, Xanthos, early 2nd century BC. The module equals 5 Attic feet, making the column spacing 10 ft and the interaxial length of the peristyle 100 ft.

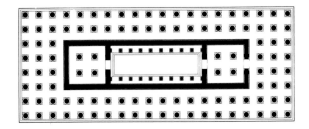

2.11 Plan of the Temple of Olympian Zeus (Olympieion) in Athens, 1 : 1500. Although the project was probably initiated in the 4th century, all the elements now standing (fig. 2.19) belong to the resumption of construction in the 170s BC which Vitruvius says was supervised by Cossutius, or its termination in the 2nd quarter of the 2nd century AD.

(since this bears on planning and optics); history (so as to explain the origin of architectural form); philosophy (for the sake of moral education); music (since this has practical applications for adjusting the tension of catapults, as well as in the field of acoustics); medicine (so as to assess the healthiness of sites and sources of water); law (so as to advise on party wall agreements and contracts); astronomy (so as to grasp the principles of sundial design and locate north, south, east and west). With allowance for changes in the curriculum, the polymath ideal is still central to modern architectural education.

Just as Cicero had done in the cause of oratory, Vitruvius suggested that architecture was really superior to the various disciplines cited, by virtue of the fact that it embraced them all. He stopped short, however, of Pytheos' claim that the architect should achieve more in all the arts than the masters of each separate one, projecting a more modest image, if not quite a 'Jack of all trades but master of none'. What enabled a single individual to assimilate such different branches of learning was, according to both Cicero and Vitruvius, an understanding of theory, the life-blood common to them all.

Six principles of design (I,2)

In the sequence that he gave them, Vitruvius' six fundamental principles are *ordinatio*, *dispositio*, *eurythmia*, *symmetria*, *decor* and *distributio*. Their origins emerge clearly enough since he supplied Greek equivalents for three of them (*taxis* for *ordinatio*, *diathesin* for *dispositio* and *oikonomia* for *distributio*), while *eurythmia* and *symmetria* are in themselves Greek. Translations of Vitruvius often render these terms by single words; in the Loeb edition, for example, they are translated as order, arrangement, proportion, symmetry, propriety and economy. On this basis ancient and modern equivalents might be set out as follows:

Greek	Latin	English
taxis	*ordinatio*	order
diathesin	*dispositio*	arrangement
eurythmia	–	proportion
symmetria	–	symmetry
prepon	*decor*	propriety (decorum)
oikonomia	*distributio*	economy

Closer inspection reveals that such simplistic matches can be positively obstructive. Symmetry, in the sense that it is universally understood today, is especially unhelpful as an equivalent to *symmetria*. Then there is the problem that Vitruvius' definitions are themselves quite obscure, and presented in a seemingly arbitrary sequence. In particular those for *ordinatio* and *symmetria*, although worded differently, are almost interchangeable, while those for *dispositio* and *eurythmia* appear to echo one another deliberately.[34] What explains such redundancies? Did Vitruvius confuse ideas he took from different sources, or is there really some underlying logic?

An interpretation attracting growing support detects a bipartite split between processes of design and the attributes they produce.[35] *Ordinatio* might be the process of calculation that gives rise to *symmetria*; *dispositio* might be the process of composition which gives rise to *eurythmia*; *distributio* might be the process of evaluation that gives rise to *decor*. Thus emerges a tripartite scheme to complement the three departments of architecture, the three categories of public buildings, the three prerequisites of good building (*firmitas*, *utilitas* and *venustas*) and the three primary orders (Doric, Ionic and Corinthian).[36]

Act of design	Attribute of result	Nature of conception
ordinatio	*symmetria*	the project as numberform and mathematical harmony
dispositio	*eurythmia*	the project as composition and visual harmony
distributio	*decor*	the project as appropriate to its social and physical context

Should this be correct, the foundations of Vitruvius' theory are *symmetria*, *eurythmia* and *decor* alone;[37] accordingly the rest of this chapter examines each of these concepts in turn.

SYMMETRIA, THE PRINCIPLE OF MATHEMATICAL HARMONY

Symmetria is arguably the most important single element of Vitruvius' theory. He used it no fewer than eighty-four times, far more than any other critical term,[38] frequently giving it an explicit emphasis (I,3,2; III,1,1; V,1,6; V,6,7; VI,2,1). In the preface to Book VII he cites several treatises on 'the laws of *symmetria*', but none on, say, *eurythmia*. Other sources too confirm *symmetria* as 'one of the most deeply-rooted and abiding features of ancient Greek thought, both artistic and philosophical'.[39]

The meaning of *symmetria* stems from *sym–*, coming together (as in sympathy, symbiosis, synthesis or the ancient Greek for a military alliance, *symmachia*), and *metron*, measure. In general terms, it is essential to understand that for the ancient mind absolute and eternal values, as opposed to relative and transient ones, were those that were measurable and therefore reproducible, a point that is forcefully expressed in the passage from Plato's *Philebus* already cited in the Introduction (p. 10). To be more specific, Vitruvius defines *symmetria* as 'a proper agreement between the members of the work itself, and relation of the parts and the whole general scheme, in accordance with a certain part selected as standard' (1,2,4). A short-hand definition might be 'the commensurability of parts',[40] or simply 'mathematical harmony', but any such label renders an inadequate picture of what is a multi-layered concept. *Symmetria* was clearly related to the Latin term *proportio*, but it evidently meant more than proportion alone. The best key to a fuller understanding of the concept is the beginning of Book III, where Vitruvius explores an analogy with the human body.

> The design of a temple depends on *symmetria*, the principles of which must be most carefully observed by the architect. . . . Without *symmetria* and proportion there can be no principles in the design of any temple; that is if there is no precise relation between its members, as in the case of those of a well-shaped man.

To illustrate this point, Vitruvius listed a series of ratios: the face takes up one-tenth of the total height; the hand, from the wrist to the fingertip the same; the head takes up one-eighth of the height, and so on, as the matrix below shows:

Principal dimensions of Vitruvian Man

		a	b	c	d	H
a	face height; hand length	1	4/5	3/5	2/5	1/10
b	head height		1	3/4	1/2	1/8
c	foot length			1	2/3	1/6
d	chest height				1	1/4
H	total height; arm span (6 feet)					1

Vitruvius next tells how a man, laid flat on his back, may be inscribed in a circle centred at the navel and in a square too, since the arm span equals the body height (fig. 2.2). Units of measurement were derived from the members of the body: the finger (*digitus*), palm (*palmus*), foot (*pes*) and cubit (*cubitus* – the length of the forearm). Finally, he says that Greek mathematicians and philosophers took the body as a source of number theory, investing six and ten with special significance because the body is 6ft tall and owns ten fingers and toes. From this it can be deduced that *symmetria* is the mathematical harmony that comes of commensurable numbers entering into form via distinct modes, principally ratio, shape, dimension and the repetition of like elements. This explains the importance given by Vitruvius to the principle of modular composition, in which a small physical element, a *modulus* or *embater*, typically the lower diameter of a column shaft or the width of a triglyph, was multiplied to govern the most significant limits of a colonnade or building.[41] This guaranteed mathematical harmony in terms of dimension, ratio and repetition.

For Vitruvius, the task of the architect was to imitate Nature, not literally, but rather by analogy. His human proportions idealized the canons of sculptors like Polykleitos;[42] awkward ratios were suppressed, and life-like ones retained only where they were simple (the bisection of the body at the genitals, for example, characterizes both Polykleitos' Doryphoros and Vitruvian Man). In fact Vitruvius' measurements produce a decidedly curious individual, and for this reason most later variants ignore the least life-like details (fig. 2.12). But of course he was not expecting anyone to use his text to produce statues; the point was that its *symmetria* reflected a cosmic order that reduced ultimately to whole numbers. The root of this conviction depended in part on mystical speculations, a case in point being the ideas surrounding the so-called Platonic solids (fig. 2.13). But rigorous research could also point in the same direction. It is well to remember that Archimedes, in his longest treatise, *On the Sphere and Cylinder*,

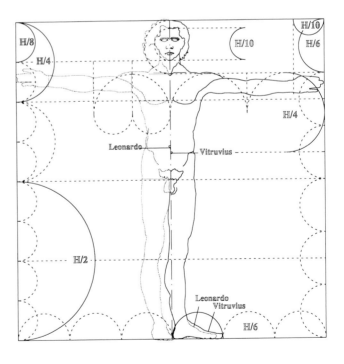

2.12 The proportions of the ideal male body, according to Leonardo da Vinci's interpretation of Vitruvius. Certain ratios were altered for the sake of a more natural result (cf. fig. 2.2).

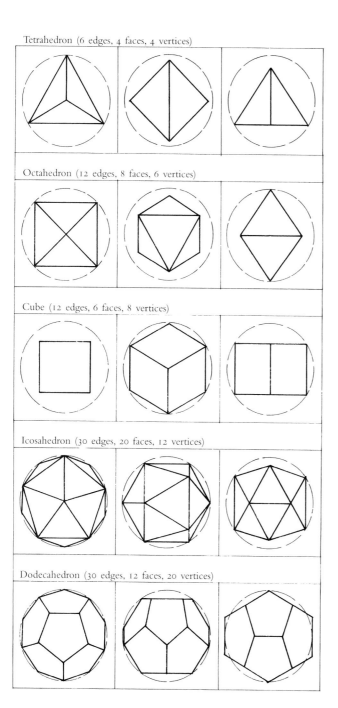

Tetrahedron (6 edges, 4 faces, 4 vertices)

Octahedron (12 edges, 8 faces, 6 vertices)

Cube (12 edges, 6 faces, 8 vertices)

Icosahedron (30 edges, 20 faces, 12 vertices)

Dodecahedron (30 edges, 12 faces, 20 vertices)

2.13   The five Platonic solids with tabulated analysis.

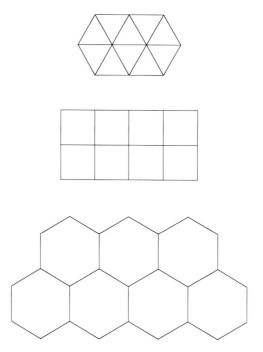

2.14   The three repeating two-dimensional patterns which may be made up exclusively of identical contiguous units: (a) the equilateral triangle; (b) the square; (c) the hexagon. In each pattern the side of the repeating unit has the same length, but the area contained varies, illustrating Pappus' point that the hexagon is the most efficient in terms of the ratio of area to perimeter.

2.15 (*right*)   A detail from the Raphael's painting *The School of Athens* (in the Stanza della Segnatura of the Vatican Palace), showing the principal musical harmonies in diagrammatic form and below this a representation of the Pythagorean decad. The ratio 6 : 12 corresponds to 1 : 2, or octave (*diapeson*), the ratios 6 : 9 and 8 : 12 correspond to 2 : 3, or major tonic (*diapente*), the ratios 6 : 8 and 9 : 12 correspond to 3 : 4, or major subtonic (*diatesseron*). The decad represents geometrically the sum of the successive rows 1 + 2 + 3 + 4, giving a total of 10, one of the perfect numbers cited by Vitruvius.

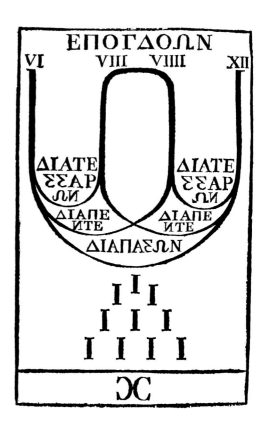

deployed for the first time the principle of infinitesimal calculus to prove that the surface areas and volumes of cylinders, cones and spheres of the same diameter were linked by ratios like 1:1, 4:1 and 3:2. This was a particular source of satisfaction, for as Archimedes himself commented in his introduction to his treatise, 'these properties were always inherent in the nature of the figures mentioned, but were ignored by earlier geometers; none of them were aware that there is a *symmetria* between these figures'.[43]

Observation of the natural world provided another impetus for the Greeks' contemplation of numerical and geometrical order. They realized that light moves in straight lines, that water at rest has a planar surface, which if disturbed gives rise to circular ripples, that the sun and moon are spherical, and that honeycombs conform to a hexagonal grid by virtue of the innate 'sagacity' of bees. (As the mathematician Pappus explained, the equilateral triangle, the square, and the hexagon are the only regular polygons that can be disposed in contiguous repeating patterns (fig. 2.14), the last being the most efficient in terms of the ratio between the length of the perimeter and the surface area contained.[44]) It is difficult to over-emphasize the importance of the discovery, usually attributed to Pythagoras, that musical harmonies match simple numerical ratios. Not only: the more striking the harmony the simpler the ratio (1:2 corresponds to the octave, 2:3 to the major tonic and 3:4 to the major subtonic). Raphael famously included a diagram summarizing these numerical harmonies in his great painting *The School of Athens* (fig. 2.15), a type of representation which has a long ancestry in manuscript copies of ancient philosophical texts by authors like Plato.[45] What pleased the ear would evidently please the eye too. Rudolf Wittkower's book *Architectural Principles in the Age of Humanism* is among many publications to have explored the musical analogy for the Renaissance period, but scholars of antiquity have only occasionally made the same connection – even though Vitruvius devotes the bulk of two chapters to harmonic analysis. It is true that his prime concern was a practical problem, namely acoustics (v,4 and v,5), but a wider interest is betrayed by the number of times music is mentioned in the opening chapter of his treatise. Given the tradition of philosophical discourse related to the harmony of the spheres, it would actually be rather surprising if some ancient architects did not use arithmetical ratios with Aristotle's concept in the back of their minds.[46] However, although Vitruvius leaned towards musical ratios,[47] he certainly did not rely on them exclusively, since he might use 2:5 for a door opening, and 3:5 or

$\sqrt{2}:1$ for the shape of a room (IV,6,3; VI,3,3). In the last analysis his guiding principle was to use the simplest possible ratio provided it was compatible with functional and aesthetic criteria.

EURYTHMIA, THE PRINCIPLE OF VISUAL HARMONY

Symmetria, then, brings abstract beauty, but not necessarily visual beauty. This is the realm of *eurythmia*, which translates as 'gracefulness', or 'the quality of being well-shaped', from *eu-*, well, and *rhythmos*, shape. It also conveys a sense of fine crafting, as with something carefully honed or well-fitted; at any rate this is its sense in a conversation between Socrates and the armourer Pistias:

SOCRATES: But tell me Pistias, why do you sell your breastplates for a higher price, although they are no stronger nor any more costly to produce than those of other manufacturers?
PISTIAS: Because, Socrates, those which I make are better fitting.
and later . . .
SOCRATES: How then do you make a well-shaped breastplate to fit an ill-shaped body?
PISTIAS: I make it fit; that which fits is well shaped.[48]

Eurythmia also makes the bridge between proportion and form. There is still a mathematical component, as Vitruvius says that *eurythmia* is found when 'the members of a work are of a height suited to their breadth and of a breadth suited to their length, and when they all respond in accordance with *symmetria*' (1,2,3), but there is a subjective aspect too. He tells us that architects could opt to leave *symmetria* aside for the sake of *eurythmia* if necessary, as for example when gauging optical refinements (VI,2,5). It is *eurythmia* that guided architects towards a limited range of proportions for visually sensitive indicators like column slenderness. One might also speak of the *eurythmia* of groups of elements like a portico or row of windows.

DECOR, THE DOCTRINE OF APPROPRIATENESS

Decor addresses what is appropriate in terms of content, ethics and style, subject to a hierarchical view of the world in which everything was ordained by custom (*consuetudine*) and authority (*auctoritas*). Each aspect of a building should reflect its social, religious and economic status, or in other words, the 'programme'. In effect, then, the concept of *decor* is the ancestor of the guiding tenet of modern design theory – form follows function – although the parallel can only be taken so

2.16 The scene which inspired the artist Kallimachus to invent the Corinthian capital, as visualized by Roland Fréart de Chambray (1650) on the basis of Vitruvius' account.

Similar ideas are expressed in Book v, when Doric columns were allowed different proportions according to the setting, 'for the dignity which should characterize them in temples of the gods is one thing, but their elegance in other public works is quite another'(v,9,3). Vitruvius was not alone in this opinion; Cicero, for example, took it for granted that a vestibule should be proportioned according to whether it stood in a house or a temple.[49]

Vitruvius' preoccupation with the derivation of architectural form has to do with another manifestation of *decor*. The question of origins is important since form was not only a function of appearance, but of content as well. For this reason he was concerned to show how the prettiness of the Corinthian capital was bound up with a specific historical explanation (fig. 2.16). Cicero too explained how form, function and symbolic charge could come to be indivisible:

> Columns support the lintels of temples and their porticoes, but this does not mean that their dignity is inferior to their utility. It was certainly not the search for beauty, but necessity, that has fashioned the celebrated pediment of our Capitol and other religious edifices. But to tell the truth, once the principle had been established of collecting the water either side of the roof, dignity came to be added to the utility of the pediment, so much so that even if the Capitol were to be set up in the heavens, where it should not rain, it could hardly have any dignity without its double pitch roof.[50]

Ancient architects resisted diluting the authority of the pediment by using it out of context. Accustomed as we are to pediments fronting everything from country mansions to shopping malls, we need to remind ourselves that in antiquity the majority of buildings met the urban frontage with horizontal parapets or eaves. Temple pediments stood out by being out of the ordinary, in keeping with the principle of *decor*.

The prerequisites of architecture (1,3)

In his next chapter, Vitruvius says that there are three prerequisites for a successful building: *firmitas*, *utilitas* and *venustas*, criteria that are applicable to all departments of architecture, not just building (*aedificatio*), but also chronometry (*gnomonice*) and engineering (*machinatio*), which included the design of military hardware.[51] *Firmitas* is strength, durability, soundness of materials and quality of construction. *Utilitas* is utility, fitness for purpose. *Venustas* is beauty, delight. As far as it goes – for it could apply to all architecture – Vitruvius' synthesis is hard to better. Indeed, it has been

far, in as much as harmony no longer constitutes the premise that it once did. Vitruvius illuminated his theme via a series of examples: outside and inside should correspond, so that a building with a grand interior should have a grand exterior. The orders should suit the programme, so that temples dedicated to Minerva, Mars and Hercules should be Doric, 'since daintiness would be inappropriate'. Mixed and hybrid orders should be avoided, as the details of one are not appropriate to another. Types of houses should suit the social standing of the occupants, while functions should suit the orientation of the site, with picture galleries requiring even illumination facing north. Materials should be chosen according to availability; fir might be the best timber for certain uses, but if it is difficult to obtain the architect can make do with another species.

paraphrased by dozens of writers from Alberti to Le Corbusier.

The strange thing about this and the preceding chapter is the autonomy of each. The reader might be forgiven for expecting a direct link between Vitruvius' six principles and the three prerequisites (for example that the former were necessary to achieve the latter), but in reality there is no such rigorous connection. The six principles bear on aspects of beauty and utility,[52] but they also have to do with mathematical issues of a more abstract nature. More strikingly still, the six principles do not address the question of *firmitas* at all – indeed, Vitruvius never explains how the Romans approached the problem of statics and the calculation of structural members, although he does raise issues that bear on stability in the broad sense of the term (I,5,1; V,3,3; VI,8).[53] His dilemma probably had its root in the difficulty of not just fitting the diverse ingredients of architecture into reasonably watertight categories, but of fitting them into triads, these being an almost unavoidable topos of intellectual speculation in antiquity. It is telling that elsewhere Vitruvius opted to bring together *venustas, decor* and *firmitas* into another group of three (VI,7,7). But if one must reduce Roman architecture to its component elements, it seems to me impossible to do without at least four: the realm of abstract (ultimately mathematical) theory; that of visual beauty; that of content, programme and communication; and that of practicality. Inevitably the boundaries are blurred by osmosis, so that *eurythmia*, for instance, has to do both with mathematical abstractions and visual appearance.

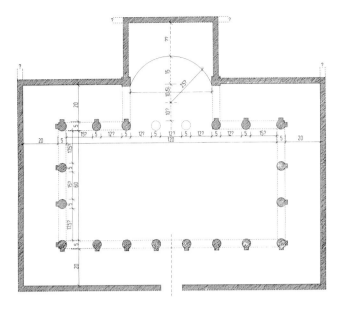

2.17 Vitruvius' Basilica at Fanum, based on his own description: (a) plan; (b) perspective reconstruction.

THE SIGNIFICANCE OF THE BASILICA AT FANUM

It is tempting therefore to seek out a more comprehensive summary of Vitruvius' theory than the account he actually gives. There are various clues at intervals throughout his book, but to my mind by far the most important is the passage dedicated to the Basilica at Fanum (fig. 2.17). This takes a special place in his treatise by virtue of his claim of authorship (V,1,6). His claim rings true through the pointed character of some of his observations, while the general viability of the project is confirmed by its similarity in some respects to real basilicas of the late republican period, of which a relatively well-preserved example is the one at Pompeii (fig. 2.18).[54] It is also highly significant that Vitruvius' basilica is the only building he describes in terms of detailed dimensions (rather than the occa-

sional dimension and a series of ratios). Presumably he was able to refer back to his own records.

In effect, Vitruvius' basilica emerges as a didactic paradigm of theory in practice. His description started with essentially a list of dimensions: the main hall measures 120 × 60 ft; the aisles are 20 ft wide; the main columns are 50 ft tall, 5 ft wide; the pilasters are 20 ft tall and 2½ ft wide on the ground storey, 18 ft tall and 2 ft wide on the upper storey. This amounts to a textbook *symmetria*. The main space fits a double square, and most dimensions are multiples or fractions of 10 or 6, the numbers he had singled out as 'perfect'. Simple ratios reverberate throughout (see the matrix below), including slenderness ratios of 10, 9 and 8 for the columns/pilasters.

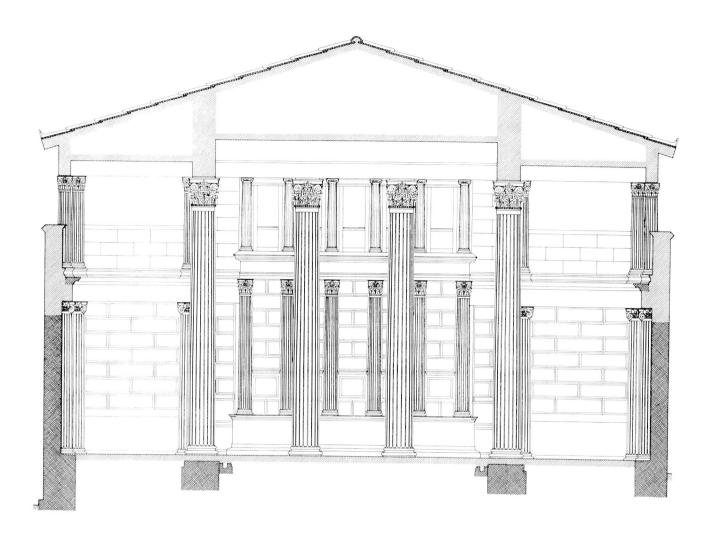

Principal dimensions of the Basilica at Fanum[55]

	2 ft	2½ ft	5 ft	18 ft	20 ft	50 ft	60 ft	120 ft
2 ft	1	4:5	2:5	1:9	1:10	1:25	1:30	1:60
2½ ft		1	1:2	5:36	1:8	1:20	1:24	1:48
5 ft			1	5:18	1:4	1:10	1:12	1:24
18 ft				1	9:10	9:25	3:10	3:20
20 ft					1	2:5	1:3	1:6
50 ft						1	5:6	5:12
60 ft							1	1:2
120 ft								1

Vitruvius then defines the disposition of the columns, which allow the reader to gauge the rhythm of solid to void, and so the *eurythmia* of the colonnades. Further details follow that bear on the aesthetic experience, such as the nature of lighting and material finishes. The final paragraphs address *decor* to some extent, but also issues associated with *firmitas* and *utilitas*, or rather, since it is perhaps unwise to put specific words into Vitruvius' mouth, with what instead might be called practicality. He describes how loads from the trusses were

2.18 (*above*)   Restored section of the basilica at Pompeii (late 2nd century BC). The reconstruction of the main order as Corinthian is conjectural.

2.19   Temple of Olympian Zeus (Olympieion) in Athens: (a) view with Acropolis in the distance; (b) detail of capital.

transferred directly to the column shafts, and how care was taken not to obstruct the view of the tribune, or the circulation in the aisles. He emphasizes how costs were reduced by the giant order (as opposed to two storeys of orders), together with the forthright expression of the timber superstructure. But he is careful to add that the huge columns made the result sumptuous and dignified all the same. Thus his basilica achieves harmony with respect to the four – not three – cornerstones of good design: theory, beauty, content and practicality. This is why Vitruvius drew attention to his own part in the project, and this is what makes his building a paradigm of the Romans' approach to architectural design.

III

THE DYNAMICS OF DESIGN

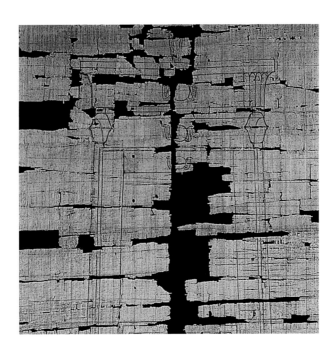

DESIGN IS A PROCESS, a dynamic interaction between concept and contingency, between the generic and the specific; it evolves progressively as multiple individual decisions are assimilated into the whole. This needs to be stated with some force in order to dispel the widespread perception that the classical grammar of forms generated more or less predictable patterns, as if by automatic pilot. It may be true that Vitruvius sometimes presented design in this fashion, but this is a failing that he was at pains to counteract on other occasions. Equally unhelpful is the common notion that creative activity takes place in a rush of inspiration. The spontaneity that Ayn Rand idealizes in her novel *The Fountainhead* is certainly one facet of architectural design, but only one of many facets. As a painter and sculptor, Michelangelo was famous for his tempestuous output – apparently completing some lunettes in the Sistine Chapel in a single day, without the help of cartoons or underpainting – but as an architect he was given to working over his designs again and again until he achieved the right effect.

Aside from the desire of artists and architects to perfect their designs, the impetus for change can come from many quarters: changes of mind on the part of the patron, budgetary and time constraints, political instability, problems of material supply and so on. In the main, ancient writers mention such things only to illustrate some other theme. For example, Augustus' reluctance to be seen as a despot reportedly led him to scale down his ambitions for his forum rather than expropriate all the necessary land; perhaps this accounts for the irregular boundary at one end (fig. 1.6).[1]

3.1 (*facing page*) Interior of the large temple at Niha, near Baalbek, Lebanon (late 2nd century AD), looking towards the adyton (see fig. 3.11).

3.2 Detail of an elevation of a portable shrine (Petrie Museum, London) on a papyrus sheet ca. 53 cm in height found at Ghorâb, Egypt (18th Dynasty).

The mutable character of the design process is self-evident to architects, but it may be less obvious to others. Archaeologists and historians tend to address the subject as a *fait accompli* rather than a process,[2] partly because the Roman period furnishes neither the wealth of Greek specifications and contracts, nor the archival documents that can be available from the late Middle Ages on. Like writings about architecture, drawings and models are intermediaries between imaginary and built realities, yet they are sometimes able to capture modes of thought more vividly than reams of text. This is why it is important to look keenly at the ancient graphic record, despite its limitations. Outside Egypt there survive no architects' drawings made on the perishable media most likely to have been used for design: papyrus, parchment and wood. Most drawings that do survive – because they were inscribed on stone – were not made so much for design as to preserve the *outcome*, being either record documents or full-size masons' templates. Meanwhile the great majority of models were votive offerings representing notional, idealized or metaphorical images of architecture. Votives such as Greek house models, Etruscan cinerary urns and Roman dice-throwers in the shape of fortified towers may be fascinating historical artefacts, but they say little about design processes.[3]

For such reasons, even those few Roman drawings and models that were known were not thought worthy of attention until recently. When excavations in the 1940s uncovered ancient drawings incised on the travertine pavement in front of the Mausoleum of Augustus (fig. 10.14), nobody was sure what they were; some scholars wondered if they described some Renaissance church façade.[4] With few exceptions,[5] it was not until the late 1960s that Roman working drawings appeared in print, namely a series of 1:1 details discovered by Haroutune Kalayan during restoration work at Baalbek (ancient Heliopolis) (fig. 3.16) and the lesser known Lebanese site of Bziza (fig. 3.17).[6] Not long after Kalayan's revelations, Lothar Haselberger came upon the magnificent set of full-size drawings at the Hellenistic Temple of Apollo at Didyma on the Ionian coast (figs 3.13 and 6.29),[7] and now archaeologists know what to look for, more examples have come to light at places like Aphrodisias (fig. 6.31), Bulla Regia, Córdoba, Pergamon, Pompeii and Priene (fig. 3.12).[8] So medieval drawing floors like those of the cathedrals at Bourges, Clermont-Ferrand, Limoges, Narbonne, Soissons, Strasbourg, Wells and York may belong to a tradition that never died out.[9]

Architectural representation

Before looking at individual drawings and models, it is worth reflecting on the question of representation in general. In an age when the use of drawings is taken for granted it is easy to underestimate the importance of the medium used for design and space conception. But in the archaic and classical periods Greek architects appear to have made remarkably little use of drawings, these being reserved primarily for full-size profiles of capitals, mouldings and the like. Instead, design depended primarily on architectonic rules and proportional canons combined with the study of preceding buildings, an approach that allowed fresh variations to be encapsulated by a verbal and numerical specification.[10] Only when architects confronted problems as complex as those presented by the Periclean buildings on the Athenian Acropolis would graphic procedures have offered significant advantages. In any event, by the late Hellenistic period scale drawings were used widely, and on the back of this experience (and contact with Egypt?), Roman architects came to depend on scale drawings and models. Indeed it is hard to see how else architects could have described the plans of centralized buildings such as amphitheatres or sections through interlocking arches and vaults. The importance of drawing may be more significant still, for neurological and cognitive studies suggest that the act of drawing nurtures right-brain specialities and the awareness of space (*topos*), without which the left-brain bias towards numerical and linguistic logic (*logos*) tends to predominate.[11] In other words, graphic skills were a prerequisite for the very conception of the three-dimensional complexities associated with mature Roman architecture.

It is significant too that architectural images were a commonplace of Roman antiquity. Vitruvius mentions plans (*orthographia*), elevations (*ichnographia*) and perspectives (*scaenographia*), but it is clear that sections were also used, since the profiles of mouldings effectively come under this category. Although his own illustrations are kept to the minimum,[12] the number of times he cites drawings, including the opening lines of his treatise, shows that he expects them to be familiar to the non-architects among his readership. Suetonius narrated how Caesar, on the eve of crossing the Rubicon, went on a round of everyday duties which included inspecting plans for a gladiatorial arena.[13] Another passing reference, this time by Cicero, discounted his brother's acquaintance with architects' drawings in giving him the following news of progress at his villa:

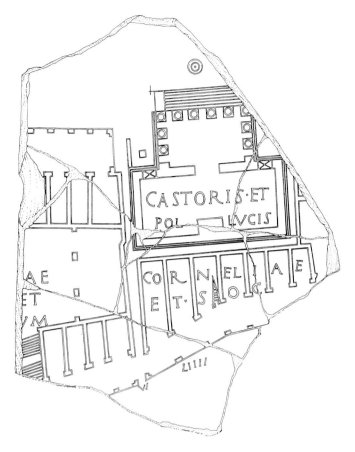

Work was going ahead with a crowd of builders. I said a few animating words to Longilius the contractor, and he convinced me that he wants to give us satisfaction. Your house will be splendid. One can see more now than we could judge from the plan.[14]

The very nature of architectural drawings on durable supports is further proof that they spoke to a non-professional audience. By far the most famous example is the so-called *Forma urbis*, a marble map of Rome in Severan times that covered one entire side of an 18 metre wide public hall in the Forum of Peace. The scale of 1:240 was large enough for noteworthy colonnades, entrances and staircases to have been visible from a distance (fig. 3.4).[15] A fragment of finer draughtsmanship showing the Temple of Castor and Pollux near the Circus Flaminius (fig. 3.3) may well have belonged to another earlier map at the same scale.[16] A marble plaque found at Perugia shows three plans at different scales (the main one shows the ground level of a tomb

3.3 Marble plan discovered in Via Anicia, Rome, showing the Temple of Castor and Pollux in the neighbourhood of the Circus Flaminius. The original scale is 1:240, becoming 1:600 here (being reproduced at ²⁄₅ life size).

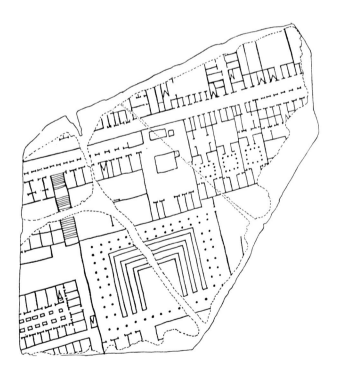

3.4a *Forma Urbis*, the marble plan of Rome dating to the Severan period: fragment with three atrium houses side by side, each with a slightly different layout.

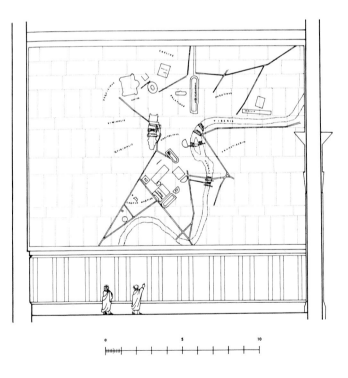

3.4b *Forma Urbis*, reconstruction of the original display as a wall map in one of the halls opening off the Forum of Peace, Rome.

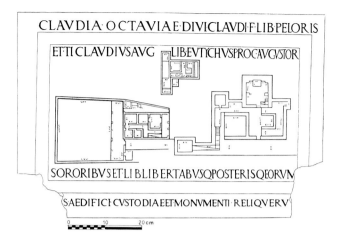

CLAVDIA·OCTAVIAE·DIVICLAVDI·F·LIB·PELORIS

ETTI·CLAVDIVS·AVG □LIB·EVTICHVS·PROC·AVGVSTOR·

SORORIBVS·ET·LI·B·LIB·ERTAB·VSQ·POSTERIS·QEORVM

SAEDIFICI·CVSTODIAE·ET·MONVMENTI·RELIQVERV

3.5 Marble plan of a tomb complex in the Archaeological Museum, Perugia, $\frac{1}{10}$ life size; their relative size can be appraised by virtue of the annotated dimensions in feet.

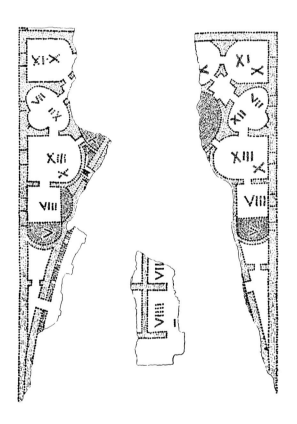

3.6 Fragments from a floor mosaic representing the plan of the bath complex of which it formed part. Room sizes are indicated by numerals of feet, suggesting a scale of 1:16.

3.7 (*facing page*) Statue group known as the Dying Gaul in the Capitoline Museums (2nd century AD copy of a Hellenistic original?), with interpretation of the diagram inscribed on its base: (a) tracing of the diagram in its actual state; (b) reconstruction of the diagram in pristine state; (c) reconstruction of its underlying geometry; (d) the diagram related to the plan of the statue; (e) the diagram related to the supposed location of the statue in its original setting in Pergamon; (f) the statue in elevation.

complex, the others the custodian's building overhead) (fig. 3.5). It seems to have been appended to a testament, to ensure that the beneficiaries faithfully followed the wishes of the deceased rather than building a cheaper project.[17] A comparable example is illustrated in figure 4.5. Another curious plan in the form of a mosaic floor shows a bath building, probably at 1:16.[18] With the plunge pools in blue and the interlocking room shapes picked out in other colours, it doubled as a decorative pattern and visitors' map (fig. 3.6). Proper architects' scale elevations from the Roman period have yet to be found, but it is important to note that frontal views of buildings were a familiar staple of the Roman relief sculptor (fig. 3.8). As for perspectives, elaborate architectural fantasies were one of the prime subjects of Roman fresco decoration, which implies that non-architects must have felt comfortable with receiving proposals in this form. Wealthy Romans were in effect surrounded by architectural representations in their own homes, a familiarity that may have helped make them more effective patrons.

Design drawings and models

After the annexation of Egypt by Augustus, papyrus became plentiful enough and cheap enough to have entered into general usage.[19] Rolls were made by gluing multiple sheets of papyrus end to end, the most common height being just 16–20cm, at least in the case of those used for script. This therefore precluded drawings of a decent size, unless they happened to be long and thin,[20] but larger surfaces were certainly feasible, since a pair of architectural drawings from the Eighteenth Dynasty belonging to the Petrie Museum in London have a height of around 53cm (fig. 3.2).[21] Architects may have had access to parchment made from animal skin, a more costly medium which allowed for greater precision and larger surfaces. At any rate there do exist medieval parchments used to design Gothic tracery in exquisite detail.[22] One ancient source tells of an occasion when Cornelius Fronto was presented with alternative projects for a bath complex on *membranulae*, a word that seems more likely to signify parchment than papyrus.[23] Representations of Roman architects sometimes show a roll of some kind in their hand, and it is tempting to think of these as drawings as opposed to written documents. It is true that the scrolls shown in a relief at Terracina (fig. 1.14) are too small to be more than a location plan, but much larger ones are represented in a relief at Sens showing a gang of decorators at work.[24] The funerary relief of T. Statilius Aper (fig. 1.12) shows him in the company of a very large roll of drawings (90cm or more tall)

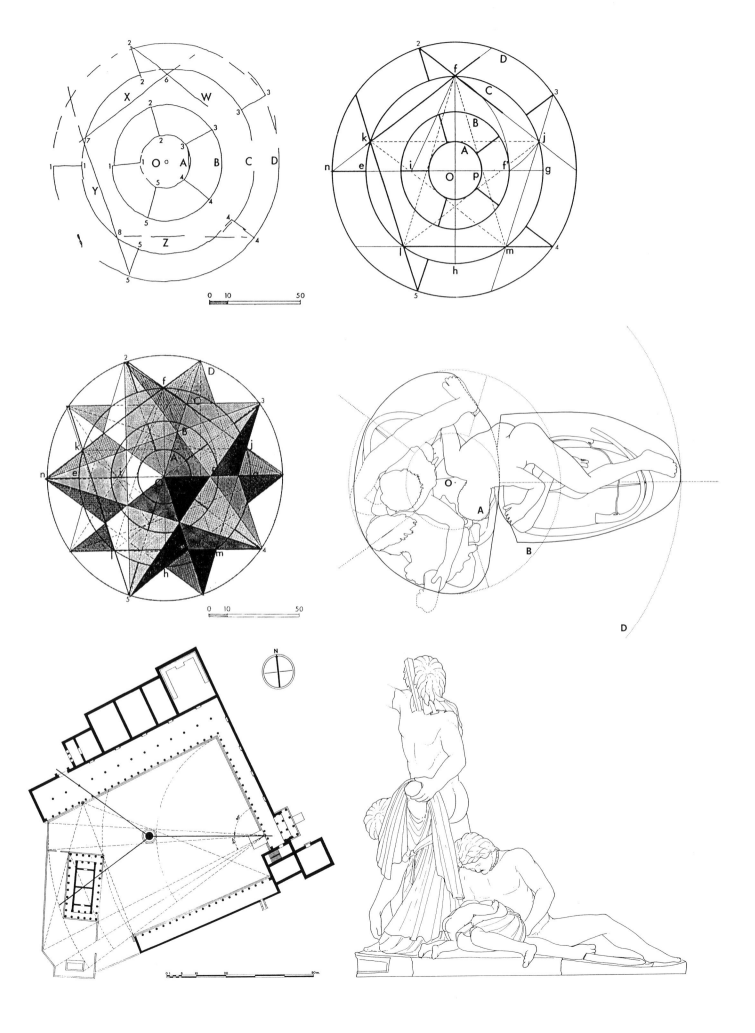

0   10   50

0   10   50

N

0·1 5 10   20   50 m.

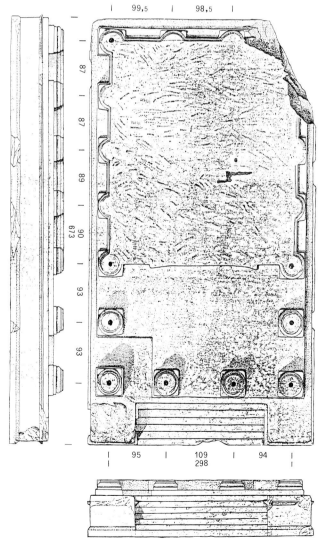

standing on the ground – still a not unfamiliar sight in today's architect's office.

The content of such perishable drawings can be visualized on the basis of comparisons, including Roman marble maps, the plan inscribed on the lap of a diorite statue of the Mesopotamian ruler Gudea (figs 1.9 and 1.10), and the papyrus plan of Ramses IV's tomb.[25] Similar draughting procedures were no doubt used for design as for the purpose of record, including the use of straight lines (whether free-hand, struck using taut strings or ruled with a straight-edge), compass-drawn arcs and annotated dimensions. Other types of drawing would have been explanatory diagrams (excluding correct wall thicknesses and so on) akin, perhaps, to Vitruvius' lost schemes for planning theatres (fig. 2.5). A diagram of this type that survives on the base of the famous statue group of the Dying Gaul (fig. 3.7) could have been used in its composition. Filippo Coarelli further argues that this same diagram was the key to the positioning of the statue group in its architectural setting.[26] Elevations are more elusive, but potential guides include sculptural reliefs with architectural backdrops from the Roman period itself (fig. 3.8), the stunning Pharaonic elevations of a portable shrine in the Petrie Museum (fig. 3.2), and the 1:24 design of a pediment found on a marble block built into the Hellenistic Temple of Athena Polias at Priene (fig. 3.12).[27] Scales like those mentioned, 1:240, 1:24 and 1:16, were no doubt used for design too, as they corresponded to simple factors in terms of the standard subdivisions of the foot, inches (or one-twelfths) and digits (or one-sixteenths).

As already stated, the reliance on scale drawing has implications for the very way in which architects design. Roman architects' frequent use of the compass in constructing and calibrating details may have predisposed them to using curves for general planning purposes. Also significant is the fact that drawings and models enhance the possibility of coming to terms with the visual consequence of a design, thus inviting a process of review and modification. As Alberti observed on the basis of his personal experience:

3.8 (*top left*) Relief elevation of an octastyle temple, probably that of Mars Ultor, from one of the marble reliefs belonging to the Ara Pietatis Augustae (dedicated AD 43), now in the Villa Medici collection, Rome.

3.9 (*left*) Plan and elevations of marble model representing a project for a temple, Antiquarium, Ostia (mid-imperial period), probably 1:24 or 1:32 (reproduced here at ⅙ life size).

I have often formed in my mind ideas of buildings that
have given me a wonderful delight, yet when I work
them out into lines I discover that in the parts which
please me most there are serious errors which must be
corrected.[28]

There are just two known detailed design models from
the Roman period, and it so happens that both of
them bear witness to processes of modification. One is
a marble model of a thoroughly conventional temple
which was found in the college of the Augustales at
Ostia (fig. 3.9). The other, this time made of a fine
limestone, shows the inner sanctum, or adyton, of the
larger of the two temples at Niha in the Lebanon (figs
3.1, 3.10 and 3.11). In each case the upper parts of the
superstructure were omitted, since they would have
prevented a close examination of the plan, and scaling
off from it.[29] The presence of dowel holes in the top
of some of the columns of the Ostia model indicates
the existence of an upper half which could have been
lowered into place.[30]

It is not known to which temple the Ostia model
related, but the general typology of the plan is familiar enough from buildings like the rectangular temple
at Tivoli and that of Portunus in the Forum Boarium
(fig. 3.26). The so-called Maison Carrée at Nîmes
follows the same principle and the same double-
square proportions, although the number of columns
is greater (fig. 3.29). The width of the model is about
one Roman foot measured from centre to centre of
the corner columns, suggesting that this measurement
was an important feature of the design. The most likely
scale is 1 : 32 (one digit to 2 ft), in which case the built
equivalent would have been similar in size to both the
Temple of Portunus and, closer to hand, the temple
behind Ostia's theatre.[31]

Three details of the Ostia model yield insights into
the vicissitudes of the design process. First of all, the
central bay of the front is wider than its neighbours.
Secondly, the column spacing along the flanks is not
regular; starting with the interval used for the front
(excluding the central bay), it gradually reduces towards
the back, perhaps because the depth of the site was
limited (fig. 3.9). Both these features suggest that a
regular organization based on a double square grid
with a 10 ft module provided the starting point for
design, just as it did for the Hellenistic temples at Teos
and Letöon (fig. 2.10), and the Temple of Portunus too
(fig. 3.26). Finally, the architect provided two alternatives for treating the stylobate and the column bases.
The area with a lowered floor on the left side of the
portico probably represented the less favoured option

3.10 (*top*) Plan of a limestone 1 : 24 scale model representing a
project for the adyton of the larger of the two temples at Niha,
near Baalbek, Lebanon (late 2nd century AD). The plan is reproduced here at 2/15 life size.

3.11 Reconstruction of the interior of the large temple at Niha.

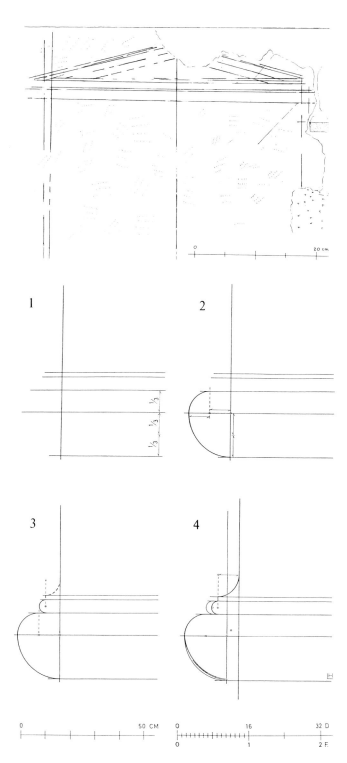

of placing the columns on individual sub-plinths, not unlike the detail used for the aedicules inside the Pantheon, for example. The rest of the model showed the more typical solution of bases resting directly on the stylobate, as they do in the Maison Carrée and countless other temples.

The Niha model offers an especially precious glimpse of the design process, for it can be directly compared with the built result (figs 3.10 and 3.11), hitherto a possibility in an ancient context only in the case of the tomb of Ramses IV.[32] The temple is in fact an interesting building in its own right, with the rich contrast between the highly articulate adyton that was popular in the Levant and the relatively austere box that contained it. The model evidently described the project as it stood just before construction began – witness the inclusion of peculiarities such as the asymmetrical stair and the entrance to the undercroft. But the executed temple diverges in respect of minor details, just as the tomb of Ramses diverges from its plan. The lower flight of steps has one step less than the upper, and the configuration at the top is different. These changes were possibly introduced during the presentation meeting, along, perhaps, with the freehand sketch of an octagonal group of colonnettes defining a sort of baldacchino. But the survival of hexagonal bases of an appropriate size suggests that the plan of this part ended up hexagonal too. In short, the design process had yet to run its full course.[33]

On-site drawings

With the commencement of work on site, architects began to lay out detailed working drawings on suitable flat surfaces, usually of stone, but plaster must sometimes have been a handy alternative, especially in the residential context.[34] The support might be floors, walls, or even the faces of particularly large single blocks (notably one of the three unimaginably huge stones built into the podium of the Temple of Jupiter at Baalbek (figs 3.16 and 8.20)). Some drawings survive because they, like this one, were immured by the next phases of construction, others because the parent masonry was never finished – usually, of course, drawings were erased during the final polishing. Due to erosion and staining, lines can now be hard to make out, but originally some draughting surfaces may have been coated in red pigment, allowing the incised lines to stand out by virtue of exposing the bright marble below.

3.12 (*top*) Elevation of a pediment incised on a marble block built into the wall of the Temple of Athena Polias at Priene, Turkey (ca. 340 BC), 1:24 (reproduced here at 1/6 life size).

3.13 Base profile for the peristyle columns of the Temple of Apollo, Didyma, Turkey (mid-3rd century BC), with hypothetical sequence of stages used to generate the design/template (4) at full size, reproduced here at 1/15 scale. Like other drawings this was inscribed on the marble wall of the adyton.

To date, the subject-matter of Hellenistic and Roman site drawings includes voussoir construction (fig. 3.15), pediments (fig. 3.12), cornice details (figs 3.16, 3.17 and 10.14), base and capital profiles (figs 3.13 and 10.14), fluting (fig. 0.12), entasis (fig. 6.29) and entire recumbent column shafts (fig. 6.31). Most examples are full size, but the 1:24 elevation of a pediment at Priene (fig. 3.12) is a reminder that the composition of the upper levels might still be outstanding during the construction phase. As for three-dimensional site mock-ups, these are known only from the Pharaonic, Greek and Ptolemaic periods,[35] but their use is likely to have continued to some extent in Roman times. It seems that full-size prototypes were occasionally sent to the quarries to guide serial prefabrication, one example being a Corinthian capital of Italian manufacture which has been found at the Proconnesos quarries near Constantinople.[36] It should also be remembered that entire buildings could act as full-scale preliminary designs for later 'copies'. No ancient building is wholly a slavish copy of another – but in a very real sense the fifth-century BC Temple of Juno-Lacinia at Agrigento was a full-size model for the Temple of Concord on the same site (fig. 3.25), just as was the Arch of Septimius Severus for Constantine's (p. 124) or Trajan's Column for Marcus Aurelius' (chapter 8).[37]

In theory, full-size drawings might be just copies of ones prepared in advance at a smaller scale; it is clear, however, that certain aspects of design remained outstanding until the last minute. Some drawings show trial and modification in microcosm: the profiles at Bziza (fig. 3.17) and Aphrodisias (fig. 6.31) were first constructed according to a simple geometry, and then adjusted to taste. This process is particularly clear in the base profile at Didyma (fig. 3.13). Lines defining the limits of the profile and points for compass centres were first laid out according to a series of simple proportions and whole *dactyls* (the standard one-sixteenth part subdivisions of Greek feet). The profile was then constructed accordingly, but the result was presumably not quite what was wanted, hence a couple of minor adjustments which meant that it no longer adhered precisely to a neat mathematical scheme. As for the drawings relating to the little cult building inside the great court, these bear witness to a more radical change of design, for it seems that the façade was broadened before construction. At the end of this book I confront the question of whether the drawings at the Mausoleum of Augustus suggest something of an original, abandoned, project for the Pantheon.

3.14 (*top*) Detail of the bottom storey of the amphitheatre at Capua (Hadrianic period). Note the indefinite character of the order, with elements deriving from the Doric, Tuscan and Ionic vocabularies.

3.15 Full-size template for setting out the arch and masonry joints of a typical bay of the amphitheatre at Capua. The building is visible in the background.

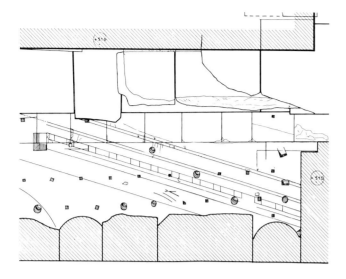

3.16 (*above*)   Full-size working drawing for the pediment of the Temple of Jupiter at Baalbek (early 1st century AD), inscribed on one of the three huge blocks known as the Trilithon.

3.17 (*below*)   Full-size profile of a pediment inscribed on the walls of a temple of imperial date at Bziza in northern Lebanon (reproduced here at $\frac{1}{15}$ life size).

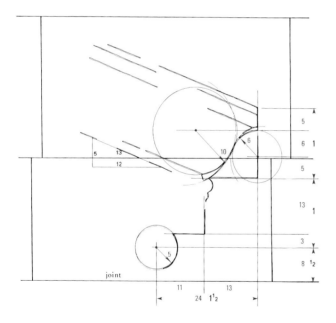

THE EVIDENCE OF VITRUVIUS

In short, a sizeable proportion of the few Hellenistic and Roman design drawings and models that survive bear testimony to a surprisingly fluid approach to design. I say 'surprising' since, as remarked at the beginning of this chapter, classical architecture, including that of the ancient world, is often perceived to be locked into relatively predictable patterns.[38] It must be admitted that the conventions of building with the orders meant that a great deal of information was encoded in words like 'Doric', 'Ionic' and 'Corinthian'. And Vitruvius certainly adopted a rather mechanical approach to categorizing temples on the basis of formulas defining column distribution. 'Tetrastyle', 'hexastyle' and 'octastyle' indicated the numbers of columns on the ends of rectangular buildings as 4, 6 and 8 respectively. 'Pycnostyle', 'systyle', 'eustyle' and 'diastyle' defined column rhythms in terms of intercolumnations equal to $1\frac{1}{2}$, 2, $2\frac{1}{4}$ and 3 column diameters. 'Peripteral', 'dipteral', 'pseudoperipteral', 'pseudodipteral', 'prostyle' and 'amphiprostyle' defined standard types of temple plans. It was possible for an architect or even an informed patron to determine the outline of a project simply by stipulating a brief list of such definitions. The instruction to make, say, 'a double-square tetrastyle pseudoperipteral temple with a 28 ft tall systyle Ionic portico' was enough to guarantee that the result resembled the Temple of Portunus (fig. 3.27). Little of strategic importance remained besides selecting materials, proportions, the rake of the pediment and the form of podium. But other building types were not nearly so constrained. Vitruvius' insistence on apparently immutable formulas (just as the writers of some cookery books concentrate on recipes as opposed to culinary principles) reflects more his personal background and his didactic programme than it does actual practice (chapter 2).

Yet Vitruvius does occasionally yield to a more flexible approach. For example, he advises that basilicas conform to a certain proportional range, 'unless the site is naturally such to prevent this and to oblige an alteration in these proportions' (V,1,4). The proportions of entablatures and other elements could be modified for optical reasons. Repeating the Platonic doctrine that the visual image is but a corruption of reality, Vitruvius argued that the architect's task was to trick the eye into conveying a 'true' impression to the brain. So the relative size of the entablature should increase in a tall building,

> for the higher that the eye has to climb, the less easily can it penetrate the thicker and thicker mass of air . . . Hence there must always be a corresponding increase in the proportions of the members, whether the buildings are on unusually lofty sites or are themselves somewhat colossal (III,5,9).[39]

Vitruvius expanded on the general problem of modification in two key passages, both of which are worth quoting at length. The first occurs in the chapter on the layout of the Latin theatre (fig. 2.5). After presenting an ideal mathematical schema, he went on to explain:

It is not possible that in all theatres these rules of *symmetria* should answer all conditions and purposes, but the architect ought to consider to what extent he must follow the principle of *symmetria*, and to what extent it may be modified to suit the nature of the site or the size of the work. There are, of course, some things which, for utility's sake, must be made of the same size in a small theatre as in a large one: such as the steps, curved cross-aisles, their parapets, the passageways, stairways, stages, tribunals . . . Again, if in the course of the work any of the material fall short, such as marble, timber or anything else, it will not be amiss to make a slight reduction or addition, provided that it is done without going too far, but with intelligence (v,6,7).

The other passage appears in the second chapter of Book VI:

There is nothing to which an architect should devote more thought than to the exact proportions of his building with reference to a certain part selected as standard. After the standard of *symmetria* has been determined, and the proportionate dimensions adjusted by calculations, it is next the part of wisdom to consider the nature of the site, or questions of use and beauty, and modify the plan by diminutions or additions in such a manner that these diminutions or additions in symmetrical relations may be seen to have been made on correct principles, and without detracting at all from the effect.

The look of a building when seen close at hand is one thing, on a height it is another, not the same in an enclosed place, still different in the open, and in all these cases it takes much judgment to decide what is to be done . . . [so] diminutions or additions should be made to suit the nature or needs of the site, but in such fashion that the buildings lose nothing thereby. These results, however, are also attainable by flashes of genius, and not only by mere science.

Hence the first thing to settle is the standard of *symmetria*, from which we need not hesitate to vary. Then establish the length and breadth of the work proposed, and when once we have determined its size, let the construction follow with due regard to beauty of proportion, so that the beholder may feel no doubt of the *eurythmia* of its effect.

What emerges are three distinct stages of design. The first aims 'to settle the standard of *symmetria*', that is to say a provisional scheme of proportions and dimensions. These were then 'adjusted by calculations', creating a more considered and elaborate stage. Thus far the design was abstract in conception, a play on mathematical principles. The purpose of the next stage brought the project down to earth, so to speak, by focusing on the 'nature of the site, or questions of use and beauty'. In other words, the architect turns his attention from *symmetria* to *eurythmia* and *decor*. There was however another, earlier, phase. At the inception of design the architect needed to have some idea of the basic character of the future building, including knowledge of its environment and rough size:

If our design for private houses is to be correct, we must at the outset take note of the countries and climates in which they are built. One style of house seems appropriate in Egypt, another in Spain, a different kind in Pontus, one still different in Rome, and so on . . . (VI,1,1).

The size of a forum should be proportionate to the number of inhabitants, so that it many not be too small a space to be useful, nor look like a desert waste for lack of population (V,1,2).

Other aspects which had to be confronted at an early stage include the choice of order, for example Doric for a temple to Hercules, Ionic for one to Venus (I,2,5). Plans had to organized so as to take into account orientation: art galleries should make use of north light; the hot rooms of bathing quarters should face south or south-west, so as to exploit solar gain (VI,4; V,10,1).

It is now possible to chart Vitruvius' four main stages of architectural design:

Vitruvius' conception of the design process

Generalities	Abstract design independent of site		Specifics
I **Inception**	**II** **Preliminary scheme**	**III** **Interim scheme**	**IV** **Definitive project**
rough idea of character, size and site of project [preliminary *decor*]	outline dimensions and proportions [preliminary *symmetria*]	mathematical and formal conflicts resolved [interim *symmetria* and *eurythmia*]	modifications to suit the site, use and beauty [definitive *symmetria*, *eurythmia* and *decor*]

Stage I: Inception

It is instructive to look for signs of Vitruvius' stages in actual buildings. Only his ideas that certain orders were best suited for particular deities are, as discussed in chapter 6, conspicuously wide of the mark; otherwise both his specific recommendations and their general tone find direct echoes in reality. The porticoes of major civic buildings in the capital do have more elegant proportions than those of Pompeian houses; the hot rooms in bath buildings do often face south or south-west, a desire that no doubt explains the diagonal bias of the Forum Baths at Ostia (fig. 3.18), and the south-west orientation of entire complexes like the Baths of Caracalla or Diocletian (fig. 1.1). To illustrate his point about the importance of the site, everything about the sanctuary at Palestrina shows that its steeply sloping setting inspired the very way the space was orchestrated. And it almost goes without saying that large buildings tend to serve large populations (Rome has the biggest circus, the biggest amphitheatre, the biggest baths). The size of a project, too, was fundamental in another sense: no architect would choose a tetrastyle front for a huge temple, or an octastyle front for a tiny one. Experience showed that the former implied unrealistically wide spans, and the latter unreasonably small passageways between the columns.[40]

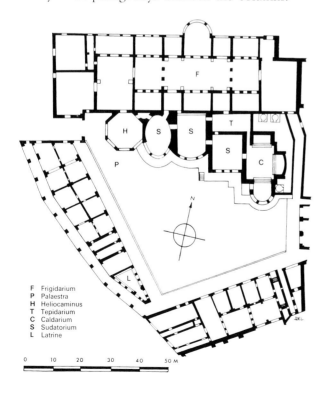

F   Frigidarium
P   Palaestra
H   Heliocaminus
T   Tepidarium
C   Caldarium
S   Sudatorium
L   Latrine

0   10   20   30   40   50 M

3.18   Plan of the Forum Baths at Ostia (AD ca. 160), 1:1250.

Stage II: Preliminary scheme

The principles guiding the choice of dimensions and proportions in practice are the focus of chapters 4 and 5; here it is enough to recall the mathematical character of Vitruvius' ideals, as represented by the Basilica at Fanum. Almost all of the dimensions quoted are simply related to one another, besides being either multiples or fractions of 6 or 10, the numbers he singled out as 'perfect' (see pp. 45–6).

Stage III: Interim scheme

The aim of this stage is to reconcile conflicts arising between different ideals posited in the preceding one. For example, a simple overall proportion for a peristyle or atrium might turn out to be incompatible with a neat column distribution, calling for one or other to be adjusted.[41] At a much larger scale it would seem that detailed considerations regarding the relationship between the main block and the perimeter porticoes of the Baths of Caracalla had the effect of distorting the nominally 1000 ft square precinct into one which actually measures 1000 by 1010 ft.[42] In round buildings a recurrent problem was the inevitable presence of awkward dimensions, due to the irrational ratio (π) between the diameter of a circle and its circumference. The Zeus-Asklepios temple at Pergamon serves as a good illustration, since it is possible to identify the starting-point for its design, namely the Pantheon in Rome. It follows its model most notably in the array of sixteen radial accents arranged as eight piers and openings. Perfect symmetry was presumably envisaged at the outset (fig. 3.19), but it must have then become clear that regular radials did not produce round dimensions for the subdivisions of the perimeter. So the initial radial geometry was abandoned in favour of a sequence involving runs of 12, 18 and 24 ft (fig. 3.19), all multiples of 4 ft, just like the 80 ft diameter; as a result the diagonal axes no longer subtend 45° with respect to the cardinal axes.[43]

Similar adjustments were normal practice in amphitheatre design. The starting-point for laying out a substantial number of monumental civic amphitheatres was one of just two geometrical schemes. These schemes located the focal points of an oval at the vertices of two 'focal triangles', one being the 3:4:5 or Pythagorean triangle, the other the bisected equilateral triangle (figs 5.3 and 5.4). Using either of these methods it was possible to generate the basic outline of an amphitheatre arena with but a few sweeps of the compass.[44] Curiously enough, however, the dimensions

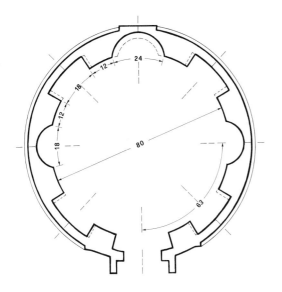

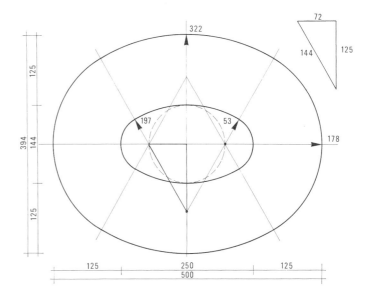

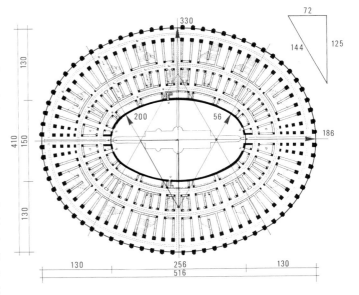

3.19 Plan of the Zeus-Asklepios temple at Pergamon, Turkey (Hadrianic period), 1:500. The dotted lines describe a perfectly symmetrical possible initial scheme.

3.20 Outline layout of the amphitheatre at Verona (early 1st century AD): (a) hypothetical initial design based on the Equilateral-triangle-and-inscribed-circle scheme and simple dimensions (cf. fig. 5.4); (b) modified scheme ensuring that the centres of the perimeter piers are spaced 20 ft apart (cf. p. 16).

utilized are almost never as simple as one might expect: the arena at Verona is quite typical in having proportions and dimensions that are almost simple, but not quite. It seems that the first step was to create a provisional scheme based on simple *linear* dimensions, one that was then adjusted to achieve the desired *circumferential* ones (fig. 3.20). It was a point of principle that the interval between successive piers on the main façade be both regular and a whole number of feet, 20 ft in this and in several other examples (fig. 6.22).

Stage IV: Use and beauty

It might seem odd that Vitruvius bracketed use and beauty together (VI,2,1), but it can be hard to divide them. A good example is the common practice of widening the central bay of otherwise regular façades, as in the case of the Ostia model (fig. 3.9), the Maison Carrée (fig. 3.30), the Temple of Saturn and the Pantheon (fig. 10.12),[45] besides numerous Hellenistic and Etruscan precursors. A wider bay had a functional purpose, by enlarging the principal circulation route, and it was for this reason Vitruvius' preferred solution (III,3,5; cf. III,3,3). It also provided a better view of the main door, and, when it was open, the cult statue

beyond. (Just such a desire is implicit in countless numismatic representations of temples with the columns shifted out of the way.) Aesthetic considerations certainly apply to the wider central bay of the short sides of the Temple of Bel at Palmyra – for the entrance was along one of the long sides. Nor does the wider axial bay in the portico of the Teatro Marittimo at Hadrian's Villa serve any practical function, as the moat of water effectively confined circulation to the portico itself (fig. 5.19).

In general, modifications to the elevation are likely to reflect a concern for its appearance. Circuses, on the other hand, offer good examples of modifications made on the basis of functional criteria. The notional model was a symmetrical U-shaped plan closed by the line of starting gates (*carceres*). This was then adapted so as to improve racing conditions: the line of *carceres* was inclined slightly and curved in a bow, giving each team an equal distance before the bottleneck at the beginning of the central barrier or spine (*euripus, spina*); a kink was introduced into the flank so as to increase the width at this critical point; the barrier was tilted to take account of the centrifugal slippage as the chariots swung around in an anti-clockwise direction (fig. 3.21).[46]

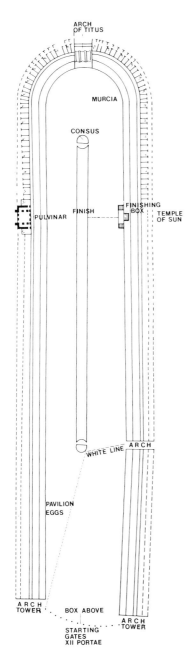

3.21   Plan of the Circus Maximus, Rome. Note how the notional symmetrical extruded U-shape plan incorporates a series of minor adjustments in the interests of improving conditions for chariot racing.

Stage IV continued: The site

Unless it was so extreme as to dictate the initial strategy, as in the case of the sanctuary at Palestrina, site topography seems to be a relatively late preoccupation, just as Vitruvius suggests. The uncertain shape of the hemicycle of Trajan's Markets no doubt represents the adaptation of a semicircle in view of problems with carving it out of the Quirinal escarpment.[47] Cramped site conditions must also account for the exceptionally compact column spacing on the flanks of the Temple of Vespasian, or the receding rhythm along the sides of the Ostia model (fig. 3.9).[48] Amphitheatres on sloping sites usually exhibit the same formal characteristics as those on flat ones, suggesting that the flat site model was adapted to suit all types of terrain. The local topography at Merida and Italica meant that the façades reached full height only towards the main axes. Otherwise they were simply cut away to fit the sloping ground, leaving the top of both buildings perfectly horizontal.

The evolution of the design of Diocletian's army headquarters, or *principia*, at Palmyra may be attributed in part to the local topography, in part to structural considerations. Once the basic organization was taken from some manual of military architecture (similar schemes are quite common), the first task was to ascertain a suitable overall size on the basis of occupancy and funding, in this case, 200 by 100 ft. The next step was to prepare a proper plan, taking into account provisional wall thicknesses of either 3 or 4 ft. At the same time the corners were cut off so as to avoid levelling works where the building met the base of a hill (fig. 3.22a). Finally, a couple of the walls were thickened up; those either side of the central apsidal room became $3\frac{2}{3}$ ft as opposed to 3 ft, presumably because the thickness was judged inadequate for the span. This change, together with a minor misalignment of the main axis, explains why the overall width worked out as 202 ft (fig. 3.22b).[49] At the other end of the empire the *principia* type was the model for the forum at Banasa in Morocco, only here the nature of the site called for the whole plan to be skewed (fig. 3.23).[50] There are in fact innumerable irregular urban complexes which bear witness to analogous processes. In the more sophisticated designs the treatment of secondary spaces and wall thicknesses according to the *poché* principle meant that primary spaces could yet present a regular experience. Good illustrations are the basilica at Lepcis Magna (fig. 3.24) and the imperial fora in Rome (fig. 1.6).

Even though such examples can be seen to fit into

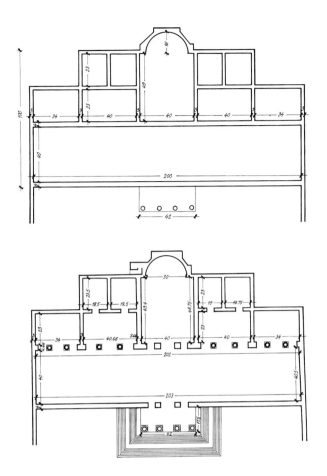

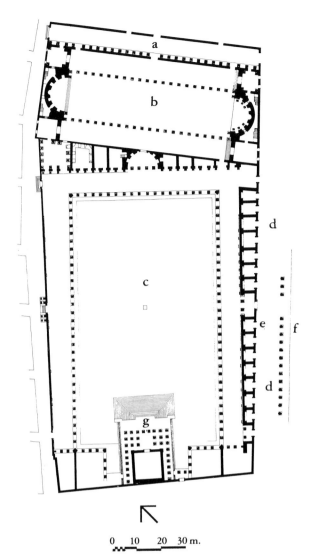

3.22 Plan of Diocletian's army headquarters at Palmyra, Syria: (a) provisional design; (b) executed version, with thicker walls where required structurally and other minor modifications.

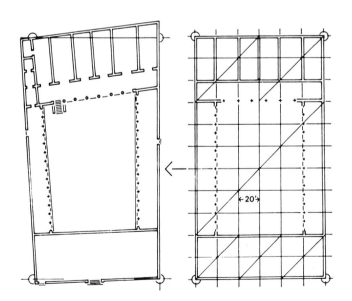

3.23 Plan of the forum at Banasa, Morocco: (a) hypothetical ideal scheme; (b) actual state.

0   10   20   30 m.

3.24 Plan of the Severan forum and basilica at Lepcis Magna, Libya (AD ca. 200), 1 : 1500. Note how the regularity of the subordinate spaces is sacrificed in deference to the hierachically more important ones: (a) side street; (b) basilica; (c) forum; (d) arcaded walkway; (e) shops; (f) boulevard; (g) dynastic temple.

Vitruvius' framework, it still bears two notable faults. Firstly, he conceives design as a linear development, moving successively from the general to the specific;[51] there is no mention of the feedback mechanism whereby the resolution of details may induce changes to the overall scheme. Secondly, he gives little hint that design continued after works had begun, implying a rather artificial split between design and construction, one which is contradicted by the graphic evidence discussed earlier. As William Wallace has remarked, 'Before the twentieth century, there was rarely a clear division between design and execution. The period of realization is, therefore, also a period of creativity.'[52]

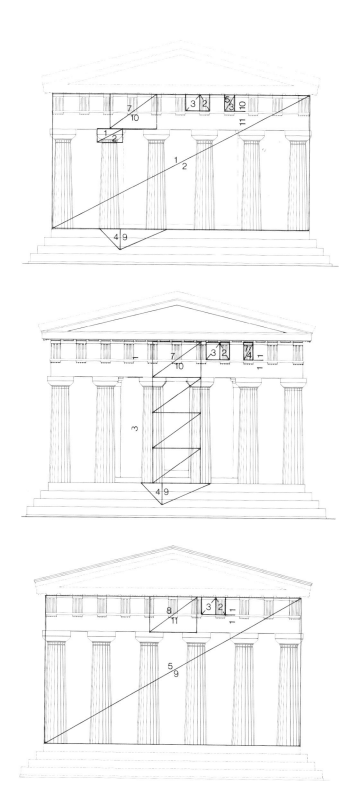

3.25 Elevations of three Doric temples at Agrigento with proportional interpretation overlaid: (a) Temple of Juno-Lacinia (450 BC); (b) Temple of Concord (430 BC); (c) Temple of Castor and Pollux (420 BC).

THE DIALOGUE BETWEEN PLAN AND ELEVATION

A fundamental characteristic of classical architecture is the interdependence of plan and elevation, largely as a function of the logic of the orders. Yet plan and elevation each have an autonomous logic too. A plan is an imaginary horizontal slice through a building, an abstract tool that serves to organize space. An elevation, on the other hand, represents a façade as if it could be seen from a distance, without perspective recession. Vitruvius distinguished between the drawing techniques that were appropriate in each case: the plan (*ichnographia*) being made 'by the proper successive use of compasses and rule, through which we get outlines for the plane surfaces of buildings'; the elevation (*orthographia*) being 'a picture of the front of a building, set upright and properly drawn in the proportions of the contemplated work' (1,2,2). So architects, then as now, operated in different ways according to the mode they were in, yet they still had to make plan and elevation match.

The impact of the plan on the elevation, and vice versa, very much depends on the type of building in question. The elevation of a Doric temple of the classical period arguably took precedence over the plan; it might be said that design was primarily an exercise in planning the elevation. The ubiquitous hexastyle temple displays a remarkably uniform façade, always with a stylobate of three or four steps, an enfilade of robust columns, a trabeation with a triglyph frieze (always two per bay), a pediment rake in the range 11–15°, and everywhere tightly controlled proportions. Plans, by contrast, were relatively heterogeneous. One configuration was favoured for temples on the mainland, another for those in Sicily and the western colonies; then there were miscellaneous variants, such as the plan of the Olympieion at Agrigento or the Temple of Apollo at Bassae (fig. 7.3). Such plans do not usually display an obvious compositional order: the cella walls may or may not align with the peristyle columns; the column rhythm on flank and front may differ; the corner bay is contracted. Such irregularities only make sense as devices to obtain a desirable appearance and a regular triglyph frieze in particular. The three temples at Agrigento illustrated in figure 3.25 show this point particularly well, but the same message could be made using most major Doric temples from the century or so following the 470s BC.

Vitruvius states that some architects reacted against what he called the 'embarrassments' and 'incongruities' associated with the Doric corner (IV,3,1). Indeed, the architects of an extended family of Hellenistic Ionic temples adopted what almost seems to be a deliberately contrasting strategy, design being essentially an exercise in elevating the plan. The plans themselves were fixed by more or less rigorous grid systems, a method learnt, perhaps, from Egyptian working practices (fig. 3.2).[53] Pytheos' Temple of Athena at Priene exemplifies this approach, with the width of the column base used as the module for a two-way grid (fig. 2.10). The axes of the peristyle delineate a double square of ten by twenty modules, while the cella walls align with the corresponding columns. Although Pytheos must have made sure that this scheme produced a satisfactory elevation, its rough proportions were effectively constrained by the plan and the detailed profile of the bases.

In the wake of numerous variations on this theme at other sites in Asia Minor,[54] the rectangular temple at Tivoli, that of Portunus (fig. 3.27), and the Maison Carrée (fig. 3.29) represent more or less standard adaptations of this scheme to the Roman context. The new common denominator is the type of organization known as pseudoperipteral, in which free-standing columns are replaced by half-columns applied to the cella wall on the back and sides. The predominant Roman formula wedded this layout to a high podium approached by a broad flight of steps, a typology which made a great deal of practical sense. The all-embracing colonnade of the Greek peripteral temple had in any case little place in Roman liturgy, which contemplated primarily a frontal approach. Retaining a full-blooded portico on the front had the effect of simultaneously emphasizing the entrance while creating a monumental urban statement. Meanwhile immuring the walls along the flanks both maximized the width of the cella while eliminating the expense of a complete circuit of columns.

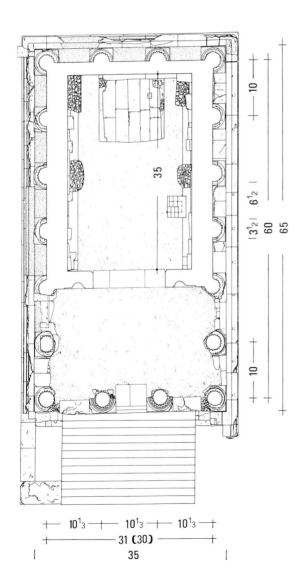

3.27　Elevation of the Temple of Portunus, 1 : 150.

3.26 (*left*)　Plan of the Temple of Portunus, traditionally known as the Temple of Fortuna Virilis, in the Forum Boarium (early 1st century BC), 1 : 250. The 30 ft width shown in parentheses indicates the likely intended value at an early stage of design.

65

The polarities of temple design can apply to other types of building; it is possible, for example, to class the typical circus as a plan-driven project and the typical Petra tomb as an elevation-driven one. In the main, however, the equilibrium was more balanced. A good illustration is the Maison Carrée at Nîmes, one of the best preserved of all ancient buildings (figs 3.28–3.31), and one which is as likely as any to represent general practice, being a thoroughly orthodox interpretation of the model Roman temple. The façade based on the Corinthian order reflected the prevailing norms for official architecture in Rome, recalling in particular Augustus' great Temple of Mars Ultor (fig. 2.4).[55]

An analysis of the *symmetria* of the temple reveals a pattern that is almost simple and coherent – but not quite. The name Maison Carrée appears singularly apt since two squares are inscribed implicitly on the front, one based on the interaxial width of the peristyle, the other on the overall width, the mouldings excluded (fig. 3.30). However, further relationships as simple as this are hard to find. One might ask why the length of the peristyle is somewhat more than double its

width? Why are the column bases not quite half the column spacing? Why is the column spacing on the front different to that on the flanks?

These 'near misses' suggest that at some stage the architect had in mind a simpler plan, but came to modify it, just as the designer of the Temple of Portunus modified a comparable double cube initial scheme (figs 3.26 and 3.27).[56] Since the Maison Carrée stands in the middle of a flat colonnaded court, it is hard to see why the site should have been the cause of modification. Instead the explanation lies in the conflicts that arose between the ideal proportions of the plan and those of the elevation. The original goals are likely to have included the following:

Plan:

- a column diameter ½ the *diagonal* width of its base
- a column base ½ as wide as the column spacing
- a peristyle ½ as wide as its length (interaxially)
- a cella ³⁄₂ times as long as its width (internally)

Elevation:

- a column height of 10 diameters
- an entablature height ¼ the column height
- a podium height ³⁄₂ times the entablature height
- a column height ½ the length of the cella
- a height of podium plus column equal to the peristyle width

There is the further possibility that the project was conceived on a modular basis, since numerous multiples of 3 ft are present. However, there is a far from consistent pattern, and in fact it is doubtful that Roman architects pursued such a markedly modular strategy as that practised by Durand, for example. In any event, the ideal plan happened to generate a slight difference with respect to the ideal elevation. Assuming a 3 ft column diameter, the plan implies a 42½ ft wide peristyle, measured from centre to centre of the corner columns (fig. 3.29a). But with the same 3 ft diameter as the point of departure, the combined height for column and podium comes to 41¼ ft

3.29 (*facing page top*) Plan of the Maison Carrée (1st decade AD), 1 : 250: (a) hypothetical ideal plan; (b) modified executed version.

3.30 (*facing page bottom*) Front elevation of the Maison Carrée, with 1 : 1 proportions overlaid: (a) hypothetical ideal design; (b) modified executed version.

3.28 (*left*) Detail of end façade of the Maison Carrée, Nîmes, France, 1 : 60.

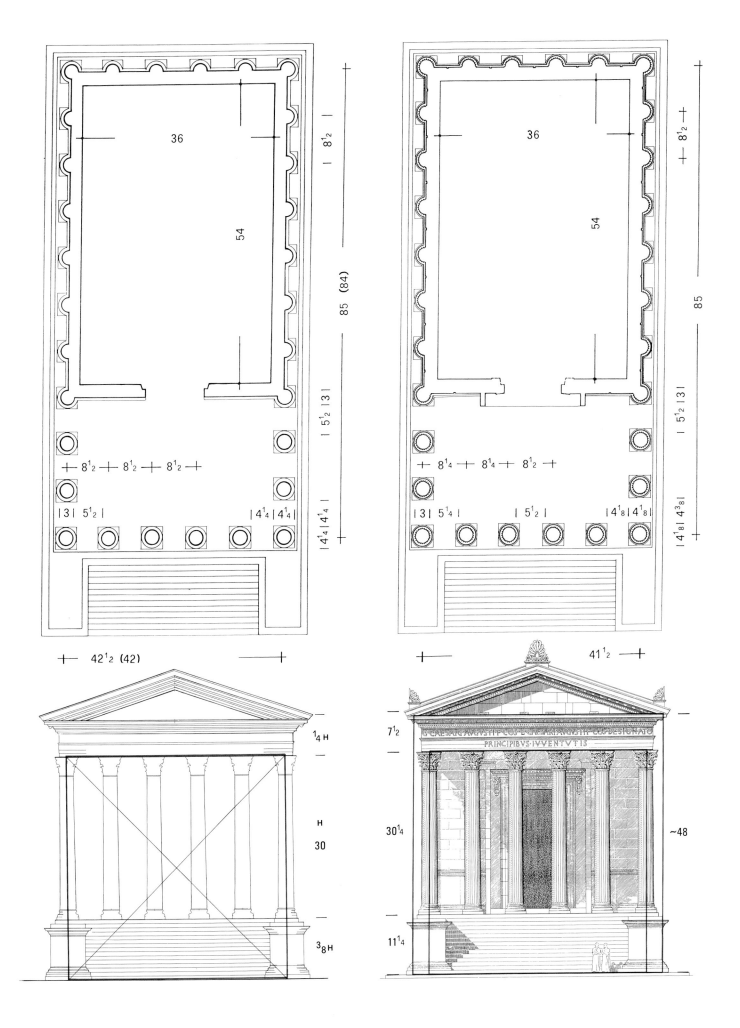

(fig. 3.30a). This last should correspond to the inter-axial width of the peristyle, but there is in fact a discrepancy of 1¼ ft. So in the next stage of design (Vitruvius' Stage III), the architect evidently elected to compromise: stretching the elevation and contracting the plan to give a perfect square of 41½ ft – a solution that was no doubt chosen because of its compatibility with a second 48 ft wide square.[57] As a consequence most of the numerical relationships changed, losing some of their mathematical harmony in the process (figs 3.29b and 3.30b). Thus the column height became no longer 30 ft but 30¼ ft, and so no longer 10 diameters tall. The column spacing front and back became less than that of the flanks, which remained unchanged.[58] Accordingly the 2:1 ratio for the peristyle as a whole ceased to be exact, as did that between the column height and the axial length of the cella. Everything is inextricably linked in three dimensions, so changing one set of proportions inevitably set off a chain reaction.

Many of Vitruvius' statements quoted earlier now find a peg to hang on, and it begins to become clear what he meant when he said 'after the standard of *symmetria* has been determined, and the proportionate dimensions adjusted by calculations . . . let the construction follow . . . so that the beholder may feel no doubt of the *eurythmia* of its effect'. Text, drawings, models and buildings tell the same story: that the dynamics of architectural design are such that unblemished proportional perfection was an elusive goal. The completion of Alberti's text on this subject cited above is a reminder that problems of this nature are a perennial burden for any architect committed to the goal of mathematical harmony:

I have often formed in my mind ideas of buildings that have given me a wonderful delight, yet when I work them out into lines I discover that in the parts which please me most there are serious errors which must be corrected. On a second examination of the design, in translating it into numerical proportions I am struck by my inadequacy. Finally, when I have turned my design into a model and re-examined its elements, I find that I am mistaken, even in the numbers.

3.31 Maison Carrée, detail of the exterior.

IV

GROUND RULES: PRINCIPLES OF NUMBER AND MEASURE

THE EXPLORATION OF THE FORMAL and mathematical intentions behind the design of any historical structure is the search for patterns that make sense at several levels. It necessarily involves the formulation of hypotheses and the testing of them against actual measurements and relationships. The nature of building is such that the 'fit' between the model and reality is hardly ever so clear as to be indisputable; moreover, the factors at play are so disparate as to elude the kind of assessments that scientists perform in laboratory conditions, which is why the subjective element – as discussed in the Introduction – is bound to be significant. It is therefore vital to have a grasp of the general questions that underlie analyses of this sort: how much tolerance should be admissible? is the proposed unit of measure likely to match that used by the original builder? are the proposed goals likely to match those of the original architect?

Tolerance Standards of accuracy differ enormously from building to building, and even within the same one. The total length of the Maison Carrée measured on either flank agrees to within 1 mm, while the column spacing varies by as much as 9 cm (3½ ins) even though the distance involved is so much smaller. It is possible to speculate about specific explanations (was the initial setting out supervised by the architect, but that of the peristyle delegated to separate gangs of masons?), but in general accuracy depended on the nature of the measurement in question. In the case of the Parthenon, ones that are supposed to match each other often do so within a tolerance well under 1 mm, but metope widths vary by up to 7 cm apparently so as to suit specific scenes.[1] Unlike the Greeks, the Romans rarely pursued precision for its own sake. The very simplicity and crispness of the geometry of the pyramid tomb of Gaius Cestius (fig. 4.8) invited an

4.1 Mausoleum of a Hellenistic monarch or potentate at Dougga, Tunisia (?2nd century BC).

4.2 Tomb of Caecilia Metella on the Via Appia, Rome (last quarter of 1st century BC).

exacting standard of setting out,[2] but in most circumstances the overriding concern was to produce the *effect* of regularity. Inaccuracies were usually permitted so long as they did not attract the eye's attention.[3] Of course, there is no shortage of instances, especially in a provincial context, where this doctrine was not upheld. Because of trouble with converting into the local Punic cubit a specification couched in Roman feet, the perimeter bays of the amphitheatre at El Jem are decidedly ragged, oscillating by as much as 15 per cent in width (fig. 0.23).[4] Normally, however, tolerances may be expected of up to 0.5 per cent for medium-to-large distances, and perhaps a bit more where the materials are brick and concrete as opposed to good quality stone.

Units of measure Most ancient units of length derived ultimately from human measures, as is shown both by their name and by the existence of Greek metrological reliefs in anthropomorphic form.[5] The Roman foot, or *pes monetalis*, is virtually identical with the Attic foot, and both may furthermore be linked to cubits of greater antiquity.[6] Its length may be deduced from bronze measuring instruments, representations of them inscribed on architects' and builders' tombs (figs 1.11 and 1.13), and metrical standards set up in public places (these were common in regions where the coexistence of different units was a potential source of confusion (fig. 4.3)).[7] Together these yield a mean value of

around 296 mm – some 4 per cent less than today's Anglo-American foot (304.8 mm), typically with subdivisions into either 16 digits (*digiti*) or 12 inches (*unciae*). Actual buildings show that the value could in practice range between 294 and 297 mm and beyond.[8] Some scholars have tried to establish techniques for inducing the precise unit used for any given building,[9] but in the last resort questions of judgement cannot be avoided. The fact that appreciably different values can be induced for parts of the same building – for example the Pantheon rotunda and portico – warns of the dangers of being overly dogmatic.[10]

Goals The mathematical goals of Roman architects and the limits to which they applied may be identified by comparing a range of buildings while bearing in mind the way in which Vitruvius framed his recommendations. As an illustration, the analysis of the Maison Carrée put forward at the end of chapter 3 may now be reviewed from this standpoint:

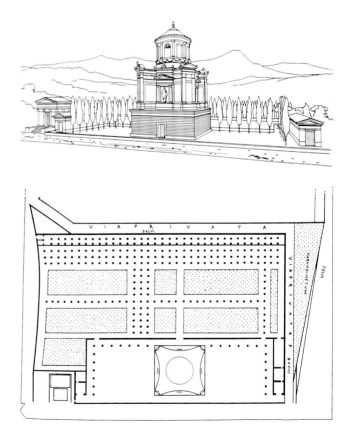

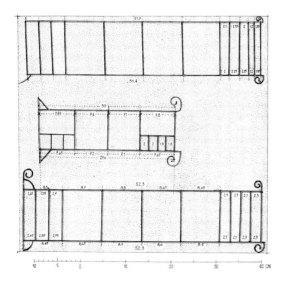

4.3 Plaque with metrological standards set up in the forum at Lepcis Magna. The smaller representation in the middle is the Roman foot, which is divided into quarters and into sixteenth parts, or digits, on the right, and twelfth parts, or inches, on the left. Top and bottom are representations of the Punic and Egyptian cubits.

4.4 (*top*) Reconstruction of the funerary complex shown in fig. 4.5.

4.5 Record plan of a Roman mausoleum and its garden inscribed on a marble plaque, found in a cemetery on the Via Labicana, Rome.

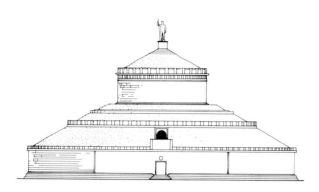

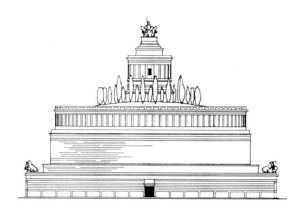

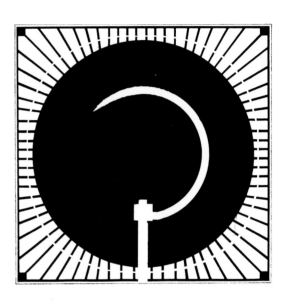

4.6 Dynastic mausolea of the emperors Augustus (a) and Hadrian (b), Rome (respectively 28 BC and AD 140).

The 1:2 ratio between the column diameter and the diagonal width of the base. This proportion was popular from Augustan times on, besides being that used in the building that exerted the most significant influence on the design of the Maison Carrée, the Temple of Mars Ultor (pp. 142–3).

The 1:2 ratio between the lateral width of the column bases and their spacing. There is a long tradition associated with just such a scheme, one that can be traced via Hermogenes' Temple of Dionysius at Teos back to Pytheos' Temple of Athena at Priene (fig. 2.10a). Both architects disseminated their ideas in influential treatises.

The 1:2 ratio between the width and the length of the peristyle, measured from axis to axis of the corner columns. The

use of this proportion also goes back to Hellenistic temples like those at Teos and Priene; directly comparable Roman examples include the republican temple at Tivoli and those of Portunus (fig. 3.26) and Apollo Sosianus in Rome.

The 1:10 ratio between column diameter and height. This is found in numerous imperial Corinthian columns, not least those of the Temple of Mars Ultor, which are exactly twice as large as those of the Maison Carrée (see Appendix B).

The 1:1 proportion of the front façade. In one form or another this appears in numerous buildings (p. 122). Although considerable scope existed for selecting the precise limits involved, the axial width of the peristyle was often among the most important.

In short, comparison confirms that the goals proposed for the Maison Carrée are perfectly plausible. On the other hand, the deviation between the hypothetical and actual proportions often reaches 2 per cent, that is to say too much to be attributed to error alone; hence the emphasis placed on the passage from an ideal scheme to a final one, and the ensuing modifications. The object of this chapter is to extend the use of comparative method so as to identify general mathematical principles that might be applicable to laying out *any* Roman building. For this purpose the centralized plan (whether circular, square or cruciform) makes a particularly good subject. In the first place it constitutes an inherently formal response to design, the result of a way of thinking that subordinates functional issues to ideals of space conception. From the point of view of analysis, the symmetry of the centralized plan serves to limit the number of measurements to be taken into consideration and facilitates cross-checking. Then there is its *romanitas*; it may have been used by other peoples before them, but it was the Romans who went on to make the centralized plan a major vehicle for expression, and their varied experiments in this field constituted one of their most important legacies for the development of Byzantine, Islamic, Romanesque and Renaissance architecture.[11]

CENTRALIZED BUILDINGS IN AND AROUND ROME

A suitable starting-point is a group of well-preserved centralized buildings in Rome and its vicinities built between 100 BC and AD 500, provided they are large (at least 10m wide) and free-standing. Large dimensions reduce the significance of errors in construction or surveying, while the restriction to free-standing buildings minimizes the potential impact of external constraints. Twenty-six buildings, most of them well known, comply with these criteria (see Table 4.1 and the corresponding section of Appendix A).[12]

Hierarchies of Design and Dimension

The overall size of these buildings manifests a preponderance of whole numbers of feet or cubits (1 cubit being 1½ft), especially multiples of 10 or 12, and to a lesser extent multiples of 16. But as Table 4.1 shows, a much sharper pattern emerges once it is realized that such 'round' dimensions are usually associated with the exterior of a building where this is more important than the interior, and vice versa. The buildings have therefore been divided into three categories according to what may be called the character of their 'orientation'. Typical externally orientated buildings are late

republican and early imperial tombs like those of Augustus (fig. 4.6a) or Caecilia Metella (fig. 4.2), which boast a grand public face but have relatively insignificant interiors. Conversely, the exterior of internally orientated buildings like the Pantheon (fig. 9.11) and the Mausoleum of Maxentius (fig. 4.9) are arguably just containers for the interior. Bivalent buildings display no overriding stress either way, examples being peripteral temples (fig. 4.13) or early Christian buildings like Santa Costanza (fig. 4.12) and Santo Stefano Rotondo.

These categories find confirmation in the type of entrance. As a rule, externally orientated buildings have entrances that thrust inwards, maintaining a geometrically pure exterior (figs 4.7a–d). Internally orientated ones have entrances that thrust outwards (often as a portico), maintaining a geometrically pure interior (figs 47e–f and 9.11). Bivalent buildings generally maintain their neutrality by having doors projecting neither one way or other (figs 47g–i). These patterns are not hard and fast (Santa Costanza may best be described as bivalent, yet the narthex interrupted the original external colonnade), but it is clear enough that Roman architects believed that access, like dimension, should acknowledge perceived hierarchies of composition. This is of course but one manifestation of their pervading sensitivity to the concept of appropriateness or *decor* in design (pp. 43–4). Similar observations apply, for example, to the way door openings were arranged in complex buildings, it being common for the usual symmetry of individual rooms to be discarded if need be out of respect for major axes and vistas.[13]

These hierarchies transcend functional divides. Although many of the centralized buildings under consideration are tombs or cenotaphs, the same function might also be housed in structures that mimicked the form of columns, altars or rectangular temples.[14] Moreover, there was a chronological trend away from externally orientated tombs towards internally orientated ones. In the late republic and the early empire variations on the cylindrical tumulus (with or without a square podium) were popular vehicles for aristocratic display, evoking perhaps the graves of mythical heroes like Achilles' favourite Patroclus, perhaps the grandiose memorials of Hellenistic rulers like those that survive at Halikarnassos, Belevi and Dougga (fig. 4.1).[15] Augustus built his own version in the Campus Martius (fig. 4.6), possibly also inspired by the tomb of Alexander the Great, and the established Roman families followed suit at a smaller scale. Prime locations were public highways like the Via Appia (fig. 4.2) or natural

4.7 Comparison of the plans of the best-preserved free-standing centralized buildings in or near Rome: (a) Tomb of Munatius Plancus at Gaeta, 1:600; (b) Tomb of the Servili on the Via Appia outside Rome, 1:600; (c) Tomb of Caecilia Metella on the Via Appia outside Rome 1:600; (d) tomb at Capua known as Le Carceri Vecchie; (e) Mausoleum of Maxentius on the Via Appia outside Rome, 1:600; (f) Tor de' Schiavi, 1:600; (g) tomb at Portus, near Ostia, 1:600; (h) tholos by the Tiber, Rome, 1:600; (i) San Stefano Rotondo, Rome, 1:1000.

landmarks like the promontory at Gaeta where stands Munatius Plancus' tomb.[16] As the marble plan illustrated in figure 4.5 shows, such tombs often stood free in a garden which provided a verdant setting for funeral banquets. Inside, however, the burial chambers were just big enough to house urns or sarcophagi in reasonable dignity; they may be irregular in shape and not even centred on the middle of the plan. Despite its lavish appointments (his will specified wall-hangings from Pergamon, ones that were typically decorated with gold thread), the sepulchral chamber in Gaius Cestius' tomb (fig. 4.8) accounts for only 3 per cent of the total floor area.[17] But with time the emphasis

4.8 Entrance side of the pyramid tomb of Gaius Cestius at Porta Ostiensis, Rome (before 12 BC). Originally located some way outside the city, the monument came to be incorporated within the Aurelian circuit of walls in the 3rd century AD.

moved inwards as a response to several factors. No longer could private families vie so ostentatiously in the market for posterity with the imperial dynasties. Meanwhile problems of overcrowding meant that good frontage on major routes was limited, and tombs often had to butt up against one another, which meant there was no advantage in designing them to be seen from all sides. Denied a congruous external setting, feasts and other ritual observances shifted to the interior, and its importance naturally came to be recognized in terms of architectonic significance and relative size,[18] a development made possible by the improved spanning capability of vaulted concrete construction. Eventually the Pantheon – the classic example of an internally orientated plan – was taken up as the prototype for late antique tombs like the Tor de' Schiavi or the Mausoleum of Maxentius.

Turning now to look at dimensional patterns in more detail, it is well to begin with five of the fourteen externally orientated buildings in the present sample group that are 100 ft wide. Of these five, Gaius Cestius' pyramid is a sheer geometric solid with 100 ft being its maximum width where it meets the pavement. Three others, the Torrione di Micara, the Casal Rotondo and the tomb of Munatius Plancus, take the form of squat cylindrical drums articulated by mouldings; in the first two the *base* is 100 ft wide, while in the third the *drum* is 100 ft wide, so the base projects further. The architect of the tomb of Caecilia Metella managed a sort of fusion, for here 100 ft located the base of the drum as well as the face of the podium below (figs 4.2 and 4.7c). Thus there was agreement about the dimension to be used, but scope in the way it was put into effect. As for the interiors, they might or might not reflect comparable simplicity, since this was a secondary rather than a primary objective.

The reverse is the case for internally orientated buildings; all members of this group have internal diameters that are multiples of 10 ft or cubits save two exceptions, Tor Pignattara and Tor de' Schiavi (figs 4.7f and 4.10). The relevant measures coincide either with the internal face of the structure, or, more usually, with the surface finish.[19] A notable variant is the Pantheon, with its clear span of 147 ft. Here the ring of columns was given a dimensionally perfect axial diameter of 150 ft (100 cubits) – appropriately enough for the starting-point of the whole design (fig. 9.11). External measurements conform to no clear pattern, suggesting that the overall size of these buildings was determined by adding the wall thickness to the chosen interior diameter, a sum that did not necessarily produce a simple number.

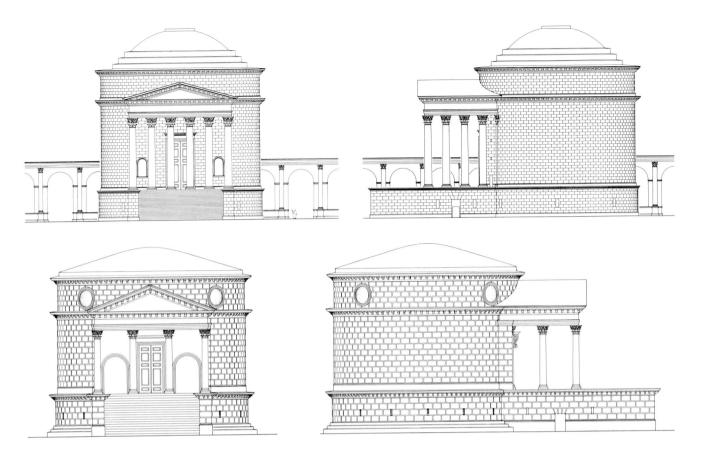

4.9 (*top left and right*)   Restored elevation of the Mausoleum of Maxentius (sometimes called the tomb of Romulus) on the Via Appia, Rome (AD ca. 310).

4.10 (*above left and right*)   Tomb known as the Tor de' Schiavi on the Via Prenestina, Rome (AD ca. 300): (a) reconstructed front elevation; (b) reconstructed side elevation.

In bivalent buildings the presence of independent rings of structure allowed the plan to be manipulated more freely, enabling round dimensions to occur both inside and out. Often they could be simply related to one another as well: the three peripteral temples all have cellae half as wide as the platform on which they stand; the inner room of Santa Costanza is approximately half as wide as the ambulatory (fig. 4.11); the central ring of Santo Stefano Rotondo is a half and a third as wide as the middle and outer rings (fig. 4.7i). In addition, the way in which dimensions were assigned to the fabric underlined the spatial conception. Appropriately enough, the perimeter of Santo Stefano Rotondo, being externally orientated (it can be seen in its entirety only from the outside), measures 150 cubits on its *external* surface. Conversely, the centre room, being internally orientated (it can be seen in its entirety only from the inside), measures 50 cubits *internally*.[20] It is interesting to see how a comparable logic was to survive (or reemerge?) in Bramante's plan for the Tempietto – a bivalent structure *par excellence*; the

internal radius of the cella is 10 *palmi*, its external radius 10 *piedi* and the axial radius of the peristyle 10 column diameters (fig. 5.11).[21]

Up until now the dimensions considered have been linear ones, measures of width or diameter. But there was another mode of measurement which might be relevant in the case of circular structures, namely their circumference. In Santa Costanza the ring of twelve double columns is based on a remarkably coherent scheme in this respect: the normal bays measure 10 ft, from centre to centre of adjacent columns in the inner ring, while the wider bays on the cardinal axes have 10 ft intercolumnations (fig. 4.11). This sort of game demanded the fine tuning of the diameter, explaining why that of the central space is 38½ ft rather than the more obvious 37½ ft, or half the overall internal diameter of 75 ft. Another exception to radial simplicity, the Tor de' Schiavi, displays a comparable focus on the circumference (fig. 4.7f).

The dimensional characteristics common to all twenty-six buildings under review can now be

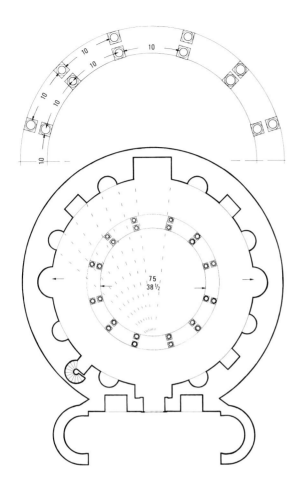

4.11 Part plan of Santa Costanza. The desire to achieve simple dimensions in terms of the circumference (top) explains why the diameter of the inner room slightly exceeds half the overall interior diameter.

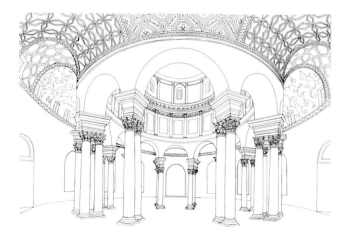

4.12 (*above and top right*) Interior of Santa Costanza, Rome (2nd quarter of 4th century AD, or later): (a) view looking into the rotunda and towards the main apse with light tower over; (b) reconstruction showing the original decoration of the central drum.

4.13 Tholos by the Tiber near the Forum Boarium, which may be identified as the Temple of Hercules Victor and possibly attributed to the architect Hermodoros of Salamis, mid- to late 2nd century BC.

summed up. Multiples of 10, 12 and sometimes 16 units (usually feet, although cubits come to the fore in Christian times) are associated with virtually all of them.[22] Units of 50, 60 and 100 are especially popular, giving rise to several coincidences (Table 4.1). The emergent pattern can hardly stem from chance, so architects must have considered it important to define the size of a building by assigning it a 'critical dimension' in such a way as to reinforce the character of the design.[23]

Table 4.1
Dimensions of centralized buildings in and around Rome

Dimensions are given to the nearest foot of 0.296 metres, unless cubits (c) are indicated. 'Critical dimensions' for setting out each building are highlighted in bold where they correspond to multiples of 10 or 12 feet/cubits.

Name of building	Width of exterior	Width of interior
Externally oriented buildings		
Mausoleum of Augustus	≈**300** (base)	?
Mausoleum of Hadrian	≈**300** (base)	?
Il Torrione	150?	?
Tomb of Lucilius Paetus	**120** (base)	
Tomb of Gaius Cestius	**100**	14 × **20**
Tomb of Munatius Plancus	**100** (drum)	**80**
Tomb of Caecilia Metella	**100** (base)	22½
Torrione di Micara	**100**	?
Casal Rotondo	≈**100**	?
Tomb of the Plautii	**80** (podium)	
Tomb of the Oratii & Curiatii	**50** (base)	?
Tomb at Falerii	≈**36**	?
Tomb at Vicovara	≈**36**	?
Tomb of the Servilii	≈**36**	18, **10**★
Internally oriented buildings		
Pantheon	188	**150**★
Tomb of Maxentius (lower hall)	122	**80**
Tor de' Schiavi (upper hall)	≈**64**	46
Tor Pignattara	94	68
Pantheon at Ostia	≈75 (**50 c**)	≈**60** (**40 c**)
Temple of Romulus	**50**	
Tomb at Portus	≈**64**	**50**
Buildings with bivalent orientation		
San Stefano Rotondo	225 (**150 c**)	75 (**50 c**)
Santa Costanza	**100**	75 (**50 c**)
Temple B	≈**64**	32
Tholos by the Tiber★★	**50**	≈25
Tholos at Tivoli	**48**	≈24

★ as measured to the axis of the ring of columns
★★ in terms of a foot of 330 mm

WIDESPREAD PATTERNS OF PRACTICE

Are these patterns widely applicable? Did the same principles influence comparable buildings far from Rome, or variants on the centralized theme − such as polygonal buildings or ones that are not free-standing? The answer is a straightforward yes. Plenty of instances could be cited, but it is enough to list the well-known tombs illustrated here: the 10 ft wide tower at Mactar in Tunisia (fig. 4.16), the one at Glanum in Provence, with its 20, 15 and 10 ft wide tiers (fig. 4.18), and the 200 ft wide tumulus in Algeria known as the Médracen (fig. 4.14). The reader may be spared the tedium of a longer list, for the trend emerges clearly enough from measurements gathered in other publications.[24]

One theme that gains definition looking further afield is the emphasis on circumferential dimensions as a response to architectonic significance, typically that of a ring of columns or semi-columns.[25] In the case of amphitheatres the importance of the fornix module on the façade is almost invariably signalled by its dimensional simplicity, and it was undoubtedly this that explains why overall measurements of length and width tend not to work out so neatly (p. 61). On some occasions plans were manipulated to satisfy both modes of measurement. The perimeter of a 70 ft wide tomb at Capua known as Le Carceri Vecchie (figs 4.7d, 4.15) has twenty-two semi-columns, an unusual number, but one that exploited the fact that $^{22}/_7$ is a close approximation to π. It meant that the 220 ft perimeter divided up neatly into 10 ft intervals marked by the axes of the semi-columns. The Médracen, the tomb of a North African monarch of the second century BC, measures 200 ft across the base, yet the drum was set back enough to yield a circumference of 600 ft − an apt dimension given that it again generates a 10 ft spacing for the 60 half-columns.

In casting the net further afield it is not uncommon to encounter pairs of closely related buildings that have the same size or nearly so. The second of the two huge royal tumulus-tombs in Algeria, the so-called Tomb of the Christian Woman, clearly took its basic form, size and number of semi-columns directly from its precursor the Médracen (fig. 4.14). But this time the critical 200 ft dimension, which had earlier defined the steps, was transferred to the drum; so the nominal size is the same, but the effective size greater. A similar kind of imitation links a pair of tombs in the Kidron Valley necropolis of Jerusalem, both of which have a square plan and a three-bay façade of Ionic columns capped with an Egyptian cornice (fig. 4.17). The 20 ft width

4.14 Royal mausoleum known as the Médracen, Batna, Algeria (2nd or 1st century BC).

4.15 Mausoleum known as Le Carceri Vecchie, Capua, Italy (probably 2nd century AD).

of the 'Tomb of Zacharias' appears in the 'Tomb of Absalom' too, except that in the second building this dimension marked the centres of the corner pilasters and not their external edges, again making the result slightly bigger. When Hadrian commissioned a variant of Augustus' Mausoleum for his own tomb, the podium was made 300 ft wide, too (fig. 4.6). The later building emulates its model by being the same size, and yet larger still, in as much as a square occupies a greater surface area than a circle of equal width.

The role of dimension in imitation is in fact more important than is generally thought. It is well known that the desire to emulate the span of the Pantheon was a fundamental constraint on the design of first the cathedral in Florence, and later of St Peter's in Rome, but the only ancient parallel that is commonly cited is the reprise of the 100 ft height of Trajan's Column in Marcus Aurelius' (chapter 8).[26] But there are comparable examples from as early as the fifth century BC, when the Temple of Concord at Agrigento was modelled on that of Juno-Lacinia on the same site (fig. 3.25), or as late as the fourth century AD, when the Arch of Constantine was modelled on that of Septimius Severus (p. 124). A 300 ft nave length, albeit measured differently in each case, may unite the three great early Christian basilicas in Rome: St Peter's, St Paul's and St John Lateran.[27] Although it is not known to which building it relates, an inscription in North Africa records the same intention, referring as it does to a 300 ft long basilica, or *basilicae centenariae tres*.[28] Lengths of 400 ft recur in one form or another in each of the imperial fora, and this was arguably the logic of

its use as the starting-point for laying out the last of them, Trajan's (fig. 8.4).[29] But should particular significance be accorded to the presence of 100 ft wide exedrae in Diocletian's Baths as well as Trajan's or to the fact that the diameter of the Teatro Marittimo at Hadrian's Villa is close to that of the Pantheon interior?[30] It must be borne in mind that the relevant key 'critical dimensions', 100, 144 and 150 ft, complement the doctrine of *symmetria*, the second pair being numerically the most attractive options between 120 and 200 ft (144 is 12^2 and 150 is $1\frac{1}{2} \times 10^2$). Unless they are supported by specific formal or programmatic links, it is well to be wary of making too much of such coincidences.

With regard to chronology, the patterns described here undergo only minor shifts of emphasis. While few centralized Greek and Hellenistic monuments survive in good condition, those that do often fit similar patterns. The Monument of Lysicrates (fig. 7.2), the Lion Tomb at Knydos, the Ptolomeion at Limyra, the mausoleum at Belevi and the tumulus nearby respectively measure 10, 30, 50, 100 and 200 ft wide.[31] Examples like these lend credence to the idea that some of the buildings that the Greeks called *hekatompeda* (literally 'one hundred footed') incorporated this dimension in a tangible way.[32] And when an attention to the dimensional neatness of perimeter rhythms is discernible in buildings as different both in character and date as the Médracen and Santa Costanza, it is clear that the cause lies in a fundamental undercurrent of continuity.[33]

Exceptions to the rule can serve to highlight points of principle. In the case of large domed halls, for

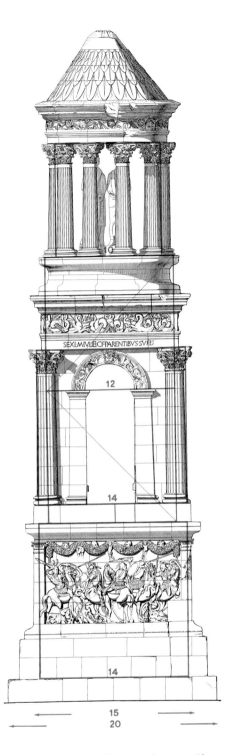

4.18 (*top right*) Elevation of the mausoleum at Glanum, France (1st decade AD), 1 : 100; one of the most elaborate Roman tower tombs to have survived, with principal dimensions and 1 : 1 proportions overlaid.

4.16 (*top left*) Tower tomb at Mactar, Tunisia (?2nd century AD).

4.17 (*left*) 'Tomb of Absalom', Kidron Valley, Jerusalem (probably first half of 1st century AD). Note the mixed order, with Ionic columns, Doric frieze and an Egyptian cornice.

example, those that break with the general pattern belong not to free-standing buildings, but to spaces incorporated into larger complexes. And the 42 ft of the so-called Tempio della Tosse was in effect imposed by the desire that the front and back walls respect alignments dictated by an earlier structure on the site. Presumably its size had to fit in with the plan as a whole, a situation that did not necessarily permit dimensional simplicity. On the other hand, the 50 ft span of the octagonal hall in the Domus Aurea underlines the fact that it was the nucleus around which its immediate surroundings were planned.

At the other end of the spectrum in civic terms are infrastructure projects such as ramparts, bridges, aqueducts and cisterns, where practical issues may be assumed to have had the upper hand. It comes as no surprise that the Cloaca Maxima, the great drain running from the imperial fora to the Tiber, fits no dimensional pattern: the cross-section, route and materials chop and change according to site conditions and phases of construction.[34] None the less, even ostensibly functional structures could be set out in a principled fashion, as was Trajan's harbour by the outflow of the Tiber – a regular hexagon 2400 ft wide.[35] The plan of the monumental cistern known as the Sette Sale (or 'Seven Rooms', despite there being nine main compartments), which fed this emperor's baths with an 8 million litre capacity, was determined by the interplay of arcs and lengths of 200, 150 and 100 ft (fig. 5.12).[36]

QUESTIONS OF STRUCTURE

Roman architecture evokes automatic connotations of constructional solidity, durability and practicality. What is more, Roman architects doubled as engineers, so it is almost unthinkable that they did not bring structural considerations to bear when assessing the size of a building. Structure must certainly have been a major concern where spans were significant, but unfortunately little is known about how Roman architects tackled statics due to Vitruvius' silence on the subject. It should also be remembered that in antiquity the general form of trabeated structures and the very language of the orders was essentially conservative in terms of statics. The proportions of stone columns and entablatures were determined primarily on tectonic and aesthetic grounds; structural difficulties intervened only at very large scales, typically because of the spanning limitations of architraves. Meanwhile the main limit on the spans of timber roofs was essentially the availability of long enough pieces of timber.

There are relatively few examples exceeding an 80 ft span and the very top of the range is in effect indicated by the admiration that Pliny expressed for the 100 ft long beams that Agrippa brought to Rome to roof the Diribitorium.[37]

The Romans certainly had no scientific basis for calculating stress and strain in concrete. The ancient mind was, however, attuned to empirical observation, the lessons of which doubtless found their way into codes of practice. In the early days of concrete vaulting, spans were increased step by step (subject to the occasional disaster), following experiments with *pozzolana*, relieving arches, buttressing, graduating aggregate densities according to levels of stress, and reducing weight by means of structural voids – culminating in that wonder of engineering that is the Pantheon. There was a broad consensus for span: wall ratios vaguely in the region of 10:1 or so for barrel vaults and 8:1 or so for domes, with a trend to more adventurous solutions over time.[38] In setting out a large circular hall the basic response was to take its internal diameter and simply add a suitable wall thickness.

When the architect of the Zeus-Asklepios temple at Pergamon took a scaled-down Pantheon as his model (fig. 3.19), he may initially have aimed at a 80 ft wide hall within a 100 ft envelope, a solution implying a span/wall ratio of 8:1. But given the relative local inexperience with vaulted construction, caution must have argued for a ratio nearer 7:1, hence a total of about 102 ft instead.[39] This would seem to illustrate the pragmatic approach for which Roman builders are renowned, but care should be taken not to credit them with notions of structural efficiency which they did not necessarily share. Buildings could be greatly overstructured for purely formal reasons. The perimeter wall of Santa Costanza (fig. 4.11) is thick enough to carry a vault over the entire building, but it supports only the annular barrel vault (since the central drum sits on the ring of columns), yielding a span/wall ratio of $1\frac{1}{4}$:1! The superfluous thickness of the wall was evidently required to accommodate the deep apses on the major axes, while at the same time allowing its exterior diameter to reach 100 ft.

NUMEROLOGY AND THE PHYSICAL ENVIRONMENT

Roman architects were apparently incapable of conceiving a project without a simple dimensional premise, unless some overriding factor argued to the contrary. Nowadays people have lost this habit, even though number is still celebrated in terms of time and personal achievement (witness the attention accorded to centenaries and other significant anniversaries). Ever since the Enlightenment, with the triumph of the metre, size has been just a relative issue. The qualities of design are perceived to be unmeasurable, and quantities merely a practical necessity; as Louis Kahn put it, architecture begins with the unmeasurable, goes through measurable means in order to be built, and ends with the unmeasurable again.[40] The Romans knew no such divide; for them the effect of a building was not only a consequence of its relative size, but of its absolute size as well.

In fixing the boundaries of their physical environment the ancient mind displayed a natural inclination towards numerical simplicity. Roman surveyors are famous for the practice of centuriation, the marking out of property in square or rectangular parcels (*centuriae*) by dividing balks and roadways (*limites*) according to a simple dimensional system,[41] while unitary dimensions like the *actus* (120 ft) often regulate town planning grids too.[42] The Romans' literal approach to measure is exemplified by the fact that the foot rules sometimes represented on builders' or architects' tombs are invariably life size (figs 1.11 and 1.13). Funerary inscriptions often record the size of individual plots, and these too typically conform to numerically neat sizes (fig. 1.13). At Aquileia, which is one of the best sites for appreciating their original context (fig. 4.19), one example reads: L(OC) M(ONU-MENTA) INFR(ONTE) P(EDES)XXIIII IN AGR(O) PED(ES) XXXII, attesting to a 24 ft frontage and a 32 ft depth (giving an aspect ratio of 3 : 4).[43] Where the original context is preserved it is possible to verify that such dimensions are not just vague approximations, but quite precise.[44] The aspirations of the monied classes were satirized by Petronius through his fictive character Trimalchio, who reckoned that a tomb taking up a 100 × 200 ft plot and planted with vines and fruit trees, marked him out as a man of substance.[45]

All around the Mediterranean civilizations made their mark by imposing on built form a transcendent order that ultimately reduces to number. Symbols of such an endeavour include the pyramids of Giza,[46] the Babylonian ziggurats,[47] Solomon's Temple,[48] and Noah's Ark, the reputed dimensions of which were 300 cubits long, 30 broad and 50 tall. Back in Italy, the mythical dimensions of the Tomb of Lars Porsena (the Etruscan king), as recounted by Pliny the Elder, shows how popular memory gravitated towards commensurability (p. 101). Legend spoke of a square podium surmounted with two tiers of pyramids, an example, in Pliny's view, of the worst sort of 'irresponsible story-

telling'.[49] However, there is nothing necessarily fantastical about the dimensions cited in this case; a podium width of 300 ft is after all a feature of both Augustus' and Hadrian's tombs. Of course numerical hyperbole was rife: besides the inflated dimensions habitually cited by Diodorus Siculus, there is for example Tacitus' ridiculous claim that 50,000 spectators perished when an amphitheatre collapsed at Fidenae outside Rome.[50] The point is that the fantasy element reflects real desires; the report that the emperor Alexander Severus started a portico of 1000 columns (1000 ft long and 100 ft wide) in the Campus Martius may or may not mirror reality literally, but it still says something about what his architects would have wanted to do if humanly possible.[51]

Decimal and duodecimal numbers permeated all walks of ancient life. Myths recount that Helen's face launched 1000 ships, that 300 Spartans died to save Greece at Thermopylae and that the city of Thebes had 100 gates. Twelve was the number of the Olympian Gods, the Labours of Hercules, the Tribes of Israel, the Christian apostles, and so on. Numerical simplicity manifests itself in the very structure of Roman institutions. The calendar was first divided into ten and later twelve months, while night and day each had twelve hours (of variable length). The size of a legion reflected organic growth, yet the notional combat units remained the century of 100 men and the maniple of 60. Building regulations were couched in terms of simple dimensions, like those that in certain periods restricted the height of urban frontage to 60 or 70 ft, or the notional width of major streets, the *decumanus maximus* and the *cardo maximus*, as respectively 40 and 20 ft.[52] And it is especially relevant in the present context that the Roman system of measurement featured 12 inches to the foot, 120 feet in an *actus*, and 1000 paces in a mile, to cite a few relations between different units.[53]

CONCLUSION

So number and measure entered into architectural planning just as they did in society at large. This said, it is equally important to realize the extent to which the patterns that have emerged in the course of this chapter mirror the ideals of *symmetria* (pp. 40–43). The shape of buildings derives ultimately from elemental geometrical forms; their overall size – or some other critical dimension – is frequently a simple dimension; the parts tend to relate one to another in either an arithmetical or geometrical sense; the numbers involved conform to the ideals of Graeco-Roman numerology. Thus Vitruvius' repeated concern for mathematical abstractions do not stand in a vacuum, but rather find a direct echo in the output of his fellow professionals. Today it is customary to conceive of theory and practicality as two distinct and often irreconcilable polarities. For a Roman architect, however, any such split was a purely academic notion, for in reality both led in exactly the same direction.

If actual practice upholds the principle of *symmetria*, it is equally clear that the concept of *decor*, propriety or appropriateness, is never far away. Time and again *symmetria* enters into the fabric of buildings in an appropriate manner. Critical dimensions locate the exterior of a structure if it is more important than the interior, and vice versa. If one side of a wall takes precedence over another, or alternatively if columns enjoy a more significant role, then this is acknowledged in dimensional terms. In other words, mathematical harmony was indivisible from other aspects of design. *Decor* affected abstract principles just as much as it did questions of form and content, so all levels of architectural design mirrored Cicero's conception of *decor* in a social context, namely doing the right thing in the right way at the right place.

4.19 Funeral architecture at Aquileia, Italy: (a) and (b) details of the monument of the Curii, now in the courtyard of the Archaeological Museum; (c) terrace of tomb plots at the cemetery.

V

GROUND RULES:
ARITHMETIC AND GEOMETRY

LIKE SO MANY MANIFESTATIONS OF TRADITIONAL architecture, Roman buildings derive ultimately from elemental geometrical forms like circles, regular polygons, rectangles and their three-dimensional counterparts. Sometimes these are expressed via bold, elemental volumes of sweeping simplicity, sometimes they are dressed in elaborate encrustations of decorative detail – but either way the power of geometry sings through, inspiring the work of modern architects as different as Tadao Ando, Louis Kahn, Leon Krier and Aldo Rossi. This said, however, *the detailed articulation of such forms was not necessarily geometrical*, in the sense of being conditioned by the manipulation of compasses

5.1 Detail of decorative paving in the House of Cupid and Psyche at Ostia, Italy (AD ca. 300), using a variety of types of stone: grey granite from Elba, Turkey, Egypt; red porphyry from *Mons porphyrites* in Egypt; green porphyry or *serpentino* from Croceai, near Sparta, Greece; *giallo antico* (*marmor Numidicum*) from Chemtou, Tunisia (ancient Numidia); *pavonazetto* (*marmor Phrygium* or *Synnadicum*) from Docimion, Turkey (ancient Phrygia); *africano* (*marmor Luculleum*) from Teos, Ionia, Turkey (first exploited by Lucullus).

5.2 Teatro Marittimo or Island Retreat at Hadrian's Villa (AD 118–125).

and straight-edge after the fashion of Vitruvius' method for setting out theatres (fig. 2.5). Indeed, arithmetic was generally the most important constraint in determining the size and shape of spaces and architectural elements, with commensurable proportions predominating roughly as a function of their simplicity. The measurements of the centralized buildings studied in chapter 4 consistently return the ratios 1:1, 1:2, 2:3, 4:5 and so on, as in so many other aspects of design (see pp. 66–8, 120–22 and 149–51).[1] It seems that the smaller the terms, the more satisfactory the ratio, although musical proportions may have had a particular appeal for some architects (chapter 2, p. 43). Meanwhile geometrical ratios, of which the most common are $\sqrt{2}$ and $\sqrt{3}$ (along with their respective approximations such as $\frac{7}{5}$ and $\frac{7}{4}$),[2] come to the fore in a substantial minority of cases.

It must straightaway be made clear that overblowing the contrast between arithmetic and geometry is a modern, post-Renaissance, preoccupation. We may be sure that ancient architects would have been puzzled by the extent of the divide in the way scholars have interpreted their designs, since not only was there originally more of an overlap between arithmetic and geometry then than there is now, but also because they

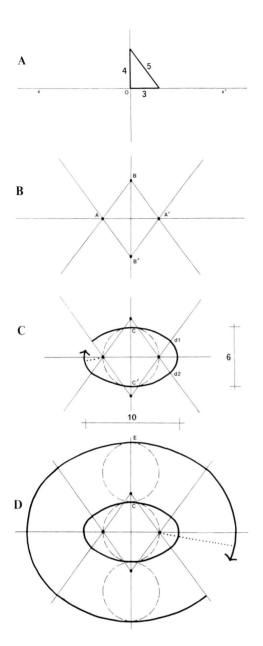

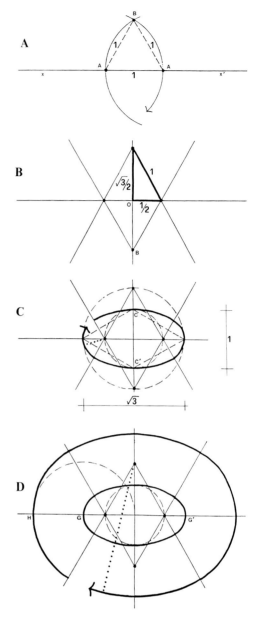

5.3 Method for laying out monumental civic amphitheatres using the Pythagorean-triangle-and-inscribed circle scheme.

1. SETTING OUT THE FOCAL POINTS AND AXES
draw triangle with sides in the ratio 3 : 4 : 5, producing an angle of 90° at the origin, O; project the major axis (x–x') and the minor axis.

2. DEVELOPING THE FOUR SECTORS
reflect the point A about origin for A'; repeat for B and B'; project lines from B and B' through and A and A' to obtain the limits of each sector.

3. FORMING THE ARENA OUTLINE
define width of arena as equal to A–A', giving C and C';
with compasses at B draw arc through C'; repeat for B' and C;
with compasses at A and then A' join ends of the arcs defined in the preceding step.

4. FORMING THE CAVEA OUTLINE
proceed in a similar manner to stage 3, having first defined the width of the cavea in relation to the dimensions of the arena. Here the widths of the cavea and the arena are made equal.

5.4 Method for laying out monumental civic amphitheatres using the Equilateral-triangle-and-inscribed-circle scheme.

1. SETTING OUT THE FOCAL POINTS AND AXES
Draw main axis, locate compass centre somwhere on it, and draw arc; where this intersects the axis place the compass centre and draw a second arc of the same size; the crossings of the two arcs gives rise to two equilateral triangles, while the line between them becomes the cross-axis at 90° to the main axis.

Stages 2, 3 and 4 follow in a similar manner to the Pythagorean-triangle-and-inscribed-circle scheme.

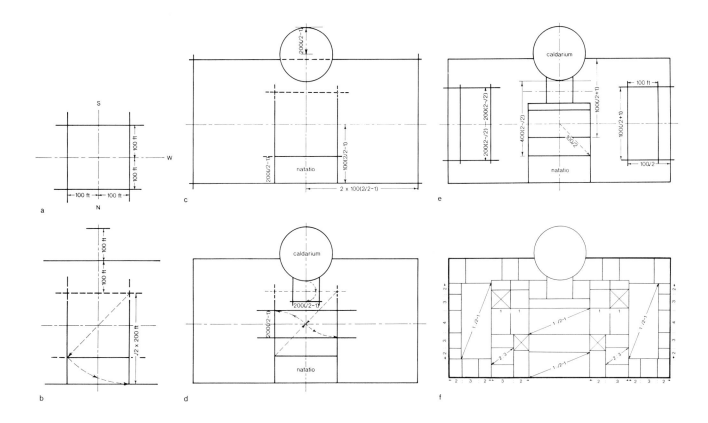

5.5 The principal geometrical manipulations for laying out the Baths of Caracalla, Rome (AD 212–216) based on a module of 100 ft, together with key arithmetical ratios used in later stages of design (f).

5.6 Plan of Corinthian column base belonging to the Temple of Hadrian, Rome (AD 140), with geometrical scheme overlaid. This relationship, with the diagonal width of the plinth being double the lower diameter of the shaft, is very common in the imperial period.

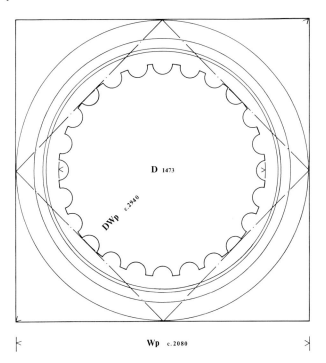

switched with dexterity from one to another. Proportions of 1:1 and 2:1 are both arithmetical and geometrical, and similarly it would seem futile to argue that a grid bears witness to graphic procedures as opposed to the numerical multiplication of a basic module. It should be appreciated how often ancient practices called for a mixture of the two approaches. Both are documented in the design for a column base from the Didymaion (fig. 3.13), where arithmetical ratios were used first to fix key guidelines and arc centres, after which compasses were taken up to generate the actual profile. The planning of amphitheatres began with geometry (figs 5.3 and 5.4), but shifted towards arithmetic for the façade (p. 121, figs 5.31–2). The plan of the Baths of Caracalla appears to have been conditioned by an admixture of $\sqrt{2}$ related ratios and arithmetical ones (fig. 5.5). Roman Corinthian columns typically have a geometrical plan (fig. 5.6), in which the lateral width of the base equals the column diameter $\times \sqrt{2}$; meanwhile the elevation was thoroughly arithmetical (chapter 7). Vitruvius too could intermingle arithmetic and geometry. As in the case of amphitheatres, the plan of his Latin theatre (V,6,6) develops from geometry, whereas its elevation conforms to simple proportions (fig. 2.5). The spiral volutes of his Ionic capital were constructed by geometrical means,[3] but the rest relied on ratios like 11:12, 7:9 and 1:12 (III,5,5–7).

It still remains important to be able to distinguish between arithmetic and geometry, and to understand what it was that led Roman architects to choose between them. For Vitruvius and the majority of his colleagues, it seems that arithmetic was the default mode for quantifying design decisions and ensuring *symmetria*. Geometry was not by any means inconsistent with this goal, but its chief value lay in solving what Vitruvius called 'difficult questions of *symmetria*' (I,I,4). To illustrate this point he used the problem of doubling the area of a square:

A square place 10 feet long and 10 feet wide gives an area of 100 feet. Now if it is required to double the square, and to make one of 200 feet, we must ask how long will be the sides of that square. . . . Nobody can find this by means of arithmetic. For if we take 14, multiplication will give 196 feet, if 15, 225 feet (IX, Pref., 4–5.).

Vitruvius went on to show how the desired result could be obtained geometrically, by making the sides of the new square equal the diagonal of the first – hence the ratio known as $\sqrt{2}$. He even dedicated one of his few (lost) illustrations to clarifying the matter, one that no doubt resembled the diagrams evoked by Plato in his *Meno*,[4] or those of the Mesopotamian surveyor's tablet shown in figure 5.7. It is true that there is no Roman documentation of *Ad quadratum* to match the handbooks of medieval designers,[5] but this is probably an accident of history. As Vitruvius intimates, problems of land measurement, and the need to divide areas conveniently into halves, quarters and so on, was one explanation for its longevity.[6] For similar reasons $\sqrt{2}$ progressions like those illustrated in figures 5.7 and 5.8 served for regulating and simplifying decorative patterns involving squares, as may be seen over a wide spectrum of mosaic and *opus sectile* work (figs 5.1, 5.9, 5.22 and 5.23). Nor is metrical analysis necessary to perceive its presence in the way the soffit was laid out at the tomb at Mylasa (fig. 5.10). The same organizational principle applied to ceiling coffers in the Didymaion, while many centuries later there is evidence of a more sustained progression in both the Cosmatesque floor pattern and the overall layout of Bramante's Tempietto (fig. 5.11). *Ad quadratum* was a mnemonic device that transcended the boundaries of surveying, building and craft, and within sensible limits of accuracy there is no reason to doubt the potential relevance of $\sqrt{2}$ in the analyses of individual monuments.[7] To a lesser extent the same applies to *Ad triangulatum*, the manipulation of the equilateral triangle (and hence $\sqrt{3}$), which was also of service to masons and decorators for such practical problems as setting out axes at right angles to one another. In part for the same reason equilateral triangles were frequently used in amphitheatre layouts (fig. 5.4), as was the 3 : 4 : 5 triangle (fig. 5.3).[8]

The ratio $\sqrt{3}$ turns up also in the so-called Sala Trilobata (fig. 5.13), the core of a fourth-century AD villa built on the roof of the Sette Sale cistern (which by then was some two centuries old). The reason this time lies in the fact that the plan is based on a hexagon – a figure that is intimately associated with the equilateral triangle. The principal planning operations may be reconstructed as follows. First of all a circle 40 ft in

5.7 Cuneiform Mesopotamian terracotta tablet with geometrical diagrams from the British Museum, London (ca. 18th century BC)

5.8 (a) *Ad quadratum* progression overlaid with concentric circles; (b) derivation of the so-called Sacred Cut.

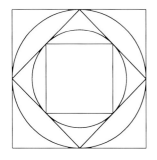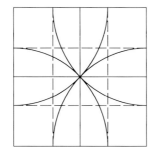

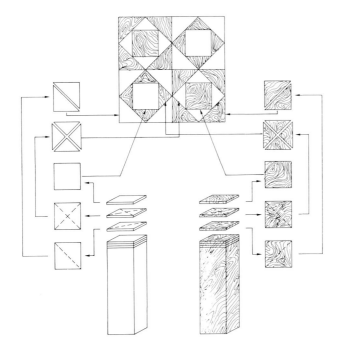

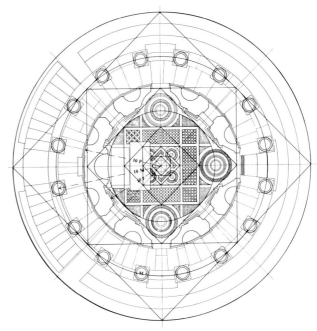

5.9 (*above left*) Scheme for the fabrication of an *opus sectile* pavement using squares of the same size of two different stones, together with 45° triangles produced by successive division of the squares on the diagonal. Along with variants on the theme, this organization was a basic staple of flooring patterns.

5.11 (*above right*) Plan of the Tempietto, San Pietro Montorio, Rome (Bramante, 1503), with annotated dimensions and *Ad quadratum* progression. This scheme finds confirmation in the inherent geometry of the Cosmatesque floor pattern.

5.10 Interior detail of the mausoleum at Mylasa, Turkey (uncertain date), the form of which is thought to have been directly inspired by the Mausoleum of Halikarnassos. Note the geometry of square and rotated square in the layout of the soffit.

radius fixes the total width of the complex, while one half this size circumscribes the central hexagon, producing facets of 20 feet. The lobes were then made about 20 ft wide too, with an internal span of 17¼ ft, that is to say smaller by a factor of $\sqrt{3}:2$. This ratio might just result from chance – a consequence perhaps of opting for standard 1½ ft bricks – but 17¼ ft corresponds to the inscribed radius of the central hall, so the architect may be visualized as transferring this to the lobes with a pair of dividers. In effect the plan unfolds via the sequential manipulation of ruler, compasses or dividers, with the ratios 1:1, 2:1 and $\sqrt{3}:2$ emerging inevitably in the process.

The lesson, in essence, is that geometry was used when it brought with it tangible practical advantages, or when it was inherent in the nature of the design exercise. This is why it was the automatic choice whenever design involved non-circular curves like those employed for the Didyma base, Ionic volutes or amphitheatre plans. In theory such curves could be defined numerically by means of a series of coordinates, but this presumes relatively elaborate mathematics. On the other hand effective approximations could be obtained by using combinations of compass-drawn arcs, a procedure that was not only more in keeping with traditional craft skills, but also more responsive to adjustment.[9] The $\sqrt{2}$ proportion of Corinthian bases arises because their *diagonal* width is double the column diameter (fig. 5.6), besides being a natural corollary of manipulating circles and squares about a common centre, just as it was in medieval *Ad quadratum*. The plan of a late antique martyrium at

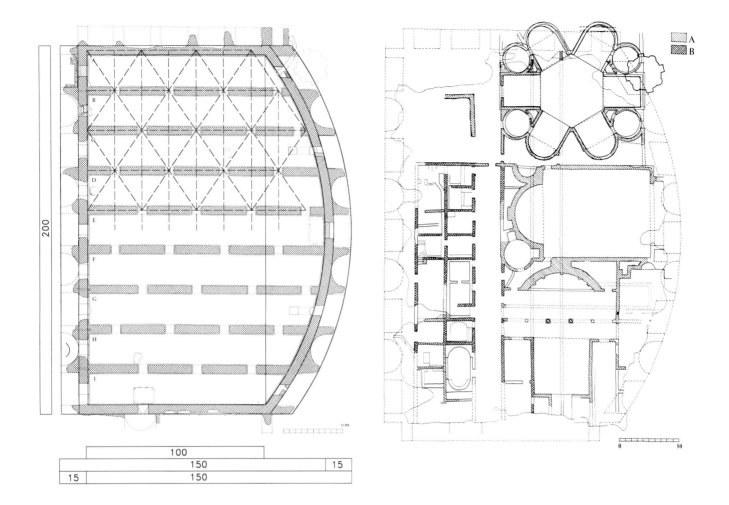

Carthage displays a receding series of interlocking squares, so it is hardly a surprise to find that its layout follows the same principle.[10] √2 appears in the plan of the Pantheon too, being the relation between the circle locating the interior columns and the square locating the portico columns (fig. 9.11). Again there is a certain logic here, in as much as the building is essentially made up of a circular mass intersected by a square one (see chapter 9 for further detail). As for the typical Roman theatre, geometry provided a convenient means for dividing the cavea into aisles on account of the circular shape of the orchestra. Once architects had compasses in their hands, it must have seemed logical to carry on using them to position the stage as well (fig. 2.5).[11]

The Hadrianic period stands out as a time when architectural geometries were enjoyed both intellectually and sensually to an extent that was hitherto unknown. The emperor's villa near Tivoli was a veritable laboratory for researching how geometry could be exploited to create new spatial forms and effects of light and shade, of curve and counter-curve (figs 5.2 and 5.14–5.19).[12] It is self-evident that many of the plans could not have been laid out save by manipulating compasses and straight-edge (fig. 5.18).[13] Here it is enough just to look at the geometrical elegance of

5.14 Reconstruction model of Hadrian's Villa, near Tivoli (AD 118), on display at the entrance to the archaeological complex.

5.15 Vestibule to the so-called Piazza d'Oro at Hadrian's Villa, with part of the characteristic scalloped or pumpkin vault still intact.

5.12 (*facing page top*) Monumental water cistern known as the Sette Sale and later accretions, Rome. The cistern originally serviced the adjacent Baths of Trajan; in late antiquity it became incorporated as the substructure to a villa. (a) Plan of the main Trajanic level with geometry and dimensions overlaid, 1:600. (b) Plan of the 4th-century villa constructed on the roof, 1:600. The centrally planned suite of rooms known as the Sala Trilobata (cf. fig. 5.13) is at the top.

5.13 (*facing page bottom*) Principal geometrical manipulations for laying out the suite of rooms known as the Sala Trilobata (cf. fig. 5.12). Note how the relevance of the equilateral triangle (and hence the ratio √3) follows naturally from the geometry of the hexagon.
top left: construct hexagon 40 ft wide using basic compass method
top middle: construct second hexagon twice as large, rotated by 30°
top right: with compasses centred on the side of the inner hexagon, inscribe circle within its radials; translate the same circle (or semicircle) to define apses
bottom left: place the same circle on the side of the outer hexagon to define the circular chambers; use the same circle again to define the width of the rectangular rooms, their length being determined by the intersection with a circle circumscribing the outer hexagon.
bottom middle: complete by symmetry
bottom right: give the wall thickness
The skeleton plan thus obtained was then adjusted to suit practical considerations; in order to align the external faces of the rectangular and circular rooms, as indicated by the dotted lines, the former was shortened and the latter shifted slightly.

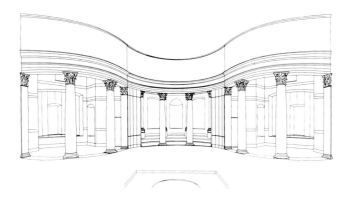

5.16 Perspectival reconstruction of the central hall of the so-called Piazza d'Oro complex, Hadrian's Villa, Tivoli.

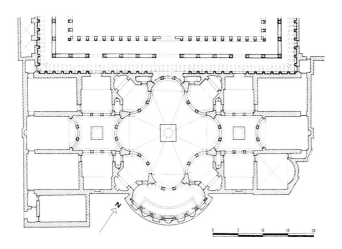

5.17 Piazza d'Oro, plan.

5.18 Plan of the so-called Accademia complex at Hadrian's Villa, with breakdown of key geometrical relationships.

5.19 (*facing page*) (a) Teatro Marittimo or Garden Retreat in Hadrian's Villa, with key geometrical scheme overlaid. (b) Sequence of geometrical operations underlying the relationship of island, moat and overall enclosure: (1) beginning with a perimeter of external diameter 150 ft and internal diameter 144 ft, an arc of the same radius is centred on the circumference of the latter; (2) a chord is drawn where the two 144 ft circles intersect; the crossing with the axis established in the previous step defines the width of the innermost circle (hence its diameter of $144/\sqrt{3}$ ft); (3) another arc of the same radius as the smaller circle is drawn centred where it crosses the axis; the intersection with the chord established in the previous step defines the width of the intermediate circle (hence its diameter of $(144 \times \sqrt{2})/\sqrt{3}$ ft). In reality construction seems to have gone ahead using $\frac{7}{5}$ as an approximation to $\sqrt{2}$.

the so-called Teatro Marittimo or the emperor's own 'Island Retreat' (figs 5.2 and 5.19). Here is a tripartite concentric layout, with a perimeter portico, an inner island rich in curvilinear shapes, and a reflecting pool which also served for swimming and assuring privacy, since access to the intricate inner sanctum was by means of a draw-bridge. The detailed resolution of the island itself is inevitably complex,[14] but the connection between the island, moat and portico was simplicity itself. The 144 ft interior diameter was first divided by $\sqrt{3}$ to give that of the island, the latter being then multiplied by $\sqrt{2}$ (or rather its approximation $\frac{7}{5}$) to locate the moat. This is but the product of a simple rationale, namely that island, pool and portico each have the same surface area. What is more, such a scheme is child's play to set out with a pair of compasses (fig. 5.19b).

THE ANNEXE AT BAIAE

A quintessential example of Hadrianic geometry is the centrally planned suite of rooms or 'Annexe' attached to the circular rotunda known as the Temple of Venus at Baiae (fig. 5.20).[15] In antiquity this was a renowned up-market shoreline resort to the west of Naples in

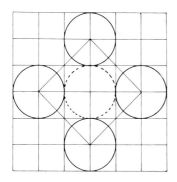
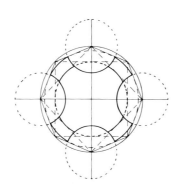
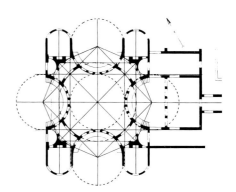

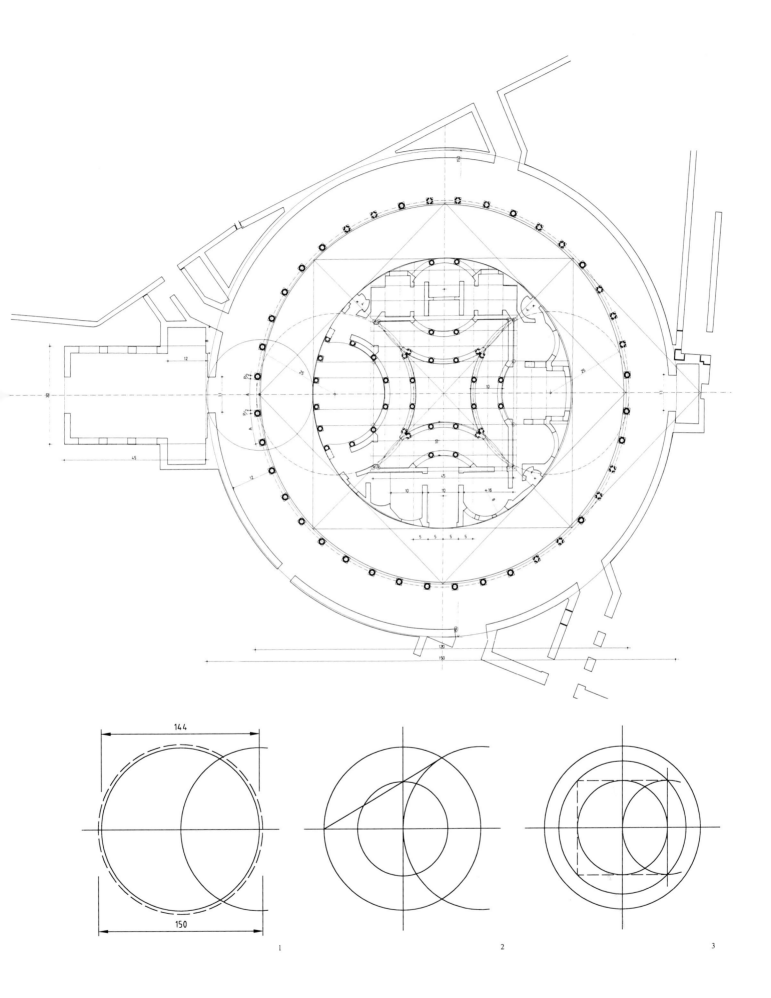

1

2

3

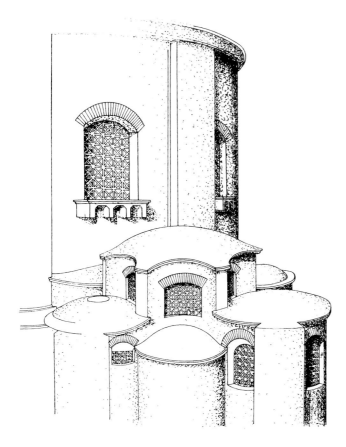

5.20 Reconstruction of the Annexe to the so-called Temple of Venus at Baiae, Gulf of Naples (AD 130s): (a) interior; (b) exterior with part of the rotunda of the 'temple'.

the region of simmering volcanic activity picturesquely known as the Phlegraean Fields – fields consumed by fire. To judge by the huge communal pool it sheltered, the Temple of Venus was no temple at all, but one of the exclusive thermo-mineral bathing establishments for which the area was famous.[16] The label 'Annexe' for the adjoining suite is just as unsatisfactory, but its precise original function has yet to be determined.

Despite the almost total loss of the decoration, there is enough evidence to show that there were never columns and pilasters, so – unlike most of its cousins at Hadrian's Villa – the Annexe is free of the shackles of the classical orders, a fact that helps explain its strikingly abstract character. The central space is outlined by alternately projecting and re-entrant arcs in such a way as to make a sinuous Greek cross, one that embraces the three circular corner chambers and the semicircular apse of the main hall. Overhead there is a lantern which takes up the form of an open umbrella (fig. 5.20).

Apart from its obvious geometrical character, the plan recalls motifs found in decorative geometrical pavements in mosaic or cut stone (*opus sectile*). The same configuration appears in a mosaic in the Augustales' headquarters at Ostia,[17] besides later examples at Acholla, Aquileia, El Jem (fig. 5.21), Ljubljana, Ravenna and Taranto.[18] And in general terms the sinuous walls present analogies with the bands of mosaic that define the figure ground. In the building their place is taken by the walls, with the tesserae transformed as the *caementa* of the concrete. Both media are capable of being moulded in an organic fashion, transforming abstract geometries into sensuous form.

While not one of the structures at Hadrian's Villa or any known mosaic reproduces precisely the same scheme as the Baiae plan, similar procedures are undoubtedly at work. A fundamental shared principle is that of an orthogonal grid. The plan of the Annexe fits a grid in as much as its 15 ft diameter corner chambers are placed 30 ft apart, and so can be inscribed within a chequerboard of nine 15 ft squares, as shown in figure 5.24. Significantly, it is also possible to overlay just such a grid of nine squares over the comparable plans of the Accademia and Piazza d'Oro pavilions at Hadrian's Villa (fig. 5.18). The use of planning grids in antiquity was widespread; they are documented by drawings from Pharaonic Egypt and Mesopotamia,[19] and may be inferred from Hellenistic temple plans (fig. 2.10), from the layout of cities and military camps, and centuriation. But in the present context it is especially relevant that grids also performed an important

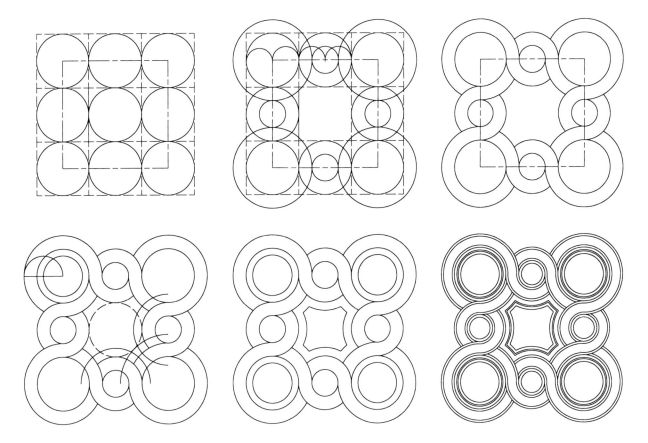

5.21 Floor mosaic from El Jem showing Diana, hunting scenes and allegories of the Seasons (Musée National du Bardo, Tunis, early 3rd century AD): (a) view of the whole mosaic (*below*); (b) simulation of geometrical operations underlying the design (*above*).
top left: lay out grid of nine squares and inscribed circles
top middle: with a width quarter as wide as the initial circles, create bands for the foliate border; in this way the smaller fields become half as wide as the larger ones
top right: edit scheme to create woven effect

bottom left: place a circle half as wide as the outermost of the corner circles so as to create the border for the larger scenes; establish the diagonal limits of the quatrefoil by the centremost circle, and create offset accordingly
bottom middle: complete pattern by symmetry
bottom right: add further elaboration by offsets to the geometry already established

5.22 (*below right*)   *Opus sectile* patterns using a common geometry.

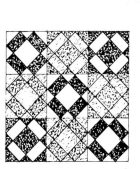

1

2

3

4

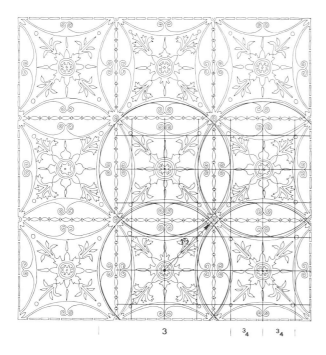

5.23 Floor pattern from one of the rooms in the so-called 'Ospitalia' or guest residence at Hadrian's Villa at Tivoli, with geometrical scheme and dimensions overlaid.

function in mosaic and *opus sectile* work. Quite apart from their detection by means of analysis, as in the case of numerous British mosaics,[20] physical evidence has been discovered in the form of preparatory grids incised in the substrate of curvilinear pavement patterns at a number of sites including Ostia, Acholla, Stabiae and Pompeii.[21] It is interesting to see too how grids were used in a pair of mosaics belonging to the so-called 'Ospitalia' – a kind of guest residence – at Hadrian's Villa. One of these is a simple pattern of touching circles of constant radius inscribed within another chequerboard of nine squares (fig. 5.23). Another offers an additional comparison with the Baiae plan, with its pattern of cusped octagons bordered by circles on the diagonal axes.[22] There is a further echo in terms of geometrical and numerical simplicity, for these circles are set out 3 ft from one another, with their internal diameter being again half as much, 1½ ft. This same relationship is present again in a closer parallel still, the mosaic from El Jem analysed in figure 5.21. The trick of all these types of design, then, was to create seductive curvilinear shapes from a simple geometrical framework.

We can now go on to drafting the complete sequence of steps used to compose the plan of the Annexe:

(i) Locate the centres of the corner rooms at corners of a square of sides 30 ft. The orthogonal and diagonal axes and centre of the whole scheme would have been specified at the same time (fig. 5.24a).

(ii) With compasses centred at the corners of the square, draw circles 15 ft in diameter to define the interior surface of the corner chambers. As mentioned, this implies a chequer pattern or grid of three by three 15 ft squares.

(iii) The centres of the lobes are defined by the vertices where four quarter octagons meet, each octagon being centred at the external corners of the 45 ft chequerboard. The simplest way of constructing this pattern is to place here a 45 ft wide square rotated at 45°, and then pick out the intersections with the cardinal axes (fig. 5.24b). This organization departs from the scheme used at El Jem (fig. 5.21) and elsewhere, but it is another that comes up frequently in decorative pattern-making, particular those involving octagons and/or rotated squares (fig. 5.22).[23]

(iv) The interior radius of the lobes was then set to touch the inner square of the 15 ft grid. At the same time their external envelope was made to reach the outer frame of the grid (fig. 5.24c). The beauty of this choice was that it set in train an extraordinary set of associated coincidences. Firstly, the outer circles meet one another at a tangent. Secondly, the centres of the lobes intersect the tangents connecting opposing corner chambers. Thirdly, the external radii of the lobes and chambers are virtually identical (the difference is just 1½ ins), producing a 'close-packed' pattern of circles.

As for the lantern, its layout proceeded as follows:

(v) Locate the points of the lantern on a circle inscribed within the original 30 ft square. This circle may then be subdivided with points placed at equal intervals on the circumference of the 30 ft circle, using a standard compasses procedure for generating an octagon (fig. 5.24e). The cusps of the octagon so obtained coincide almost exactly with the points of transition between the lobes and the 'shoulders' of the main space below.

(vi) To produce the counter-curves for the perimeter of the umbrella, two rotated squares were extrapolated from the sides of the octagon constructed in step (v). With compasses centred on the vertices of these squares, arcs are drawn to join pairs of points on the initial circle to produce the interior profile of the lantern. Its exterior surfaces are

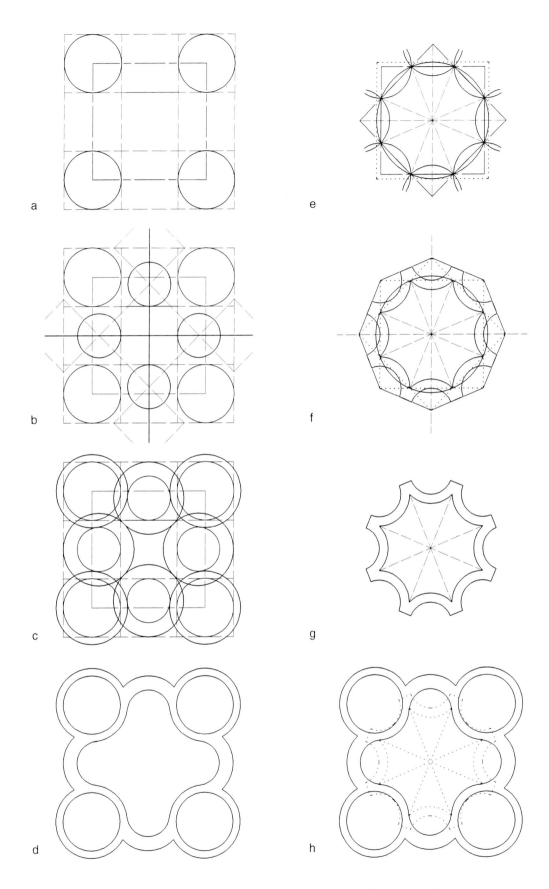

5.24   Sequence of geometrical operations underlying the generation of the plan of the Annexe to the so-called Temple of Venus at Baiae (AD 130s?).

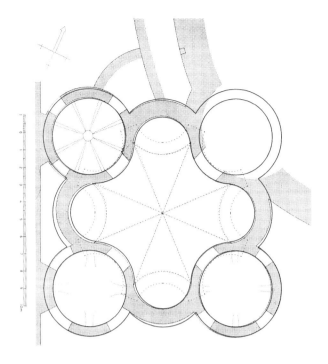

5.25 Plan for the Annexe to the Temple of Venus overlaid with the outcome of the geometrical sequence shown in fig. 5.24.

defined by arcs drawn from the same centres so as to meet the octagon at a tangent (fig. 5.24f).

It so happens, however, that this last step produced a geometry that did not fit precisely over that of the ground floor, since step (ii) and step (vi) generated different shapes for the counter-curves, or shoulders, of the central space. Before finalizing the design, the architect must have given careful thought to this problem, since a unified solution was clearly superior not just in terms of theory but also for the sake of spatial quality. So a compromise was chosen: whereas the corner rooms were retained at the corners of the original 30 ft square, the shoulders have as their centres the points set out in step (vi), so as to harmonize with the lantern layout (fig. 5.24h).

It is this last dilemma that explains one of the singular oddities of the Annexe plan, namely that the curving stretches of wall mediating between the main space and the corner chambers are not uniform in thickness as reasonably might be expected, resembling instead portions of a crescent moon (fig. 5.25). (Complex Roman buildings are, it is true, full of amorphous walls which are effectively the leftovers determined by the shape of the space they contain, but the peculiar thing here is that the geometries either side are so similar.) Another curiosity that contradicts common sense is the great thickness of the lobe walls,

for they carry only tiny vaults and nothing else. The surplus to requirement is highlighted by the fact that the counter-curves supporting the upper storey are only half as wide despite the greater loading. Again, the answer lies in the geometrical steps just described, ones that gave rise to a concatenation of geometrical niceties and a coherent *symmetria*. To underline the last point, it should be remembered that many parts of the building fit the sequence 15 : 30 : 45 ft. The dimensions 15 and 45 ft are respectively ½ and 1½ times the size of the basic 30 ft square and circle, while each of these is a fraction of 90 ft, the interior diameter of the main hall to which the Annexe is attached. All other dimensions were yet related to the key 30 ft by simple geometry (giving rise to ones that today might be expressed as $\sqrt{2} \times$ 30 ft or $(2\sqrt{2} - 1) \times$ 30 ft). This is a reminder of one of the fundamentals of Roman planning, as explored in the previous chapter, namely the use of an appropriately resonant round dimension as the starting-point for design. Indeed, there is good reason to doubt any geometrical proposal that is not locked into a simple metrical premise as at the Annexe at Baiae, the Teatro Marittimo, the amphitheatre at Verona (fig. 3.20), the Baths of Caracalla (fig. 5.5), the Sette Sale (fig. 5.12) and the Sala Trilobata on top of it (fig. 5.13). In the case of the Pantheon, it is this simple lesson that discriminates between the scheme actually used (fig. 9.11) and a rival candidate with which it shares much in common.[24]

VIEW PLANNING

The circumscribed decagon on the base of the Dying Gaul (fig. 3.7) yields a tantalizing glimpse of geometry in the hands of a Hellenistic sculptor. If such a diagram was used to locate the statue group in relation to its setting – and this 'if' is quite a big one – then geometry presumably came into play because it offered a means of organizing vistas and privileged lines of sight. Similar concerns have been invoked to explain the asymmetrical or eccentric arrangements that are often found in Greek urban spaces,[25] which may imply that view planning was less relevant to Roman civic design, given the preference for symmetry and for alignments following the cardinal axes north-south, east-west, where site conditions permitted.[26] Within the confines of a complex, a clear enough example of view planning occurs in the Forum of Augustus, where the axes between the great opposing exedrae pass in line with the front of the temple. On entering the precinct it was impossible even to be aware of the existence of these exedrae, for sight of them was barred by the serried lines of columns seen in perspective (fig. 2.4); glimpses between the columns expanded as the visitor moved forward towards the temple, and finally a frontal view through to the head of each exedra came when entering the temple itself. This axis was also of fundamental importance in iconographical terms, for it locked the temple front, with its pedimental statuary and dedicatory inscription, in an intimate relation to the statue groupings in the exedrae.[27] So composition, views, movement and programme all contribute to a single dramatic climax. In as much as this sort of orchestration is the domain of urban planning it goes beyond the scope of this book, but it is well to note hints of similar principles at work both in the plan of the Sette Sale cistern (fig. 5.12), and that of Santa Costanza, where an unimpeded view of several niches at once can be had only at the moment the visitor penetrates the central space (fig. 4.11). Perhaps it is this that explains the lack of radial alignment between the ring of twelve columns and sixteen niches/accents on the perimeter, a feature that so puzzled Renaissance observers.[28]

Once geometry had served its purpose, architects tended to gravitate back towards arithmetical calculation, just as Vitruvius does. Some scholars, however, sustain that many of the arithmetical ratios in Vitruvius' treatise are really approximations to geometrical ones.[29] But while this is quite plausible on occasions, as a generalization it makes little sense. In Book VI Vitruvius cites several ratios for establishing room proportions, most of which are arithmetical ratios like $3:2$, $4:3$ or $5:3$. It is significant too that when he does use $\sqrt{2}$ (VI,3,3) he is explicit about its geometrical nature. He shows a marked propensity towards arithmetic in the key theoretical passages on the *symmetria* of the human body (p. 41) and the Basilica at Fanum (pp. 45–6), just as the tacit ideals of myth-makers emerge in the reputed dimensions of lost monuments like Lars Porsena's tomb.

To recapitulate, where geometry was used it was either inherent in the nature of the exercise, or it offered a convenient means for, as Vitruvius put it, 'resolving difficult problems of *symmetria*'. This should be the litmus test for modern analyses, for Roman architects did not normally indulge in complexity for its own sake. Such is their enthusiasm for geometry, however, that some scholars get carried away to the extent of presenting a quite distorted view of ancient practice. The reasons are various, ranging from an over-evaluation of the importance of the Euclidean tradition – which was not by any means the only mode of ancient mathematics – to the legacy of Romanticism's flirtation with geometry, not to mention its appeal to those who feel at home with compasses and theorems. In any event, the scepticism surrounding concepts like Hambidge's Dynamic Symmetry has not been enough to warn everybody of the dangers (p. 4). Kalayan, for example, sees the proportion $6\sqrt{2}:5\sqrt{3}$ in a tomb at Petra measuring $5.9 \times 5.77\,\text{m}$, but surely the original intention was simply a 20 ft square, as in the case of another comparably irregular rock-cut tomb, that of Zacharias in Jerusalem.[30] A recent analysis of the imperial fora confirms the recurrence of certain simple relationships and round dimensions (fig. 8.4), which is all well and good until the underlying cause is revealed to be a cosmic diagram reminiscent of those advocated by Brunés, Gardner (fig. 0.8) and others, as opposed to principles of *symmetria* combined with the desire to emulate precedent.[31]

THE GOLDEN SECTION

No treatment of architectural proportion would be complete without some mention of the golden section, the irrational ratio approximating to 1.618 which is commonly represented by the Greek letter Φ. The unique mathematical properties associated with this ratio have been an enduring source of fascination,[32] of which the most important may be briefly summarized as follows:

If two quantities or line segments are related by Φ the smaller stands to the larger as the larger stands to their sum. This can be expressed as

$$a:b = b:a + b = \Phi = 1.618 \text{ (fig. 5.26)}.$$

From this it follows that

$$1/\Phi = \Phi - 1 = 0.618.$$

The principal dimensions of the tomb of Lars Porsena (as reported by Pliny the Elder)

	50	75	100	150	300
50 ft podium height	I	⅔	½	⅓	⅙
75 ft pyramid width		I	¾	½	¼
100 ft pyramid height (2nd)			I	⅔	⅓
150 ft pyramid height (1st)				I	½
300 ft podium width					I

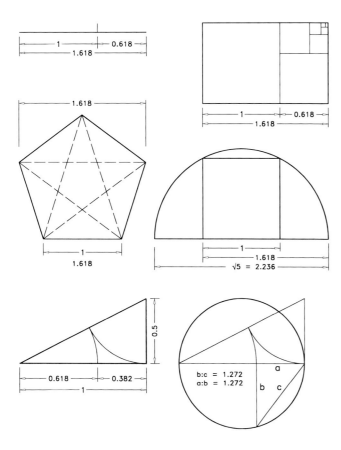

$$\sqrt{\Phi} \times a = b, \text{ while } \sqrt{\Phi} \times b = c$$

5.26 Derivation of the golden section ratio (Φ or approximately 1.618), and its square root ($\sqrt{\Phi}$ or approximately 1.272) and their relation to selected geometrical figures.
top left: division of a line into its 'mean and extreme proportion', with the smaller portion standing to the larger portion as the larger portion stands to the whole.
top right: golden rectangle progression. Any rectangle with an aspect ratio corresponding to the golden section contains a square and a smaller golden section rectangle.
middle left: derivation of Φ, or ($\sqrt{5}$ + 1)/2), from a regular pentagon.
middle right: derivation of Φ from the figure of a square inscribed in a semicircle. Note that the overall width of the semicircle is $\sqrt{5}$ times that of the square.
bottom left: derivation of Φ from a right-angled triangle with a height equal to half the base.
bottom right: use of the previous figure to derive the so-called Diophantine triangle, this being the only right-angled triangle in which the height (a) relates to the base (b) as the base relates to the hypotenuse (c), the ratio being in each case $\sqrt{\Phi}$.

And also that

$$\Phi^2 = \Phi + 1 = 2.618.$$

The square root of the golden section, $\sqrt{\Phi}$ or approximately 1.272, is furthermore the ratio applicable to the only right-angled triangle (the so-called Diophantine triangle) in which the hypotenuse (c) stands to the longer of the other two sides (b) as the latter stands to the shortest side (a), i.e.:

Despite the acclaim that has flowed from these and other properties (fig. 5.26), there is no firm evidence that the golden section found favour in the eyes of Roman architects. Its detection by means of metrical analysis is in the first place fraught by the problem of distinguishing it from $^{8}\!/_{5}$ (1.600), since the difference amounts to only 1 percentage point. Advocates of the golden section may regard $^{8}\!/_{5}$ and even $^{5}\!/_{3}$ as approximations, but how can we be sure when these arithmetical ratios were not intended in their own right?[33] Then there is the problem that Vitruvius does not apply the golden section at all – and to claim it was really a well-kept secret is a limp defence. It is true that ancient geometers knew it as the 'mean and extreme ratio', and that it is associated with the geometry of the pentagon and the dodecagon; but Euclid gave these figures no special emphasis in his study of polygons, just as he placed no special mystical significance on the ratio that did not become 'golden' until the Renaissance. The pentagon and pentagram are rare in ancient planning, a notable exception being the diagram used to set out the Dying Gaul statue group (fig. 3.7). Here the ratio in size between two of the concentric circles (the second and third) is indeed equivalent to Φ, but it is a moot point whether this is anything other than the consequence of manipulating a pentagon. Another avenue of critical interest centres on the purported aesthetic appeal of the golden rectangle progression (fig. 5.26b), but here again there is no evidence of its architectural application in antiquity. In short, the golden section is an exquisitely intellectual concept which has little in common with Roman uses of geometry, ones which were always appropriate to the matter in hand or rooted in convenient solutions for specific problems. It is hard to see what possible practical aid the golden section could have offered in setting out circular plans or ones based on the more popular forms of polygon (the square, hexagon and octagon).[34]

The whole historiography of proportional studies (as outlined in the Introduction) shows that assessments like this must remain a matter of opinion. In fact in 1996 Fabrizio Esposito and Antonio Michetti staked out a diametrically opposed thesis, namely that the ratios $\sqrt{\Phi}$ and Φ lay at the heart of Roman architects' habitual strategies for determining the wall thickness of circular halls, the Pantheon being a case in point.[35] $\sqrt{\Phi}$ is shown to be the ratio between the interior and exterior diameter of the rotunda, while the Diophantine triangle is supposed to be responsible for the resolution of the section (fig. 5.27). Both proposals are just as accurate as my own, whether for the plan (fig. 9.11) or elevation. Unless the two trains of thought are somehow mutually compatible – which on the face of it seems unlikely – here is a classic divergence of approach.[36] They see the wall entering into a sophisticated geometrical conception, I see its thickness (20 ft) as the most suitable whole number consistent with the Romans' experience of statics. If a proportion was important, this would be the 5:4 ratio between the external diameter and that of the column ring (notionally 187½:150 ft), and not the √Φ ratio between the former and the internal span (notionally 187½:147½ ft). But such debates come down to opinion, and the onus must remain with the reader to weigh the evidence and adjudicate accordingly. There are of course numerous instances where quite different analyses seem to fit equally well – that other much-studied building, the Parthenon, being a notorious example. In the last resort the real question is whether a particular proposal effectively resonates with the tenor of ancient thought and society in general.

THE THOLOS AT TIVOLI

It seems unfair to those readers who want to get to grips with the present subject constantly to have to skim over the nitty-gritty evidence while being referred to publications that are often only available in specialist libraries. So, for didactic purposes, it is well to conclude this discussion by comparing arithmetical and geometrical proposals for a single building with the support of sufficient documentation to allow them to be evaluated with respect to the other. The peripteral temple or tholos at Tivoli (fig. 4.13) is chosen for this purpose, since my arguments for arithmetic (fig. 5.28) can be compared with those that Herman Geertman puts forward in defence of geometry (fig. 5.29).[37] The building also makes a suitable vehicle for debate since it is both quite well preserved and has been the repeated subject of surveys that agree with one another within a negligible margin.

The undisputed key to the mathematics of the composition is the 1:2 relationship between the height of the columns, 24 ft, and the overall diameter of the podium, 48 ft. Next it seems significant that the internal diameter of the cella exceeds 24 ft by just 5 inches, so if allowance is made for the lost stucco dressing it seems highly likely that the whole foot dimension was the original clear width.[38] Thus we have a 24:24:48 ft, or 1:1:2 sequence, and two further proportions that

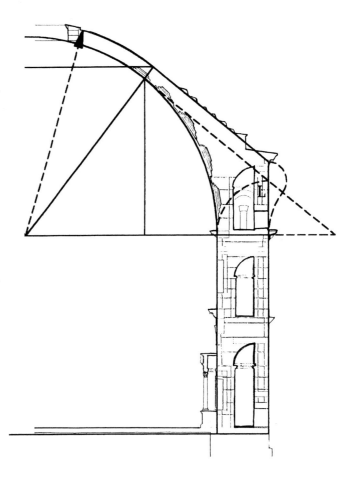

5.27 Geometrical interpretation of the section of the Pantheon cupola according to Esposito and Michetti. The external diameter of the drum is greater than its internal diameter by a factor of √Φ, while the resolution of the haunch of the dome and its stepped external profile is determined by the Diophantine triangle EHL.

evoke highly pertinent comparisons. The 1:2 ratio between the width of the interior and that of the podium occurs in other centralized structures of bivalent orientation (Table 4.1).[39] Meanwhile the 1:1 ratio between the width of the interior and the column height was specifically recommended by Vitruvius for this type of building (IV,8,2).

Arguably 1:1 and 1:2 ratios could reflect a geometrical mode of conception as much as an arithmetical one, so the real test is the nature of further relationships. Geertman interprets the positioning of the cella as follows: he sees the external and not the internal diameter as the critical limit, taking his cue from another Vitruvian ratio found in the same passage as that just cited, that this dimension be about ⅗ the diameter of the podium. In his view Vitruvius used the word 'about' to signify that ⅗ approximated the irrational ratio (2 − √2)/1, a ratio derived from

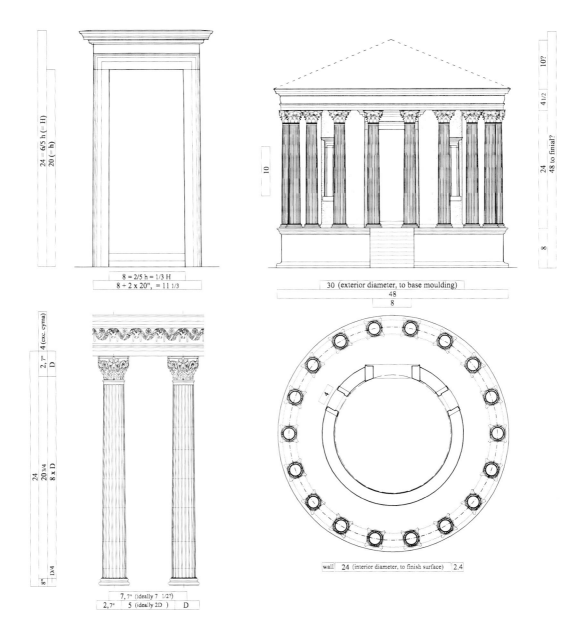

5.28 Key arithmetical relationships in the design of the tholos at Tivoli, according to author.

the geometrical scheme illustrated in figure 5.29.[40] But the actual exterior diameter measures substantially more than either the value predicted by geometry or Vitruvius' ratio, apparently because of the attraction of another approximation which better suited the metrical resolution of the project as a whole, namely 11:18.[41] In my view, however, Vitruvius could have used 'about' to reflect the fact that the exterior diameter was not fundamental, but rather the sum of the internal diameter and the wall thickness, the latter being a technical detail that was left to the discretion of individual architects, subject to the type of construction in question.

Geertman then perceives a geometrical bond between plan and elevation (fig. 5.29), following the

observation that the exterior radius of the cella equals both the height of the window sill above the ground, and the (reconstructed) height from the architrave to the summit of the whole building. But these are not limits of any great architectonic value; by contrast simple fractions of 24 and 48 ft recur in recognizably important elements in both plan and elevation. The window openings are 4 ft wide; the portal opening is 8 ft wide and 20 ft tall; its entablature is 4 ft tall; the podium is 8 ft tall. As the matrix below shows, the principal dimensions of this building thus follow in the

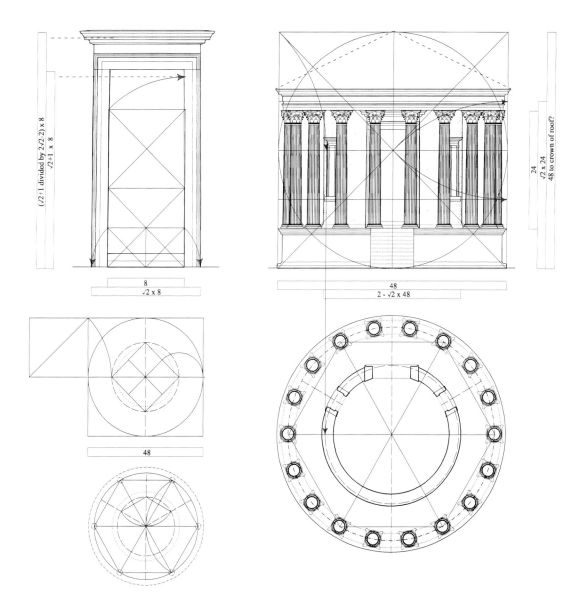

same mould as the idealized *symmetria* of Vitruvian Man (p. 41), Vitruvius' Basilica at Fanum (p. 46) or Lars Porsena's tomb (p. 101).

5.29 (*above*) Key geometrical relationships in the design of the tholos at Tivoli, according to Herman Geertman.

The principal dimensions of the tholos at Tivoli in feet

	4	8	20	24	48
4 ft	I	½	⅕	⅙	⅛
8 ft		I	⅖	⅓	⅙
20 ft			I	⅚	5/12
24 ft				I	½
48 ft					I

5.30 Tholos at Tivoli, analysis of doorcase.

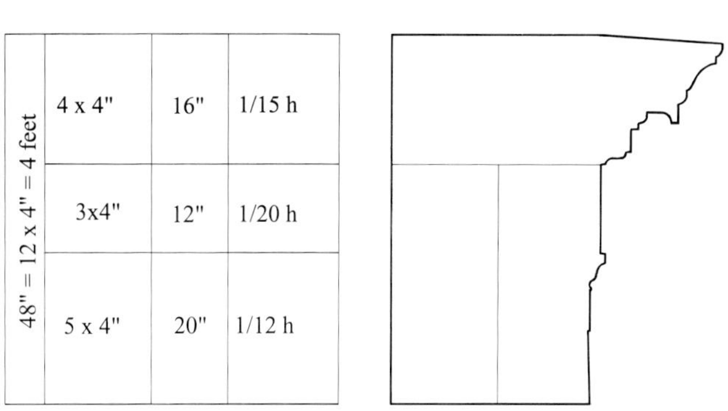

The only significant exception to this pattern is the height of the entablature of the peristyle, about 4½ ft. But since 4 ft would have been so very suitable, this likely represented the *initial* aim of the architect. The extra fraction was probably judged necessary in order to avoid what would have been an exceptionally slight proportion (one sixth) in relation to the column height. (As it happens neither is there an immediately impelling geometrical explanation for the particular dimension chosen.) In any event, the rest of the design of the peristyle certainly argues more in favour of arithmetic. The columns were accurately divided into their constituent elements by a modular scheme, with the heights of the base, capital and shaft corresponding to $\frac{1}{4}$, 1 and 8 column diameters.[42] Meanwhile the gap between adjacent columns is very close to twice their diameter, that is to say the standard spacing which Vitruvius refers to as 'systyle' (p. 120).[43] This, no doubt, was the reason behind the choice of eighteen columns. In fact it is surely significant that a ring of eighteen columns cannot be constructed on the principles of Euclidean geometry, for although every third column can be located by equilateral triangles, just as Geertman's diagram shows (fig. 5.29),[44] the trisection of the resultant angle of 60° into three equal parts eludes a rigorous construction by means of compasses and straight-edge. In other words the spacing can be established only by trial and error, trigonometry, or by subdividing the circumference arithmetically.

The disposition of radial elements is in fact a useful key for distinguishing between arithmetic and geometry. Where geometry was used there should be radial arrays consonant with figures like the equilateral triangle and the square (and hence angles such as 60°, 30°, 15° or 45°, 22½°, 11½°) as in Vitruvius' theatre layout (fig. 2.5). But angles like these are frequently absent in the arrangement of apses, niches and other radial accents in centralized buildings, the logic being the subdivision of the circumference in terms of whole dimensions.[45]

As for the details of the portal, these again correspond well with Geertman's geometrical diagram, but the same result is none the less predicted more accurately still by arithmetical relationships like 6:5, 2:5, 1:12 and 3:4:5 (fig. 5.30).[46] In fact both the overall and detailed dimensions of the portal interrelate in a harmonious manner, and it is again possible to construct a matrix of striking simplicity, as shown below.

The principal dimensions of the portal of the tholos at Tivoli

	Height	12 ins	16 ins	20 ins	4 ft	20 ft	24 ft
12 ins	*frieze*	1	$\frac{3}{4}$	$\frac{3}{5}$	$\frac{1}{4}$	$\frac{1}{20}$	$\frac{1}{24}$
16 ins	*cornice*		1	$\frac{4}{5}$	$\frac{1}{3}$	$\frac{1}{15}$	$\frac{1}{18}$
20 ins	*architrave*			1	$\frac{5}{12}$	$\frac{1}{12}$	$\frac{5}{72}$
4 ft	*trabeation*				1	$\frac{1}{5}$	$\frac{1}{6}$
20 ft	*opening*					1	$\frac{5}{6}$
24 ft	*total*						1

It now remains only to apply Occam's razor. At each turn arithmetical procedures offered simpler alternatives to geometrical ones. The architect of the Tivoli temple could have roughed out a skeletal design with 'back-of-an-envelope' arithmetical calculations. This process would have rapidly yielded a series of subordinate ratios and measurements for detailed aspects of design (column spacing and slenderness, entablature proportions etc.) which could have been verified in the light of personal experience or specific precedents, and modified if necessary. Finally, it may be noted that drawings were at no stage essential for this endeavour, although of course they could have helped in visualizing the effect. As in earlier Greek practice (p. 50), drawings were needed only for determining profiles of mouldings and the like – and it is no coincidence that the Tivoli temple conforms to a long-standing and thoroughly predictable type of design going back to Greek prototypes of the sixth century BC.[47] For a building such as this, all its main characteristics could have been quite adequately described in words and numbers, that is to say in a more detailed version of the sort of recipe that Vitruvius supplies. The nature of the problem placed it a world apart from the geometrical intrigues created at Hadrian's Villa and Baiae by the emperor and his architectural entourage.

5.31 (*facing page top*)   The amphitheatre at Nîmes.

5.32 (*facing page bottom*)   The Colosseum at Rome.

VI

COPING WITH COLUMNS:
THE ELEVATION

THE IMPORTANCE OF THE ORDERS cannot be overstated; they are the DNA of classical architecture, the core of the mnemonic system by which its forms evolved and were transmitted. The design of countless façades is in large part a question of distributing and tailoring the orders; indeed the archetypal Graeco-Roman temple presents to the world essentially a run of columns and entablature, plus a flight of steps, a pediment and associated sculpture. The character of the elevation therefore revolves around the choice of order and the way it is treated: its size, materials, details and proportions. Where more elaborate designs use two or more orders, the effect depends on the dialogue between them. And even when they are absent, their memory may live on in the form of vestigial mouldings, allusions, or the scansion of repetitive elements like doors, windows and niches.[1]

The just equilibrium between the authority vested in the orders and their potential for variety was central to Roman architects' efforts to confer individuality on each single construction. It is hard to see this equilibrium as the ancients did, for the modern viewer is conditioned by the legacy of Renaissance attitudes, and the familiar synoptic image of the five orders, Tuscan, Doric, Ionic, Corinthian and Composite, graded sequentially in terms of proportion and ornament (figs 0.4 and 0.5). The very word order – with all its attendant implications of logic and discipline – was a Renaissance invention. Vitruvius himself used *genus*, rather in the spirit of botanical classification, and this continued to be popular in the fifteenth century along with custom, manner, mode, sort and species.[2] It was Raphael, or someone in his circle, who first adopted order (*ordine*),[3] which went on to become a veritable international standard following the publication of Vignola's treatise. It would seem futile to try and turn back the clock in favour of Vitruvius' outmoded terminology.

6.1 Rock-cut tomb at Petra, Jordan, known as the Khasneh, detail.

6.2 Rock-cut tomb at Petra known as El Deir (?early 2nd century AD), detail.

The Renaissance codification of the orders is symptomatic of the then prevailing urge to define architecture in terms of conceptually clear patterns. In reality ancient usage eludes such neatness. Columnar proportions conform only vaguely with an ascending scale from Tuscan to Composite, and no order possessed its own pedestal. What is more, it is doubtful that ancient architects ever put Composite and Tuscan on the same level as Doric, Ionic and Corinthian. Composite was just a variant of the Corinthian capital, without its own entablature, despite sixteenth-century efforts to assign it one.[4] Vitruvius dismissed such variants briefly, without naming them (IV,1,12), while he referred not to a Tuscan *genus*, but rather its *dispositiones*.

CHOOSING BETWEEN THE ORDERS

There was certainly no smooth progression in terms of quantity. In the middle and late imperial periods Corinthian represented the almost automatic choice, for reasons that will be examined in the next chapter. The Composite capital (fig. 7.21) offered an alternative when even greater elaboration was required, although Alberti and more recently John Onians may be right in detecting nationalistic sentiment as well.[5] It is as if by grafting Ionic volutes onto the Corinthian capital that the Romans sought to better the Greeks at their own game. Doric, meanwhile, suffered an inexorable decline, it being progressively snubbed from major projects as being too stark, too cumbersome and, perhaps, too Greek. The fact that the rules for composing the triglyph and metope frieze restricted the configuration at corners was an 'embarrassment', as Vitruvius puts it (IV,3).[6] Meanwhile Ionic was tarred by the same brush to some extent, in as much as the sides of the capital differ from the front and back. The corner solution was usually to butt together two fronts and two sides, producing a lop-sided abacus. And although a variant, sometimes known as the canted capital, was designed to solve this dilemma by presenting fronts on all faces (figs 0.6 and 7.3), its popularity was limited. As for Tuscan, it is hard to know exactly how Roman architects distinguished it from Doric, and indeed textbooks do not agree which to call the bottom order of the Colosseum (fig. on p. vi). The capital may be Doric, but the bases, by their very existence, are un-Doric. The real litmus text is the absence of that essential ingredient of Doric, the triglyph and metope frieze, which makes the result more Tuscan by exclusion, although the Ionic flavour of the entablature suggests that it is best to speak of a mixed order.

Doric and/or Tuscan occur most frequently in miscellaneous civic porticoes of subordinate importance, or in the domestic realm, a context where the saving in cost was a relatively weighty factor. Tuscan – or what might be called 'Greekified' Tuscan, by virtue of its Doric and Ionic components – was, however, by far the most popular choice for the amphitheatre. No doubt its simplicity suited the forthright nature of this type of building, but in addition Tuscan may have carried nationalistic or military overtones,[7] ones that were seen to be appropriate given the origins of gladiatorial combat. The amphitheatre was the only building type that the Romans invented from scratch, and undiluted Doric or Ionic arguably would have introduced an unwant foreign note.[8] The triglyph and metope frieze is, in fact, practically unknown in this context, while Ionic is only securely documented in the case of the Colosseum. The orders on the façades of the ten best preserved monumental amphitheatres are as follows:

Amphitheatre	1st	2nd	3rd
Pola	Tuscan	Tuscan	
Verona	Tuscan	Tuscan	Tuscan
Arles	Tuscan	Corinthian	
Nîmes	Tuscan	Tuscan	
Colosseum	Tuscan?	Ionic	Corinthian
Pozzuoli	Tuscan	Tuscan	?
Capua	Tuscan	Tuscan	Tuscan
Salone	Tuscan	Ionic?	?
Italica	Tuscan	?	
El Jem	Corinthian	Composite	Corinthian

Vitruvius promoted an anthropomorphic reading of the orders, associating squat Doric columns with manly strength, moderately slender Ionic columns with feminine grace and more slender Corinthian ones with virginal purity (IV,1,6–8). Logically he advised that Doric should be used for the temples of virile gods like Mars and Hercules, and Corinthian for delicate goddesses like Venus and Flora (1,2,5), but there is little sign that such ideas had much currency in either the Greek or the Roman periods. In archaic and classical times the use of Doric and Ionic divided predominantly on regional and political lines, and where Doric was preeminent it was as likely to have been used in connection with a female deity as a male one. Two of the grandest Corinthian temples of the Hellenistic period, at Athens and Diocaesarea, were dedicated to Zeus. The most delicate Corinthian columns in Rome belong to the tholos by the Tiber (figs 4.13 and 7.13), which in sympathy with Vitruvian notions was traditionally known as the Temple of Vesta; now, however, a dedication to Hercules seems much more likely.[9] And

Augustus, the prime target of Vitruvius' polemic, evidently ignored it when he chose Corinthian for his Temple of Mars Ultor. The common practice of adopting Corinthian when reconstructing damaged temples that hitherto had been Doric or Ionic is yet another indication of the irrelevance of this sort of symbolism in the imperial period.

When combining different orders Roman architects on occasions followed Hellenistic precedent by exploiting the Doric-Ionic-Corinthian scale to register programmatic polarities, such as exterior versus interior, or commonplace versus special.[10] Such manifestations include the basilica at Pompeii (where Corinthian marks out the tribune from the Ionic aisles (fig. 2.18)), the Parthian Arch of Augustus (where Corinthian marks out the central arch from the Doric flanking arches) and the triad of temples at the forum at Sbeitla (where Composite marks out the central temple from the flanking Corinthian ones (fig. 6.19)).[11] An emblematic example from late antiquity is Old St Peter's, with its progression from an Ionic atrium via a Corinthian nave to a Composite transept.[12] As for vertical arrangements, it can hardly be a coincidence that a monument as iconographically charged as the Sebasteion at Aphrodisias employed Corinthian on the top storey. This was the level housing images of the imperial family and gods, a position that was programmatically superior with respect to the middle, Ionic, level with its Grecian pantheon, and the bottom, statue-less Doric level.[13] So the implications seem clear: Rome had triumphed over the Greek world, just as Corinthian had triumphed over the other Greek orders.

With time, the usual predominance of Corinthian meant that hierarchies of intention were typically highlighted not so much by changes from one order to another but rather by gradations of ornament. Fluting could be enriched by mouldings applied to the fillet, it could take a spiral form or be omitted altogether;[14] columns in the round could be juxtaposed with half-columns, piers or pilasters; plain marbles could be played off against expensive ones, and so on. Contrasts like these remained fundamental for the deployment of recycled elements, or *spolia*, in late antique and medieval architecture.[15]

THE LIMITS OF ORTHODOXY

The words 'order' and 'canon' are put together so often that it requires a positive effort to appreciate the fluidity of ancient practice. It is far from certain that Roman architects ever reached consensus on what constituted normal Doric. On rare occasions (as at the propylaea to the Roman agora in Athens (fig. 2.7) and the sanctuary at Eleusis) imperial architects were instructed to reproduce classical models for political motives,[16] but otherwise these were shunned. Most Roman versions are variants. The canonic Doric frieze, with square metopes one and a half times as wide as the triglyphs, ceased to be obligatory. 'Tetra-glyphs', or triglyphs with four bars, appear very occasionally, as indeed they had in Greek times, while a set of 'bi-glyphs' were used to decorate an altar at the Nabataean sanctuary of Khirbet et-Tannur, not far from Petra. The echinus of the Doric/Tuscan capital was sometimes adorned with egg and dart, as at the Parthian Arch of Augustus, Trajan's Column and that of Marcus Aurelius (fig. 8.19). In the so-called Hall of the Doric pilasters at Hadrian's Villa the *guttae* were attached to the triglyphs, on the 'wrong' side of the junction with the architrave (fig. 2.9). Proportions could vary widely; the members of this last example or the Temple of Hercules at Cori would have seemed outrageously flimsy to Greek architects.

MIXED ORDERS AND HYBRIDS

Mixed orders are the most striking manifestation of the late Hellenistic and Roman taste for variety, a taste that contradicts received stereotypes. The combined volumes on Greek, Roman and Etruscan architecture in the Pelican History of Art series illustrate only four examples of mixed orders; John Ward-Perkins's *Roman Architecture* illustrates three; Frank Sear's book of the same title illustrates two, as does William MacDonald's twin volume *The Architecture of the Roman Empire*. A recurrent example is the rock-cut façade of the El Deir tomb at Petra (fig. 6.2), and students might be forgiven the mistake of thinking that mixed orders were limited to such out-of-the-way locations, a tangible sign perhaps of a cultural remove from the Graeco-Roman mainstream.

Hybrids may be defined as individual elements that fuse details from different orders (as in the Composite capital or the 'Doric' cornice of the Theatre of Marcellus, with its Ionic dentils). Mixed orders are those that are made up of heterogeneous separate elements (as when a Doric frieze is combined with an Ionic cornice). In the archaic period hybrid cornices were quite common in Magna Graecia.[17] In Hellenistic times the principal order of the Bouleuterion at Miletos represents one of the most sustained essays on

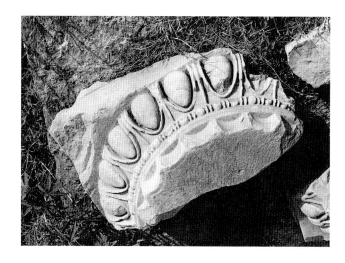

6.3 Capital from the Bouleuterion or Council House at Miletus, Turkey (1st quarter of 2nd century BC).

the Doric-Ionic theme. The capitals are Doric but enriched by Ionic egg and dart, the shafts combine shallow, Doric, flutes with Ionic fillets (fig. 6.3), while the entablature brings together a Doric frieze and an Ionic cornice, so that it is both a mixed order as well as a mix of hybrids.

While Vitruvius explicitly rejected mixed orders in one passage, in another he paradoxically allowed the Corinthian column to support either a Doric or an Ionic entablature (I,2,6; IV,1,2). This reflects in part his ambivalence towards Corinthian, which, although a distinct *genus*, did not in his day have the authority of Doric and Ionic, and in part the realities of contemporary practice. Before the consolidation of the modillion cornice (pp. 141–2), Corinthian columns generally supported Ionic entablatures or, to a lesser extent, Doric ones. Alternatively Doric friezes might be placed over Ionic capitals, or Ionic cornices over Doric friezes. In Labraunda, Alexandria and the funeral architecture of Tripolitania mixed orders seem to have been almost more popular than unmixed ones.[18] Back in Rome, however, Vitruvius' strictures may have found a sympathetic audience, for the lively experimentation of the early Augustan period came with time to be swallowed up by the emergent orthodoxy (chapter 7, p. 141).

To give a rough idea of the chronological and geographical range of mixed orders, selected Hellenistic and Roman examples are listed below according to the four most common combinations. Some examples fit more than one category, such as the tomb of Absalom at Jerusalem (Ionic capitals, Doric frieze and Egyptian cornice), or the Augustan temple at Philae (Corinthian

capitals, Doric frieze, Ionic cornice). Others elude categorization altogether. A case in point is the exterior order of the theatre at Arles, with its Corinthian cornice and 'Doric' architrave — if such a solecism as an architrave covered by tetraglyphs may be called by this name (fig. 6.4).[19] The dates range from the third century BC to the third century AD; within each group entries are arranged in roughly chronological order:

(i) Ionic capitals with Doric frieze

Labraunda, Andron 'A' and 'B'	
Agrigento, 'tomb of Theron'	
Canosa, temple[20]	
Samaria, Deir-el-Derb, tomb[21]	
Pompeii, portico of Temple of Apollo	
Beida, Asklepieion[22]	
Pergamon, Stoa of Athena	
Ptolemais, Palazzo delle Colonne[23]	fig. 2.8
Jerusalem, 'Tomb of Queen Helena'[24]	
Jerusalem, 'Tomb of Absalom'	fig. 4.17
Baalbek, vaulted rooms in substructures	

(ii) Ionic capitals with Egyptian cornice

Dougga, mausoleum	fig. 4.1
Sabratha, Mausoleum B[25]	
Tombe de la Chrétienne	
Jerusalem, 'Tomb of Zacharias'[26]	
Jerusalem, 'Tomb of Absalom'	fig. 4.17

(iii) Corinthian capitals with Doric frieze

Alexandria generally	
Arak el-Amir (Jordan), Palace of Hyrcanus[27]	fig. 6.6
Rome, tomb near Porta Maggiore[28]	
Philae, Temple of Augustus[29]	fig. 6.7
Aosta, triumphal arch	fig. 6.5
Arles, arch over the Rhône[30]	
Cyrene, Caesareum, temple	
Tripolitania generally, e.g. Tomb F at Ghirza[31]	
Apamea, colonnade	

(iv) Corinthianizing capitals with Doric frieze

Paestum, Doric-Corinthian temple[32]	
Eleusis sanctuary, lesser propylon	
Petra, El Deir	fig. 6.2
Petra, Palace Tomb door	
Ghirza, Tomb A (North)	
Alexandria, Sciatbi necropolis	
Tuna el-Gebel, funerary temple[33]	
Pompeii, Garland Tomb	
Kalat Fakra (Lebanon), tomb[34]	
Lepcis Magna, colonnaded street[35]	

6.4 Entablature belonging to the ground storey of the theatre at Arles, France (Augustan period).

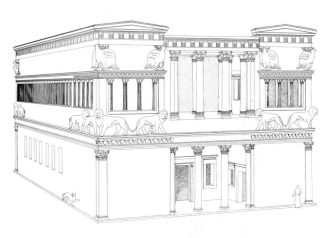

6.6 'Fortress Tyros' (Qasr il 'Abd), the Palace of Hyrcanus at Arak el-Amir (Iraq el Emir), Jordan (2nd or 1st century BC).

6.5 Detail of the Corinthian-Doric order of the triumphal arch at Aosta, Italy (Augustan period).

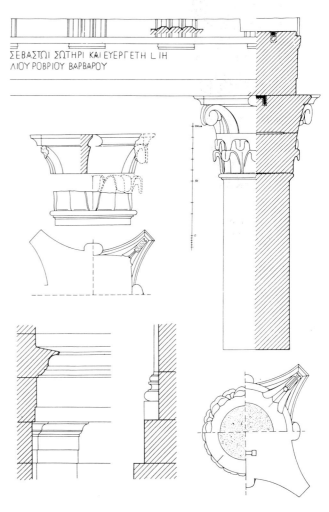

6.7 Corinthian-Doric order of the Temple of Augustus at Philae, Egypt (Augustan period).

6.8 Detail of the column screen in the so-called Marble Court of the Bath-gymnasium at Sardis, Turkey.

6.9 Library of Celsus at Ephesos, Turkey (ca. AD 117–120) detail.

Of all the myths surrounding the orders, there is none so pervasive as the sequential superimposition of Doric, Ionic and Corinthian. But although numerous buildings, classical and Hellenistic stoas especially, do have Ionic over Doric, the full trio is rare indeed. Aphrodisias is quite exceptional in having three examples (the Bouleuterion, the *scaenae frons* of the theatre and the Sebasteion), since many major sites lack even one such sequence. There is no major surviving monument in Rome with Doric-Ionic-Corinthian, although in its original state the Theatre of Marcellus is a highly likely candidate, and the Theatre of Pompey could well have been its model.[36] The Colosseum façade is often held up as the archetypal model of 'correct' usage, but the true sequence is 'Greekified' Tuscan, Ionic, Corinthian, Corinthian. As for the so-called Tabularium, this is typically restored with the existing Doric capped by an Ionic one (fig. 0.1), but it could equally have been Corinthian.

Although convention put more slender columns over less slender ones, superimposition could embrace almost all permutations of the five orders. For example, Ionic orders stood on top of Corinthian in a few cases, beginning with the Temple of Athena Alea at Tegea in the fourth century BC, and continuing in the Roman period with the basilica at Pompeii (fig. 2.18), the interior of the Basilica Ulpia[37] and the towers flanking the entrance to the sanctuary at Baalbek. In terms of slenderness Composite columns stood on a par with their Corinthian cousins and so could go under as well as over them, as at the Porta dei Leoni in Verona (fig. 6.12), the South Market Gate at Miletos, the Library of Celsus (fig. 6.9) and the Gate of Hadrian at Ephesos. But the Romans' most popular mode of superimposition (aside from amphitheatres, as mentioned above, p. 110) was, inevitably, Corinthian on Corinthian.

In more complex compositions the orders could be intermixed; in the apse of the Severan basilica at Lepcis Magna Corinthian columns were juxtaposed with tiers of smaller Ionic ones, while there is the converse arrangement in the *natatio* of the Baths of Diocletian. At first such a differentiation seems to have been permissible only when the shift in scale was fairly extreme, but in late antiquity the approach was less inhibited. Different types of column were united under a single entablature at the Baths of Diocletian again (in the *frigidarium*, where Composite occupies the central bay, Corinthian the rest), the so-called Marble Court at Sardis (fig. 6.8) and the Lateran Baptistery.

Another myth supposes that multi-storey displays of columns should always stand directly one upon the

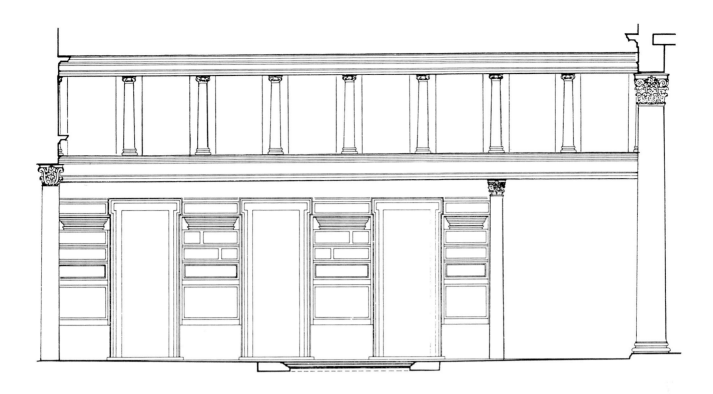

other. Francesco di Giorgio provides one of the clearest statements of this dogma:

> As a general rule to be observed without exception . . . voids must go above voids, solids above solids, piers above piers, columns above columns, and generally every element should sit in a straight line over its like.[38]

6.10 Side elevation of the atrium of the so-called House of the Faun, Pompeii.

6.12 (*below*) City gate known as the Porta dei Leoni at Verona, Italy, reconstructed elevation.

6.11 Elevation of the so-called Great Tomb at Lefkadia, Greece (?3rd century BC), with 1 : 1 proportion overlaid.

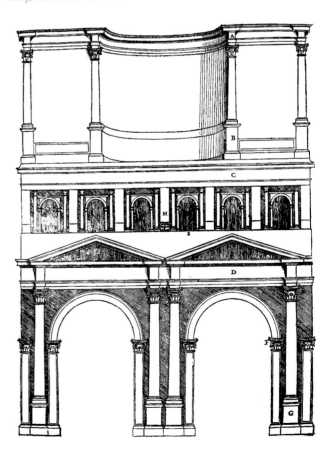

Without doubt the default mode of Roman architects was to proceed just as Francesco di Giorgio advised. This was in any event a structural necessity when using free-standing orders (as in the *scaenae frons* of a theatre) or heavily loaded *fornices* (as in the façade of an amphitheatre). Yet where structure did not dictate the solution, lapses of alignment were entertained – provided that there was a substantial contrast in scale. Hellenistic buildings in which small attic pilasters do not mimic the rhythm of the principal order include the Great Tomb at Lefkadia (fig. 6.11), the Gate of Zeus and Hera at Thasos,[39] a house at Pella,[40] the Palace of Hyrcanus at Arak el-Amir (fig. 6.6), and the peristyle court of the Palazzo delle Colonne at Ptolemais (fig. 2.8).[41] Parallel phenomena may be seen in the residential architecture of the republican period at Pompeii. In the atrium of the House of the Faun the architect contrived to resolve an asymmetrical composition by aligning some pilasters in the usual manner, but others were just divided into the residual intervals (fig. 6.10). In another example of so-called '1st style' decoration, the attempt to align some false stonework joints under pilasters produced a hiccup in the pattern which only served to draw attention to the general lack of coordination.[42]

Several Augustan city gateways, including those at Aosta (fig. 6.13), Autun, Fanum and Turin (fig. 0.3), have high-level arcades of pilasters and/or arches that answer only to the central axis of symmetry below, but otherwise fail to synchronize with the ground floor.[43] Two gateway façades from the mid-imperial period, the Porta dei Borsari (fig. 6.14) and Porta dei Leoni (fig. 6.12), each have a third storey organized on yet another principle.[44] Although the Pantheon in Rome presents the most famous example, non-canonic compositions of this sort were most in vogue in the eastern Mediterranean. The decoration on the back wall of the Kasr el Bint at Petra is arranged so that only the central axis of

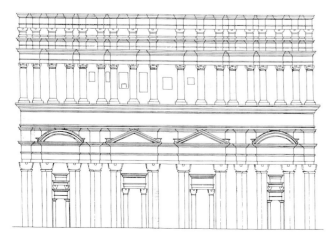

6.13 (*top left*) City gate known as the Porta Praetoria at Aosta, Italy (Augustan period), elevation.

6.14 (*centre left*) City gate known as the Porta dei Borsari at Verona, Italy (Hadrianic period), elevation.

6.16 (*facing page*) Long section through the *frigidarium* of the Baths of Caracalla, Rome (AD 212–216), with 1:1 and 3:1 proportions overlaid.

6.15 (*left*) Rock-cut tomb at Petra known as the Palace Tomb.

the pedimental group responds to the pattern of the relief panels below. The Palace Tomb in the same city, examined below (fig. 6.15), presents an accomplished alternation of rhythms rather like the meeting of two wave patterns. The interior articulation of a grandiose third-century temple-tomb at Palmyra is another testimony to the longevity of this approach to design.[45]

EXTENDING THE VOCABULARY OF FORM

The possibilities for manipulating the orders were further enhanced by a range of formal devices:

Columnar companions. Columns in the round could be married to, or substituted by, semi-columns, three-quarter columns, recessed columns, heart-shaped columns, *antae* (square piers treated like columns (fig. 10.7)) and pilasters. Pilasters normally match the full width of their companion columns, but they could be half as wide at corners, or somewhere in between. Pilasters could also be 'stretched', as it were, to suit unusual circumstances, as when they adorn the great piers at the entrances to the hemicycles of the Forum of Trajan, or the stair towers of the Temple of Bacchus at Baalbek (fig. 7.33).

Ressauts. These are repeating units made up of a free-standing column, usually in front of a pilaster, and a section of projecting entablature.[46] Generally, ressauts were linked by a run of entablature, rather like a file of columns (Forum Transitorium, Library of Hadrian (fig. 1.17)). In late antiquity, however, they might have no such link (Basilica of Maxentius, *frigidarium* of the Baths of Diocletian (fig. 1.1)), an omission that enhanced the vertical continuity between the column and the vaults they helped (or seemed to help) support.

Paired columns, or paired column and pilaster. These were used to terminate a file of single columns/pilasters (Basilica Aemilia), to face up piers which were so wide that a single column would have looked feeble by comparison (triumphal arches at Pola and Djemila or the bridge at St Chamas), or simply to intensify the richness of ornamentation (nymphaeum of Herodes Atticus at Olympia).

Giant orders. These are so called because they substantially exceed the scale of other orders to which they are intimately connected. The most common applications were in basilicas (as in that at Pompeii (fig. 2.18) and Vitruvius' one at Fanum) and in the *frigidaria* of bath complexes, where the main order dwarfed the columnar screens leading to subsidiary spaces (fig. 6.16). Sometimes the expressive effect of a giant order was obtained by means of juxtaposing large columns with stacked storeys of aedicular niches, as in the interior of the Temple of Bacchus at Baalbek (frontispiece), or the *natatio* façade of the Baths of Diocletian (fig. 1.1).

Pediments. Apart from the traditional triangular form, these could be segmental or partly flat and partly segmental (Baalbek, great court of sanctuary), they could be pierced by an arcuated lintel (Temple of Hadrian at Ephesos, the adyton of the temple at Niha (fig. 3.11)), and they could be 'split' (Trajan's Markets (fig. 1.18), the Sebasteion at Aphrodisias, the Khasneh and El Deir at Petra (figs 6.1 and 6.2)).

Rustication. Columns and/or pilasters could be 'imprisoned' by bands of rusticated stone (Temple of Claudius, the amphitheatre at Verona (fig. on p. 16)), or they could be left intentionally unfinished, or even, as at Porta Maggiore, be made up of what appear to be tiers of unfinished capitals (fig. 6.17). The juxtaposition

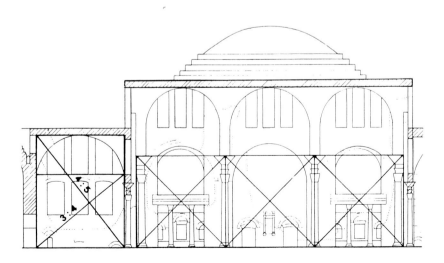

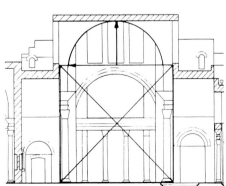

of raw or 'natural' stone with refined, man-made mouldings heightened the effect of both.

ORCHESTRATION AND AXIALITY

The freedom to manipulate this repertoire rested on the realization that columns did not have to be used for support alone – another Hellenistic discovery that the Romans were to exploit to the full.[47] When the orders were used to dress a more massive structure behind, the actual load on columns was reduced to little more than short stretches of trabeation. Moreover, this trabeation, being built into the main wall, acted in part as a cantilever, making the columns themselves structurally redundant. Indeed, there are plenty of ruined façades that have lost their columns, but where entablatures and pediments still hover in their original position. Then there are late antique buildings, such as the Arch of Janus in Rome, where the orders were attached to the main structure only by metal cramps, a technique that betrays a purely decorative role.

The term 'Baroque' has sometimes been given to ancient architecture that employs devices like those just listed in ways that anticipated the work of architects such as Borromini, Bernini, Giacomo della Porta and Hawksmoor.[48] Indeed words associated with the seventeenth and eighteenth centuries like layering, juxtaposition, crescendo, frame and theatricality enter naturally into critiques of compositions such as the Library of Celsus (fig. 6.9), the adyton of the temple at Niha (fig. 3.11) and many of the tombs at Petra (figs 6.1 and 6.2).

There are dangers, however, in isolating ancient Baroque as a movement apart from other modes of design, for it is really an extension of strategies applicable to buildings decked in more conventional clothing. Take the devices that emphasize the importance of the central temple of the forum at Sbeitla with respect to the lateral ones (fig. 6.19): Composite capitals as opposed to Corinthian; semi-columns instead of flat pilasters; and a slight increase in size. These are all relatively subdued, even timid, moves, yet they combine together effectively to create a crescendo on the central axis. This was in fact a principle with a long pedigree, especially in the case of buildings that had a significant presence in terms of urban design. In essence 'Baroque' features achieve similar ends by more explicit, eye-catching means.

Axial emphasis was reinforced by formal groupings and readings of like elements. These come into play as soon as elevations move beyond the uniformly spaced rhythms of the 'typical' classical temple. Designating the standard bay by the letter A, the front of a hexastyle temple reduces to A–A–A–A–A. There are just two main ways of apprehending a design of this type: the individual repeating bays and the whole. The triumphal arch is the Romans' most simple composite composition, that is to say one that combines a minor bay, A, and a major one, B. So each of these can be read separately or as part of a unity, typically a tripartite group with its axis of symmetry in line with the principal circulation route: A–B–A. This type of composition is stated in its most basic form in single arches such as that of Titus in Rome or that of the Sergii at Pola. Triple arches (figs 6.23–6.27) combined two such readings at different scales. The lateral arches may be represented again as A–B–A, while the wider central arch can be notated as A–C–A. In combination, the whole reads A–B–A–C–A–B–A.

The presence of an even number of bays, as at Porta Maggiore (fig. 6.18), introduces a certain ambiguity. Each half still scans as A–B–A, but the central aedicule is also framed symmetrically by the main arches, thus creating the unit B–A–B. Taken as a whole, however, the composition breaks down to A–B–A★–B–A, where the asterisk stands for the extra width given to the central pier. In the façade of the Library of Celsus two groups of alternating rhythms are laid one on top of each other, exactly out of phase (fig. 6.9). By designating the aedicules B and the space between them A, and adding either t for a triangular pediment or s for a segmental one, the composition reads as follows:

upper floor $\qquad B^s$–A–B^t–A–B^s
lower floor $\qquad B$–A–B–A–B–A–B.

Further emphasis on the entrance is provided by the enlarged central bay and door opening. At the same time the isolated ressauts terminating the upper storey reinforce the unity of the whole, since only in this way are the local asymmetries resolved. Ressauts were used to similar effect at the propylon of the Sebasteion at Aphrodisias, the nymphaeum at Miletos, the Porta dei Borsari (fig. 6.14), El Deir (fig. 6.2) and the *natatio* of the Baths of Diocletian. Split pediments work in an allied manner, by setting up local assymetries that beg to be resolved at a larger scale. The upper level of the hemicycle of Trajan's Markets disposes no fewer than three sets of such groups which mark the principal and diagonal axes (fig. 1.18).

More complex interactions are created when the lineaments of different storeys do not align with one another, as may be seen at the Palace Tomb at Petra

6.19 Two of the three temples in the forum at Sbeitla, Tunisia (last quarter of 2nd century AD); the meeting between the central and one of the flanking temples.

6.17 Porta Maggiore in Rome (inaugurated AD 52), detail. The deliberately unfinished structure carries the conduits of the aqueducts Aqua Claudia and Anio Nova over two roads, the Via Prenestina and the Via Labicana.

6.18 Porta Maggiore, Rome.

(fig. 6.15). If the elements of the lower storey are defined as *A* for the ressauts, *B* for the aedicules with segmental pediments and *C* for those with triangular pediments, the principal readings for this part are:

two groups of   *A–B–A*
one of   *A–B–A–C–C–A–B–A.*

Meanwhile the upper floor may be defined in terms of four more distinct components (*d*, *e*, *f* and *g*) and characterized as:

two groups of   *d–e–d–e–d–e–d*
one of   *d–e–d–e–d–e–d–f–g–f–d–e–d–e–d–e–d.*

The two patterns only line up one above the other with respect to the central axis and the intermediate ressauts, which in effect introduces yet another reading by dividing the whole façade into four equal sections, thus reclaiming an element of underlying simplicity for a design that risks becoming too clever for its own good.

119

PROPORTION

Now it is opportune to shift attention from the visual to the mathematical aspects of composition, or from *eurythmia* to *symmetria*. It is well to concentrate on the Romans' two most enduring and distinct compositional strategies. One took a repetitive component and generated the whole by aggregation; the other assigned a specific proportion to the whole, and adjusted its components to suit. Both approaches could be applicable over a wide time span.

The principle of aggregative composition is at the heart of Vitruvius' account of temple design (III,3). Here the basic repeating unit is the columnar interval, which in turn was defined by multiples of the lower column diameter (see Table 6.1).

Table 6.1
*Vitruvian intercolumnations and interaxial bay widths
expressed in terms of column diameters*

	Intercolumnation	Axial width
pycnostyle	$1\frac{1}{2}$	$2\frac{1}{2}$
systyle	2	3
eustyle	$2\frac{1}{4}$	$3\frac{1}{4}$
diastyle	3	4
araeostyle	3 plus	4 plus

This system was clearly not just an academic notion, for seven of the ten best preserved Corinthian orders belonging to religious buildings in Rome concord reasonably well with either the pycnostyle or systyle schemes (see Table 6.2).

Table 6.2
*Peristyle rhythms for the best-preserved Corinthian orders
from temples in or near Rome*

Temple	Column diameter in feet	Inter-columnation in terms of D	Nominal value
Mars Ultor	6	1.48	$1\frac{1}{2}$
Apollo Sosianus	5	1.48	$1\frac{1}{2}$
Castor	5	1.54	$1\frac{1}{2}$
Hadrian	5	1.63	$1\frac{5}{8}$
Pantheon exterior	5	2.05	2?
Antoninus & Faustina	5	1.51	$1\frac{1}{2}$
Vespasian (front)	$4\frac{3}{4}$	1.55	
Vespasian (flank)	$4\frac{3}{4}$	1.31	
Pantheon interior	$3\frac{3}{4}$	1.55	
Tholos by the Tiber	$3\frac{1}{4}$	1.53	$1\frac{1}{2}$
Tholos at Tivoli	$2\frac{7}{12}$	1.97	2

A compact spacing is typical for monumental temples, while rhythms slacken as scale and civic importance decrease. Thus the portico surrounding the Maison Carrée, with its $2\frac{1}{2}$ ft columns set out on 10 ft centres, corresponds to a diastyle rhythm, that is to say one much looser than that of the temple itself. More airy spacing still is characteristic of smaller-scale work and/or the domestic realm, where the superstructure might be made of lighter materials like timber and terracotta. This gradation on the one hand expresses the principle of appropriateness, or *decor*, by virtue of which Vitruvius allowed the proportions of Doric columns to vary according to their context (p. 44). On the other hand it is a reflection of cost – for columns are expensive – as well as structural necessity. As the scale grows, load increases more rapidly than strength (doubling the size of a colonnade multiplies loads eight-fold but resistance to them only four-fold).[49]

Used in tandem with standard columnar proportions (chapter 7), such formulas allowed architects to generate predictable compositions with neither risk nor imagination. With good materials and skilled craftsmen routine solutions guaranteed façades along the lines of the Temple of Portunus, if there were to be four columns on the front (fig. 3.27), the Maison Carrée at Nîmes if there were to be six (fig. 3.30), or the Temple of Mars Ultor if there were to be eight (fig. 2.4). Fortunately Roman society called for only a minority of such thoroughly predictable edifices.

Vitruvius' system based on the column diameter was certainly not the only means of defining rhythms. There was a long tradition that made the gaps between adjacent bases the same as their width (p. 73), a scheme that implies intercolumnations between $1\frac{2}{3}$ and $1\frac{7}{8}$ diameters, with the exact value dependent on the profile of the base itself.[50] The bay width might also be a simple fraction of a major limit of height, either that of the column or that of the order; the column intervals used in the Basilica Ulpia, for example, correspond to half the column height. It was sometimes possible to satisfy more than one objective simultaneously: the 10 ft column spacing of the forum temple at Assisi is double both the width of the bases and quarter the height of the order.[51] Similarly, the 15 ft bays of the Temple of Mars Ultor are pycnostyle at the same time as being a quarter of the 60 ft column height.[52] Moreover, the frequent presence of whole-number dimensions like these is a reminder that this might be an important criterion in its own right. Superimposed tiers of orders introduced further rhythmical relationships, unless the upper orders have the same diameter as the lower one, a case in point being the Colosseum (figs on p. vi and 5.31). Some degree of reduction in size was more common, the precise ratio being chosen, it seems, according to the merits, both aesthetic and mathematical, in each instance.

The aggregative principle did not apply only to files of columns. It also entered into the design of runs of *fornices*, the *fornix* being a repeating column plus arch unit, as typified by the Colosseum. A celebrated early example is the front of the Tabularium (fig. 6.20), where the intercolumnations proper, 16 ft, correspond to 4 column diameters. But the 20 ft wide bays divide into 8 ft piers and 12 ft openings, a rhythm that could be termed another sort of pycnostyle. Around four centuries later the same attention to both types of rhythm can be seen in the portico surrounding the Mausoleum of Maxentius (fig. 6.21). Here the 24 ft intercolumnation is equivalent to eight pilaster widths, while the archways are twice the width of the piers supporting them.

The elevations of many theatres and amphitheatres follow similar patterns. The principle of defining the bay as a whole-number dimension is well illustrated by the recurrence in the largest amphitheatres of 20 ft for either the intercolumnation or the axial width (figs on p. 16 and 6.22). As a reflection of their relative importance, both structurally and visually (figs 5.31–2), it was again common for the openings to relate to the pier width as 3:2 or 2:1, viz. 'pycnostyle' and 'systyle'.[53] Because of the subordinate nature of the columns, intercolumnar rhythm was not a prime consideration. A third type of proportion related an important limit in plan to one in elevation. The following are the most noteworthy examples:

(i) height of impost equals the span of the arch it carries: Rome, Verona, Nîmes and Arles;

(ii) height of pier up to impost equals the width of pier: El Jem, Nîmes and, very approximately, Verona;

(iii) storey height is double the intercolumnation: Rome, Verona and Nîmes;

(iv) column height equals the width of bay, measured to outer edges of the columns/pilasters: El Jem, Verona, Arles and, approximately, Nîmes.

These are just the most common among a cascade of arithmetical relationships which are too numerous to mention individually.[54]

Aggregative design clearly gave no guarantee of proportional simplicity for the whole. This, however, was clearly a major aim for many architects throughout the Hellenistic and Roman periods. Thus, for example, the perimeter of the amphitheatre at Verona attained a total height of 100 ft, a dimension equal to five bay widths.[55]

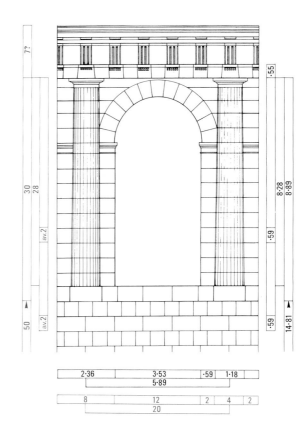

6.20 Typical bay of the so-called Tabularium, Rome (late to mid-1st century BC), elevation with principal dimensions and proportions overlaid, 1:150.

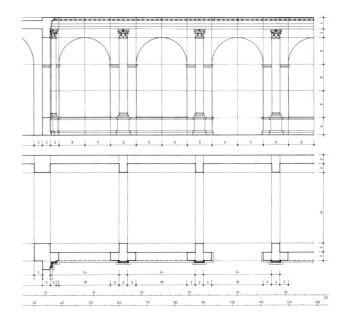

6.21 Restored elevation of the precinct of the Mausoleum of Maxentius on the Via Appia, Rome (AD ca. 310), showing key proportions and compositional principle based on a square grid.

As for the 163 ft height of the Colosseum, in all probability this originally equalled the clear width of the arena. To underline this point it is enough to list a number of façades illustrated in this book that, in one way or other, conform accurately to the simplest proportion of all, 1:1.[56] (The list is arranged in chronological order, from the late fourth century BC to the late fourth century AD.)

Although the aggregative and unitarian strategies represent the two principal poles of composition, the one did not exclude the other. The Maison Carrée (figs 3.29 and 3.30) is a prime example of how an architect might adjust component proportions so as to make the façade fit into two squares, while the Temple of Antoninus and Faustina attests to a similar process.[57] Meanwhile the Doric-Corinthian temple at Paestum – at least according to scholarly reconstructions – fits not only two types of 1:1 relation, but also two types of modular system, one based on the column diameter, the other on the width of the triglyph.[58] In short, the more harmony the better.

6.23 and 6.24 (*facing page*)   Arch of Constantine, Rome (dedicated AD 315), and detail of the entablature.

6.22 (*below*)   Typical bays of the amphitheatres at: (a) Arles (Flavian period); (b) Nîmes (Flavian period), with 1:1 and 1:2 proportions overlaid, 1:200.

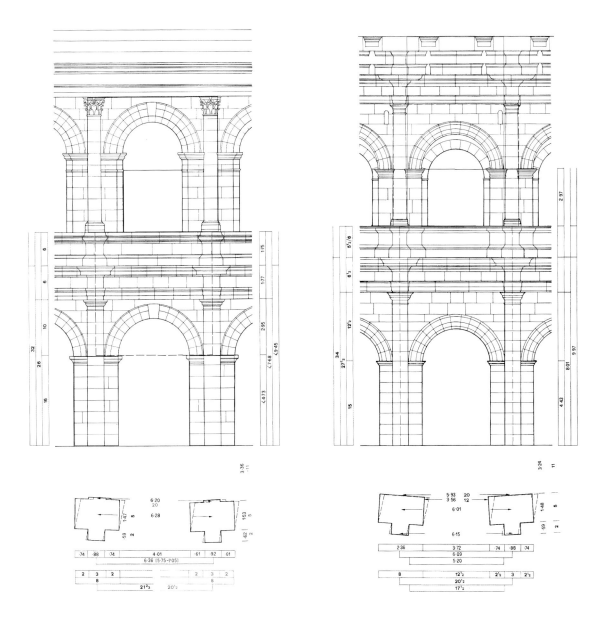

THE ARCH OF CONSTANTINE

The possibility of reconciling different types of proportion is well illustrated by the Arch of Constantine (figs 6.23 and 6.24), all the more so because this was achieved in spite of the tight constraints imposed by the incorporation of *spolia* from earlier buildings. The second-hand elements comprise the columns, most of the main entablature, many mouldings and ashlar blocks, and an extraordinary sculptural repertoire, including the great Trajanic friezes in the main passageway; the Hadrianic circular reliefs, or *tondi*, over the flanking passageways; and the relief panels from an arch of Marcus Aurelius in the attic. There is a lively controversy over the date when all this was put together, but the idea that the building was the result of adding to an earlier, possibly Hadrianic, arch[59] can be confidently rejected in favour of a single Constantinian campaign.[60] For present purposes the key point to appreciate is that one of the prime functions of the new design was to weld a heterogeneous collage into a harmoniously integrated whole.

The logistics of re-use mean that many details fail to stand up to close scrutiny. The height of the frieze under the *tondi* is raggedly irregular; the *tondi* themselves are not true circles; the main cornice is put together with little regard for the continuity of the dentils and egg and dart; there are frequent lapses of symmetry in the distribution of minor elements like the modillions. Continuity of detail is subordinated to the effect of the whole, an approach that is symbolized by the recutting of the heads of Trajan and Marcus Aurelius with Constantine's portrait, an act not of negligence or disrespect but rather a conscious attempt to convey a political message, that is to say the identification of the latter with the 'good emperors' of the past. Against this background, it might seem that proportions were unlikely to be high on the agenda, but in fact they were very much so. The principal proportional 'propositions' are listed below, and keyed to the accompanying illustration (fig. 6.25):

Proposition 1: The width of the flanks, measured to the column axes, equals the column height.

Proposition 2: The height of the central imposts equals the column height.

Proposition 3: The central intercolumnation equals the column height.

Proposition 4: The depth of the central passage equals its clear width.

Proposition 5: The overall length front and back is three times the column height.

Proposition 6: The height of the façade up to the entablature is half its overall length.

Proposition 7: The width of the lateral fornices is half the height of the façade up to the entablature.

Proposition 8: The width of the central fornix is $^3/_2$ that of the lateral fornices.

Proposition 9: The height of the order is half the axial length of the three *fornices* combined.

Proposition 10: The total width of the building is half its total height, measured to the topmost cornice.[61]

Proposition 11: The height of the main cornice off the ground is $\sqrt{3}$ times the column height.

Proposition 12: The overall length is $\sqrt{3}$ times the height of the main cornice off the ground.[62]

So here are several strategies working in concert. First are those ratios that define the whole: the flanks are double squares (*Proposition 10*), as is the front, measured up to the entablature (*Proposition 6*). The whole building, taking only the columnar zone into consideration, is a triple cube (*Propositions 1* and *5*). Second are a series of 1 : 1 and 1 : 2 ratios that govern the individual bays or subordinate relationships, rather as discussed in the context of amphitheatre façades. Third is an implicit modular system, for the fact that so many of the key relationships involve the column height suggests that this may have been conceived as a sort of module.

In any event, the column height was certainly the starting-point for quantifying the whole design, especially because the availability of shafts was a fundamental physical constraint for any building made up of *spolia*. There cannot have been that many possibilities for obtaining a finer set than this one: eight fluted two-part monoliths of *giallo antico* (the salmon-gold colour suited the polychromy of red porphyry, green porphyry and purple-veined *pavonazetto* used elsewhere). The particular column height, 28¾ft, is the outcome of coupling standard shafts 3 ft in diameter and 24 ft tall with suitable bases and capitals.[63] This size was also extraordinarily apposite from another point of view, for it matches that of the (Composite) ones belonging to the Arch of Septimius Severus. The two monuments also share the same width for the central *fornix*, suggesting that the earlier building represented not just a precedent in general terms,[64] but the specific basis for Constantine's project. Evidently the aim was to emulate quite literally the Severan arch, the site of which, at the heart of the Forum Romanum, made it Rome's triple arch *par excellence*. It seems highly likely that the later architect overlaid his own design over drawings of the earlier building. This goes a long way to explaining the very success of the new composition: with so much predetermined, he could concentrate his energies on improving the prototype and accommodating the various *spolia*. So the attic became no longer flat, but modelled by the Dacians to respond to the tripartite main storey. One of the stepped bands under the columnar pedestals, arguably an inelegant feature, was removed. The side passages were widened, to give sufficient width for the pairs of *tondi*. Such adjustments made the proportions even more 'classical' than those of the earlier arch, presenting an intriguing counterpoint to the otherwise innovative character of contemporary architectural developments.

The ideal proportional scheme must have come under review whenever the architect came to select

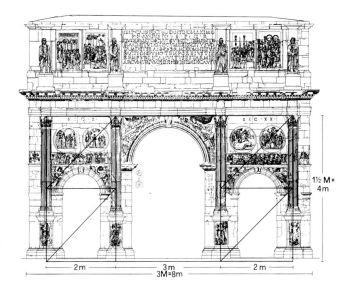
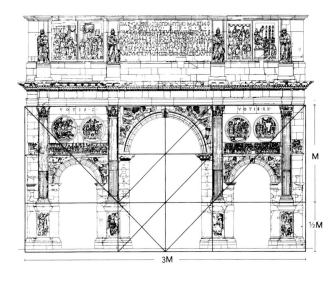
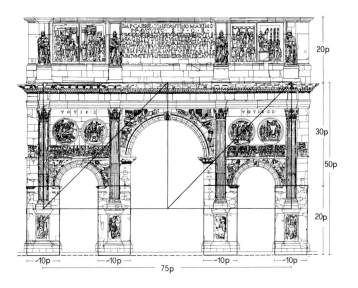
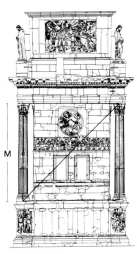
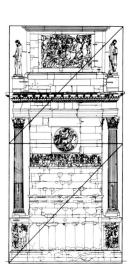

6.25 Arch of Constantine, elevations with proportional interpretation overlaid.

specific second-hand elements and to define detailed dimensions and profiles. Conflicts were bound to arise in so complex an endeavour; one example is the central intercolumnation, which should equal on the one hand the column height of $28\frac{3}{4}$ ft (*Proposition 3*), and on the other nine-eighths of the column height less its diameter, or $29\frac{1}{4}$ ft (*Propositions 5, 6, 7 and 8*). Hence the compromise value of 29 ft, and a series of minor discrepancies that flowed in its wake. Metrical simplicity was further assured by adding a small plinth under the column base, a device which among other things allowed the main cornice to reach a height of 50 ft from the ground.[65]

As it happens 50 ft equals the column height (M) multiplied by the square root of 3 (*Proposition 11*) as well as the overall length of the monument divided by the same (*Proposition 12*). In other words, 50 ft is the geometrical mean between these terms,

| since | $28\frac{3}{4}$ | 50 | $86\frac{1}{4}$ |
| relate as | M | $\sqrt{3}$M | 3M. |

Consequently both the front and the flanks, excluding the attic, fit $\sqrt{3}$ rectangles (figs 6.28 and 6.29).

It is impossible to know whether $\sqrt{3}$ entered into the design out of intent or chance. If the former is the case then here is a composition of unusual mathematical sophistication. But even if this geometry should be a happy fluke, the orchestration of all the various other types of proportion still represents quite an achievement, an astonishing one, given the

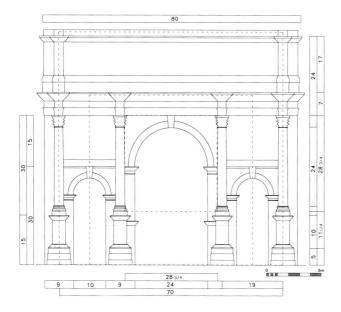

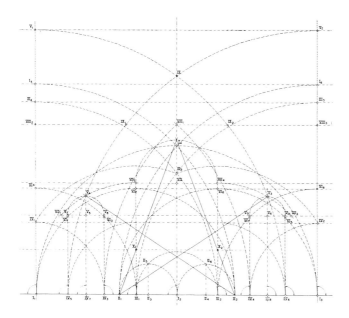

6.26 Proportional interpretations of the Arch of Septimius Severus: (a) elevation with arithmetical relationships; (b) geometrical diagram by Richard Brilliant (1967).

complexities of reconciling them with the chosen *spolia*. Sensibility to the issue of proportion continued to be a consideration in late antiquity.[66] It is almost as though the impossibility of achieving a satisfactory *eurythmia* (in the sense of that which is well fitted) propelled architects to lavish special zeal on *symmetria* – witness the proportional coherence of the Temple of Saturn, Santa Costanza (fig. 4.11) and later Santo Stefano Rotondo (fig. 4.7). Metrical harmony stood for the triumph of intellect over contingency, a triumph that, in the case of the Arch of Constantine, responded

to the spirit of the whole enterprise as declared by the inscription: to celebrate his victory over chaos and strife thanks to 'divine inspiration and greatness of spirit' (INSTINCTV DIVINITATIS MENTIS MAGNITUDINE).

ARITHMETIC AND GEOMETRY

The potential aptness of $\sqrt{3}$ in the context of a triple cube composition such as Constantine's Arch cannot be denied; it recalls the use of this ratio in laying out the Teatro Marittimo at Hadrian's Villa, where as a result the three major components of the plan each have the same surface area (p. 94). What is more, studies of the arches at Orange, Pola, Rimini and Susa seem to confirm Georg Dehio's belief in the use of the equilateral triangle (and hence $\sqrt{3}$),[67] so there may plausibly have been some long-standing association between this proportion and this type of building. In addition, an elaborate geometrical scheme has been proposed for the Arch of Septimius Severus by Richard Brilliant (fig. 6.26), which raises the question whether geometry might have supplanted arithmetic as the basis for the whole design process.

It is wise to guard against jumping to such conclusions without reservation. While geometry certainly provided the discipline for generating certain types of plan, the evidence in favour of geometrically inspired façades is at best ambiguous. For example, Brilliant's interpretation of the Arch of Septimius Severus must be only part of the story, given the presence of so many simple arithmetical proportions like $1:1$, $3:1$, $3:2$, $5:4$ and $6:5$. Meanwhile, the purported $\sqrt{3}$ ratio at the Arch of the Sergii at Pola is really closer to $7:4$. Can it be certain that the architect did not use this ratio for its own merits, and not merely as an approximation?[68] As for the Colosseum, the accurate $\sqrt{3}$ ratio between the width and height of the second and third storeys (fig. 6.22a) could well be just the fortuitous outcome of choosing 40 ft for the height, half as much for the intercolumnation (20 ft), and 3 ft for the column diameter.[69] My concern here is not to insist that irrational ratios like $\sqrt{2}$ and $\sqrt{3}$ were never used in elevation, but only that Roman architects were unlikely to have indulged in the sort of optimistically intricate schemes reproduced here in figures 0.7, 0.8, 0.9, 0.10 and 6.26.

As Dinsmoor's and Eco's remarks (p. 4) remind us, it is all too easy to trace lines over elevations and convince ourselves of patterns that did not necessarily occur to the original architect. In reality Roman architects were less likely to use geometrical procedures in

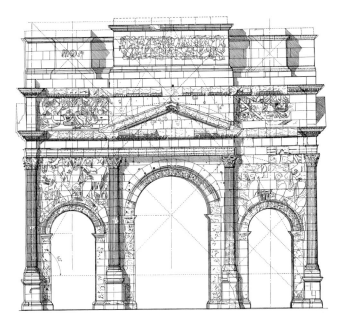

6.27 Front of the triumphal arch at Orange, France (AD ca. 25), with geometrical interpretation overlaid.

composing elevations than plans. By their very nature plans are abstract and geometrical, representing what would be seen by cutting through a building horizontally. On the other hand the prime purpose of an elevation is to simulate the final appearance. Vitruvius makes this distinction clear: 'A groundplan is made by the proper successive use of compasses and rule. . . . An elevation is a picture of the front of a building, set upright and properly drawn in the proportions of the contemplated work' (I, 1,4). Accordingly he used geometry to set out the plan of the theatre, but arithmetic alone for its elevation (v,6). Similarly, equilateral triangles were often used in planning amphitheatres for eminently practical reasons (fig. 5.3), but their elevations consistently display simple arithmetical ratios (fig. 6.22). It may also be noted that, while the accurate layout of groundplans may in some cases have been resolved by swinging lengths of chain (as when exploiting the geometry of a 3:4:5 triangle to guarantee orthogonality), such procedures were impracticable up in the air.[70]

ENTASIS AND THE CALIBRATION OF COLUMN SHAFTS

There is a very definite place for the use of geometry in elevation, and that is in the design of details. The volutes of the Ionic capital are emblematic of the way in which compasses could be used to generate the sensuous, curvilinear forms so vital to the classical lexicon.

Geometrical procedures came to the fore too for the most minute and exacting problem faced by ancient architects, the calibration and execution of the various so-called refinements. These are minor, sometimes imperceptible, deviations from the straight and regular; indeed it is this virtual quality that imbues them with particular fascination, distinguishing them, say, from the mundane inward batter of fortifications.

Progressively introduced during the sixth and fifth centuries BC,[71] refinements animated the cubic volumes of Greek architecture, either correcting or enhancing optical phenomena associated with the experience of temples, treasuries and stoas.[72] By contrast, Roman buildings tend to involve more complex spatial forms, a context in which refinements were arguably too subtle to be effective. This is not to say, however, that the Romans never indulged in them. Vitruvius mentions the principal manifestations,[73] of which most turn up on occasions in actual buildings: the peristyle of the Hadrianeum inclines inwards; the stylobate of the Sebasteion at Aphrodisias is slightly convex; the floor inside the Pantheon is a shallow dome (fig. 9.12); the elevation of the Library of Celsus at Ephesos boasts a *tour de force* sequence of both convex and concave curves.[74] But entasis (and the shaft diminution that it invariably accompanied) was the only refinement used as a matter of course in Roman times – or indeed in any later period. It is true that they could be omitted from square pilasters and *antae*,[75] small-scale shafts, half-columns applied to arcuated structures (fig. 0.23) and even the occasional monumental example like the Column of Marcus Aurelius (fig. 8.13), but such exceptions hardly detract from the vast majority of columns in prestigious buildings that taper with entasis in the time-honoured fashion.

In setting out entasis and other fine curves circular arcs were out of the question, because even at a reduced scale the radii implied were huge. Ever since the issue re-surfaced in the Renaissance it was a perennial subject of expert debate, remaining one of the 'quatre principaux problèmes d'architecture' covered by François Blondel in his book of this title published in 1673.[76] But once the investigation of Greek refinements in the first half of the nineteenth century revealed their subtlety and precision,[77] scholars were soon persuaded that Renaissance methods were too crude, and the search was on for more sophisticated ones. It was well known that the Greeks were familiar with the hyperbola and parabola, both of which elegantly define the flattening of a curve towards a straight line, and Francis Penrose's surveys of unparalleled precision seemed to present unassailable evidence in their favour.[78] When Gorham

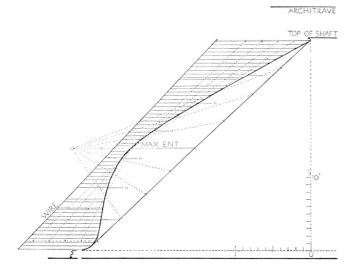

6.28　Method for setting out the entasis of the columns belonging to the tholos by the Tiber, according to Gorham Stevens. The proposed profile corresponds to a pair of hyperbolas which meet at the point of maximal swelling.

6.29　Working drawing inscribed on the north wall of the adyton of the Temple of Apollo at Didyma, defining the entasis of the peristyle columns (?mid- to late 3rd century BC). The horizontal scale is full size while the vertical scale is 1:16, or one *dactyl* to the foot. This has the effect that, when executed, the horizontal lines become a foot rather than a *dactyl* apart, thus generating a shallow curve corresponding to part of an ellipse.

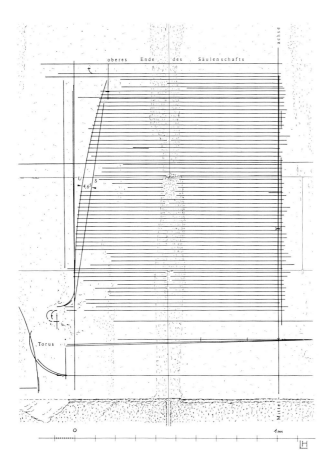

Stevens later turned to the analysis of columns in Rome he not surprisingly – such was the climate of respect for both Penrose and the intellectual achievements of the Greeks themselves – produced similar results. He even advocated pairs of hyperbolas in some cases (fig. 6.28).[79]

Only recently have ideas about curvature had to turn a full circle in the light of archaeological evidence. It so happens that one of the working drawings discovered at the Hellenistic Temple of Apollo at Didyma (pp. 50 and 57) defines the profile of the peristyle columns (fig. 6.29). The geometrical principle is actually similar to that used by Serlio (fig. 0.15b), although the Didymaion strategy is capable of greater precision. The trick was to keep the horizontal scale full size while compressing the vertical scale 1:16, or one *dactyl* to the foot. This ingenious device enabled the curvature to be pronounced enough to be drawn with nothing more elaborate than a sweep of a compass. When executed, the arc became transformed into a much more shallow curve, part of an ellipse in fact.

On the other hand, it is apparent even to the naked eye that shafts belonging to the propylon of the sanctuary at Baalbek and the Hadrianeum in Rome do not curve at all. Measurements of the latter reveal a cranked profile uncannily like Alberti's (fig. 0.15a); the lower part rises vertically and the upper part tapers in a straight line (fig. 6.30). It is true that there is a transitional curve between these linear sections, as well as hints of curvature at the very top and bottom, but these are minor adjustments aimed at creating a fluent effect. This method too has now been confirmed by ancient working drawings. The most complete example belongs to the *scaenae frons* of the theatre at Aphrodisias, while a few scratched lines at Pergamon suggest a similar approach.[80] The Aphrodisias drawing defines the outline of a small shaft by just pairs of lines at an oblique angle to one another (fig. 6.31). The result might be simplistic, but it is hard to imagine anything easier to execute.

So the purported use of parabolas, hyperbolas and suchlike turns out to be an elaborate modern fiction. Instead of Stevens's two tangential hyperbolas, the shafts of the tholos by the Tiber fit two straight lines, that is to say a Hadrianeum-like profile.[81] Meanwhile, instead of parabolas and hyperbolas, the smoothly swelling shafts from monuments in Rome such as the Basilica Ulpia fit profiles akin to the Didymaion model. As

6.31 (*facing page bottom*)　Working drawing defining the profile and entasis of shafts belonging to the *scaenae frons* of the theatre at Aphrodisias (2nd half of 1st century BC or later). The drawing is inscribed on the exterior marble facing of the stage building.

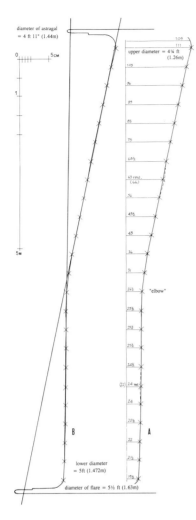

diameter of astragal
= 4 ft 11" (1.44m)

0   5см

1

5м

upper diameter = 4¼ ft
(1.26m)

"elbow"

B   A

lower diameter
= 5ft (1.472m)

diameter of flare = 5½ ft (1.63m)

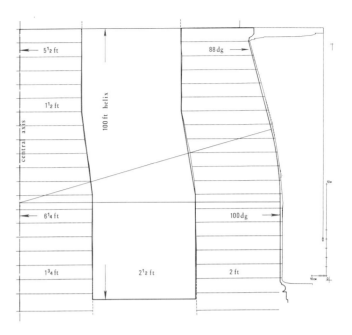

central axis

5½ ft

1½ ft

6¼ ft

1¾ ft

100 ft helix

2½ ft

88 dg

100 dg

2 ft

6.32   Survey of the entasis of Trajan's Column, with hypothetical
design overlaid; horizontal scale 1:25, vertical scale 1:400.

6.30 (*left*)   Survey of the entasis of the Temple of Hadrian (Rome,
AD ca. 140); horizontal scale 1:6¼, vertical scale 1:100 (equivalent
to a scale compression of 1:16, as used at Didyma). Note the simplicity of the 'cranked' profile, and the absence of curvature except
at the transition between the two main straight sections: (a) profile
as surveyed; (b) same profile with straight lines overlaid.

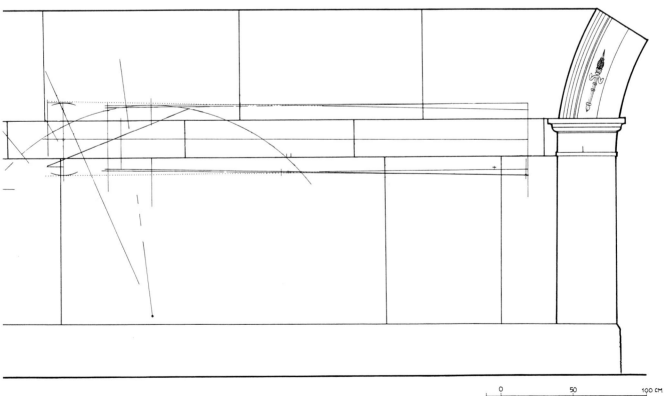

0   50   100 CM

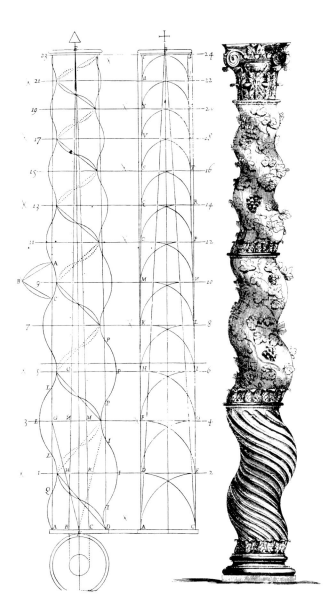

6.33 Survey and analysis of an ancient corkscrew column now in the Vatican.

To understand the success of the Didymaion and Hadrianeum methods it is necessary to grasp the attendant technical advantages. All the main competing curves (ellipse, parabola, hyperbola, conchoid and helix) were investigated by ancient mathematicians, and the very existence of corkscrew columns like those that Bernini copied when creating the baldacchino at St Peter's shows that ancient architects could master taxing problems of projective geometry (fig. 6.33).[83] But what interested them most were the practicalities of how such shapes could be produced and transmitted. Rather than resort to calculation and schedules of the measurements so derived, the key thing was to be able to represent graphically the shaft section at full size, for drawings like those at Didyma or Aphrodisias have the immense benefit of acting simultaneously as templates. To find the width of the shaft at any given height, masons had but to read it off with dividers, and then scratch it on the surface to be calibrated. There was no need to translate distances into dimensions in terms of feet and inches or digits, so no precision was lost in so doing.

While cranked profiles could have been designed using drawings like the ones found at Aphrodisias and Pergamon, it was actually possible to circumvent advance planning altogether, using an *in situ* technique. Unfinished shafts from all around the Mediterranean testify that where they were made out of drums the end mouldings were cut first, with the rest being finished only when the complete column was up (for the sake of achieving perfect smoothness). So it is surely significant that the lower part of the Hadrianeum shafts aligns with the astragal at the top, while the upper part aligns with the flare at the bottom (fig. 6.30). Having first cut the mouldings, the upper part could have been defined by cords stretched between the flare (DF) and the neck (d), while the lower part could have been defined by cords stretched between the astragal and the lower diameter of the shaft proper (fig. 6.34). Once both the upper and lower parts of a shaft were trimmed parallel to these cords the junction could then have been smoothed off.[84]

If the disadvantage of the Roman *in situ* procedure was its relatively crude shape, the advantage was its speed. Greek builders painstakingly dimensioned column drums with reference to a template before erection, having then to make sure that each one took up its correct sequential position.[85] The *in situ* technique, by contrast, allowed the drums to be thrown up quickly, without more than a rough control over their

for Trajan's Column, it represents a composite or compromise solution, with an ample arc sandwiched between two straight sections (fig. 6.32). Surveys of shafts in places as far away as Baalbek or the *cipollino* quarries in Euboea return similar results, variation after variation on the Didymaion and Hadrianeum methods. As in the case of fluting (pp. 7–9), no two solutions are the same, which suggests that architects eschewed slavishly sticking to some fixed formula, but worked freely around principles that were thoroughly embedded in their experience.[82]

6.34 Temple of Hadrian, Rome, hypothetical constructional sequence leading to the definition of entasis: (a) column erected with prefabricated base and capital but with the shaft as yet rough, except for the mouldings; (b) and (c) cutting the body of the shaft parallel to cords stretched from top to bottom; (d) finished column, with fluting.

size. Cutting the profile parallel to stretched cords in a second operation would have been both efficient and foolproof, provided the top and bottom mouldings were accurately aligned with respect to the column axis. Such considerations were doubtless attractive to Imperial builders given their record for remarkably short contract periods (p. 14). On the other hand, monolithic shafts never have cranked profiles, precisely because of the practicalities of manufacture. Prefabricated shafts were left unfinished at either end, leaving the quarries with protective collars out of which the mouldings would be cut at the destination (figs 6.35–6 and 6.38). Without sharply honed limits to act as a guide, the Hadrianeum method was unworkable. The profile was probably transferred by measuring offsets from a stretched cord, in which case the cranked form

6.36 Hypothetical stages in the fabrication of a fluted monolithic shaft based on a broken half-shaft from the Forum of the Corporations at Ostia (cf. example at Pompeii in fig. 0.11).

6.35 Detail of two shafts of differing length (24 ft and 40 ft) in the *cipollino* quarries at Kylindri above Karystos, Evvia (ancient Euboea), Greece. While the entasis has already been cut, the ends of the shafts remain rough as protective collars for the sake of minimizing damage during handling and transportation. When the shafts reached their desination, the collars were trimmed off to suit the precise lengths required.

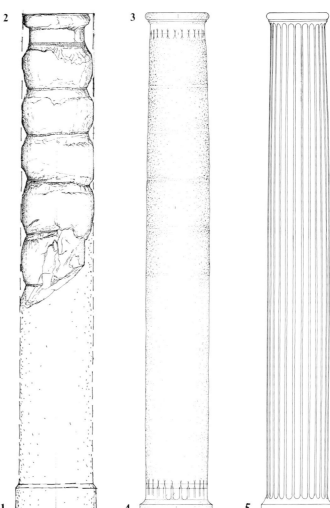

offered no particular advantage over a curve, and a curve was, of course, aesthetically superior.[86] The Romans' solutions to the problem of entasis stands for their whole stance *vis-à-vis* the architecture of the Greek period: time and again they adopted their fore-runners' achievements, but they brought their own brand of practical intelligence to improve on them and make an art out of constructional common sense. Here, then, is geometry at the service of efficiency.

To return in conclusion to the theme of arithmetic and geometry, it may once again be emphasized that while geometry served a vital purpose for the design of details such as entasis, fluting, volutes and miscel-laneous types of moulding, arithmetic was otherwise the 'default' mode of design. Earlier in this chapter I described how the orders were disposed in terms of intervals and rhythms based on commensurable ratios. And the design of orders themselves certainly had little to do with geometries like those that Texier superim-posed on that of Hadrian's Library (fig. 1.16). Indeed, the whole thrust of the next chapter shows that columns were fashioned by arithmetical reasoning of startling simplicity.

6.37   Temple of Antoninus and Faustina, Rome (AD ca. 150). The portico has a set of eight 40 ft *cipollino* shafts comparable with the larger Kylindri examples (cf. fig. 6.38), but less slender.

6.38   Set of semi-finished monolithic shafts abandoned in the *cipollino* quarries at Kylindri. Lengths range from 11.85 to 12.05 metres, or an average of 40 ft plus a surplus of about half a foot assigned to the protective collars.

VII

A GENIUS FOR SYNTHESIS: THE CORINTHIAN ORDER

CORINTHIAN IS THE ROMAN ORDER. At a guess two-thirds or more of all imperial columns are Corinthian or variants on this theme, Composite included. This represents a dramatic reversal of the situation in the middle of the fifth century BC when, in a world dominated by Doric and Ionic, Corinthian made its tentative appearance on the architectural stage. It is sometimes speculated that the new capital originated in the Parthenon, either in the room at the west end, or as part of the column supporting the outstretched hand of the colossal statue of Athena Parthenos herself.[1] Tantalizing as these theories may be, the first known example stood at the head of the cella of the Temple of Apollo at Bassae in the Peloponnese (figs 7.3 and 7.4).[2] Here clearly is the germ for the future developments, but of course there was as yet no sign of other elements that were later to be associated with Corinthian; the new invention simply substituted the Ionic capital of its companion columns, and shared the same entablature.

After some sporadic experiments, by 360 BC the capitals inside the Tholos of Epidauros were a long way down the road to the definitive solution (fig. 7.19a). Corinthian columns went on to be used externally, first in the little Monument of Lysicrates in Athens (330 BC) (fig. 7.2),[3] and by the first quarter of the second century were chosen for the exterior of major temples, notably those dedicated to Zeus at Athens (figs 2.11 and 2.19) and at Diocaesarea in Seleucia (Turkey).[4] They went on to gain wide acceptance while continuing to borrow the entablature from Ionic or, less frequently, Doric, just as Vitruvius allowed (IV,1,2). It was in the Augustan period that Corinthian emerged not only with all the apparatus of an order in its own right, but also as the Roman order *par excellence*.

What was the secret of its success? Why were Roman architects content to embrace Corinthian rather than invent their own order? The explanation lies in a number of convergent factors; content, form and proportion all enter into the equation. It is

7.1   Detail of the peristyle of the Temple of Mars Ultor, Forum of Augustus, Rome (10–2 BC).

7.2 (*above*)   Monument of Lysicrates, Athens (ca. 330 BC). Like other monuments in the Street of Tripods leading to the sanctuary of Dionysius, this was built to commemorate a victorious performance at a choregic festival; the acanthus finial orginally supported the bronze tripod prize.

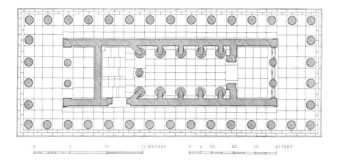

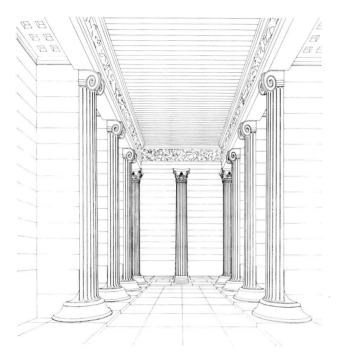

7.3 Temple of Apollo at Bassae, Peloponnese, Greece (ca. 450 BC): (a) plan, 1:500; (b) perspective reconstruction showing the first known Corinthian column at the end of the cella, and the original location of the Battle Frieze.

7.4 Temple of Apollo at Bassae, reconstruction of the Corinthian capital on the basis of drawings made before its disappearance.

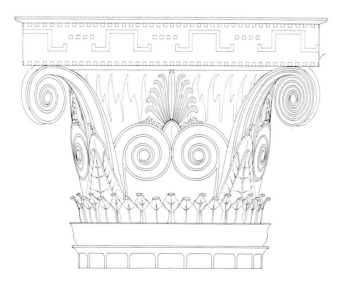

appropriate to dedicate a whole chapter to this phenomenon, since understanding it is essential to understanding Roman attitudes towards architectural design in general.

ORIGIN AND MEANING

The question of origins is important since, according to Cicero, Vitruvius and Pliny, the beauty of art was not only a question of appearance, but of content as well. To achieve *decor* and *maiestas*, form had to answer to the combined authority (*auctoritas*) of tradition and Nature.[5] One natural theme that applied to all columns was the analogy between columns and the human body. Echoing Hellenistic theories, Vitruvius likened the Doric column to an upright man, the Ionic to a woman, and the Corinthian to a virginal girl (IV,1,6–8). The etymological links between capital (*capitulum* in his terminology) and head (*caput*) are all too obvious. Vitruvius (X,10,4) uses *caput* to describe the capital of the central post supporting a catapult, while Euripedes had Iphigenia dream of a column with a human voice, and with golden hair streaming from the capital.[6] However, Doric lacked a base/foot, and both Doric and Ionic capitals are much squatter than the human head. By contrast, Corinthian and Composite proportions lend themselves better to the sort of literal parallel that was more likely to appeal to the Roman mind (fig. 7.5). As a percentage of the total height, the base corresponds roughly to the human foot, measured up to the ankle bone, while the capital corresponds roughly to the head.[7]

As for the Doric and Ionic vocabularies, the logic behind them was lost in a haze of collective amnesia. Vitruvius described the former in terms of the petrification of timber construction (IV,1,6), but it is doubtful that triglyphs originated in this way, and they may have been derived in part from tripods instead.[8] Vitruvius likened Ionic volutes to ringlets of hair, but this too is a rather feeble image. They might better evoke Aeolic forerunners,[9] the horns of sacrificial rams,[10] or perhaps a scroll of some sacred text, but the point is that by Roman times no one could be certain why Doric and Ionic were as they were. From this viewpoint one aspect in favour of the Corinthian capital was its recognizable source imagery, a tile-capped basket shrouded by acanthus foliage, flowers and other plant motifs.

Vitruvius (IV,1,9) relates that the new capital was the result of a specific event. Following the death of a girl from Corinth, her handmaiden put a few of her possessions in a basket, covered it with a tile, and placed it on her tomb – or, as it happened, just over the root of an acanthus plant. With time the acanthus was forced to grow out and around the basket, a pretty scene that caught the eye of Kallimachus and inspired him to create a new prototype (fig. 2.16). The mention of Kallimachus, a renowned Athenian sculptor who was active around the time when the Parthenon and the temple at Bassae were built, hints at some element of historical veracity, but most scholars side with Alois Riegl in dismissing the whole story as 'obviously fictitious, though admittedly charming'.[11]

But even if the details of Vitruvius' creation myth are spurious, this does not delegitimize it altogether. Behind the make-believe, all myths embrace aspects of reality in disguise, which in this case relate to fifth-century Greek burial custom. It seems that offerings at the head or foot of tombs were frequently deposited in a basket, or *kalathos*. Some lekythoi, the slim painted vases that were popular as grave offerings in the fifth century, show baskets and/or acanthus associated with columnar tomb monuments, and sometimes placed on top of them (fig. 7.6).[12] A stele capital at Megara Hyblaea dating to around 500 BC may lack acanthus, but it is significant that it already has the slender proportions, the moulded abacus and the volutes that went on to become essential ingredients of Corinthian or its variants (fig. 7.7).[13] The funerary connotations of acanthus are apparent from other sources too; gold acanthus leaves, for example, wrapped around the Ionic columns of Alexander's funeral car.[14]

It might seem that the funeral imagery would constitute a negative attribute in other contexts. But, like other plants, acanthus stood not for the triumph of death, but the triumph over death, and so for cycles of life, rebirth and regeneration. Moreover, in Mediterranean climes some varieties of acanthus do not die back in winter (as does, say, the vine), but maintain a lustrous green. So at a more general level, acanthus imbued the Corinthian capital with a certain vigour and optimism. As the specificities of its symbolism gave way to broader associations, Corinthian came to be

7.5 The human analogy as applied to the Composite capital by Francesco di Giorgio.

7.6 (*above right*) Detail from a white-glazed Attic lekythos (late 5th century BC). The tomb shown is of the type in which such vases were deposited along with the deceased. Similar representations of acanthus leaves or plants at the bottom or top of piers or column-shaped tombs are not uncommon.

7.7 Corinthianizing limestone capital from a funeral monument at Megara Hyblaea, Sicily (ca. 500 BC), now in the Archaeological Museum of Syracuse. Although acanthus is not present, there are several parallels between this and later Corinthian capitals.

7.8 Reconstruction of the interior orders of the Temple of Apollo Sosianus, Rome (20s BC). The ground level capitals are not straight-forward Corinthian, but Corinthianizing variants: ones with the Apolline symbols of tripod and python for the main columns, ones with double palmettes and 'sofa' volutes for the aedicules.

7.9 Ara Pacis, Rome (13–9 BC), detail of the ornamental relief of scrolled acanthus and other vegetal motifs.

used for other functions. In the Monument of Lysi-crates (fig. 7.2), a structure that celebrated a victory at the Athenian choregic festival, there was arguably a tri-umphalist symbolism behind the choice of Corinthian capitals and acanthus ornament for the finial support-ing the crowning tripod prize. As for Rome, Corinthian first found favour as a vehicle for the pro-paganda of generals returning home from triumphant campaigns abroad.[15] And if it is correct to identify the tholos by the Tiber (fig. 4.13) as the temple that Mummius commissioned after his defeat of the Corinthians,[16] is it pushing things too far to wonder if the Corinthian order was chosen by virtue of its very name – troping as it were a trophy?

The new design brought with it architectonic benefits too, being notably more flexible than its pre-decessors, particularly with regard to the corner con-dition (chapter 6, p. 110). This made it better suited to relatively complex column groupings,[17] while the concave Corinthian abacus lent itself to curvilinear plans and angles other than 90°, and the upward and outward motion of the leaves made a suitable prelude to any vaulting overhead. Being more organic, the Corinthian capital was also more adaptable. Compos-ite is the best-known variant (fig. 7.21), but Roman architects introduced countless others with vegetal, animal or human motifs substituted for the usual acan-thus (fig. 7.22), especially in small-scale work, interiors and the private realm. This introduced scope for icono-graphical reference, as in the case of Corinthianizing capitals inside the Temple of Apollo Sosianus which bear the god's Delphic attributes, the tripod and python (fig. 7.8). The geometry too could be altered, with one ring of leaves not two, or twelve leaves per ring not eight; the abacus could be made octagonal or pentagonal; the whole capital could be stretched, as it were, so as to dress unusually wide piers or projections such as the stair towers in the Temple of Bacchus at Baalbek (fig. 7.33). As Borromini later liked to do, the volutes could be turned upside down, and so on.[18]

Finally, Corinthian was simply more luxuriant, more sensuous and more impressive than the other orders. It opened up new possibilities for exploiting contrasts, contrast between structural force and filigree delicacy, contrast between light and shadow, and hence oppor-tunities for expression hitherto unexplored using Doric and Ionic. It was the natural choice for build-ings encrusted in marble ornament, while on the other hand a run of a few Corinthian capitals could give a touch of splendour to buildings that were otherwise plain. All told, it is hard to imagine a better vehicle for Roman architects' aspirations.

AUGUSTUS AND THE CORINTHIAN ORDER

Apart from the advantages it brought to Roman architects, Corinthian suited their emperors too. The first of them, Augustus (fig. 2.3), pursued a building programme that was geared to propagandistic aims of some sophistication.[19] He promoted a civic image that was both new and yet redolent of a golden past; he encouraged normative codes of behaviour in the interest of moral and political cohesion; he sought to show that, under his aegis, Rome was a match for Greece culturally – the only arena in which his people felt themselves to be inferior. These themes affected architecture in several ways. One was the transformation of Rome, as Augustus famously boasted, from 'a city of brick to one of marble', that is to say one with a Greek face. Another was a tendency towards standardization in architectural and urban typologies, as exemplified by the ascendancy of the permanent civic amphitheatre. Then there was the use of Corinthian (a style that required marble for the best results); the new order was embraced in official monuments not just in Rome, but with surprising rapidity throughout the empire.

For Augustus' purposes Corinthian was Greek enough to evoke the classical past, but not too Greek. The name recalled its geographical origins, but it had none of the racial overtones of Doric-Dorian and Ionic-Ionian.[20] Nor was acanthus linked to a particular divinity, thus leaving Augustus' advisers scope for promoting an appropriate set of connotations. In fact acanthus was utilized in a variety of modes, including the frieze of entablatures like that of the Maison Carrée (figs 3.28 and 3.31) and the magnificent lower register of that quintessential model of Augustan art, the Ara Pacis (fig. 7.9). In the latter setting in particular, it is clear that acanthus played more than a merely decorative role.[21] It is distinguished from its companion elements of the Hellenistic floral repertoire by providing the structure of the composition. In contradistinction to ivy and the vine (with their intimations of Dionysiac chaos), acanthus stood for an ordered growth, in which each element had its due place.[22]

Although acanthus was not one of Apollo's own symbols (like the bow, laurel, python or tripod), its associations with healing made it a suitable complement, and it was in his Apollonian guise that Augustus healed old wounds and brought unity to a world riven by decades of civil war. As mentioned above, acanthus symbolized renewal too – and Augustus' programme also cast him as a new Romulus, or Caesar reborn.[23]

This accumulation of meanings made Corinthian an ideal vehicle for the Augustan regime. It was the best of orders for the best of all possible worlds. Statues and portrait busts of the *princeps* – idealized, Grecian, ever youthful, semi-standardized (fig. 2.3) – were diffused throughout the empire,[24] and it is not too far-fetched to see the Corinthian column as an architectural foil to these images, a sort of impersonal embodiment of the Augustan spirit. Occasionally, as in the case of the Sebasteion at Aphrodisias, such an idea seems to fit the iconographical programme for a specific complex (p. 111). Otherwise it comes through in general terms, given the sheer statistical domination of Corinthian beginning with the early imperial period. In any event, its hegemony during the gestation of the empire guaranteed its future popularity, making it an almost automatic choice in the absence of specific motives for using one of the other orders; there are countless buildings with Corinthian (or Corinthianizing) throughout, like the Pantheon or the Temple of Apollo Sosianus (fig. 7.8), not to mention column displays with successive tiers of Corinthian such as the scene buildings of the theatres at Arles, Jerash, Lepcis Magna, Mérida, Orange and Sabratha (fig. 7.10). Later emperors and

7.10 Reconstructed stage-building (*scaenae frons*) of the theatre at Sabratha, Libya (last quarter of 2nd century AD).

their supporters often found it expedient to underscore their allegiance to the proto-emperor, and Corinthian did this in a way that Doric and Ionic did not. Thus the Corinthian order became a declaration of imperial order – a declaration that never slipped from fashion as long as Rome's power lasted.

FORMAL DEVELOPMENT

The Augustan period was also decisive for the morphological definition of Roman Corinthian. The preceding decades had seen already a decline in the Italic version of the capital, which had predominated since the third century BC both in Italy and some other parts of the Mediterranean (figs 7.11–7.12).[25] The emphasis shifted towards Hellenistic models which differed from the Italic pattern in giving a more prominent role to the volutes and helices, together with the ribbed stalks from which they spring. One particular Hellenistic type, in which the volutes and helices spring from a single cauliculus, went on to become the Romans' preferred choice, earning the name 'Normaltyp' or 'Normalkapitell' from German scholars. This elegant fiction introduced a delightful tension between the cardinal axes (where terminated the helices) and the diagonal axes (where terminated the volutes). The result was vital and exuberant in a way that Italic capitals rarely matched. The 'normal' variant had a more satisfying architectonic character too. In contrast with that of the Italic form, its *kalathos* is clearly visible, providing a credible support for the load it carried. At the same time the *kalathos* recalled explicitly the mythical origins of the capital (fig. 2.16), which must have made it preferable in the eyes of Vitruvius and like-minded theorists.

The normal Hellenistic capital appeared in Rome in the second half of the second century BC, notably in the Tiber tholos (fig. 7.13). These and other capitals made by Greek craftsmen out of Greek marble acted as models for native masons to imitate.[26] The new model overtook its rival in the second half of the first century BC, riding the wave of skilled labour from Attica and Asia Minor that came to Rome to work on the projects of Caesar, Pompey and then Augustus.[27]

7.11 (*top left*) A Corinthian capital in the Italic mode from the so-called House of the Faun, Pompeii (late 2nd or early 1st century BC).

7.12 Pair of small-scale Italic Corinthian capitals from the House of Augustus, Rome (30s–20s BC). For their plan and elevation, see fig. 7.21c.

After a period of experimentation, when architects could choose between an array of competing options,[28] a consensus emerged in the capitals of the Temple of Mars Ultor, at once delicate yet strong, sculptural yet architectural (fig. 7.14).[29] The fleshy foliage of the Italic capital spoke too clearly of its earthy origins, and by the end of the century it seems that architects in Rome had come to associate it with poor materials, crude workmanship and provincialism. Just as in Britain the red squirrel lost the fight against the imported grey breed, so the Italic capital faded from sight.

THE CORINTHIAN CORNICE

Of other contemporary developments, the most important was the affirmation of a type of cornice enriched by modillions and coffering. The modillion was a decorative bracket that supported the corona of the cornice – or appeared to support it, since the structural function is negligible except in stucco work. It derived from simplified Doric mutules and assorted flat or S-shaped brackets developed by architects from Pergamon, Rhodes, Delos and Alexandria in the early second century.[30] But although its origins cannot be traced back directly to a constructional system, this is not to say that architects were insensitive to such allusions. In multi-storey displays, modillions sometimes appear only in the topmost cornice, a position in which they bring to mind the projecting ends of roof timbers.

Modillions appeared in Italy at the start of the first century BC. For some time they were confined to a handful of public monuments such as the Corinthian temple at Cori, and the domestic domain, notably real and painted architecture at Pompeii.[31] It is hard to say if at this stage they were linked expressly to Corinthian,[32] but in due course this came to be the case. Once architects had Greek or Carrara (Luni) marble to work with, they experimented with more elaborate types of modillion for the Corinthian

7.13   Capitals from the tholos by the Tiber: (a) one belonging to the original construction (mid- to late 2nd century BC); (b) one substituted in restoration works of the early 1st century AD following fire damage. Note how the proportions shift, particularly of the leaf range. The original set were among the first examples of marble Corinthian capitals of high-class Greek craftsmanship, and as such were important models for the future development of the so-called 'normal' type in Rome and Italy.

7.14   (*right*)   Capital of the Temple of Mars Ultor, Forum of Augustus, Rome (10–2 BC).

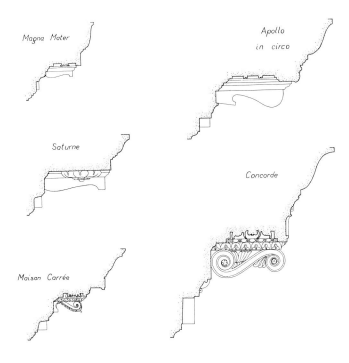

7.15 A selection of cornices with modillions: (a) Temple of Magna Mater, Rome; (b) Temple of Apollo Sosianus, Rome (ca. 20 BC); (c) Temple of Saturn or Regia, Rome (ca. 40 BC); (d) Maison Carrée; (e) Temple of Concord, Rome (AD 2–10).

temples of Apollo Sosianus (fig. 7.15c) and Mars Ultor, along with the occasional building outside Rome, such as the Arch of Augustus at Rimini. With time the classic scrolled form used in the latter and in the Temple of Concord (figs 7.15e and 7.16) became the establishment option – classic also in the mimesis of Athenian consoles, in particular those of the north door of the Erechtheion.[33] A final, Corinthian, touch was the acanthus leaf added to the underside. The great majority of later modillions follow in this vein, with the exception of a rectangular bracket which became popular in the Hadrianic period (fig. 1.16).[34]

The success of modillions was founded on several reasons. They provided a play of light and shade under the corona, and enlivened the entablature seen from below – a factor of considerable importance in an age of increasingly tall columns. They added a rhythmical scansion somewhere between the extremes of the Doric triglyph and the Ionic dentil. More importantly, perhaps, modillions served to create a distinctly Corinthian cornice, for otherwise the base, shaft, architrave and frieze remained interchangeable with Ionic. Other trends led towards more slender capitals (if never quite so slender as those of the Tiber tholos), and a taller base, thanks to the addition of a plinth. The first major surviving building that displays all the vital ingredients of Roman Corinthian proper was Augustus' Temple of Mars Ultor (figs 7.1, 7.14 and 7.18), the showpiece of his grandiose forum (fig. 2.4). This was a key point of reference for future projects in Rome and other cities such as Nîmes, Vienne or Cherchel.[35] Ironically, the quality of work back in Greece suffered from the haemorrhage of skills to Rome, as is apparent in the workaday carving of the capitals of Agrippa's Odeon in Athens (fig. 7.17). The Corinthian vocabulary may have originated in the Greek world, but it was the Romans who synthesized them into a unified whole. As in so many other fields, they soon became masters of the outcome – and the Corinthian age was born.

7.16 Detail of the cornice block from the Temple of Concord, Forum Romanum, Rome (dedicated AD 10). This is now on display in the Tabularium.

7.17 Detail of a capital from the Odeon of Agrippa, Athens (ca. 15 BC). In contrast to examples in fig. 7.13, the surplus stone between the volutes and the associated leaves is not hollowed out, while the termination of the volute does not twist outwards as the spiral closes in.

PROPORTION

The background

Perceptions about the design of the orders divide fairly cleanly into two opposing camps: for and against proportion. Vitruvius and his Renaissance followers shaped the orders according to mathematical ratios tied to the lower diameter of the shaft (figs 0.4 and 0.5). But the infamous gap between such rules and actual practice naturally induces a certain scepticism about their validity. Indeed, modern specialists often take pains to reject the relevance of proportional rules in no uncertain terms, as discussed in the Introduction (p. 6).

The diversity of Roman Corinthian is certainly striking. So many versions have little in common apart from this type of capital, one that was in any case open to a wealth of variations, as illustrated in the examples reproduced in figures 7.19 and 7.22. Bases, shafts and capitals can be slender or squat; columns may be spaced close together or not; entablatures may be light or heavy and assembled from a wide range of mouldings.[36] Yet all the same there do exist tell-tale signs of just the sort of normative patterns that many scholars deny. For example, is it coincidence that columns with identical proportions to those of the Temple of Mars Ultor appear later at the Maison Carrée, the Trajanic arch at Timgad, and the Hadrianeum in Rome? Does not the fact that these columns are accurately 60, 30, 20 and 50 ft tall, and ten times their diameter besides, alert us to a mathematical principle of some sort? We might still imagine that some architects followed rules

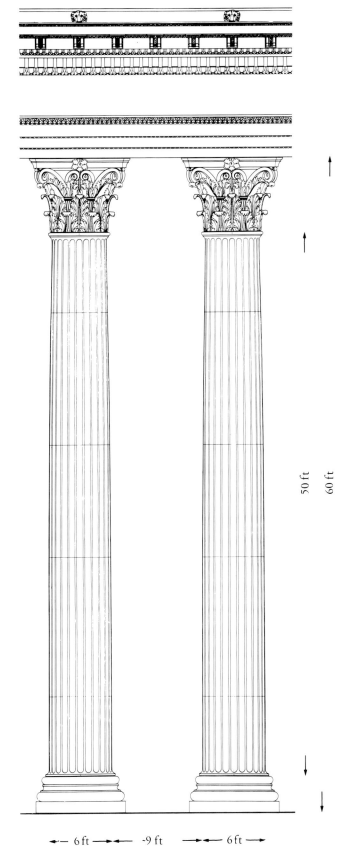

← 6 ft → ← 9 ft → ← 6 ft →

7.18 Elevation of a typical bay of the Temple of Mars Ultor, Rome (10–2 BC).

7.19 (*above*)   Plans and elevations of selected Corinthian and Composite capitals from a wide chronological range which accurately fit the cross-section rule: (a) Tholos of Epidauros (360–340 BC); (b) Solunto, Sicily (late 3rd to early 2nd century BC); (c) House of Augustus, Rome (30s–20s BC) – the right-hand side illustrates the unfinished and the left the finished state; (d) temple of unknown divinity, Sabratha (mid-2nd century AD); (e) Arch of Caracalla, Ostia (early 3rd century AD); (f) 'Wind-blown' capital from Deir Sambul, Syria (5th century AD).

7.20 (*below*)   Cross-sections of three Corinthian capitals. Each conforms accurately to the cross-sectional rule, as indicated by the overlaid squares: (a) Tholos by the Tiber (mid- to late 2nd century BC), 1 : 30; (b) Temple of Vespasian and Titus (AD ca. 90), 1 : 40; (c) Temple of Hadrian (AD 140), 1 : 40.

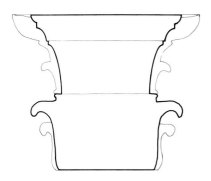 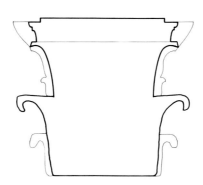 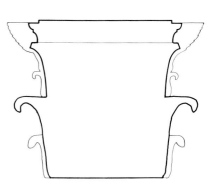

of design, while others did not – and that would be the end of the matter. But to do so misses the subtlety of the Romans' approach: for it was their aim somehow to reconcile the apparently contradictory ideals of rule and variety.

The design of the capital

The Corinthian capital encapsulates the dialogue between rule and variety in microcosm. It would seem natural to begin any study of its design with an analysis of Vitruvius' model, but this is in fact an unreliable starting-point, given that it represents an idealized and half-digested conflation of chronologically disparate elements.[37] It is ironic that he omitted to mention the most consistent of all ancient rules, one that applies to around two-thirds of all Corinthian capitals, whether Hellenistic, Roman or Byzantine. This demanded that *the height of the capital equals the axial width of the abacus* (as measured on the orthogonal axes, excluding the flowers). Since it effectively governs the shape of the capital in section (fig. 7.20) I have called this the 'cross-section rule'. The proof of its existence lies primarily in the accuracy with which it is borne out in a large number of examples.[38] However, the occasional presence of masons' marks defining

the cross-sectional width is another sign of its importance, as is the fact that it was often one of the earliest limits to be established in the process of fabrication (fig. 7.31).[39]

The origins of the cross-section rule appear to go back to the Tholos of Epidauros (fig. 7.19a), since here the key pair of measurements match one another to within 2 cm. Although several subsequent capitals (such as those of the Monument of Lysicrates) do not comply, the rule reasserted itself in the Hellenistic period in places such as Olympia (Stadium and Gymnasium) and Miletos (Bouleuterion). The Epidauros model also had a decisive impact on the development of the Italic capital, in terms both of morphology and of proportion, so it is no surprise to find that it too tends to fit the rule. In fact I know of only three sets of Italic capitals that do not.[40] All others I have examined do, whether they are found in mainland Italy, Sicily, France, Spain or Tunisia (figs 7.11, 7.12 and 7.19b–c).

7.21 Pair of Composite capitals from Santa Costanza. The capital on the right dates to the early Augustan period, while that on the left dates to a century or more later. Note the considerable variation in size of both shafts and capitals.

The cross-section rule happened to be one of the few points in common between the Italic capitals and the first examples in Rome of the 'normal' Hellenistic type, those of the tholos by the Tiber (figs 7.13 and 7.20a), and this was no doubt a crucial contribution to its future success. The great majority of later capitals keep to this proportion, right down to the coarse early fifth-century versions of San Paolo fuori le Mura, among the last products of large-scale new manufacture in the city.[41] Naturally enough, there are exceptions.[42] For example, the designers of some Composite capitals gained space for the volutes by extending the elevation without altering the plan. Conversely, a set from the Atrium Vestae were reduced to one tier of leaves by the simple expedient of eliminating the bottom one. In both cases, of course, the cross-sectional rule could no longer apply.

Ever since the Renaissance, architects' handbooks and scholarly studies treat proportion as a means of defining and transmitting form. It now takes a mental effort to realize that objects with the same proportions do not necessarily look the same. In fact, the Romans put their faith in the cross-section rule precisely because it suited two key principles: it did not govern the appearance of the capital except within broad limits; and there were other proportions (such as slenderness) which had a more immediate impact on appearance.

7.22 Selection of so-called 'Corinthianizing' capitals from the Capitoline Museums. Each accurately fits the cross-section rule: (a) capital with double volutes, uncertain provenance (?2nd century AD); (b) 'Sofa' capital with palmette and ovolo motifs from the Via Eleniana (?2nd century AD); (c) figured capital with birds instead of volutes, uncertain provenance (?2nd century AD); (d) figured capital in Egyptian style, uncertain provenance; (e) composite capital, uncertain provenance.

7.23 (*bottom right*) Corinthianizing capital with animal and human forms in place of volutes, from the cathedral complex of Pisa (early 13th century AD).

Designers were free – indeed obliged – to adapt secondary proportions for the sake of avoiding monotony. The cross-section rule allowed for a slender capital provided the arcs of the abacus were shallow (fig. 7.19b), or a squat one provided the arcs were relatively tight (fig. 7.19c). It could apply equally well to capitals belonging to pilasters, even those that do not diminish in width with height as columns do. (While the body of the capital can dilate accordingly, the abacus has to remain unchanged, since visual conformity was essential at the junction with the architrave.) Other proportions too could be altered, as long as the architect understood the consequences of so doing. Finally, capitals were given their own identity through myriad variations in detail and style. This explains how all those illustrated in figures 7.11–7.14, 7.19–7.23 and

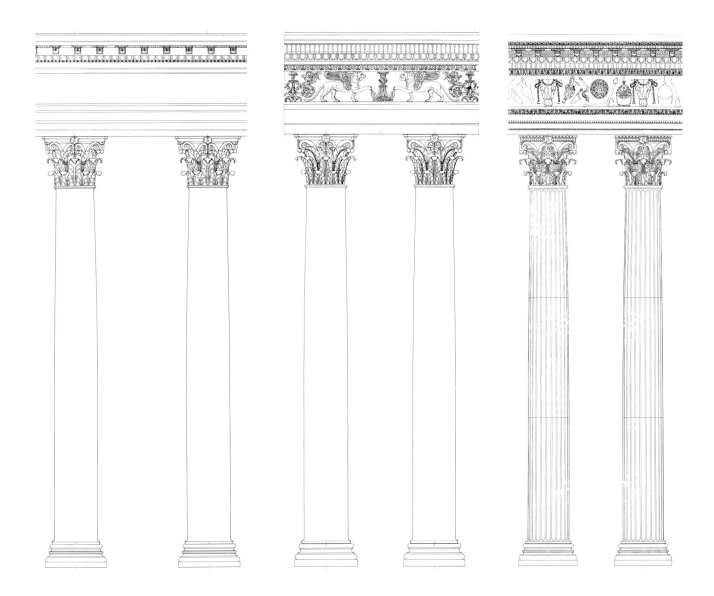

7.24 Typical bays of three of the best-preserved monu-mental Corinthian temples in Rome at the same scale of 1:125. Each shares a common height of 48ft for the whole column and 40ft for the shaft, while the slenderness varies (with a nominal ratio of 9⅗ for the first two, and 1:10 for the third): (a) Pantheon, portico (AD ca. 120); (b) Temple of Antoninus and Faustina (AD ca. 150); (c) Temple of Vespasian and Titus (AD ca. 90).

7.28 can match a single rule and yet look completely different. How appropriate, after all, was the Vitruvian term *genus*, standing as it does for a family of individuals rather than an 'order'.

The design of the column

A similar paradigm applies to column design. In orthodox imperial Corinthian *the ratio between the height of the column and that of its shaft is 6:5*. This rule applies to six out of the eight best-preserved orders belong-ing to imperial temples in Rome, and a substantial per-centage elsewhere (for measurements and analysis, see Appendix B, Table 1):

Table 7.1

A selection of well-preserved Corinthian columns from temples in Rome, with their average height, that of their shafts, and the resulting ratio. Nominal dimensions are given in feet and inches, using Roman feet from 295.1 to 296.6 mm (see Appendix B, Table 2 for metric values)

Temple	Column Height, **H**	Shaft Height, **h**	**H : h**	Percentage difference
Mars Ultor	60	49, 11 (50)	6 : 5	+0.16
Apollo Sosianus	50	42, 3		
Castor	50	42		
Hadrian	50	41, 8	6 : 5	+0.03
Pantheon exterior	48	39, 11½ (40)	6 : 5	+0.13
Antoninus & Faustina	48	39, 11 (40)	6 : 5	+0.25
Vespasian	48	40, 1 (40)	6 : 5	+0.09
Pantheon interior[43]	36	30	6 : 5	

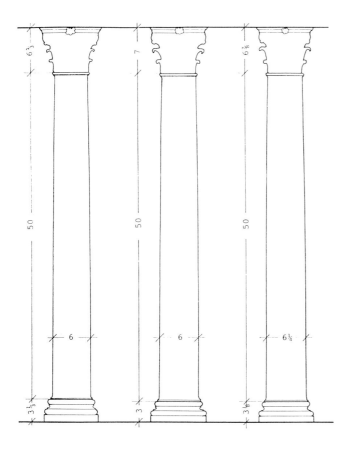

	Scheme A		Scheme B		Scheme C	
Lower diameter	6	H/10	6	H/10	6¼	h/8
Height of base	3⅓	H/18	3	D/2	3⅛	D/2
Height of shaft	50	5/6H	50	5/6H	50	5/6H
Height of capital	6⅔	10/9H	7	7/6D	6⅞	11/10D
Height of column	60		60		60	

7.25 Diagrams showing the orthodox Schemes A, B and C applied to a common column height of 60 ft, with principal associated proportional ratios.

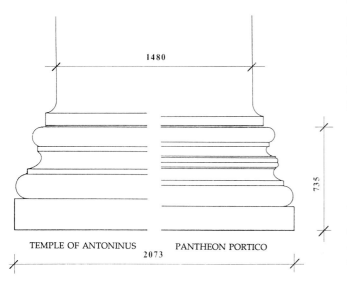

TEMPLE OF ANTONINUS   PANTHEON PORTICO

7.26 Comparison of the bases from the Pantheon portico (AD 118–126) and the Temple of Antoninus and Faustina (AD ca. 150). The dimensions and principal proportions are virtually identical (both sets of columns conform to Scheme C), yet there is an appreciable difference in terms of the mouldings.

Apart from the accuracy with which the 6:5 rule is executed – often to a tolerance within 0.25 per cent (2½ cm or 1 inch for columns 10 metres tall) – there is other supporting evidence. Firstly, discrepancies are roughly balanced either side. Secondly, many columns are suitable heights, that is to say multiples of 6 ft, so that the shafts are automatically multiples of 5 ft. The Temple of Mars Ultor (fig. 7.18) is a classic example, having 60 ft columns with 50 ft shafts, while 48 ft columns with 40 ft shafts (fig. 7.24) was the next popular size.

The third argument in favour of the 6:5 rule is the fact that it was a common denominator of the most popular proportions for the column as a whole, schemes that I have labelled A, B and C. To see how these compare, each have been applied to a uniform height and compared graphically in figure 7.25. The relatively squat proportions of Scheme C give it a robust quality which explains why this was a favoured option for columns with monolithic shafts.

Renaissance formulations occasionally come close to ancient schemes; in particular, one of the two solutions that Vignola proposed corresponds to Scheme B.[44] But be this as it may, there is still a conceptual gulf between the two periods, for Vignola's shaft, just like those of his contemporaries, is the 'left-over' determined by the proportions given to the base and the capital, and not a prime concern in its own right.

In the imperial period the autonomy of the shaft is underlined in terms of both proportion and construction. The majority of monolithic ones have a slenderness ratio of 8:1, a fact that is endorsed by Roman surveyors' formulas that survive in a medieval codex in Munich.[45] It was also usual for columns to divide neatly and unambiguously into their constituent parts, whereas earlier the distinction between base, shaft and capital had been comparatively blurred (when poorer grades of stone were used, the joints were often disguised by a coating of stucco). Contrasts between materials and polychromy were often deliberately accentuated, and it became entirely normal for the shafts to come from different quarries than those that supplied the bases and capitals.

Like the cross-section rule, the 6:5 rule operated in a more subtle way than Vitruvian and Renaissance canons, by allowing secondary proportions to vary. It did *not* define columnar slenderness, which therefore could be relatively squat or elongated. Nor did it define the size of base and capital individually, but only in combination. This is not to say that no importance was attached to proportions based on the column diameter in the Vitruvian mould; in fact these continued to be employed. A comparison of Schemes A, B, C and related ones[46] reveals how such proportions entered into the hierarchy of decisions that underpinned column design:

1 Establishing the height of the column. This had to fit its intended home, of course, but all things being equal multiples of 6 ft were preferred.

2 Establishing the height of the shaft. This should be five-sixths the height of the whole column. As a consequence, the combined height of base and capital equals one-fifth that of the shaft (or one-sixth that of the column). Thus a tall base had to be accompanied by a short capital, and vice versa.

3 Establishing the diameter of the shaft (measured above the flare). This could be thick or thin, but in the most popular schemes it is either one-tenth the height of the *column* or one-eighth the height of the *shaft*.

4 Establishing the height of the base. Although this was allowed to vary, in both Schemes B and C it is half the shaft diameter. In Scheme A it is five-ninths the same, while more or less equal to half the diameter of the *flare* (DF). Thus a 1:2 relationship occurs in one sense or other. These proportions apply equally well to the attic or the double scotia forms (fig. 7.26).

5 Establishing the height of the capital. This could vary considerably, since it had to suit the decisions already taken. As a result its proportions tend not to be as simple as those described so far, although in Scheme A, and on other occasions as well,[47] the height of the capital is twice that of the base.

An independent and yet complementary set of dimensions is related to either the shaft diameter or to that of the flare (fig. 7.28).

6 Dimensions that match the lower diameter of the shaft (D).
(i)   the diameter of the astragal at the top of the shaft (DA).
(ii)   half the diagonal width of the plinth of the base (½DWP); as a result the lateral width = √2D.

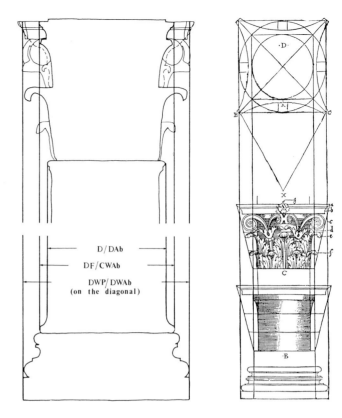

7.27   Diagram showing the principal relationships in section of a Corinthian column: (a) according to Sebastiano Serlio; (b) as in the orthodox imperial schemes.

(iii) half the diagonal width of the abacus of the capital (½DWAb).
(iv)   the height of the *kalathos* (HKal), approximately.

Meanwhile, the lateral width of the capital (LWAb) is often one-and-a-half times the diameter of the shaft.[48]

7 Dimensions that match the diameter of the flare of the shaft (DF).
(i)   the height of the capital.
(ii)   the cross-sectional width of the abacus/capital (CWAb).
(iii) the upper diameter of the kalathos (UDKal).

It is important to grasp the clarity of organization in the *vertical* sense. The fact that the diameter of the astragal is the same as that of the body of the column is tantamount to saying that the one sits precisely over the other. At the same time the rim of the *kalathos* sits over the flare of the shaft, while, on the diagonal axes, the abacus sits over the plinth. Thus a series of imaginary vertical lines run from bottom to top, similar to the spirit, if not the letter, of Serlio's scheme (fig. 7.27).[49] It should also be noted that the flare of the shaft may have played a more important role than is

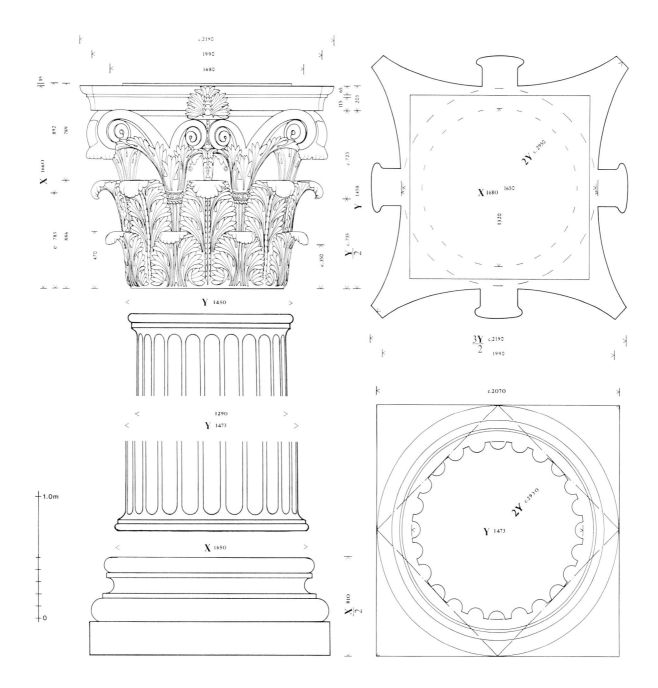

7.28 Hadrianeum, Rome (AD 140), plan and elevation of the main order, showing the principal dimensions for design and specification. Each of these dimensions can be simply expressed in terms of 'x' or 'y', respectively the lower diameter of the shaft, measured just above the flare, and the diameter of the flare itself (where it meets the base).

generally thought. One of the formulas in the Munich codex mentioned earlier referred to the flare, while some of Vitruvius' recommendations may make better sense in terms of this dimension rather than the diameter measured in the traditional way. For example, he says that the height of the Corinthian capital should equal the lower diameter of the column, a proportion

that finds an echo in imperial practice only if the latter measurement corresponds to the flare.[50] However several republican and Hellenistic capitals do match the 'normal' diameter, and I have just shown how important this was for the design of the orthodox imperial column.[51] In effect, both measures of shaft thickness were significant. But in any case it is clear that while the column diameter – in whichever way it is measured – was of considerable importance in antiquity, it never played such a dominant role as it did in the hands of Renaissance and later advocates of modular design methods. The principal features of the imperial framework for Corinthian design may now be summarized as in the chart below (cf. fig. 7.28).

IN ORTHODOX IMPERIAL CORINTHIAN COLUMNS
the shaft height is five-sixths that of the column,
this being the key to a series of proportional schemes.

Meanwhile
the diameter of the shaft is often either
one-tenth of the total height
or one-eighth that of the shaft (especially if monolithic).

A FAMILY OF ELEMENTS
D, DA, $\frac{1}{2}$DWAb
and often $\frac{1}{2}$DWP, HKal
are the same dimension, 'y'
(while LWAb equals $1\frac{1}{2}$y).

A FAMILY OF ELEMENTS
HCap, CWAb
and often DKal, DF
are the same dimension, 'x'.

In addition
the height of the base may be $\frac{1}{2}$ 'x', or $\frac{1}{2}$ 'y'.

'x' must vary with respect to 'y'
so as to suit the overall column proportions.
With Schemes A, B and C in particular,
x:y is respectively 10:9, 7:6 and 11:10.

Applying the framework in practice

Choice and flexibility were built into this framework; it did not set out a single all-encompassing recipe that architects could apply mechanically. As discussed in chapter 3, design involved a dialogue between idealized conceptions and specific details, between primary and subordinate proportions. Theory was always subject to review should it produce something that was unattractive or impracticable.

It is now appropriate to illustrate this dialogue with particular reference to a representative colonnade of the mid-imperial period, that of the Hadrianeum (fig. 7.28). At this time an abacus that occupied about one-eighth of the capital height was consistent with conventional taste, yet the mathematics of Scheme A called for the same ratio to be one-tenth. In practice compromises were introduced to resolve such conflicts, and this explains why these capitals have an abacus that is an inch and a half thicker (and a *kalathos* an inch and a half smaller) than theory predicts.[52]

Metrical considerations could also argue against ideal proportions. Ancient foot rods were divided into digits ($\frac{1}{16}$ parts) or inches ($\frac{1}{12}$ parts), but not usually into smaller units. Where calculation produced non-unitary dimensions they were often rounded off. The need to do so was most marked where column heights were not multiples of 6 ft, as again in the case of the Hadrianeum (see Table 7.2). Rounding off was bound to affect proportions to some extent, explaining for example why the columns of the Temple of Vespasian exceeded the ideal slenderness ratio of 10.[53]

Stone-cutting too involves tolerances. Marble can be honed to within half a millimetre or less – as the Parthenon proves – but the Romans never took precision to such extremes (p. 71); profiles and standardized components had to be accurate enough only to *appear* perfect. Circumstance or error conspired to make one of the shafts in the Hadrianeum almost 2 inches shorter than its companions, but this is hard to make out from the ground. However since the eye is relatively sensitive to the straightness of a continuous element, this discrepancy had to be absorbed before the architrave was put in place, that is to say by adding extra height to the capital. The organic shape of the Corinthian type made it perfectly suited to such tasks, masking even quite considerable discrepancies.[54] In capitals prefabricated at the quarries a margin of tolerance was often provided by a raised ledge on top of the abacus, which could be pared down or not as necessary – a feature that also ensured that loads were not transmitted to the vulnerable corners. (Variations of shaft length are typically more substantial in sets of monoliths – as is understandable given that these might be made in two or more separate quarries.) Given these and other factors that potentially could have led to the modification of the ideal model, the executed version of Scheme A as it appears in the Hadrianeum constitutes a pretty good approximation (see Table 7.2).

Table 7.2

Measurements of the Hadrianeum columns in feet and inches compared with hypothetical values produced by Scheme A (cf. fig. 7.25) (the assumed foot length is 0.2966 metres)

		Ideal	Actual
H	Total height	50	50,0
h	Height of shaft (5H/6),	41,8	41,8
D	Lower diameter (H/10)	5	4,11$\frac{1}{2}$
DA	Diameter of astragal	5	4,11
HKal	Height of kalathos	5	4,10$\frac{1}{2}$
LWAb	Lateral width abacus (3D/2)	7,6	7,4$\frac{1}{2}$
DWAb	Diagonal width abacus (2D)	10	9,11$\frac{1}{2}$
DWP	Diagonal width plinth	10	9,10
LWP	Lateral width plinth ($\sqrt{2}$D)	7,1	7,0
HB	Height of base (H/18)	2$\frac{7}{9}$★	2,9
HCap	Height of capital (H/9)	5$\frac{5}{9}$★★	5,7
CWAb	Cross-sectional width	5$\frac{5}{9}$	5,8
UDKal	Upper diameter of kalathos	5$\frac{5}{9}$	5,6$\frac{1}{2}$
DF	Diameter of flare	5$\frac{5}{9}$	5,6,$\frac{1}{2}$

★ 2$\frac{7}{9}$ ft equals 2 ft 9$\frac{1}{3}$ ins
★★ 5$\frac{5}{9}$ ft equals 5 ft 6$\frac{2}{3}$ ins

How widespread were the practices observed in monumental temples in Rome, and when did they come into play? Measurements from fifty buildings, listed in Appendix B, show that the orthodox framework reached its peak in the first half of the second century AD, and is increasingly irrelevant the further one moves away from this period.

The key ingredients appeared in stages: the earliest was the cross-section rule for the capital; the next was the equality of the diameters measured at the astragal and the lower body of the shaft, a relationship that had become fairly standard by the end of the second century BC. At this time other proportions could still differ widely, witness those of the tholoi at Tivoli and the Forum Boarium. The 6:5 relationship occurs in just one surviving Hellenistic building, the Olympieion at Athens in its reincarnation begun by Antiochus IV in 174 BC (figs 2.11 and 2.19). It may be significant that Antiochus employed a Roman architect, Cossutius. Was it he who made the conceptual jump of relating the two main measures of height, only for the idea to lie dormant until someone else turned to the Olympieion as a model? In fact architects in Rome would have been familiar with its columns, since Sulla, reputedly, had some of them removed and re-erected on the Capitoline.[55] But since the 6:5 rule does not seem to affect other columns until the Augustan period, this is the most likely date for its invention (a supposition that helps explain its omission by Vitruvius).[56] In any event Augustus' architects were the first to grasp the full potential of the new approach. It was they too who made plinths a normal part of the base, which is important since tall bases suited the 6:5 rule better than shallow ones.[57] And as mentioned above, this was also the time when the 'normal' capital and the modillion cornice were perfected, completing the morphological definition of Roman Corinthian.

The apogee of orthodox practice and Roman building activity occurred during the first half of the second century, a period in which countless public works embellished cities all around the Mediterranean. The Corinthian orders in Trajan's Forum, the Pantheon and the Hadrianeum set the official standard, while equally 'correct' echoes replied from as far away as Timgad and Mactar in Africa; Athens in Greece; Euromos and Ephesos in Ionia; Byblos, Scythopolis and Baalbek (Frontispiece and fig. 7.34) in the Levant. Because of the widespread preference for standard sizes there are some notable coincidences: for example, the columns of the Pantheon could be interchanged with those of the Temple of Antoninus and Faustina (fig. 7.26); the columns of the Library of Hadrian at Athens could be interchanged with those of the altar court at Baalbek (see Appendix B).[58]

The decline began in the third century. Some Severan colonnades appear to be fairly orthodox,[59] but in the rebuilding of the Portico of Octavia the capitals and bases are decidedly too tall for the 6:5 rule. The Severan buildings at Lepcis Magna display a marked variation in shaft length, so much so that it can be difficult to be sure what proportions were originally intended.[60] From this time on standards generally felt the impact of the worsening military and political climate. The chain of production beginning with several of the imperial quarries came to be interrupted or definitively broken, ushering in an era of recycling. This is not to say that in earlier periods materials were not recycled – note, for example, the frequent practice of incorporating broken-up decorative elements from dismantled buildings in the concrete foundations of their replacements, or the cutting up of inscribed slabs to make marble roof tiles for the Pantheon[61] – the critical point is that only from this time was it acceptable to re-use elements with a function comparable with their original one. Even where care was taken to assemble matching sets of bases, shafts and capitals, as at Santa Costanza (where the inner ring of capitals come from a single early Augustan building, the outer ring from a mid-imperial one), proportions still tended to suffer (fig. 7.21). Recycled bases and capitals typically take up a greater share of the total height, as may be seen throughout Diocletian's Palace at Split, for example. While this might signal a new desire to emphasize the decorative elements of the column, it probably had as much to do with making *spolia* fit into colonnades that were lower than the original ones. It was, after all, always easier to cut down shafts than make them taller. As for capitals and bases, cutting them down was an ugly business and so avoided.

For such reasons, sets of columns as orthodox as those of the Arch of Constantine are hard to find in late antiquity (see Appendix B). Proportional norms survived, however, in a substantial percentage of capital production, despite marked shifts in terms of style and technique. The cross-section rule continued in use at Proconnesos, one of the few main Roman quarries to stay open into Byzantine times.[62] It even crops up in fifth-century 'wind-blown' capitals in Syria (fig. 7.19f), sets of tenth-century basket capitals in Venice, and a figured capital dating to the early thirteenth century from the great cathedral complex of Pisa (fig. 7.23).[63]

Regional factors were also important. Nonconformist proportions are the rule on the fringes of the empire, in Portugal, Syria and Britain (fig. 7.29). The most wayward Corinthian capitals are found at sites such as Petra and Philae (figs 6.1 and 6.7), places where indigenous traditions were well established before the Romans arrived.[64] In Pergamon, too, a city with its own vigorous traditions, architects were ill disposed to succumb to foreign ideas; the Corinthian columns at the gymnasium seem to be almost a conscious essay in how to design *not* according to the usual parameters. By contrast, imperial norms penetrated further where local traditions were weak. In much of North Africa the Romans' methods were adopted wholesale by the local workforce; several sites in Tunisia have not a single capital that contradicts the cross-section rule.

In parts of the empire where local traditions were stronger than in Tunisia, yet not so strong as at Pergamon or Petra, orthodox and unorthodox coexist side by side. Some of the main sites in the Levant show this particularly well. In civic buildings the orders generally follow conventional patterns, but an exceptionally tall plinth was popular – a detail that necessarily meant that the 6:5 rule could not apply, as for example in the case of the Temple of Jupiter at Baalbek (fig. 8.20). Conversely, the columns of the Hadrianic nymphaeum at Scythopolis fit the 6:5 rule, but have unorthodox capitals proportionally speaking. At sites like these proportions reflect the materials used, or rather their place of production. At Scythopolis imported marble capitals from Proconnesos or Phrygia tend to fit the cross-section rule, while those of local stone tend not to. The most canonic columns in Baalbek, those of the great court, use shafts from the imperial quarries of Aswan (Syene) in Egypt. At Byblos imports were more sustained, thanks to its coastal location. The architect of the theatre had the simple task of erecting a colonnade from a matching set of prefabricated components (shafts from the Troad, bases and capitals from Proconnesos), producing almost inevitably an entirely conventional result. On the other hand local idiosyncrasies – mixed perhaps with half-digested glimpses of official styles – persisted everywhere in the private sphere (fig. 7.30).[65]

7.29 Elevation of the Temple of Minerva Sulis at Bath, England (mid- to late 1st century AD). The columnar proportions share little with orthodox imperial practice.

7.30 (*left*) Elevation of a tomb at Dosene, near Diocaesarea, Cilicia, Turkey. Note the extremely squat proportions of the Corinthian columns, and the unusually tall capitals.

Augustan architects inherited a Corinthian order that was substantially resolved in terms of design, having evolved out of centuries of Hellenistic experience. But they also made a decisive contribution towards the establishment of a fresh orthodoxy. This contribution has three distinct aspects. In terms of *decor* (content and appropriateness), Corinthian took on Augustan and then imperial associations besides more general ones of triumph or vitality; in terms of *eurythmia* (visual harmony), its language of forms was perfected and brought together in a new synthesis; in terms of *symmetria* (mathematical harmony), its proportions achieved a rationality and coherence that was lacking from previous practice. The very popularity of Corinthian in the Roman period has its roots ultimately in the balance it achieved between the Vitruvian triad of design principles (p. 40).

It is true that orthodox Corinthian bears little resemblance to Vitruvius' detailed proportional recommendations, but it does echo his views on design theory in general, and especially his conception of *symmetria*. As discussed in chapter 2, he held that Nature's design of the human body was a supreme model of proportional harmony (figs 2.2 and 2.12). There are indeed striking similarities between the *symmetria* of the body and the *symmetria* of orthodox Corinthian columns. Is it just a coincidence that so many of them are multiples of 6 ft tall, the notional body height? More to the point, the proportions of the most popular schemes for Corinthian columns, as set out in the following matrix for Scheme A, imply a web of simple ratios not unlike those applicable to Vitruvian Man (p. 41).

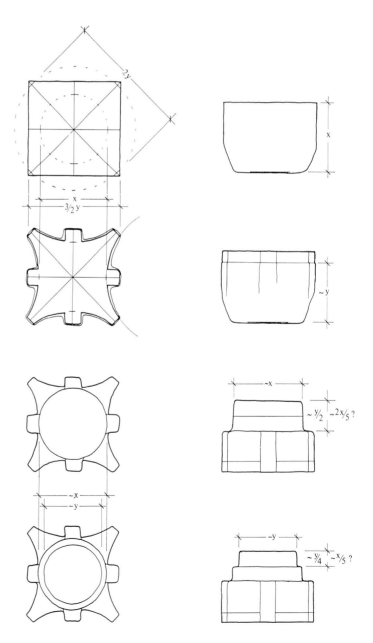

The principal proportions of Corinthian columns following Scheme A:

		HB	D	HCap	DW	H
HB	base height	1	5:9	1:2	5:18	1:18
D	shaft diameter		1	9:10	1:2	1:10
HCap	capital height			1	5:9	1:9
DW	diagonal width				1	1:5
H	total height					1

As already noted, the integration of the height of the shaft within the new proportional system was the key to achieving consistent harmony. And it is here too that a sense of *decor* enters into the *symmetria*, for there is something singularly appropriate in a concern for this dimension; the column is after all a *vertical* element, and it is the shaft that gives it its verticality.

PRACTICALITY

The orthodox system brought notable practical advantages too. Simple, predictable proportions were easy to memorize, and no doubt became a matter of habit. At major quarries like Carrara or Proconnesos, quarry workers roughed out capitals using coarse tools, the pick, point and mallet, while still working near the rock-face.[66] One of the most astonishing of all Roman artefacts, a huge partly finished capital in the latter quarries, is a particularly eloquent testimony (fig. 7.31). Moreover, formative capitals must have passed through many hands on their way to completion, and a common repertoire of rules of thumb based on ratios like 1:1, 1½:1 and 2:1 must have greatly reduced the risk of misunderstanding and error (fig. 7.32). Indeed, the predominance of the orthodox framework lay in its inherent compatibility with the volume supply of marble upon which the imperial building machine depended. Among other things, it allowed architects to define clearly and efficiently primary proportions (those with architectural implications), while leaving individual craftsmen free to fashion secondary proportions according to decorative or iconographic concerns.

One of the hallmarks of the imperial period is the extensive use of monolithic shafts. Following Alexander's conquest of Egypt, monoliths of marble, granite and other fine stones appeared in wealthy cities like Delos, finding their way to Rome first in dribbles and eventually – after determined efforts to eliminate piracy – in a flood. By the second century AD marble imports reached almost every major metropolis close to the Mediterranean.[67] Shafts were generally shipped in a partly finished state, often with the entasis already cut (figs 6.35 and 6.38), a system that not only saved weight during transportation, but time as well, since work at the destination was essentially a question of assembly. In his studies of the Roman marble trade, John Ward-Perkins highlighted a trend towards dimensional standardization, particularly shaft lengths in multiples of 5 or 10 ft.[68] It is surely no coincidence that these sizes perfectly suit the 6:5 rule, yielding total column heights that corresponded also to whole numbers of feet. But production was not restricted to these sizes alone. Lengths could also be:

- Multiples of 4 ft, particularly 8, 12, 16 and 24. Coupled with the popular slenderness ratio 1:8, these heights matched diameters of 1, 1½, 2 and 3 ft for the body of the shaft and the astragal at the top.
- Any other whole numbers of feet up to 20 ft (e.g. 9, 14 and 18 ft).[69]
- None of these: architects were free to choose alternatives. Shaft lengths were sometimes tailored to achieve specific column heights: 16⅔ ft shafts, for example, are not uncommon since this is the size that suits 20 ft columns.[70]

Standardization no doubt streamlined operations at the quarries, as it must have done the dialogue between architects, patrons and suppliers. Everyone was presumably familiar with the ramifications of using, say, 25 ft as opposed to 20 ft shafts. What is less clear is whether production was geared to commission or the creation of stockpiles. In the late republic, when imported columns were still a rarity, stockpiling is out of the question. The fact that Cicero ordered shafts for his daughter's tomb even before he had bought the site suggests long consignment times.[71] In the imperial period, on the other hand, quarry products were not necessarily used straight away, which is a possible if not certain proof of stockpiling.[72] Very large projects, however, probably always represented special orders.

Stockpiling or no, once the imperial framework was in place much could have been resolved by the briefest of instructions, the equivalent to saying: 'Provide a set of roughed-out 40 ft shafts, with bases and capitals of such and such a stone, all so as to fit Scheme C.' We get a wonderful glimpse of 'mail-order statue shopping' in a letter by Arrian, the governor of Cappadocia, to the emperor Hadrian. Having inspected a newly finished project at Trebizond he reported:

> As for the statue of yourself, it is fine as regards the pose – pointing towards the sea – but it is a poor likeness and not good work. Please send a statue in this same pose. . . . If you think fit, please send a fresh Hermes about 5 feet high . . . and one of Philesios, 4 feet high.[73]

The quasi-industrial serial production of the mid-to-late imperial period could, however, act against proportional harmony. 1 ft bases and 2 ft capitals turn up all over the Mediterranean, and although according to the orthodox schemes these should accompany 15 ft shafts, it is not uncommon for them to go with 14 or 16 ft ones. This phenomenon is most marked in cities like Perge, where colonnaded streets consumed large numbers of prefabricated imports. This was the architecture of mass consumption, where ideals took second place to expediency.

7.31 (*facing page top*) Unfinished Corinthian capital abandoned at the rock face of the Proconnesos quarries near Constantinople. The diagonal width is approximately 3.55 metres, making it suitable for a 60 ft Corinthian column (50 ft shaft).

7.32 Principal stages of working involved in making a Corinthian capital such as the one illustrated in fig. 7.31.

7.33 Interior of the Temple of Bacchus, Baalbek, Lebanon (mid-2nd century AD), detail of the corners at the rear end of the cella showing one of the pilaster-faced stair towers either side of the entrance.

RULE AND VARIETY

No amount of theoretical and practical justifications would have persuaded Roman architects to persist with systems that did not produce an attractive result. In this sense the salvation of the Corinthian orthodoxy lies in a certain disjunction between form and proportion. To appreciate this point it is enough to compare the orders of the Pantheon portico and the Temple of Antoninus and Faustina, which are identical in terms of proportions and size (fig. 7.26). Yet they *look* quite different, thanks to variations in materials, mouldings and style. In fact, the orthodox framework codified only those proportions that did not stifle diversity. To repeat what was said in the context of capitals, Roman architects put their faith in rules for column design only so long as, firstly, they did not govern the appearance of the column and its components except within broad limits, and, secondly, there were other proportions that had a more immediate impact on appearance.

The 6:5 rule allowed shafts to be thin or thick, capitals and bases to be squat or slender. By contrast, rules that would have imposed visual homogeneity were conspicuously shunned. One that fixed the height of the entablature in relation to that of the column would have been oppressively boring, and it is for this reason that the ratio could normally range between 1:4 and 1:5, with no shortage of more extreme solutions.[74] For the same reason column spacing was regulated only by a range of preferences, as discussed in the previous chapter.

Experience must have taught the Romans the virtues of this approach, but perhaps they learnt from observing Nature too. Any living organism is a unique entity, yet an oak tree, for example, still conforms to an underlying pattern of oak-ness. Nature's handiwork that Vitruvius exhorted architects to study above all other was the human body. Just like the 6:5 and cross-section rules, two of Vitruvian Man's simplest proportions, the equality of height to arm-span and the bisection of the height at the genitals, have relatively little impact on appearance (figs 2.2 and 2.12). We notice far more whether people are slim or stocky, or have some characteristic feature, be it unusually broad shoulders, a particular hairstyle or a big smile. Ancient sculptors had to come to terms with paradoxes like these, and the lessons they learnt may have percolated down to architects, or indeed vice versa. Each and every version of the Corinthian order was given its own identity by the manipulation of secondary proportions, materials and miscellaneous decorative details – the architectural equivalents of distinctive physiognomic traits.

In this happy conjunction of common sense and design sensibility, we can see the Romans' genius for synthesis at work. The Corinthian order stands for the essence of their architecture: grand, ornate, founded upon mathematical principles which were tailored to serial repetition, and yet adaptable to a variety of tastes and programmes. Theory, beauty, content and practicality come together as one.

7.34 Detail of the peristyle of the Temple of Bacchus at Baalbek. The 50 ft shafts are typically made out of either two or three pieces held together by metal dowels, a technique which explains the integrity of the inclined dislodged column.

PART II

VIII

TRAJAN'S COLUMN

STUDIES OF ROMAN ARCHITECTURE often overlook the Column of Trajan, regarding it as the province of specialists in sculpture, history or military matters. Everyone's attention is mesmerized by the extraordinary 200 metre long relief that winds around the shaft. A document of exceptional artistic and historical importance, it narrates the story of the Dacian wars via a succession of minutely detailed scenes, embracing not just the military action but a wide spectrum of related events.[1] Depictions of the horror of a mass Dacian suicide are contrasted with legionaries tending crops or constructing buildings (fig. 8.3); thus the propaganda of war proclaimed the benefits of a Roman peace. The pedestal too is covered by sculptural reliefs, this time showing armorial trophies won from the opposing tribes piled up like a mountain of loot (figs 8.6 and 8.7).

Yet the Column is much more than a vehicle for sculpture. The simple formula of an honorific column masks a building – for that is what it is – of some complexity, incorporating an entrance door, a vestibule, a chamber, a stair, windows and a balcony in the form of a capital. Indeed, as a work of architecture in its own right, it has been imitated widely. The copies made for Marcus Aurelius and Napoleon may have been inspired largely by the reliefs, but others mimicked the architecture alone. Works related to this theme include Wren's Monument to the Fire of London, dozens of lighthouses, and reams of paper projects by such architects as Ledoux and Boullée.[2]

8.1   Forum of Trajan, Rome (AD 105), view of Trajan's Column looking through the re-erected columns of the Basilica Ulpia façade.

8.2 (*above*)   Reconstruction of the Forum of Trajan, showing the relationship of the Column to the Basilica Ulpia when seen from the far end of the main court.

8.3 Scene from the shaft of Trajan's Column showing Roman soldiers at work on a building site.

Trajan's Column merits an architectural exploration for many reasons. It is the principal remnant of Trajan's Forum (figs 8.1, 8.2, 8.4, 8.5), by all accounts one of the most magnificent places in ancient Rome, if not, in the words of Ammianus Marcellinus, 'the most exquisite structure under the canopy of heaven, and unanimously admired even by the deities themselves'.[3] It is one of the best preserved of all ancient monuments, thanks in part to the technical excellence of its construction (earthquakes down the years have but shifted it half a degree out of plumb), in part to assiduous restorations under Popes Paul III and Sixtus V (it was the latter who claimed it for Christianity by placing a statue of St Peter on the summit, where one of Trajan had originally stood). Another reason for studying Trajan's Column is the opportunity of comparing it with Marcus Aurelius' full-size copy (figs 8.12 and 8.13). The value of this comparison lies in the fact that the latter is not a straight reproduction, but a thoughtful reinterpretation. The second architect kept only what he admired most, changing what he did not – thus leaving behind a unique critique by a practising Roman architect.

Before looking at the Column in detail, it is well to understand the background of Trajan's Forum as a whole. This was the culmination of the so-called imperial fora, the grand sequence of urban set-pieces that took their cue from Caesar's Forum (fig. 1.6), the original 'overflow' from the congested republican forum. First came Augustus', with its long axis running northeast, at right angles to Caesar's, ending in the imposing Temple of Mars Ultor (fig. 2.4). Sixty or so years later followed Vespasian's Forum (known as Templum

Pacis or the Temple of Peace even though it was predicated on Rome's military prowess just like the other fora), with its main axis again parallel to Caesar's. Then Domitian transformed the ancient thoroughfare in the space between the two preceding complexes into the Forum Transitorium, a project concluded by Nerva. Although Domitian may have planned something similar, it was finally Trajan who completed the sequence with a grandiose complex not much smaller than all the rest put together. The new forum extended the axis of the Temple of Peace, while the sense of unity with the other fora was reinforced by a series of compositional devices (most notably the exedrae on the cross-axis), and the reprise of certain key dimensions like 50, 150 and 400 ft (fig. 8.4).[4] Continuity is also manifest in terms of the repertoire of prestigious marbles such as *giallo antico, africano* and *pavonazetto* (cf. fig. 5.1), and in particular the paving motif of large squares framed by relatively narrow bands.

What was the role of the Column in this context? Most visitors to Trajan's Forum must have entered the main porticoed space at the south-east end, having arrived from the other imperial fora or Trajan's Markets. Ahead, the Basilica Ulpia presented its long side to the viewer, an unusual transverse orientation which was possibly derived from the layout of military encampments or *Principia*.[5] Such an organization could only provide a relatively muted emphasis on the main axis, and paradoxically – for most of it was out of sight – the Column added reinforcement. It held aloft the huge bronze statue of Trajan, grasping a warrior's spear and orb, symbol of his *imperium*, thus giving a theatrical vertical fillip to the axial progression and signalling the extension of the complex beyond. This, admittedly, is a matter of opinion, since many reconstructions of the basilica put its roof high enough effectively to occlude a view of the Column from the main court.[6] To my mind a lower level, as proposed by James Packer and Kevin Sarrinen (figs 8.2 and 8.5), feels more convincing. At any rate, once inside the basilica the visitor would have been beckoned by the light from the open court around the base of the Column.

According to most reconstructions, this court doubled as a vestibule to the temenos of the Temple of Deified Trajan and Plotina which concluded the north-western end of the project (figs 1.6 and 8.4), but recent investigations have failed to find substructures massive enough to take the temple, leading to the hypothesis that this was really at the other end of the forum.[7] Quite apart from this uncertainty over its location, controversy also surrounds the very conception of the Traianeum. It was not completed until

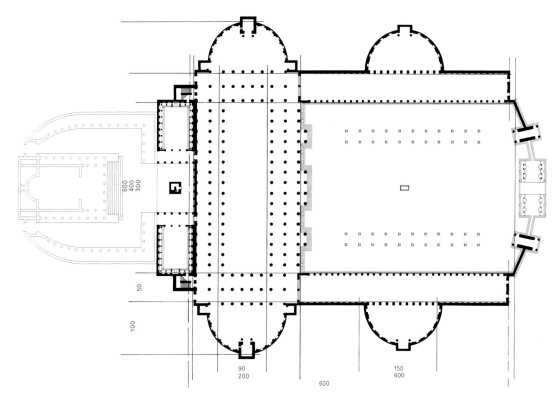

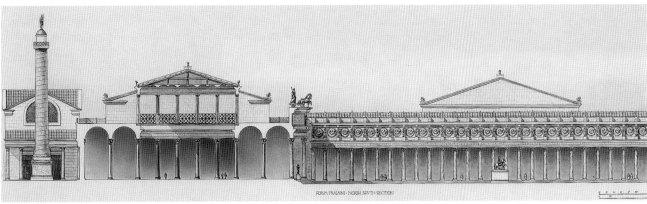

around fifteen years after the inauguration of the main complex in 112, a fact that has led many scholars to judge it entirely an addition of Hadrian's as opposed to just being completed by him. This supposes that a temple cannot have been planned for Trajan while he was still alive, since emperors were not deified until after their death, and then only upon ratification by the Senate.[8] But others regard it as a logical conclusion to the forum, given that a temple is the principal focus of all the other imperial fora. According to this line of thinking it must have been planned from the outset, on the premise that the deification of the *princeps optimus*, the best of emperors by popular consent, was a foregone conclusion even in the prime of life.[9]

8.4 (*top*) Plan of the Forum of Trajan with principal dimensions overlaid.

8.5 Sectional elevation through the basilica on the long axis of the Forum of Trajan.

A related question is the function of the Column itself when it was dedicated in May 113. It was to become Trajan's tomb after his death in 117, with the golden cinerary urn housed *sub columna*, probably in the chamber concealed within the pedestal (figs 8.6–9).[10] But was this the original intention when the forum was initiated?[11] Again there is a school of thought that holds that the Senate's unprecedented decision to concede Trajan burial inside the city

8.6 Pedestal of the Column of Trajan seen from the south-west.

8.7 Elevation of the pedestal of the Column of Trajan, entrance side.

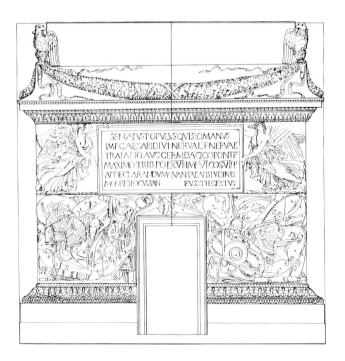

boundaries cannot have been taken during his lifetime. So did the chamber start life as a repository for Dacian trophies, that is to say the physical counterparts of the booty carved on the outside of the pedestal?[12]

Whatever the truth behind them, such disputes have the merit of forcing one to think about the other functions of the Column. It participated in the iconography of the complex, with the narration of the Dacian wars sustaining the panegyric to Trajan, the Roman Empire and its army. The forum was built *ex manubiis*, from the spoils of conquest, and the reliefs of the Column recounted how those spoils were won. Framed by the books in the Greek and Latin libraries either side of the main axis, here was a visual story offering a more refined commentary than the statues of captive chieftains around the main court. As already observed, the Column played a major role in compositional terms, reinforcing the axis in common with the Temple of Peace. Its height was crucial to this function as an axis marker, just as was that of obelisks (which in ancient Egypt were likewise placed hard up against buildings rather than in the middle of open spaces). In as much as it enabled the crowning statue of Trajan to be visible from beyond its immediate confines, the Column also functioned as a gigantic statue base.

The Column, then, was the support for narrative, a compositional device at the urban level and a statue base; but there was more to it than that. The enigmatic dedicatory inscription over the entrance (fig. 8.7) alludes to other aspects of the programme which had something to do with height. After listing Trajan's many titles, and stating that the Column was set up in his honour by the Senate and the People of Rome, the text tells of one of the ostensible purposes of the structure: *ad declarandum quantae altitudinis mons et locus tant[is oper]ibus sit egestus.* The ambiguity of the Latin permits translations with different nuances, perhaps 'to show how high a hill and area were removed for such great works', perhaps 'to show how high a mountain – and the site for such great works was nothing less – had been cleared away'.[13] Precisely how this aim was fulfilled has long been a subject of speculation. Dio Cassius launched the popular tradition that the Column marked the height of a hill that was cut away,[14] making it a sublime version of the plaques recording the 120 ft depth of the rock cutting for the Via Appia at Terracina.[15] It is too nice an idea not to be continually repeated, but it is difficult to reconcile with the possibly earlier road uncovered near the bottom of the Column by early twentieth-century excavations.[16] Presumably, then, the hill in question did not stand directly on this spot; instead it might be identified with the Quirinal escarpment before it was trimmed back to make way for the terracing of the markets. Otherwise the inscription invites a still less literal interpretation. The local terrain, while hardly mountainous, was surely far from flat, with spurs descending from the Quirinal to cover a large part of the forum. In one sense the Column showed off the feat of levelling the site by providing a fabulous view of it from the capital-platform at the top: could this be what the text alluded to?[17]

In fact, the belvedere-cum-stair-tower probably struck the ancient visitor as the most technically daring and impressive feature of the project. The panorama from the top is breathtaking enough today, but it must have been even more so in antiquity when the ground level was around 4 metres lower, and when the view towards the Campus Martius was still intact. In the other direction was the gilded roof of the Basilica Ulpia, with the imperial fora unfolding beyond, and the Colosseum looming in the distance. In his brief list of Rome's principal architectural wonders, Ammianus Marcellinus called the columns of Trajan and Marcus Aurelius 'exalted pillars', bearing 'platforms to which one could climb'.[18] That the stair was meant to be used by visitors, and not just for maintenance purposes, is confirmed by the presence of forty windows, ten on each cardinal axis, sufficient to ensure an adequate illumination throughout the climb (figs 8.8, 8.9 and 8.11). In the third century Emperor Gallienus supposedly dreamt of a statue of himself more than twice as tall, with a spiral stair that would take visitors to look out of the eye-sockets.[19] It is further significant that when Ammianus guided Constantius II through the city for the first time in 357, the emperor celebrated his visit to the top of Trajan's Column by having his name carved inside the stair (initiating a long line of graffiti).[20] Several of his successors based at Constantinople built monumental honorific columns on a similar principle.[21]

While its function as statue base and belvedere seems to demand that the top of Trajan's Column rose above the Basilica Ulpia, further significance was added by its specific height: namely 100 feet for the column proper (excluding the pedestal and statue base). In reality, however, this measurement is $100\frac{1}{2}$ to 101 ft, depending on the value used for the foot (see Appendix A for measurements).[22] It is possible, in theory, to get around this problem by invoking units other than the normal Roman foot, but the alternatives are frankly improbable from a historical point of view.[23] So the building appears to be a sort of dimensional mirage, rather like

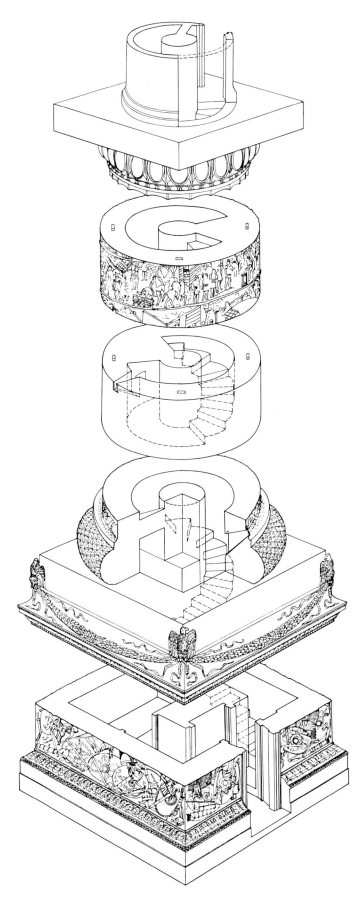

8.8 Exploded perspective of the Column of Trajan.

165

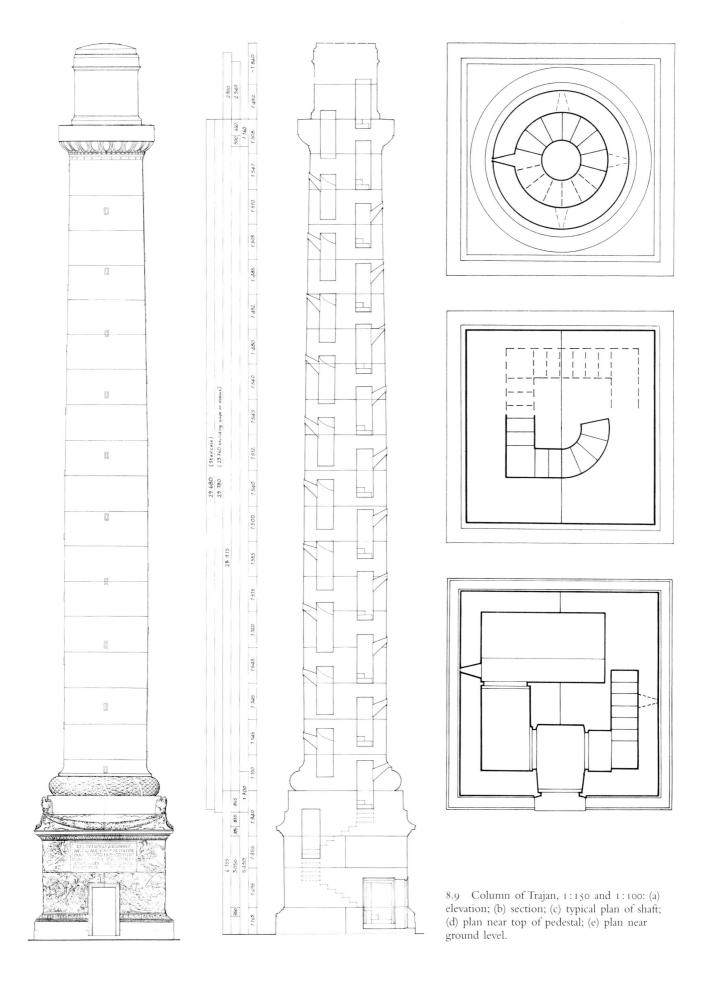

8.9 Column of Trajan, 1:150 and 1:100: (a) elevation; (b) section; (c) typical plan of shaft; (d) plan near top of pedestal; (e) plan near ground level.

the *hekatompedon* Parthenon. This is odd for a number of reasons. The diameter of the shaft (measured to the outside edge of the window frames) is 200 digits. Besides complementing this dimension numerically and proportionally (being eight times greater), 100 feet would have conveyed an appropriate sense of grandeur and perfection, just as it did in other Roman monuments (chapter 4). It would also have suited the planning of Trajan's Forum as a whole, to judge from the 600 × 200 ft basilica, the 400 ft wide court, the 50 ft porticoes and 50 and 30 ft column shafts.[24] What is more, multiples of 50 or 100 ft were recurrent ingredients of the other imperial fora,[25] while the admittedly irregular hemicycle of Trajan's Markets approximates to a semicircle 100 feet in radius.[26] Evidently the Column was intended to maintain this theme in the vertical sense. Most significant of all, Marcus Aurelius' Column was known as *columna centenariae* by virtue of its height.[27] Does not the fact that it measures 100 ft exactly (29.62 m) suggest that the model it imitated *should* have been the same, even if in practice it is not?

Might there be a link between the failure to achieve 100 ft and the informal character of the scrolled frieze winding around the shaft, with its ragged borders and evidence of improvisation?[28] The potential problems that might have interfered with the smooth running of the project include the inherent conflict of building a tomb for Trajan when he was still alive;[29] vacillation on the part of a senatorial planning committee;[30] and two phases of work.[31] But such things are hard to pin down. Could it be that Trajan's builders were simply not worried about exactitude? Inaccuracies would multiply if work were rushed – and haste is another explanation sometimes offered for the character of the relief. There is, however, nothing casual or improvised about the architecture of the Column. The 'feel' of the monument is reminiscent of the crisply executed pyramid-tomb of Gaius Cestius, where the 100 ft width varies by only 2 cm in spite of the remarkably short contract period (330 days is cited in an inscription on one side). The carving of the mouldings is of the highest quality; the entasis follows a quite definite design (fig. 6.32); the jointing of the blocks is razor sharp (figs 8.10 and 8.11). The staircase is also a marvel of precision engineering and a quantum leap in spatial quality compared with earlier examples like those in Temple A at Selinunte, or later ones like those in the Baths of Diocletian. Its soffit forms a continuous surface, a perfect helix comparable with Archimedes' Screw.[32]

Trajan's Column, then, was a highly tuned work of a highly proficient architect – a master of composition,

8.10   Column of Trajan, junction of shaft and torus, with the first window (author). The relative prominence of the construction joint above is due to the effect of spalling near the surface.

8.11   Column of Trajan, detail of window embrasure seen from inside the staircase.

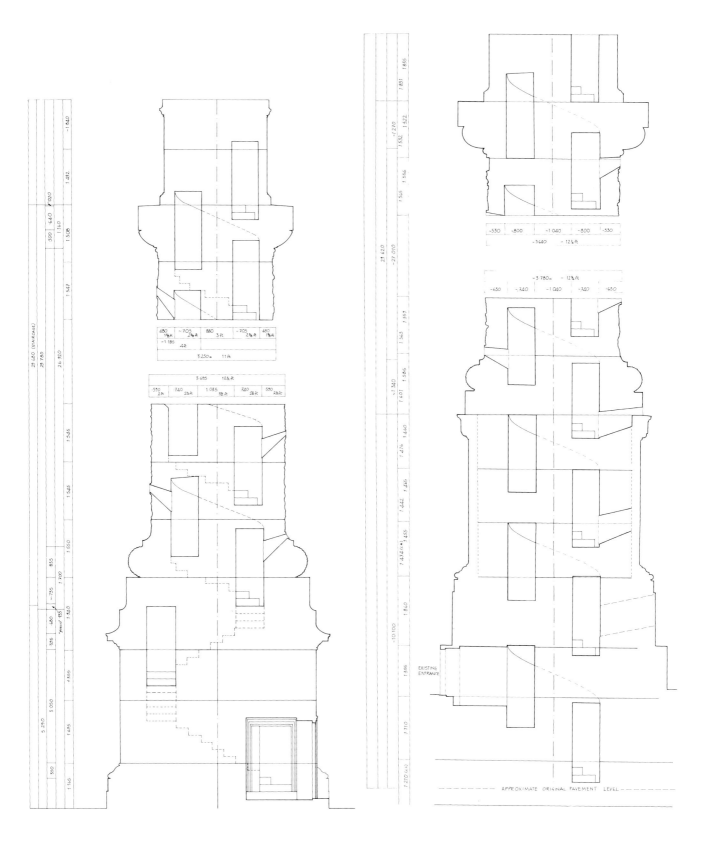

stereometry and construction. There is no reason to doubt its traditional attribution to Apollodorus, as part of his responsibility for the whole forum,[33] although there is no evidence to say that he doubled as master sculptor too.[34] If there is any truth in it, Dio Cassius'

8.12 (*above left*)   Column of Trajan, cut section on entrance axis, 1 : 100.

8.13 (*above right*)   Column of Marcus Aurelius, cut section (west-east), 1 : 100.

story about Apollodorus' quarrel with Hadrian (chapter 1, pp. 23–4) portrays the architect as a tough, uncompromising personality, and he doubtless kept an eagle eye on site supervision. All the more unlikely, then, that sloppiness of design or execution contributed to the outcome. One might even perceive a link between the exceptionally high quality of the stair and Apollodorus' origins in the Levant – assuming to be correct the single source that cites Damascus as his native city. In Baalbek, Jerash and other nearby sites, stairs consistently attained high standards, and it is notable how much care was lavished on the staircase in the Niha model (fig. 3.10).[35] In particular, the monumental tower-altar at Baalbek, with its staircase giving access to the ceremonial roof platform (fig. 8.18), could have provided the inspiration for at least the pedestal part of the Column.

The stair certainly merits further scrutiny. It is made up of a square part corresponding to the pedestal and thereafter a spiral or, to be more accurate, a helix (figs 8.9 and 8.12). It so happens that this helix does measure accurately 100 ft tall, which can hardly be a coincidence in the light of all the foregoing observations. What is curious here is the fact that the Column, externally, is not the same. While the top of the capital does align with the top of the stair, the base starts about half a foot below the start of the helix. Moreover, this is only one of a number of peculiarities. The division between the pedestal and the column does not take place at a structural joint, breaking the unwritten rule that stonework joints should reflect limits of architectonic importance. Nor does a joint coincide with the transition between the two major components of the stair; that this should occur in the middle of a block is decidedly perverse. As for small-scale dimensions, the typical course height is $5\frac{1}{8}$ ft, not 5, while that of each step is consistently $10\frac{1}{4}$ digits, not 10. Since everything about Roman architects' work implies that they had little interest in complexity for its own sake, it is legitimate to wonder if the actual project had its origins in a simpler *initial* conception, rather as explored in chapter 3. Can a mental autopsy of the monument reveal the original intentions, and why they were modified?

THE INITIAL DESIGN

If dimensional simplicity was indeed Apollodorus' original goal, then his sketch design might have included the following characteristics (fig. 8.15a):

- a Tuscan column 100 ft tall (not $100\frac{1}{2}$ ft)
- a square stair for the pedestal, a helical stair for the column (making the latter 100 ft tall as well)
- a slenderness of 8:1, giving a diameter of $12\frac{1}{2}$ ft or 200 digits (as at present)
- a normal course height of 5 ft (not $5\frac{1}{8}$)
- a pedestal 20 ft wide and 20 ft tall (not 21)
- a typical stair tread 10 digits tall (and not $10\frac{1}{4}$).

Upon embarking on detailed design, the stair called for careful attention, given that this was the most innovative and complex aspect of the project. The square part was not particularly taxing, the main requirement being that the total rise matched the height of the pedestal. The helical part was more constrained, since the shaft had to maintain its structural integrity. The detailed solution was determined by two factors, the width of the staircase and the number of steps per gyration. Apollodorus chose a set of convenient measurements, with the core, the stairway and the casing starting out at the bottom as $3\frac{1}{2}$, $2\frac{1}{2}$ and 2 ft wide respectively (fig. 8.12). On the other hand, he rejected the simplest radial geometries, those with twelve or sixteen divisions (schemes that can be produced by successively bisecting an equilateral triangle or a square respectively). Twelve steps were impracticable for the simple reason that a tall person had insufficient headroom unless the risers were uncomfortably tall, while sixteen would have made the stair unnecessarily steep. So a fourteen-part geometry was preferred, in spite of the fact that it called for a relatively painstaking procedure; indeed it is impossible to construct using ruler and compasses alone.[36] The result is certainly much more comfortable than most ancient stairways, and conforms well with modern building codes.

So far, so good. But a fundamental question had yet to be confronted: the precise relationship of the stair to the exterior skin of the monument. Detailed examination would have thrown up a serious dilemma – *there was inadequate headroom at one critical point in the stair.* This was not an issue in the helical part, since the soffit turns automatically with the treads, maintaining a constant 7 ft tall passage. Nor was it in the pedestal, where the headroom could be carved out, as it were, from its great mass. The problem arose at the point of transition, or rather at the landing just before the start of the helix. Here the hypothetical project broke down quite simply because it did not provide sufficient stone to cover the soffit; in effect the top of the stair passage would have burst through to the open sky.[37]

This problem is not an easy one to understand, and Apollodorus may have become aware of it only when

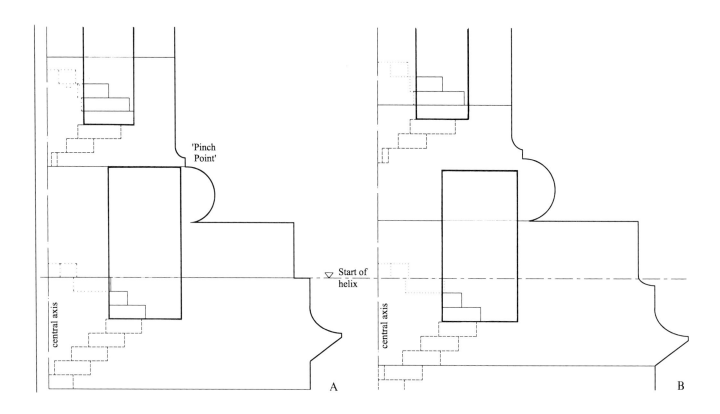

A

B

8.14 Diagonal section through the pedestal of Trajan's Column, 1:50: (a) as implied by hypothetical initial scheme; (b) as executed.

the project had reached an advanced stage. He may well have drawn out sections through the Column on the main axes, but in projections like this the critical landing does not appear. In fact the headroom problem emerges only in a diagonal section (fig. 8.14), that is to say in a type of drawing that no architect normally uses.[38] The whole issue probably surfaced when detailed specifications were compiled for the individual blocks, or even when work was put in hand in the Carrara quarries themselves.

In any event, at some stage Apollodorus was forced to modify his design. The answer was to increase the height available over the critical landing (fig. 8.15b), a solution that demanded a base at least 6 ft tall. Once this decision had been made, it was in theory possible to keep to the 5 ft modular courses, but this would have created a joint in the middle of the torus – an unheard of detail (fig. 8.15c). An alternative would have been to depart from the module, making the base a 'special', that is to say a taller block than the rest. This amendment might seem a valid alternative, but it actually raised a difficulty of a different nature: that of tackling the great weight implied.

This last point is the key to understanding the subsequent course of the design. Until the 1980s,[39] few scholars paid much attention to the construction of the Column; the cast in the Victoria and Albert Museum, for example, faithfully reproduces the sculpted surface but edits out the joints. Both Trajan's Column and its Aurelian successor are in fact wonders of heavy engineering. They stand apart from their modern imitators chiefly by their monolithic character; whereas Wren's Monument in London is made of some five hundred blocks, Trajan's comprises just twenty-nine. Structural integrity was possibly one consideration in keeping the number of joints to a minimum, but it was no doubt also important to bolster the sense of mass (discussed further in chapter 10) and to provide as seamless as possible a surface for the relief. Accordingly the stair is hollowed out of drums traversing the entire cross-section rather than being assembled from separate elements for the core, treads and outer ring (fig. 8.8). Each block comprises half a turn of the stair, a choice that, together with the standardization of height, facilitated serial production at the quarries.[40] For such an enterprise to succeed, one of Apollodorus' most pressing tasks would have been to evaluate ways of dividing up the blocks so that their weights remained within the bounds of feasibility. A 5 ft module generated weights that are impressive and yet realistic: about 32 tons for the drums of the shaft and 55 tons for the capital.

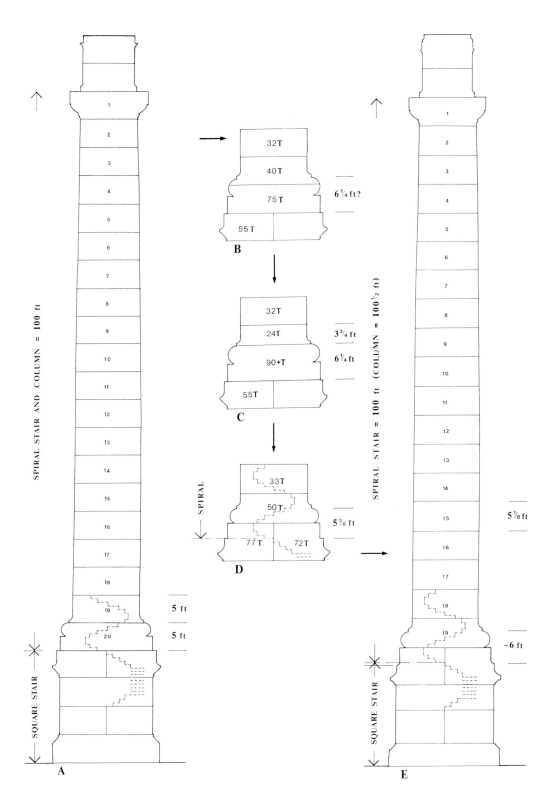

8.15 Hypothetical stages in the design of Trajan's Column: (a) initial design based on regular 5 ft tall courses; (b) rejected alternative for a taller base, with a joint in the middle of the torus; (c) rejected alternative for a taller base, with varying course heights; (d) the introduction of a joint between the torus and the plinth, assuming that the bottom of the plinth aligns with the start of the helical stair; (e) the executed design. For the sake of its proportions the base is taller than in (d), hence the bottom of the plinth no longer aligns with the start of the helical stair.

Apollodorus' initial idea was surely that the base also be a single piece of stone – as, significantly, is the case in Marcus Aurelius' Column. But the finished weight of a monolithic base 6¼ ft tall (this particular dimension matches a whole number of 10 digit risers) would be some 90–95 tons, and substantially more in its rough state. It seems quite simply that such monstrous loads

171

8.16 Detail of the sarcophagus of the Haterii family (late 1st century AD), showing a cage winch in operation. Vatican Museums.

were ruled out for this particular project, a decision that was to bring in its train a whole series of ramifications.

A weight of this magnitude might not at first sight seem to represent an insurmountable obstacle, bearing in mind the staggering capabilities of the Egyptians and the Phoenicians, and that fact that the Romans themselves shipped several obelisks of 200 tons or more back home, and re-erected them.[41] However, weights like these were never actually *lifted*, but manœuvred into position by means of ramps and colossal gantries (fig. illustrated on p. 158).[42] Such cumbersome methods had no place on usual Roman construction sites. As in modern usage, blocks were *lifted* clear of the ground and *lowered* into place. This point is borne out at Baalbek, a place with a strongly rooted local tradition of megalithic building. A series of gigantic stones were dragged from the nearby quarries to the podium of the Temple of Jupiter, of which three – the so-called Trilithon – average about 800 tons apiece (figs 3.16 and 8.20).[43] The superstructure overhead was doubtless as heavy as the available technology would allow, but the entablature blocks typically weigh 'only' 60 tons,

while the surviving corner element weighs around 100 tons (fig. 8.17).[44]

With the benefit of the Hellenistic discovery of the mechanical advantage of pulleys and winches,[45] combined with their own formidable practical experience and organizational skills, the Romans came to handle giant architraves, capitals and column shafts as a matter of course. By the end of Trajan's reign 50 ton monolithic shafts were quite common, while ones weighing 100 tons were used on rare occasions (chapter 10, p. 209). The largest cornice block known in Rome, a vestige of the enormous Quirinal temple, also weighs not far short of 100 tons,[46] a fact that confirms this as the notional top limit for 'normal' Roman building operations. A heavier unfinished block is known in the Proconnesos quarries, one that was probably destined for Emperor Theodosius' honorific column.[47] A simple cylinder 4.45 metres (15 ft) in diameter and 3.3 metres tall, it now weighs around 140 tonnes, indicating a final figure in the region of 105–20, once allowance is made for trimming the exterior and cutting out the stair. The fact that it was abandoned – ostensibly due to a crack that became visible during fabrication – illustrates the risks associated with such gargantuan ventures.

The maximum capacity of individual sets of heavy duty lifting gear (tread-wheel plus winch plus pulleys plus jib) was in the order of 8 tons or so.[48] Heavier weights would have been lifted by linking a number of sets together, perhaps in conjunction with counterweights. As at any modern urban construction site, the main problem here was one of logistics. Domenico Fontana's treatise of 1590 on the raising of the Vatican obelisk shows just how vast a surrounding area was required.[49] But the site of Trajan's Column was confined on three sides by the Basilica Ulpia and the library wings, so free space was available on one side only, towards the Campus Martius. Where were multiple sets of equipment to be located? It may be that instead of jibs like that shown on the Haterii relief (fig. 8.16), lifting gear was harnessed to a special scaffold of a type mentioned by Hero of Alexandria, but even so there was probably a limit to the number of tread-wheels that could be linked to it.[50]

It is in this light that we should understand Apollodorus' reluctance to entertain a 90–95 tonne monolithic base. For the same reason none of the courses making up the pedestal is monolithic, being divided instead into pairs of blocks running alternately parallel or orthogonal to the main axis, thus keeping the largest block of all under 75 tonnes. So the architect's choice fell on the option of making the base too out of more than one piece. A joint was duly introduced between plinth and torus, a position in which it had the virtue of being practically invisible. At the same time it neatly separated the circular monolithic courses from the square bipartite ones (fig. 8.15d).

THE MODIFIED DESIGN

The modification to the base inevitably called for the whole column to be redesigned (fig. 8.15e). The arithmetic that led to the final outcome may be reconstructed as follows:

(i)   The helical stair could still be 100ft tall, but it now comprised nineteen blocks of eight risers, plus an extra portion of the block which included the plinth and the top of the pedestal.

(ii)   Four steps made an appropriate choice for this extra, being equivalent to half a regular block.

(iii)   This makes a total of 156 steps (19 × 8 plus 4) for the helix, rather than the 160 of the initial scheme. Dividing 156 into the target of 100ft yields 10¼ digits for each step, and hence 5⅛ ft for each of the nineteen blocks of the shaft.

(iv)   This scheme produced a 97½ ft tall column, excluding the plinth. 3 ft was an appropriate height for the latter (any less would have made it look too flimsy), so the total for the complete column worked out as about 100½ ft.

At this point it is appropriate to take note of the little curved flare, about half a foot in height, at the bottom of the plinth (fig. 8.12). An unusual feature, it was surely invented so as to eliminate the main flaw of the final scheme. If one mentally excludes it, accepting only the vertical face of the plinth as part of the column proper, its height returns to the 100ft ideal.[51] That architects should have bothered themselves with this sort of frippery may seem absurd, but this is the only reasonable explanation for such a coincidence.

The reconfiguration of the base of necessity demanded the redesign of the pedestal too. Construction joints ideally had to match whole numbers of steps and coordinate with the mouldings. Thus the first joint occurs where the socle meets the die, while the third occurs at the bed of the cornice (fig. 8.12). Practical considerations also explain why the second joint does not divide the die into equal halves: this would have made the soffit of the vestibule unrealistically thin, inviting the danger of cracking.

While Vitruvius admitted that it might be necessary to 'give up *symmetria* so as not to interfere with utility',

he also advised that 'diminutions or additions' be made in such a way as to minimize the disruption of proportional harmony (v,6,7; vi,2,1). The modified pedestal respects this doctrine, for its cubic form was retained, albeit with sides now measuring 21ft (including the plinth of the column base). Other dimensions were revised in sympathy, so that the result had a certain schizophrenic quality: some dimensions followed the logic of the original design (being factors of 100ft) while others followed that of the modified one (being, like 21ft, multiples of 7ft).[52] The problem was hardly an easy one. Apollodorus had to reconcile the demands of form, theory and practicality, demands that happened here to contradict themselves.

Why did Apollodorus only tinker with the initial project rather than opting for a radical redesign? Perhaps he simply agreed with Vitruvius, and was happy to accept a compromised *symmetria* where circumstances demanded. But it is also possible that work was already in hand in Carrara before he came to understand the tricky geometry near the start of the

8.17   Comparison of the upper parts of the Column of Trajan and the Column of Marcus Aurelius.

8.18 Corner cornice block from the Temple of Jupiter at Baalbek. Its original weight was in the region of 97 tons.

8.19 Cut-away perspective of the monumental altar in front of the Temple of Jupiter, Baalbek.

helix. In fact the change of height from 5 ft to 5⅛ ft for the drums of the shaft was so slight as not to have necessitated a fresh order for any of these, because he would have been able to exploit the practice by which large quarry blocks normally had a surplus mantle of stone, a device which provided both a degree of protection and a margin of tolerance. On the other hand, the blocks for the base and the upper part of the pedestal would have been ordered afresh, offering a potential reason why the Column was inaugurated some sixteen months later than the rest of Trajan's Forum.

In conclusion, it is interesting to see how the architect of the Aurelian Column judged Apollodorus' work. If imitation is the best form of flattery, then the new project was flattery indeed. It repeats the main elements of Trajan's Column: the square pedestal, the Tuscan column, the narrative scroll and the helical stair rising to a capital-cum-balcony at the top. The prototype was reproduced with the same cross-section, the same fourteen steps per turn, and the same block height (fig. 8.13), constituting perhaps the most unashamed instance of copying in the whole history of Roman architecture.

However, some changes were introduced. The sculpted scroll was given fewer turns and greater depth in relief, making its contents more legible from a distance; the pedestal (and so the monument as a whole) was made taller; the capital was widened so as to create a more substantial viewing platform, reaching the formidable weight of 72 ton (fig. 8.17).[53] An apparently minor and yet very significant modification corrected,

as it were, the contorted junction between the pedestal and the column base: *the base was made out of one piece.* As a result, a joint could now fall in its natural position, at the junction between the column and the pedestal, and there was no longer any obstacle in the way of achieving the desired 100 ft height. This was made possible by carrying the helical stair down to the ground, a decision that eliminated the headroom problem encountered in Apollodorus' project.

The combined effect of keeping the base block to the normal module, and carving the flare of the shaft from the same block, made the base itself relatively squat. Its width too was made less than its equivalent at Trajan's Column, helping to keep the weight of the block within feasible bounds (around 70 tons). The visual effect may be less satisfactory, but it is hardly catastrophic; the architect must have considered this a price worth paying for the realization of one of the fundamental aims of the whole enterprise, the *columna centenariae.* Perhaps Apollodorus would have disagreed, judging, in sympathy with Vitruvius' ideas, that it was more important for *symmetria* to bend to utility and beauty and not the other way around. History has come down on the side of Apollodorus; when later architects came to imitate the concept of the column-cum-stair-tower, it was always to Trajan's Column – and not its more predictable successor – that they looked for inspiration.

8.20 (*facing page*) Flank of the Temple of Jupiter at Baalbek (begun early first century AD).

IX

THE ENIGMA OF THE PANTHEON: THE INTERIOR

THE PANTHEON ATTRACTS SUPERLATIVES like no other Roman building, being the most famous, the most magnificent, the best preserved, and the one with the biggest span. Yet the brightest star in the Roman firmament has its dark side. Its genesis, function and design are all open questions, ones that ancient sources answer only in riddles. Indeed, the silence that shrouds the early history of the Pantheon seems almost conspiratorial: its image is completely absent from coins, while the few known literary references are at best cryptic and at worst confusing. Modern understanding of the building therefore hangs to a large extent on the analysis of its physical fabric, which happens to be notoriously problematic.

An emblematic obstacle is the prominent inscription in the frieze over the portico (fig. 10.2). M·AGRIPPA·L·F·COS·TERTIVM·FECIT. It thus declares the building to have been founded by Marcus Agrippa and completed during his third round as consul, in 27 or 25 BC. But near the end of the nineteenth century archaeological evidence emerged to prove that the real patron of the existing structure was Hadrian. This, in fact, is the third Pantheon on the site: Agrippa's first incarnation burnt down in AD 80, to be replaced by a Domitianic version which burnt in its turn to make way for the definitive solution begun (or at least conceived) around 118, and completed some eight or more years later. So despite the fact that Hadrian rebuilt it

9.1   Interior of the Pantheon by Giovanni Paolo Pannini (ca. 1734), showing the attic as it appeared before the alterations of the 1750s. National Gallery of Art, Washington.

9.2 (*above*)   Detail of the main order of the interior of the Pantheon. Note the exquisite carving of the capital and the strong contrast created by the band of red porphyry in the frieze.

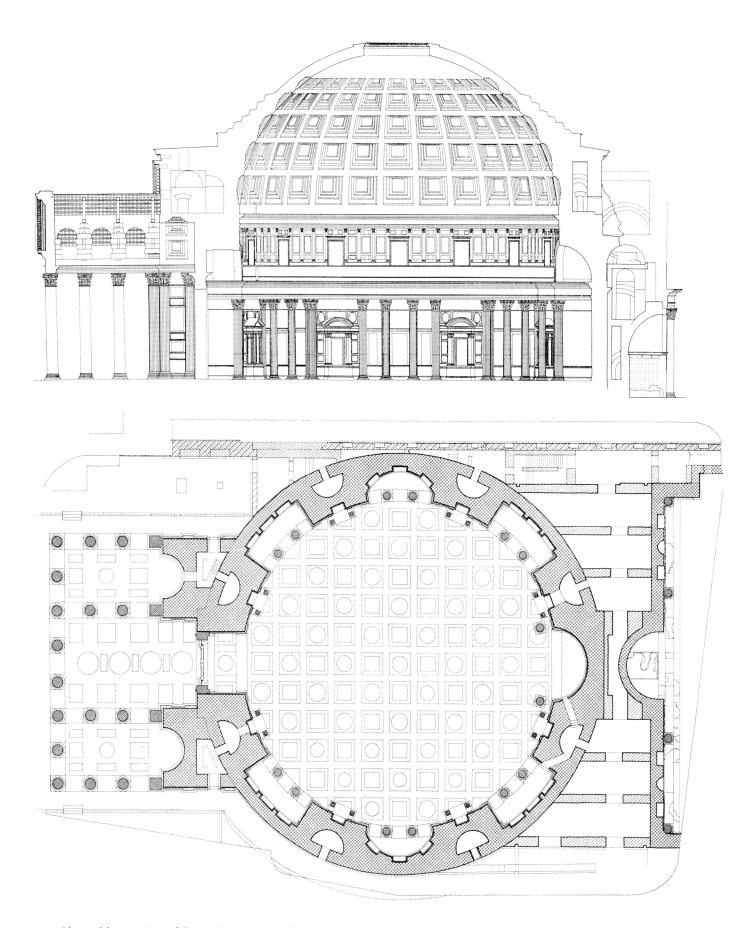

9.3 Plan and long section of the Pantheon, 1:500. The section reconstructs the original form of the attic.

from start to finish, he apparently put up the inscription commemorating the original patron as a show of respect for tradition.

As for the name, *Pantheum* in Latin, Πάνθειον in Greek, this is equally curious, for it was not the official original title, but rather a sort of nickname.[1] Its meaning was already a subject for speculation in a passage from Dio Cassius' histories which is another puzzle in itself. Evidently fooled by the inscription, he gave the building to Agrippa. Dio's mistake may be understandable, but it hardly inspires confidence in his testimony:

> Also he [Agrippa] completed the building called the Pantheon. It has this name perhaps because it received among the images which decorate it the statues of many gods, including Mars and Venus; but in my opinion the name derives because the vaulted roof resembles the heavens. Agrippa, for his part, wished to place a statue of Augustus there also and to bestow upon him the honour of having the structure named after him; but when the emperor would accept neither honour, he placed in the temple itself a statue of the former Caesar [i.e. Julius Caesar] and in the porch statues of Augustus and himself.[2]

So Dio simultaneously provides two readings, one deriving from celestial symbolism, the other from statues of multiple divinities, consistent with the common perception of the Pantheon as a temple to all the gods (from the Greek *pan*: all; and *theios*: of a god). But in many ways it eludes this definition. The inscription is unlike the usual form for temples, in as much as it omits to mention the god or gods concerned.[3] A passage in the *Historia Augusta* which cites buildings that Hadrian restored excludes the Pantheon from the list of temples.[4] Then there is the form of the great domed interior; it resembles that of no other temple, but finds parallels in imperial baths and palaces, and later mausolea. Few temples were circular, and those were relatively small. The question of size is relevant since interiors were intended primarily as homes for cult statues rather than for group worship (which focused on the altar outside), so large dimensions were not inherently necessary. Tradition demanded single occupancy, that is to say one divinity per room, explaining why temples to the Capitoline triad have three rooms and why the Temple of Venus and Rome has two (fig. 1.8).[5] So the Pantheon, with its single vast canopy, is unlikely to have been a temple in the strict sense of the term, although this does not rule out a spiritual realm of some kind and temple-like associations, as indeed the presence of the great pediment would seem to imply.[6]

AGRIPPA'S PANTHEON: THE 'SPHINX OF THE CAMPUS MARTIUS'

So what then was the Pantheon? This slippery question forces us to try to get to grips with a non-existent building, namely Agrippa's. It is thought to be significant that the gods mentioned by Dio were associated with Augustus' family, the *gens Iulia*.[7] The intention to set up a statue of Augustus inside the building along with Caesar (his adopted deified father) and Venus (the mythical *Genetrix* or founder of the Julian line) echoes Hellenistic *Pantheia*, where divine images were disposed around that of the reigning sovereign.[8] Augustus' refusal of Agrippa's proposal is characteristic of his studied respect for traditional Roman values and the rejection of the trappings of absolute monarchism, with its attendant political dangers. So while overt worship of the living Augustus was out of the question, here none the less was a dynastic celebration as unambiguous as Augustus' Forum, where the image of the proto-emperor enjoyed an intimate relation with the gods connected to the Julian family.[9]

9.4 Map of the Campus Martius showing the principal structures in existence in Augustus' day.

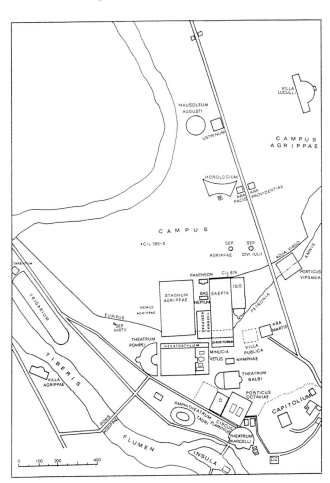

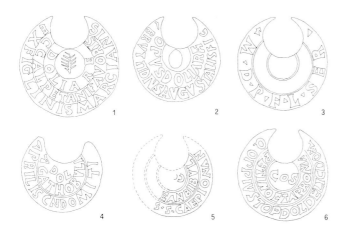

9.5 Selection of brickstamps from the Hadrianic period; 1–4, the Pantheon, 5–6, Hadrian's Villa.

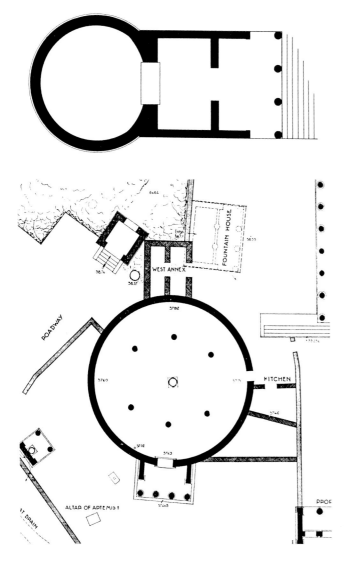

9.6 Precedents for the Pantheon plan: (a) heroon at Stymphalos, Greece (uncertain date), 1:200; (b) tholos at Athens in its late Hellenistic form, 1:400.

Dio's text makes it clear that there were many other gods on view in the Pantheon apart from the ones he mentions, and it is reasonable to suppose that Romulus was among their number, as at the Forum of Augustus. Legend had it that Romulus, transformed as the god Quirinus, ascended into the heavens above the *palus caprae*, the marshy area around the site of the Pantheon (fig. 9.4). Conceivably, by making a formal link between them, the Pantheon promoted Augustus as a new Romulus, the founder of a new Rome.[10] With time, the original complement of gods in Agrippa's building was no doubt supplemented by later deified emperors, for the Pantheon in its later reincarnations became a celebration of the imperial institution rather than its individual dynasties. In addition, Hadrian is supposed to have held court in his rotunda, which was a fundamental justification for such a large covered space; it surpassed Domitian's *Aula Regia* in the Palatine palace while putting the emperor's justice on display in a public place. On such occasions the main apse must have doubled as a tribune where sat the emperor.[11]

The idea that the Pantheon originated as a dynastic monument finds support in various strands of evidence. Its very name, as opposed to 'Augusteum', might be viewed as a smokescreen intended to disguise such a very un-Roman phenomenon as a building that accorded divine honours to a mortal. It seems significant too that the building bestrides the axis from the Baths of Agrippa to the Mausoleum of Augustus (fig. 9.4), the latter being the resting-place of the Julian family, to which Agrippa was related by marriage.[12] Then there is the circular form of the plan, which, as mentioned, would be exceptional for a straightforward temple.

That none of this is a foregone conclusion is underlined by the fact that one scholarly interpretation sees Agrippa's building as the 'missing' Temple of Mars *in Campo*.[13] The potential for such divergent views exists primarily because the shape of Agrippa's Pantheon continues to be a matter of dispute. It has been so ever since 1892, when the brickstamps collected by Georges Chédanne showed that the structure above ground belonged to Hadrian's reign (fig. 9.5).[14] Where then was the building announced by Agrippa's famous inscription? Traces of its foundations were duly uncovered in the ensuing excavations directed by Luca Beltrami and Pier-Olinto Armanini. Most authorities follow Rodolfo Lanciani's view that the evidence pointed to a T-shaped structure of the type illustrated in figure 3.3, positioned where stands the existing portico, with the entrance facing south onto an open

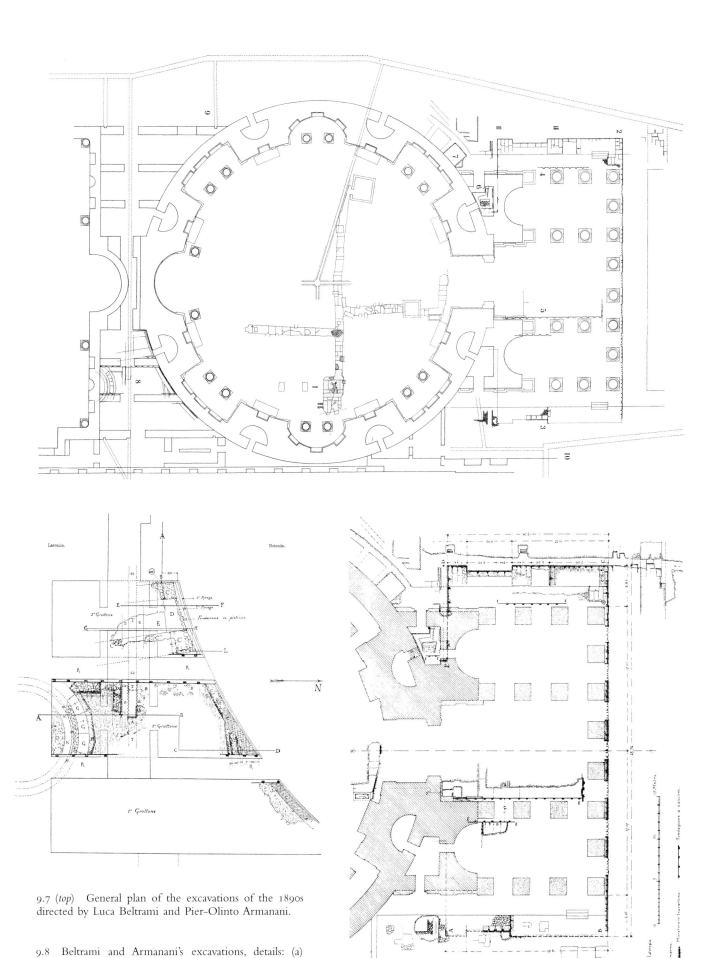

9.7 (*top*) General plan of the excavations of the 1890s directed by Luca Beltrami and Pier-Olinto Armanani.

9.8 Beltrami and Armanani's excavations, details: (a) south-east sector of rotunda with buttress walls; (b) portico and transitional block.

forecourt (fig. 9.7).[15] But the opposing school of thought, that Agrippa's building incorporated a rotunda not unlike the present one, is progressively gaining momentum.[16]

This question has important ramifications for the genesis of the existing building, for either Hadrian's replacement was a radical new departure, or it followed its predecessor's lead. To my mind there is more to be said for the second option. The hypothesis of a T-shaped Agrippan building rests on little besides the uncovering of a projection on the south side of the structure under the portico (figs 9.7 and 9.8), but there is nothing at all to show this projection was not merely a link to a rotunda. It is true that this theory has the attraction of explaining the absence of Pantheon-like buildings before Hadrian's time, but this may be an accident of archaeology, and nor is it complete. At Stymphalos in Greece is a little heroon with a comparable plan which certainly dates from before Agrippa's day (fig. 9.6a), while a less obvious but more important precedent was the tholos of the Athenian agora; although this was initially circular, it had gained a rectangular porch by about the time of Caesar (fig. 9.6b).[17]

There is a series of arguments in favour of an Agrippan rotunda,[18] but it is enough to mention just three here. Firstly, the restoration of Agrippa's inscription in the pediment of Hadrian's building (fig. 10.2) implies quite forcefully that both projects had more in common than just the site.[19] In fact Hadrian's reconstruction work in the Campus Martius was otherwise respectful of the Augustan character of the area,[20] while his mausoleum mimicked not just the typology of Augustus', but also its dimensions (Table 4.1). Is not all this inconsistent with a Pantheon which broke radically with its forerunner? Secondly, there are traces of two earlier floors below the existing interior one, the uppermost presumably Domitianic, the lowest Augustan. The thinness of the Domitianic paving (only 5 to 8 cm), and the types of marble used (including *pavonazetto*) strongly suggest a covered space of some sort, one that was apparently as wide as the existing one.[21] Thirdly, excavations begun in May 1996 have revealed two flights of stairs leading up from the forecourt to the portico, one superimposed over the other. Pending publication of the report (and the possibility of a secure dating on the basis of small finds), the levels suggest that the lower stair should belong to either Domitian's or Agrippa's Pantheon. Thus at least one of these was orientated north, just like Hadrian's. In short, there are hints of continuity everywhere.

If Hadrian's Pantheon did indeed mimic Domitian's or even Agrippa's this raises the quandary of the original rotunda. Perhaps it was substantially open to the sky, save for an ambulatory around the perimeter.[22] The possibility of a roof spanning the entire space runs up against the problem of its sheer immensity. A concrete vault was out of the question, since the necessary technology was as yet in its adolescence in the Augustan period; besides, the seriousness of subsequent fires evokes timber instead. A span somewhere in the region of 43 metres would have been far in excess of anything known, so it seems strange that Pliny, whose admiration was attracted by the 100 ft (29½ m) roof timbers in Agrippa's Diribitorium nearby, made no mention of it.[23] Alternatively, there could have existed columns analogous to those supporting the tholos at Athens (fig. 9.6b) that somehow eluded Beltrami's and Armanini's trenches. In all of this the only sure thing is a little concentric portion of *opus reticulatum* at the base of the existing rotunda documented in Beltrami's report (fig. 9.8a).[24] It may be impossible to know if it was originally part of an open court or a full-blooded building, but either way it is a remnant of the structure which conditioned both the position of Hadrian's rotunda and its great size.

CELESTIAL AND TERRESTRIAL THEMES

The chief novelty of Hadrian's Pantheon was the incomparable dome (fig. 9.10). At one level its function was simply to astound the Roman populace; at another it spoke of a universal cosmology, representing, as Dio intuits, the celestial home of the gods.[25] While the specific original intentions may remain elusive, it seems inconceivable that this was a dumb masterpiece of technical, aesthetic and spatial experience: it communicated unequivocally at the level of symbol and rhetoric too. This was certainly a factor that had an influence, and sometimes a determining influence, on the form of Roman architecture, and as such a subject which bears on design, even if it must remain at the fringes of the present discussion. It is however worth signalling here the sort of interpretational problems that come to the fore, by looking just at the reasoning behind the orthogonal grid for the paving pattern, a choice seemingly at variance with the circular plan. Might the uncentred expanse of the floor be identified with the earth's limitless horizon, and the rotunda with the perfect imperial order that bounds and shapes it?[26] Or could it be seen instead as an almost automatic response based on precedents in the imperial fora, and in particular the apses of the Basilica Ulpia? My point here is twofold. Firstly, as stated repeatedly, architectural design is an inclusive, multi-faceted activity; space can be moulded to answer quite disparate concerns, so that in the field of interpretation it is, theoretically at least, possible to have one's cake and eat it too. Secondly, that any specific readings must always be subordinate to the coherence of the project in its own right; as explained below, the play-off between the che-querboard floor and its cylindrical container is actually a vital part of the formal resolution of the whole interior.

Number symbolism doubtless made some contribution to the message of the rotunda. The articulation of the groundplan according to a sixteen-part geometry recalls, as does Vitruvius' radial city plan, the sixteen-part Etruscan sky, placing the Pantheon implicitly at the centre of a celestial scheme.[27] On the other hand, the successive bisection of the cardinal axes (fig. 9.11) is an almost instinctive, commonsense way of creating radial rhythms. Meanwhile, the coffering of the cupola is divided into twenty-eight parts, the same number as that of the columns and pilasters belonging to the main order.[28] Twenty-eight was considered 'perfect', one of a very limited set of numbers that equal the sum of their factors.[29] Being also a rough approximation to the number of days in the lunar cycle, twenty-eight perhaps invoked a cosmic iconography too.[30] And if the twenty-eight vertical divisions represent the moon, the oculus the sun, and the five horizontal rows of coffering the remaining five planets, then all the seven elements of the solar system then known are present. Is it also relevant that the Pantheon has seven exedrae (including the apse on the main axis), one for each of the associated divinities?[31] Did the sunbeam from the oculus mark astronomical cycles and events?[32]

The oculus undoubtedly contributed in a more general sense to the mystical quality of the main space (fig. 9.9). Since it provided all the illumination, windows were unnecessary at a lower level, and their absence was in fact vitally important. Being denied visual contact with surrounding buildings puts the visitor in a realm removed from everyday reality (luckily nothing came of a sixteenth-century project to cap the oculus by a lantern and to introduce windows at a lower level).[33] At the same time, the single source of light provides a wondrous sense of drama. As the sun moves across the sky, so the pool of sunlight strokes the cupola, the walls and the floor, acting as a magnet for the viewer's attention (fig. 9.1). Each day its course is different, and the effect changes too with the weather and the seasons. The sun reaches the floor around midday between May and August, bathing the

9.9 Oculus of the Pantheon.

9.10 View of the cupola of the Pantheon seen from below. Note how the central field of the coffers appears to be centrally positioned within the overall frame of the ribs, an effect which is achieved thanks to the assymetrical profile of coffering in section.

whole interior in glorious reflected light and providing optimum conditions for reading sculptural detail and gradations of colour. It is a constant surprise how good the level of illumination is, despite the dirty grey render that now covers the cupola.

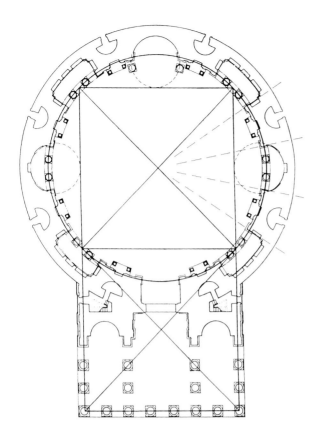

9.11 Plan of the Pantheon with geometrical interpretation overlaid, 1:750.

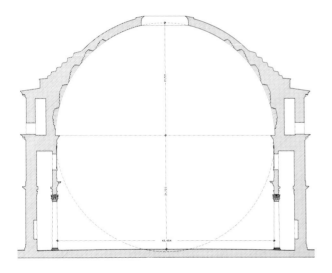

9.12 Section through the rotunda, with ideal circle overlaid. Note the convexity of the floor.

The rising curve of the floor is one of the most subtle features of the whole project. Some think it is due to settlement,[34] while Lanciani thought that it was a legacy of Agrippa's project, where it supposedly served to drain rainwater towards the edge of an open-air space.[35] But this convexity was most likely an optical refinement, one that treads that fine line between being noticed or not: it is clearly visible once you look out for it, but not nearly so prominent as that of Michelangelo's pavement on the Capitoline hill.[36] While there are holes for drainage right under the oculus, the curve may also have helped to encourage dispersion and hence evaporation; at any rate it is remarkable how quickly the floor dries off even after a thunderstorm. Nor is it inconceivable that the convexity of the floor recalled that of the earth, just as the dome recalled the heavens, thus reinforcing the numinous symbolism of the Pantheon as *templum mundi*, a celebration of the Roman world, with Rome and the emperor at its centre.[37] The same message was arguably reinforced by the provenance of the marbles decorating the space – Greece, Asia Minor, Egypt and Numidia (Tunisia) – providing tangible proof of Rome's terrestrial domain.

GEOMETRY AND STRUCTURE

It is now time to move on to less elusive issues, beginning with geometry. The interior distils into a hemispherical dome and a cylinder of the same height, which is the same as saying that the whole space is as wide as it is high, or that it contains within its embrace the figure of a sphere (fig. 0.10). Here is an idea of such portentous simplicity that it has been commented on repeatedly, coming to the attention of non-architects as early as the time of Rabelais; what is more, recent checks have shown that this relationship is quite accurate (fig. 9.12).[38] It should also be noted that a 1:1 cross-section characterizes other Roman circular halls, such as the Domitianic rotunda at Albano and the Tor de' Schiavi (cf. figs 4.7f and 4.10), while other configurations work on a similar principle, such as the rectangular chamber in the Pyramid of Gaius Cestius, where the height equals the width of the shorter sides.[39]

The geometry of a dome on a drum brings to mind one of antiquity's most celebrated tracts, Archimedes' *On the Sphere and Cylinder* (pp. 41–3). He rated the series of proofs published therein among his greatest achievements, for he had the device of a sphere and cylinder set up over his tomb.[40] One of the theorems established the equality in surface area of a hemisphere and cylinder with the same radius and height – as at the Pantheon. Thus the surface area of the Pantheon cupola matches that of the wall supporting it.

The starting-point for relating geometry to the fabric of the building was the 150 ft (100 cubits) ring

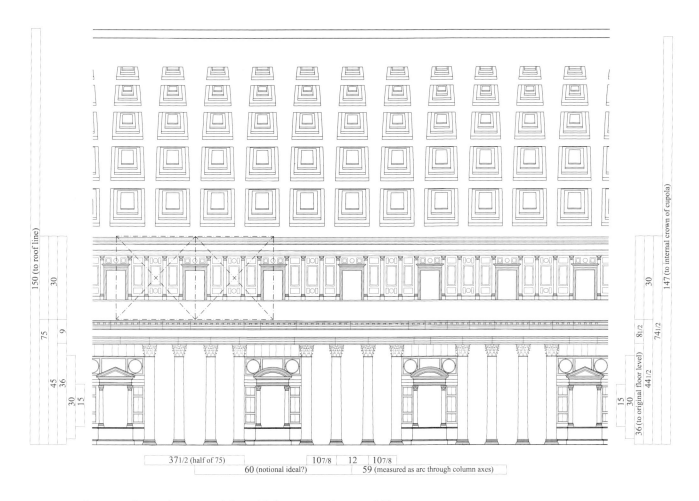

150 (to roof line)
30
75
9
45
36
30
15

371/2 (half of 75)
60 (notional ideal?)
107/8 12 107/8
59 (measured as arc through column axes)

147 (to internal crown of cupola)
30
81/2
74/2
15
30
36 (to original floor level)
44/2

9.13   Part elevation of rotunda, projected flat, with key proportions overlaid, 1:400.

defining the axes of the interior columns. As mentioned in chapter 5, the importance of this circle is
confirmed by the way a square inscribed in it doubles
up to locate the axes of the portico colonnade (fig.
9.11). Meanwhile the height of drum and transitional
block is also approximately the same, thus making a
nearly perfect square in elevation (fig. 10.16). In effect
the volumetric proportions of the whole project can
be reduced to a hemisphere, a cylinder of the same
height and a double cube. All this is incredibly apposite given the architectonic nature of the whole
project, that is to say the union of a cylindrical/
spherical mass – the rotunda – and a cubic one – the
portico. This grand simplicity also gives the lie to the
unnecessarily complex and often irrelevant tracings of
the type illustrated in the Introduction.

The layout of the lateral exedrae also relates to the
basic diagram, for the circles that contain them touch
the inscribed square. Then the clear height of the interior was made equal to the clear span of about 147 ft,
as measured to the face of the columns/pilasters. But
the diameter of the cupola itself remains nearer 150 ft,

so it is in fact not a perfect hemisphere, while a portion
of the implied sphere is cut off by the floor (fig. 9.12).[41]
In any event, the 150 ft dimension returns as the
approximate height measured to the top of the oculus,
thereby creating two sets of equal dimensions: one set
of 147 ft ones, another set of 150 ft ones. In this way
the architect sought to legitimize the lack of geometrical purity and deal with the problem that architecture has thickness, unlike the line drawings used
by geometers and mathematicians. As is only to be
expected, other modifications were made during the
course of detailed design. The main openings off
the rotunda are not, for example, completely regular;
the entrance passage is smaller than the similarly barrel-
vaulted exedrae on the diagonal axes because it faced
a tougher structural task.[42]

When it came to elaborating the interior elevation,
geometry ceased to play the driving role, as is so often
the case in Roman architecture (pp. 120–22, 126–7).[43]
Geometry had indirect effects, of course; fixing the
width of the exedrae, for example, conditioned the
rough column size, since there was a play-off between

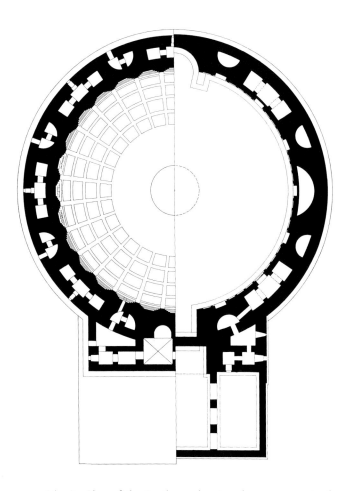

9.14 (*above*) Plan of the Pantheon showing the arrangement of structural voids: (a) at attic level; (b) at the level of the springing of the cupola, 1 : 750.

this and the intercolumnation. But the composition was defined arithmetically. The elevation was determined by the key decision to split the notional 75 ft cylinder into five parts, giving two to the attic and three to the main order (fig. 9.13). The resulting dimensions partake of a comprehensive *symmetria* based on fractions of 150 ft (e.g. 75, 30, 15, 5, 3¾ ft) and/or multiples of 5 ft (e.g. 45, 40, 20 ft).[44] The portal is emblematic of the same quest, with its 40 × 20 ft (2 : 1) opening, its architrave 2½ ft wide (an eighth of the opening) and its trabeation 8 ft tall (a fifth of the opening).

Any solution had necessarily to marry with the structure, for it was this, after all, that made the magisterial interior possible. Comfortably surpassing its nearest ancient rival, the 120 ft rotunda known as the Temple of Apollo near Baiae, the huge span demanded a complex response, and any similarity with simple concrete shells like the Temple of Mercury at the same site is purely superficial. There is nothing unusual about the relative thickness of the drum (p. 82); what is exceptional is the way the wall was treated. Together

9.15 Sections across the rotunda, with features of the construction and materials indicated: (1) foundation of concrete with aggregate of travertine; (2) concrete with aggregate of alternating layers of travertine fragments and lumps of tufa; (3) concrete with aggregate of alternating layers of tufa and fragments of tiles; (4) concrete with *caementae* of predominantly broken bricks; (5) concrete with aggregate of alternating layers of bricks and tufa; (6) concrete with *caementae* of alternating layers of light tufa and volcanic slag.

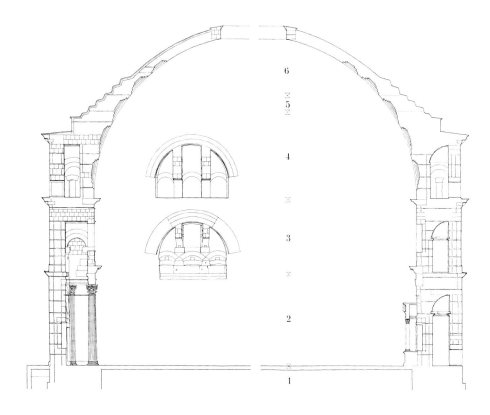

9.16 Cut away of the main structural elements of the rotunda.

with the entrance passage and the apse, the six exedrae punch into its depth, reducing the structure to eight principal areas of support. In the middle of each of these were inserted a series of half-moon chambers orientated towards the exterior, and a similar arrangement was repeated at high level in the haunches of the dome (fig. 9.14). Combined together, these structural voids save considerable amounts of weight without reducing the buttressing action of the wall, which depends primarily on the overall depth. The loads pressing on these voids were transferred via a series of solid brick relieving vaults which take up the entire thickness of the structure (figs 9.14–9.16).

The viability of the structure was further improved by the gradation of types of aggregate, ranging from travertine, brick, tufa through to pumice; that is to say from the strongest at the bottom to the lightest at the top (fig. 9.15).[45] The presence of the oculus eliminated material from the crown of the dome, a vulnerable area where compressive forces are weakest. It may be no coincidence that oculi were used in some of the very best-preserved Roman cupolas (like those of the Temple of Mercury at Baiae, the rotunda at Albano and the octagonal halls in the Domus Aurea and the Baths of Diocletian). This is not to deny that the oculus was valued for its cosmological connotations and as a source of light: illumination, meaning and structure went hand in hand. Nor should proportion be left out of the equation, since its 30 ft diameter equals both the height of the attic and the shafts of the main order, while also dividing sweetly into the 150 ft diameter of the column ring. So the oculus wonderfully symbolizes the Roman genius for synthesis (last discussed at the end of chapter 7). At one and the same time it responded to the demands of theory, beauty, content and practicality.

PRAISE AND CRITICISM

The splendour of the Pantheon has long ensured it a special place in Rome. When Ammianus Marcellinus listed the principal buildings of the city in the fourth century (cf. p. 162), he likened the embrace of the Pantheon to a 'city district'. Its impact was second only to that of the Forum of Trajan, ranking with the Colosseum and the Temple of Jupiter on the Capitoline. While other antiquities were pillaged for building materials, the Pantheon was transformed into a church, thus guaranteeing its survival. None the less to medieval eyes it was the work of the devil – a back-handed compliment if ever there was one; who else

9.17   Pantheon interior, seen from the portal.

9.18   Pantheon interior as it ought to be, according to Francesco di Giorgio.

could have raised a dome of such awesome dimensions? The *Legenda aurea* also contained the story that the cupola rested on a mountain of earth until construction was completed, one that was eagerly removed by the Roman poor, thanks to the money that had been mixed in.[46] In any event, more than twelve centuries were to pass before a comparable feat was attempted. The cupolas of first Florence Cathedral and later St Peter's were undoubtedly planned to match the span of the Pantheon while exceeding its height.[47]

With the rehabilitation of pagan culture in the Renaissance the Pantheon came to be seen as not only superior to all other antiquities, but also to anything

more recent. There is a straight line between fifteenth-century and nineteenth-century eulogies, from Flavio Biondo's declaration that the Pantheon 'surpasses all other churches of Rome' to Henry James's remark that St Peter's, by comparison, 'is absurdly vulgar'.[48] Every architectural treatise gave the Pantheon pride of place when it came to appraising the ancient legacy. Along with the Parthenon it is the ancient building that has had the greatest influence on the subsequent practice of architecture.

Paradoxically, there exists a vigorous parallel current of negative criticism. Hostility is only to be expected from the nineteenth-century champions of Greek or Gothic architecture, since attacking things Roman was an almost inevitable corollary. (For Viollet-le-Duc the Pantheon typified the 'dishonesty' of the Roman approach to design, using the orders to conceal vaulted construction.[49]) Criticism is more intriguing when it comes from quarters otherwise disposed to praise,

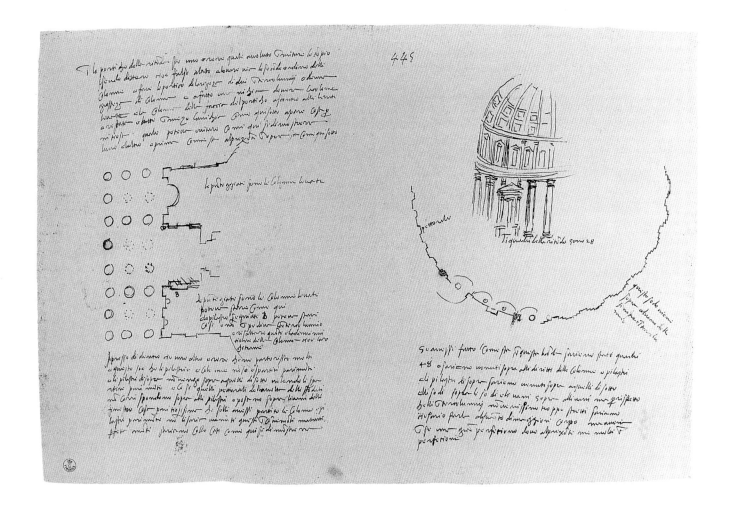

and there is plenty of it. Architects as distinguished as Antonio da Sangallo, Michelangelo, Palladio and Desgodets judged the building a flawed masterpiece. Apart from the portico (the subject of the final chapter) dissatisfaction focused on the apparent lack of unity between the constituents of the interior elevation: the main order, the attic and the dome. Critics pointed unfavourably to the lack of correspondence in scale and composition, and especially the fact that the attic pilasters fail to line up with either the columns below or the coffers above (figs 9.13 and 9.17). As seen in chapter 6, this was directly at odds with Renaissance theory, as summed up by Francesco di Giorgio:

> As a general rule to be observed without exception . . . every element should sit in a straight line over its like.[50]

Until the publication of Palladio's *Quattro libri* it was rare to illustrate the Pantheon as it actually was. Architects and artists tended, consciously or unconsciously, to correct its perceived shortcomings.[51] Francesco di Giorgio's sketch showed everything lining up as he thought it should (fig. 9.18); by reducing the number of verticals and splitting the attic into two zones, he

9.19   Annotated sketch of the Pantheon interior and part plan of the portico by Antonio da Sangallo the Younger, with accompanying written critique.

9.20   Drawing of the interior of the Pantheon by Raphael and an anonymous artist, showing the state of the building before the alterations to the attic of the 1750s, but omitting one of the principal exedrae.

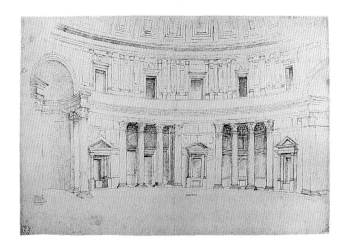

also ensured that the arch over the apse did not cut off any of the attic pilasters. Antonio da Sangallo sketched an alternative proposal, adding in a note that the lack of tectonic rigour was 'a most pernicious thing' (fig. 9.19).[52] Since the drum was subdivided by four, eight and sixteen radial divisions (fig. 9.11), he thought the cupola should follow on the same principle, with thirty-two or forty-eight coffers, not twenty-eight. Serlio followed with an adjusted elevation showing the attic pilasters aligned over the columns and pilaster below.[53] Numerous later buildings, to cite just San Francesco di Paolo in Naples, were created in this 'corrected Pantheon' mould.[54] A series of perspectives of the Pantheon interior, among them one attributed to Raphael, are often held up as faithful depictions,[55] yet even these show the attic pilasters to be taller than they really are (fig. 9.20). It seems that until recent times only Bernini is known to have taken a positive view of the attic, apparently realizing that the grouping of its pilasters into bunches of four echoes the distribution of the main columns below.[56] The floor was much admired for its great slabs of coloured marble, but this feature too was sometimes edited. A characteristic ambivalence may be seen in Pannini's eight paintings of the rotunda dating to the early eighteenth century. In most of them, including the version now in Washington (fig. 9.1), the floor is represented faithfully; but two other canvases create a radial organization in sympathy with that of the cupola.[57]

So the unqualified praise that Procopius of Caesarea heaped on Justinian's Hagia Sophia: 'proud in its inexpressible beauty; superb in its volume and harmony of proportions, having nothing in excess nor anything defective' could hardly be directed at the Pantheon.[58] On the contrary, the idea that its composition could be improved became so deeply rooted that eventually it was transformed into action. Using the need for repairs as an excuse, the attic was completely remodelled in the middle of the eighteenth century. The offending pilasters were dismantled, making room for the heavy pedimented windows and framed panels designed by Paolo Posi which conform more to Neoclassical rather than Roman tastes. The result came in for criticism; some thought that it would have been better to keep about a quarter of the ancient pilasters, that is to say just those which did align over the columns below, and it seems that Piranesi was the author of a proposal that sought to reintegrate these pilasters with a second set artfully overlaid.[59] But Posi's scheme remains, with the exception of a small portion of the ancient arrangement towards the south-west recreated by Alberto Terenzio in the 1930s (fig. 9.17).

To avoid the uncomfortable conclusion that the architect of the Pantheon was not very good at his trade, many turned to historical explanations. As Giorgio Vasari narrates, the theory went round that different parts were built at different times and/or by different architects. This information appears in an interesting passage citing Andrea Sansovino's use of the Pantheon in defence of his own work at Santo Spirito in Florence. According to Vasari, Sansovino

> made a barrel vault with richly and variously carved compartments, a much admired novelty. It is true that the work would be better if the compartments forming the divisions of the squares and circles had been in line with the columns, a thing which it would have been easy to do. Some of his old friends, however, have informed me that he defended this, saying that he had copied the Rotunda at Rome, where . . . the ribs are not in line with the columns. He added that if the builder of the Rotunda, which is the best designed and proportioned temple in existence, did not take these things into account . . . it was even less important on a smaller scale. However, many artists, and Michelangelo among them, are of the opinion that the Rotunda was built by three architects, the first carrying it up to the cornice above the columns, the second doing so from the cornice upwards . . . because this portion differs from the lower part, the vaulting not corresponding with the lines of the divisions. The third is believed to have done the beautiful portico. Thus modern masters ought not to excuse themselves like Andrea.[60]

A century or so later Desgodets elaborated further on the faults of the pilasters:

> they are so slight compared with the entablature and pedestal that one can scarcely call it an order, this badly ordered assembly of parts. They are not fit for an attic at all, which ought not to have the characteristics of an order, thus preventing it from being called an attic, unless one supposed that once there was some such (plain) one here, to which were later added the pilasters, an architrave, and a frieze.[61]

Carlo Fontana published a reconstruction of the supposed original rotunda before these and other changes (fig. 9.21).[62] According to his interpretation, the attic was just a minor aspect of a dramatic series of transformations. The existing building was held to be the outcome of three distinct phases: the first, republican one, with a much lower floor level and no columns; the second, Agrippa's reworking, featuring the set of caryatids reported by Pliny;[63] the third and definitive reconstruction.

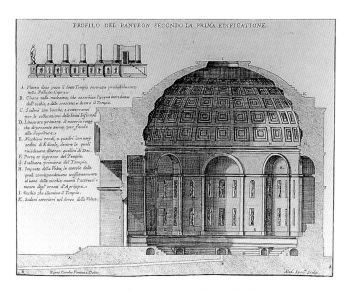

9.21 Carlo Fontana's interpretation of the Pantheon interior as the result of successive phases of construction: supposed first phase prior to the addition of the main order.

several enormous cracks running from its base to well up into the dome, which evidently appeared immediately on completion (fig. 9.21a).[65] (This cracking pattern is a common feature of Roman domes, since the concrete had negligible tensile strength to cope with 'hoop tension'. The result behaves less like a monolithic shell than a collection of masonry arches arranged as orange segments; it is the need to combat the thrust from these arches that gives rise to the characteristically thick wall construction.[66]) The magnitude of the cracking demanded other remedial measures, including the likely addition of the rows of walls linking the Pantheon with the basilica to the south. It seems they were invented to act as buttressing – certainly it is difficult to see what was the purpose of the windowless spaces in between.[67] In the interior, however, there are no signs of modifications of comparable significance.[68] In short, the idea that the present structure results from change or adaptation appears to be a mirage.

Once it was understood that the structure as a whole belonged to Hadrian, chronological explanations such as these had to be trimmed back or abandoned altogether.[64] So what, then, might explain the various shortcomings of the interior? It should not be forgotten that design is a process, and that the outcome of a project may be the result of modifications and compromise (chapters 3 and 8). But while it may be legitimate to speculate about an original or ideal solution, its credibility rests on identifying *specific causes* for its alteration. Could the cause here have a structural nature? The superstructure of the rotunda displays

TOWARDS AN ANCIENT AESTHETIC

In the last few years some scholars have started to shrug off the shackles of Renaissance theory and look at the articulation of the interior in a more positive light.[69] The apparently conflictual disposition of the main order, attic and cupola may now be seen to be an inspired solution that avoids a static, sterile effect. The dislocation between the coffering and the rest of the structure contributes to the indefinable, but none the less palpable, impression that the dome hovers over the drum as opposed to weighing it down. By their

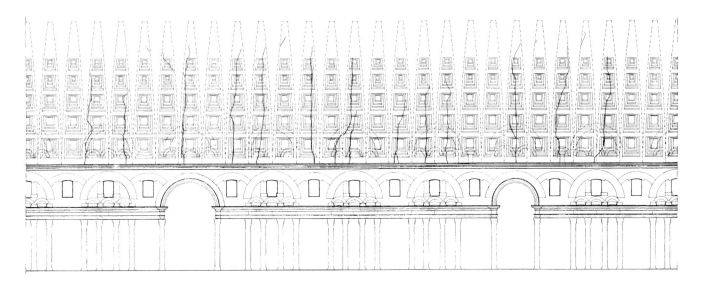

9.21a Elevation of the rotunda, projected flat, showing the principal cracks in the structure.

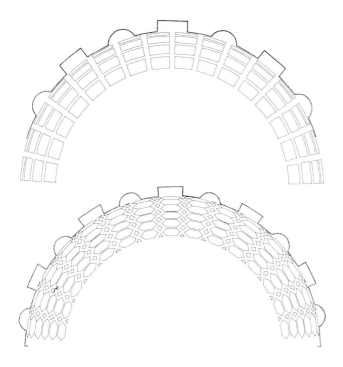

9.22   Pair of hemicycles in the Baths of Trajan (AD 105). Note the arrangement whereby the niches line up with the coffering overhead only on the orthogonal and diagonal axes. As in the Pantheon, the centres of niches can align with the centres of ribs rather than coffers.

small size and distribution the attic pilasters contribute positively to this sense of detachment, as do other details such as the use of red porphyry in both friezes so as to create strong horizontal bands separating one level from another.

When Roman architects superimposed rhythmic elements upon one another, their default mode was to place like upon like just as Francesco di Giorgio and Antonio da Sangallo advised. Yet lapses of alignment were admissible – *provided there is a substantial change of scale*. As discussed in chapter 6, small attic pilasters that do not respect the rhythm of the principal order characterize a surprising number of Hellenistic and Roman façades. Such an organization was a typical feature of numerous city gateways (figs 0.3 and 6.13), while two of the best-known examples, the Porta dei Leoni and Porta dei Borsari at Verona, boast – as at the Pantheon – three levels each working on a different compositional principle (figs 6.12 and 6.14).[70] Other manifestations of the tendency to break away from predictable vertical alignments are the column displays in the nymphaeum at Miletos and the Library of Celsus at Ephesos, where the aedicules crisscross over one another (fig. 6.9). So it seems that a minority of ancient architects – just as Andrea Sansovino was in the minority in his own time – consciously searched

to free façade design from the academic straitjacket of good Vitruvian manners.

While the foregoing examples serve to put the Pantheon attic in the general context of ancient practice, more direct parallels can be found in Rome in the years immediately before and after its construction. The exterior of the Praetorium of Hadrian's Villa has small pilasters at high level positioned with scant regard for the openings below. The coffers of the barrel vault inside the Hadrianeum fail conspicuously to line up with the scansion of the walls that support it.[71] More significant still is the design of three exedrae at Trajan's Baths, which at 100 ft in diameter are not that much smaller than the Pantheon rotunda. In each case the coffering aligns only with the niches below on the main axis and on the diagonal (fig. 9.22). Moreover, the centre of a niche sometimes aligns not with a coffer but with a rib – a relationship analogous to that occurring on the diagonal axes of the Pantheon.

APOLLODORUS – ARCHITECT OF THE PANTHEON?

This last comparison raises intriguing questions, since ancient sources name Apollodorus as the designer of Trajan's Baths, while he has also been attributed with the Pantheon by Wolf-Dieter Heilmeyer.[72] Just supposing that the relations between Hadrian and Apollodorus were not so hostile as Dio makes out (p. 24), who would be better qualified than he to take charge of the Pantheon project? As Donald Strong observes:

> the continuity of tradition in the major public buildings during the later years of Trajan's and the early years of Hadrian's reign is reasonably explained by the fact that Trajan's architect, Apollodorus, continued to act as general overseer of public works under Hadrian.[73]

Although the word 'fact' seems misplaced, the basic point is sound, especially if one drops the insistence on Apollodorus and Apollodorus only, as opposed to a like-minded group of colleagues. However Heilmeyer's attribution has generally fallen on stony ground, mainly because of the failings of his arguments in favour of an earlier date. Perhaps the undoubted stylistic affinities between mouldings in the Pantheon and Trajan's Forum betray a common bond not in the figure of the architect but in the workshops entrusted with their execution. None the less, the Apollodorus connection is worth exploring further. Excellence in engineering was certainly at the root of Apollodorus' fame, so in this respect he is a prime candidate for conceiving the

Pantheon's structure. Next there is the question of the syncopation just observed in the exedrae of his Trajan's Baths. Then there is Trajan's Column, a likely product of Apollodorus' hand, which displays a subtle form of syncopation in the helical stair: the *edge* of a step aligns with the main axis, while the *centre* of one aligns with the cross-axis (fig. 8.9). Moreover the choice of fourteen steps per turn is unusual in as much as this number, like the twenty-eight sets of coffers in the Pantheon, is a multiple of seven.[74] The difficulties of establishing the authorship of Trajan's Markets has already been discussed in chapter 1, but just supposing their designer was either Apollodorus or one of his collaborators, it is interesting that the hemicycle again displays a play upon local asymmetry and axial symmetry (fig. 1.18).

Do articulate strategies like these represent Apollodorus' signature, as it were? Or was he just the foremost exponent of a broader movement committed to animating an architecture that through its very success risked becoming heavy and simplistic? The evidence is meagre, but perhaps just enough to suggest that those in Apollodorus' 'school' or 'circle' worked in a different idiom from their fellow architects at Hadrian's Villa. Rather than articulate simple plan-forms in complex ways, as at the Pantheon, the Tivoli team impregnated plans with a geometrical sophistication that carried up into the vaulting (fig 5.15; cf. fig. 5.20a). This approach had consequences for the elevation, which usually followed the rhythms set up by the vaulting in the interest of avoiding visual confusion.[75] So it is possible to discern two antithetical schools of thought: one committed to simple plans and sophisticated elevations, the other the converse. Whether the driving forces were respectively Apollodorus and Hadrian himself must remain a matter for speculation, especially since the contrast responds in part to a sense of decorum appropriate for official public projects in Rome on the one hand, and the emperor's 'private' domain on the other. In any case the final chapter adds a further twist to this tale, and until then the Apollodorus and Hadrian question must be left up in the air.

THE LOGIC OF THE INTERIOR

Contrary to Renaissance and Neoclassical wisdom, there is nothing arbitrary about the resolution of the floor, the main order, the attic and the cupola; each contributes quite definitely to the same theme. In general terms, the aim was to model space so as to avoid a uniform radial treatment of the circular plan,

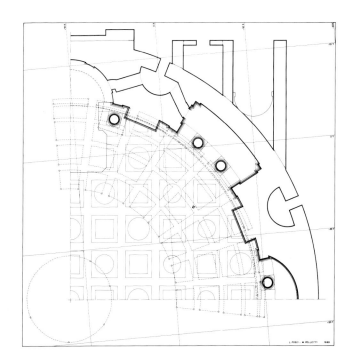

9.23   Plan of the south-west quadrant of the rotunda, showing the arrangement of the coffering as dotted lines superimposed on the floor.

9.24   The coffering of the rotunda interior, detail.

which would have drawn the eye inexorably to the centre and nowhere else. This intention also explains why the coffering profile takes up an asymmetrical form; the chosen solution ensured that the central field of each coffer is visible from all parts of the plan (figs 9.9 and 9.24).

The experience of the main space was modelled by a dominant emphasis on the main axis, a lesser one on the cross-axis, a still lesser one on the diagonal axes and virtually none elsewhere. The interaction between the sixteen- and twenty-eight-part geometries is the prime component of this strategy. It ensures that only on the cardinal axes do voids sit over voids, just as Francesco di Giorgio and Sangallo advised (figs 9.23, 9.26 and 9.28). It also ensures that the relationship on the diagonal axes, with a rib sitting over the centre of a window, is yet a considered one (figs 9.23, 9.27 and 9.29).[76] The twenty-eight-part division of the cupola was thus a formal device of prime importance, besides being a possible allusion to the lunar cycle. It goes without saying that it also produced coffering of a happy size in terms of appearance.[77] Design, after all, is the art of finding a single solution to multiple desires.

The surprising thing about the floor, from a post-Renaissance viewpoint, is the absence of a radial system akin to the cupola. In the ancient context the choice is not so strange, for, as intimated earlier, the alternation of squares and narrower bands is a commonplace of the imperial fora, while Apollodorus added roundels to alternate squares in Trajan's Forum. Such a pattern puts most emphasis on the cardinal axes, but some on the diagonal axes too – a corner-to-corner alignment, as in the bishop's move on a chess-board. Away from these axes, the junction between wall and floor is arbitrary and discordant, just as it is between the attic pilasters and the coffers (figs 9.23 and 9.25).[78] So it is that the composition of the rotunda weaves a magical dance around a syncopated, almost jazzy, rhythm and not the more obvious 4/4 march band beat associated with academic architecture, whether ancient, Renaissance or Neoclassical.

So the floor pattern, the main columns, the attic pilasters and the coffering combine to work toward the same end: they summate on the major axes and cancel each other out elsewhere. The entrance axis took priority, thanks to the full expression of the apse and the positioning of sentinel columns to either side. Next came the cross-axis with its semicircular lateral exedrae, and then the diagonal axes with their trape-zoidal exedrae. A further accent is provided by the arrangement of the two types of aedicules, those with triangular pediments and those with round-headed ones: the former stand either side of the main axis, the latter either side of the cross-axis. This sequence gen-erates a reduced emphasis for the diagonal axes since

9.26   Detail of the attic on the cross axis.

9.27   Detail of the coffering on the diagonal axis.

9.25 (facing page)   Part elevation of the rotunda, projected flat, with hierarchy of formal axes and alignments.

there is no symmetry in this respect, but rather a round-headed pediment to one side and a triangular one to the other (fig. 9.25).

To recapitulate, the composition sets up the following hierarchy:

On the main axis, emphasis is conferred by:
- The opposition of the apse, with its flanking columns, and the portal
- The expression of the vaults overhead, interrupting the attic revetment
- The alignment of void over void (coffer over vault and apse)
- The alignment of the floor pattern (with a linear run of squares)
- The symmetry of the flanking aedicules (both have triangular pediments)

On the cross-axis, emphasis is conferred by:
- The curved exedrae (with their vaults expressed behind the column screens?)
- The alignment of void over void (coffer over window over exedra)
- The alignment of the floor pattern (with a linear run of squares)
- The symmetry of the flanking aedicules (both have round pediments)

On the diagonal axes, emphasis is conferred by:
- The trapezoidal exedrae
- The alignment of vaulting ribs over the exedrae and attic windows
- The alignment of the floor pattern (from corner to corner of successive squares)

On eight minor axes, emphasis is conferred just by:
- The aedicules and the blind attic windows

Everywhere else the composition confers no emphasis at all, so the eye naturally migrates back to the privileged points of the compass.

Colour provided another source of articulation, although it has long been hard to discern due to a film of dirt which reduced everything to a muddied, murky palette. Conservation work is now reclaiming some of the polychromatic beauty of the Pantheon, but irreversible damage was caused by the 'cleaning' of the main columns with corrosive acids in the eighteenth century, which left the white- and purple-veined shafts of *pavonazetto* on the main axes virtually indistinguishable from the ochre-salmon ones of *giallo antico* on the diagonals. Worse still, the original pattern has been substantially altered by a process of selective substitution during the seventeenth- and eighteenth-century 'restorations'. For example, most of the prized red porphyry shafts of the aedicules were replaced with ones of granite.[79] It is possible, however, to reconstruct the original polychromy: the aedicules with triangular pediments flanking the main axis have fluted *giallo* shafts, while the aedicules with round-headed pediments flanking the cross-axis have unfluted red porphyry ones (figs 9.28 and 9.29). At the same time the faces of one set of pediments were picked out in mottled light-green *verde antico* to go with

the paler *giallo* shafts, the other in deep green porphyry (*serpentino*) to go with the deep red porphyry ones. Who knows how many other aspects of the decoration, including the placement of statues and fittings, participated in this subtle play of form and colour?

Thus the idea that the rotunda was designed by different architects of differing ability, or in different phases, or that something was modified in the course of construction, now looks distinctly improbable. There remains, however, a minor puzzle: the cornice of the main order collides uncomfortably into the frieze of the main portal (fig. 9.3 and 9.29). A not dissimilar condition occurs where a cornice of the boundary wall of the Forum of Augustus meets the Temple of Mars Ultor, but a neater arrangement might be expected within a single building. Was this detail the outcome of some sort of conflict?[80] In such an ambitious design it would be surprising if there was not something that proved more awkward than was first anticipated. The problem is, after all, quite insignificant compared with those that afflicted the exterior.

9.28 (*facing page top*) The interior of the Pantheon seen from high level, in line with the cross-axis.

9.29 (*facing page bottom*) The interior of the Pantheon seen from high level, in line with the diagonal axis.

X

THE ENIGMA OF THE PANTHEON:
THE EXTERIOR

THE EXTERIOR OF THE PANTHEON presents one of the most debated problems in the history of architectural history. Like the interior, it has always attracted a mixture of praise and criticism, but the balance of opinion is less favourable. In part this reflects a general perception that the blank outer skin of the rotunda is essentially a grand container for the wonders within, while the portico too is but a prelude to an experience that really begins only on stepping through the portal. When Stendhal used the Pantheon as a sort of aesthetic litmus, judging the extent of being 'ravished' by it as a measure of a person's artistic sensibility, it was the interior he had in mind.[1] Then there is the per-

sistent tradition, one that stretches virtually unbroken from the fifteenth century to the present day, that the façade has something wrong with it. Time and again, admiration has been tempered by consternation over its lack of compositional unity. Critics from a variety of backgrounds, antiquarian, artistic, architectural and archaeological, have puzzled over the stunted scale of the portico relative to that of the rotunda, and the clumsy handling of the junction between them, as manifest in the failure of major elements to align with one another (figs 10.1 and 10.3–10.5).

The shortcomings of the design might be seen as the consequence of attempting to unite two entities –

10.1 *(facing page)* Detail of the Pantheon from the south-east, showing the awkward junction between the rotunda and the portico.

10.2 Pantheon seen from the piazza in front. Note how the top corners of the transitional block appear to stick out from the top of the portico. Although the view from the same point originally differed, the ancient pavement being around 2 metres below the existing one, a similar appearance would have presented itself to an observer standing slightly farther away.

10.3 (*above left*) Pantheon seen from the north-east.

10.5 (*above right*) Detail of the junction between the rotunda and the transitional block seen from the east. Note how the entablature of the portico and transitional block collides abruptly with the rotunda.

a 'Greek' portico and a 'Roman' rotunda – that were historically and conceptually distinct. But the most persistent objections have been directed not so much against the very concept of the Pantheon as the manner of its execution. Early criticisms found indirect expression in the way the building was represented. The Pantheon was the inspiration for the temple dominating the skyline of Benozzo Gozzoli's fantasy city of Babilonia, but the painter showed a 'corrected' version, with a taller portico and the trappings of the Florentine Quattrocento.[2] A century or so later Serlio expressed a similar judgement when he made the portico somewhat higher than it really is, and again removed the second pediment (fig. 10.6a). In his text, however, he suppressed any reservations he might have had, describing the Pantheon as 'the most beautiful, the most whole, and the best considered' of all ancient buildings.[3]

Other writers too refrained from finding faults with such a hallowed building, but none the less sought to explain them away. Just as in the case of the interior, the problem was thought to lie with the chronology of its construction. Palladio interpreted the famous inscription over the portico to mean that Agrippa added it to an earlier, republican, structure. Carlo Fontana took up the same idea, showing the façade he imagined had existed earlier (fig. 10.6b).[4] Desgodets agreed with this sequence, but interpreted the smaller

10.4 Pantheon seen from the north, at high level.

inscription in the architrave to mean that the bulk of the building was Agrippa's, with the portico being a Severan addition.[5]

Another matter of dispute was the position of the supposed break in construction, the main possibilities being either the joint between the rotunda and the rest, or the joint between the portico and the rest. To some the 'transitional block' in the middle had more in common with the portico, to others it had more in common with the rotunda. One line of reasoning identified three phases of construction, the rotunda alone being built first, the transitional block second and the portico last.[6]

The disparities between the portico, transitional block and rotunda continued to overshadow the first proper archaeological investigations initiated by Georges Chédanne's discoveries (p. 180). The brick-stamps he collected not only dated to the Hadrianic period, they were also surprisingly homogenous no matter from which part of the building they came. Beltrami's and Armanini's subsequent excavations showed that the foundations under the portico and the transitional block are continuous, a fact that is equally difficult to reconcile with different phases (fig. 9.8b). So logic dictates that the entire structure was built at the same time.

Logical as it might be, this conclusion was not to everyone's liking. A single, Hadrianic, campaign was seen to be at odds not only with the lack of architectonic coherence, but also with the inscriptions naming Agrippa and the Severan emperors, and not Hadrian. For a while Beltrami continued to believe that the portico was a later addition, an idea supported by Josef Durm, who published a fanciful reconstruction of the hypothetical pre-existing front (updating, as it were, Fontana's version) (fig. 10.6c).[7] A sceptical Lanciani ventured to reconcile the evidence by proposing that the colonnade of Agrippa's Pantheon was re-used in the Hadrianic project.[8] Neither theory was particularly convincing, and thirty years later Giuseppe Cozzo, the engineer specialized in Roman construction technique, returned to the problem to show that the portico and the transitional block really were coeval. But he saw the fact that the latter butts up, at high level, against the rotunda (fig. 10.5) as proof that this came first. In his mind the history of the northern end of the building, where the present entrance is, was intimately linked with that of the southern end. He imagined that the original entrance faced south but came to be blocked up to prevent collapse – the rotunda, it is true, does have sizeable cracks in this area (p. 191). The need for a new entrance far away from the

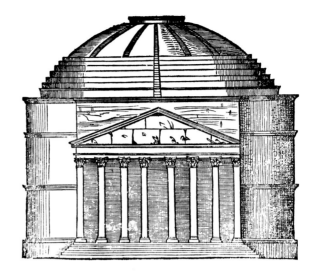

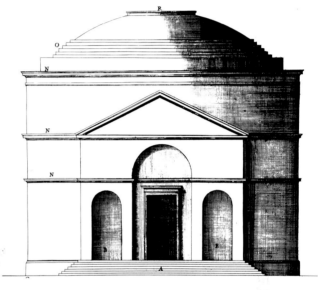

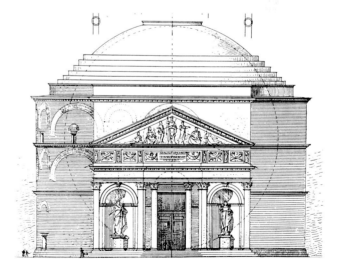

10.6   Reinterpretations of the Pantheon portico by: (a) Sebastiano Serlio (1540); (b) Carlo Fontana (1694), showing the façade of the transitional block as it may have appeared before the supposed addition of the portico; (c) Josef Durm (1905), showing a variation on (b).

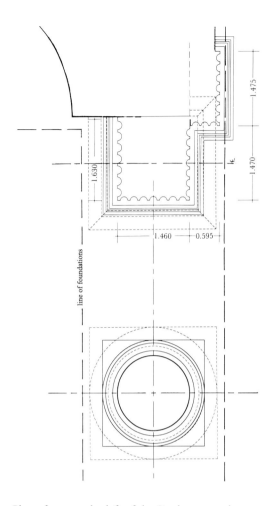

10.7 Plan of *anta* to the left of the Pantheon portal, 1:50.

10.8 *Anta* seen from the side towards the adjacent niche. Contrary to normal practice, the capital is not centred over the middle of the shaft.

damage was supposed to have given rise to the present portico. It is difficult to imagine a sillier mix of fact and fiction.[9]

Theories of this kind finally had to be abandoned in the face of an overwhelming accumulation of evidence – not just from the brickstamps and foundations, but also from literary sources and constructional details – which proved that the whole of the Pantheon really was constructed by Hadrian, beginning in either AD 117 or 118.[10]

The vexing issue that had once provoked so much controversy was now something of an embarrassment, one to be sidestepped as neatly as possible. William MacDonald questioned whether the modern mind can ever really grasp Roman architects' intentions, since what appears faulty to us might not have appeared so to them[11] – a point confirmed it would seem by the reception of the interior. It has also been argued that even if the collision of the rotunda and the portico were unsatisfactory, it could only be perceived from a few viewpoints, and hardly at all from the frontal approach which was dictated by the rectangular forum-like forecourt (fig. 10.2). Alternatively, the difficulties have been highlighted of uniting, perhaps for the first time on a monumental scale, two elements so different in character.[12] It has even been suggested that the idea belonged to Hadrian himself, so that any ineptitude could be attributed to his inexperience as an architect![13] John Ward-Perkins simply downgraded the whole issue, by putting it in a broad perspective:

> The junction of the two elements (rotunda and portico) is in detail so clumsily contrived that it is not surprising that scholars have been tempted to see in them the work of two different periods. In reality, however, the difference is one of function, not of date. The porch is the architect's concession to tradition. This was the sort of face which a religious building should present to the world. It could be – and still is today – forgotten the moment one stepped across the threshold into the cella.[14]

Where everyone agrees is that if the Pantheon was built at one time, it must be as it was intended to be. The Romans were superb builders, and the economic power of the emperors was virtually unlimited. So why would they have put up with second best? But this is not to say they were infallible, and second best certainly seems to have been accepted from time to time, witness the inconsistencies of buildings as important as the Temple of Venus Genetrix, the Baths of Caracalla, the amphitheatre at Nîmes (Introduction, pp. 11–14) and Trajan's Column. The Romans too were made of mortal flesh. Indeed, a detailed inspection of the exterior fabric of the Pantheon confirms the presence of a series of features that are sufficiently unusual or perverse as to suggest that they may not have been desirable even to the apparently uncritical Roman eye. The following is a list of the most significant:

(i) The transitional block is faced with an accessory pediment that is partially cut off by the main roof. No ancient building copies this arrangement (although it did inspire the façades of Palladio's Venetian churches, San Giorgio Maggiore and Il Redentore).

(ii) The entablature of the portico terminates abruptly at the rotunda, failing to align with the mouldings of the latter.

(iii) The portico pediment is exceptionally tall in relation to the height of the order, to judge by the proportions of other Roman buildings, especially those of the likewise octastyle temples of Mars Ultor (fig. 2.4) and Bacchus at Baalbek (fig. 8.20).

(iv) The cornice modillions of the portico pediment are smaller and are spaced at more frequent intervals than those of the upper pediment, despite the fact that both pediments are the same size.

(v) The gaps between the columns, or intercolumnations, are relatively large compared with the column diameter, to judge by the columnar rhythms of other monumental imperial buildings (Table 6.2).

(vi) The antae in the portico are oddly unbalanced (fig. 10.7). The sides facing the pronaos niches are more than half a foot wider than the rest, which, as is normal, match the column diameter. None the less the capitals are the same size on all three faces, and as a result the one over the wider side fails to align as it should with the fluting below (fig. 10.8).

(vii) The central aisle of the portico becomes narrower where it enters the transitional block (figs 9.3, 10.7), where there is a peculiar grouping of pilasters and antae (fig. 10.9). As a consequence, the barrel-vaulted ceiling here would have been lower than that of the portico.

(viii) Where the portico meets the transitional block the entablature steps out by a small amount, one neither so small as to be insignificant, nor so big as to constitute a positive feature (fig. 10.10).[15]

(ix) The brickwork of the transitional block is bonded with the rotunda only in the lower levels of the building. In the upper parts, the transitional block merely runs up against the rotunda, which, as Cozzo demonstrated, must have been built first.[16]

Taken individually, each of these points might not signify that much. Many reflect subjective judgement, and it cannot be certain whether they would have been

10.9 Capitals belonging to the *anta*-pilaster group flanking the vestibule to the entrance. Note how the capital of the pilaster (on the right) butts up against that of the *anta* (on the left), rather than the expected symmetry with respect to the diagonal.

10.10 Portico and transitional block seen from the north-west.

seen in the same light in antiquity. None the less, taken collectively, they add up to quite a mess. Is one to believe that Hadrian and his architects really intended the building to turn out as it did?

Intuition suggests that the present building is the outcome of modifying a more coherent project with virtually the same plan, except for larger columns (fig. 10.12a).[17] This produces a quite significant effect in elevation, with a taller portico rising to the level of the existing upper pediment (fig. 10.12b). This hypothetical project is much better resolved than the compromised version, with a rotunda that gracefully embraced its portico. The intended design worked better from an urban viewpoint too. Seen from ground level, a larger portico would have concealed the rotunda completely. Thus the surprise of entering the great domed interior – a quality blessed with universal approval – would have been even more dramatic

10.11   Pantheon seen from the south-west.

than it is today. There would no longer exist the unfortunate effect, from some viewpoints, that the upper corners of the transitional block appear to stick up from the existing pediment (fig. 10.2). Most important of all, a taller portico would be more akin to the vast rotunda. The present one may appear large enough at close quarters, but seen from a distance it is dwarfed by the rotunda (fig. 10.11).

As a working hypothesis it may be assumed that the compromise project came into being only once the original one was on site, thus explaining why the result is a mix of features belonging to both designs. One can review the list of shortcomings with this idea in mind, observing how each may be connected with the scaling down of the portico. In the original design:

(i) The ancillary second pediment would not have existed at all (fig. 10.12b). It is rather the vestige of the original version, besides being a feature that was created so as to tie together the ends of the middle cornice of the rotunda.

(ii) The cornice of the portico would have run into the middle cornice of the rotunda, creating a single unifying datum (fig. 10.12c).[18]

(iii) The height of the pediment seems more reasonable in relation to taller columns. The proportions of the portico as a whole thus resemble more closely those of other monuments, notably the Temple of Mars Ultor and that of Bacchus at Baalbek.

(iv) The size and spacing of the modillions belonging to the entablature could have matched those of the brackets everywhere else (fig. 10.12b).

(v) The columns would be relatively closely spaced, with intercolumnations approximating to the pycnostyle arrangement used in so many other monumental temples.[19]

(vi) The *antae* would not have had the peculiarities of the existing ones (fig. 10.7). Indeed, these can be understood as the consequence of reducing the column size. The *centres* of the new columns remained on the centres of the original ones, but the edge of the new pilasters, where they face the niches, had to butt against the brickwork, the position of which could not change. The result was the asymmetrical configuration of the *antae*, with the face towards the niches being about $\frac{5}{8}$ ft larger than the others.[20] Asymmetrical capitals were not admissible, hence the lack of alignment between them and their pilasters.

(vii) The central aisle need not have narrowed at the transitional block. Lines of evenly spaced columns and pilasters could have continued all the way up to the door, just as Antonio da Sangallo envisaged (fig. 9.19).

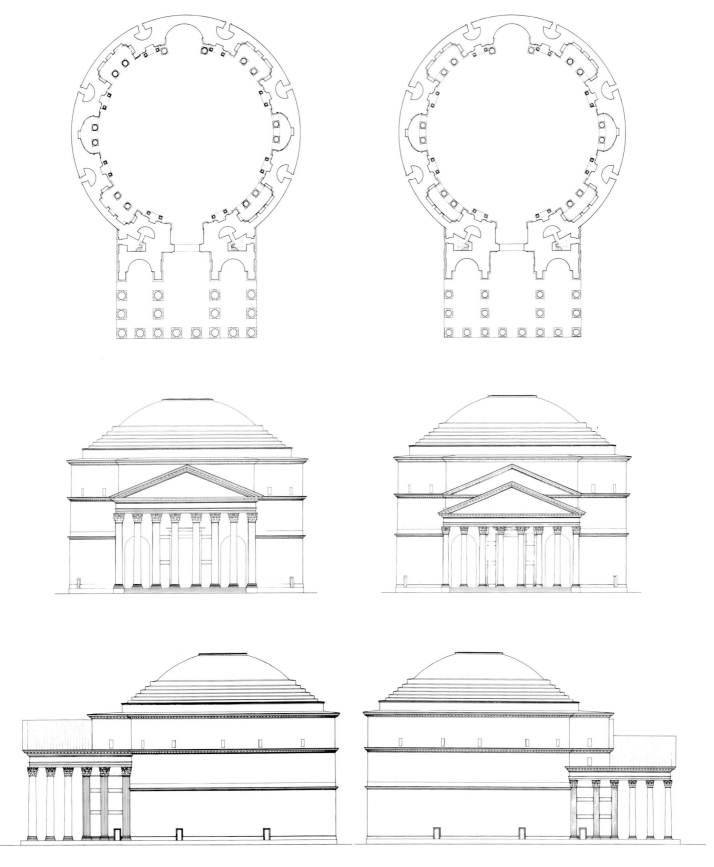

10.12 Comparison of the hypothetical original project for the Pantheon (left) and the building as executed (right): (a) plan; (b) front elevation; (c) side elevation. The hypothetical project is based on a portico with 50 ft column shafts, as opposed to the existing set of 40 ft ones.

The existing clusters came into being partly to avoid a change in pilaster width in such a prominent position. At any rate, the pilasters in the vestibule certainly look like afterthoughts. This is clear from the way the pilaster capitals are crudely butted up against those of the *antae* (fig. 10.9), rather than forming a neat 45° re-entrant corner. More significantly still, the foundations run straight, failing to take any account of the present arrangement, so that the pilasters oversail their supports (fig. 9.8b).

(viii) Owing to the wider columns, the overall width of the portico would have been about a foot greater than that of the existing building. The flanking entablature could have aligned with the entablature of the transitional block, thereby eliminating the existing projection where they meet.

(ix) There need have been no interruption in the brickwork bonding. This surely signals the moment the original project was arrested; subsequently work would have proceeded on the rotunda alone, the rest being held back pending resolution of the problem. When construction resumed the later masonry could only butt up against the former.

It is impossible to predict the original form of the upper parts of the transitional block, since what can now be seen above the level of the columns may be the result of extensive remodelling.[21] One possibility was for it to have taken the same overall shape and size as the present one. Alternatively, the portico and the transitional block could have been covered by one and the same gabled roof (fig. 10.12c). If anything this is the more natural solution, a composition repeated in ancient derivatives of the Pantheon such as the Tor de'

10.13 Rotunda of the University of Virginia at Charlottesville by Thomas Jefferson.

Schiavi (fig. 4.10), the Mausoleum of Maxentius (fig. 4.9) and a numismatic representation dating to the third century,[22] besides much later reinterpretations like those by Canova at Possagno and Thomas Jefferson at the University of Virginia (fig. 10.13).[23] The present solution may have been created only when the design was revised, the aim being to avoid the disastrous appearance of two gabled roofs stacked one above the other.[24] There was also a potential functional consideration, for in this way the staircases could continue to give access to the rotunda roof, as they could no longer have done if this part was covered by the portico roof at its revised lower level.[25]

It is a testimony to the resilience of the original conception that the compromised outcome was relatively successful. Some might say that 'the exterior is a dismal failure' and that 'the porch looks as though it had just been added on haphazardly',[26] but the Pantheon remains a wonderful experience. Whoever proposed the lowered portico, whether Hadrian or his architect, no doubt had to convince others that the result would not be too awful. The fact that the junction between the rotunda and the portico is not visible from a frontal approach must have been an important argument. The decision to create a second pediment now appears as an improvisation, one inspired, perhaps, by the Propylaea to the Athenian Acropolis, which presented a not dissimilar image from a distant vantage point.

THE PANTHEON BLUEPRINTS

Quite apart from the arguments advanced so far, a hint of proof comes from quite unexpected quarter, namely a set of architectural drawings near the Mausoleum of Augustus (fig. 10.14).[27] They include full-size part-elevations of two pediments, like the one drawn on the Trilithon at Baalbek (fig. 3.16), along with a part plan of a Corinthian capital. On the basis of the column spacing, the size of the mouldings, the slope of the raking cornice and the modillion distribution, the larger of the two pediments has with good reason been attributed to the Pantheon (fig. 10.15). The explanation for this location – about 700 metres away – lies in its proximity to the Tiber wharfs, where stone for the building was docked.[28] Flat areas for drawing, setting out and cutting up stone may have formed part of the facilities lining the river. Presumably space temporarily ran out and permission was granted to make use of the adjoining area of pavement by the mausoleum.

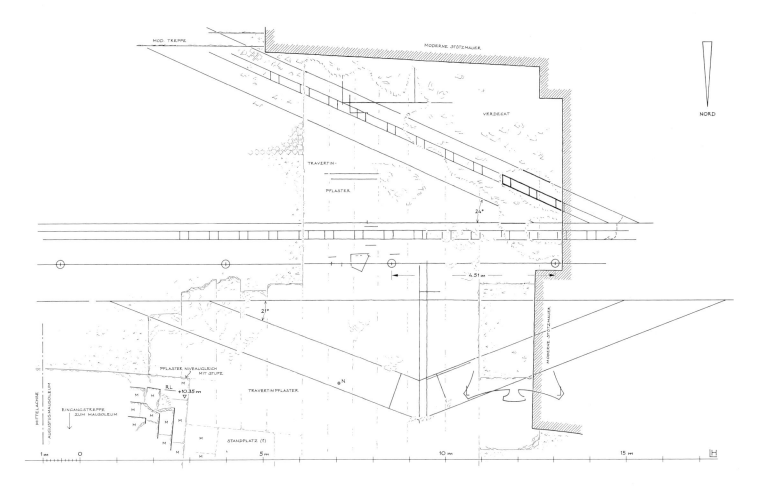

10.14 (*above*) Full-size working drawing and masons' template incised in the pavement near the entrance to the Mausoleum of Augustus, 1:10.

10.15 The west end of the Pantheon portico superimposed with the larger pediment of the drawing shown in fig. 10.14.

Curiously, the plan of the capital is too large – actually just large enough to fit over 50 ft as opposed to 40 ft shafts.[29] Is this, then, the capital for the original Pantheon? Haselberger is right to point out that it could belong to another building, provided it was more or less contemporary with the Pantheon – such activities can have been allowed to come so close to such a significant monument as the mausoleum only on exceptional and short-lived occasions. He mentions the Temple of Matidia as a possible candidate, but in point of fact the shafts of this building are no bigger than those of the *existing* Pantheon, and therefore too small.[30] This maverick capital may provide, then, a tantalizing glimpse of the Pantheon that Hadrian's architect really had in mind.

UNITY OF PROPORTIONS

Another point in favour of the original project is its proportional coherence. As noted in the previous chapter, the composition is based on the interplay between circle and square, between sphere and cube, while the dimensional starting-point was the 150 ft circle locating the rotunda colonnade. The portico locks into this scheme via a square or 1:1 relationship between the axes of its colonnade and the total height (fig. 10.16). Such wondrous geometry is shared by both the intended and the actual projects, but thereafter the proportions of the abandoned project are decidedly superior. The cornice of the portico would have aligned with the middle one running around the rotunda, that is to say a height of approximately 75 ft off the floor.[31] The apex of the pediment would have risen to a height of about 100 ft, or 4:3 the 75 ft order, 5:3 the 60 ft column height and double the 50 ft shaft height. The resulting sequence of dimensions (100, 75, 60 and 50) relate simply to the key 150 ft diameter, as is manifestly not the case with the existing equivalents (85, 59, 48 and 40 ft). One might further speculate that the desire to achieve the 100 ft peak is likely to have been the key factor determining the pitch of the pediment, one that was inherited in the actual design despite the fact that its height was relatively great for the smaller columns.[32]

THE SOURCE OF THE PROBLEM

The dimensions of the colonnade are in fact the key to the change of design. As discussed in chapter 7, 60

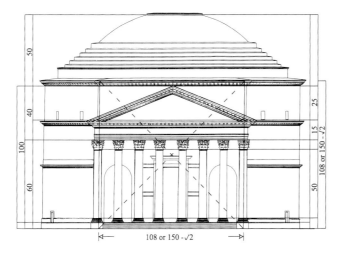

10.16   Front elevation of the Pantheon as originally intended, with the principal hypothetical proportions overlaid, 1:750.

ft columns with 50 ft shafts represent *the* optimum size for the Corinthian order, since these dimensions not only fit the 6:5 rule but are both multiples of 10 ft. The shafts are also the largest standard size, the *non plus ultra* of the sequence 20, 30, 40 and 50 ft. A handful of buildings did have still larger shafts: the Temple of Jupiter at Baalbek (fig. 8.20) and the *frigidarium* of the Basilica of Maxentius both had ones of 55 ft, while values of over 55 ft can be reconstructed for the temple on top of the Quirinal and Hadrian's extraordinary temple at Cyzicus.[33] But as far as is known the next full multiple of 10 ft was achieved only in a single case, the lone free-standing column in Alexandria known as Pompey's Pillar (although it was really erected by Diocletian).[34] In Rome itself 50 ft shafts were used in a few select projects like the temples of Mars Ultor, of Concord and of Venus and Rome.[35] Indeed, with the same number of columns spaced at virtually the same intervals, the front of the first of these is the obvious model for the Pantheon. The resemblance is confined to form and dimensions, however, since the shafts of Augustus' temple were not monoliths, but were of white marble and made up of drums.

Column size is a crucial ingredient of classical design in general, and it must have been particularly important where monolithic shafts were involved because of the time lag between placing an order and receiving it. Thanks in part to standardization, procedures in Hadrian's day were surely faster than in those of Cicero – who to avoid delays commissioned monoliths for his daughter's tomb even before he had purchased the site.[36] The 40 ft shafts of the Pantheon portico are made of two varieties of Egyptian stone: grey granite (or tonalite) from the Mons Claudianus quarries in the front row, and rose granite from the Aswan quarries in the other rows. But while shafts of 40 ft are relatively common, monolithic ones of 50 ft were used on just three occasions, each in Rome: one for the Column of Antoninus Pius, a set of eight for Trajan's Baths, and a set for Trajan's temple, of which one lies broken at the foot of Trajan's Column. It is true that the 50 ft shafts of the Temple of Bacchus at Baalbek were supposed to convey a monolithic 'feel', but they actually have one or two joints (fig. 7.34).[37] With regard to the shafts of Trajan's Forum and Baths, these were extracted in the decade before the Pantheon was started, and the same is true of the Antonine shaft, despite the fact that it was not put to use (or at least its final use) until half a century later.[38] In short, a consignment of 50 ft monoliths represented an effort that was both quite exceptional and yet one that Hadrian could reasonably have entertained.

The appeal of monoliths was in part a factor of sheer mass. As noted in the context of Trajan's Column, the Romans considered a single block of stone superior to one of the same shape made up of smaller pieces, even if they did not share the depth of the Egyptians' obsession. The more resources that were expended in construction, the greater the impact on popular opinion.[39] Sometimes there were technical advantages in monolithic construction: for structural reasons architraves cannot be divided in mid-span, and capitals must have been easier to carve as one block. However, in some imperial projects megalithic construction must be seen as part of an orchestrated show of bravado. The portal of the Pantheon is a case in point, with its threshold, 1.52 × 7.4 metres, being possibly the largest piece of *africano* known, and its cornice, 8.6 metres in length, possibly the longest piece of Pentelic known.

The combined architrave and frieze blocks of the portico weigh around 40 tons, and in the intended project the equivalent pieces would have been almost twice as heavy (since weight increases by the cube of the linear increase). Meanwhile 50 ft shafts would have approached 100 tons. Such enormous weights would have stretched the Romans' capabilities, but they are not inconceivable, witness the 75 ton capital of the Column of Marcus Aurelius and the cornice blocks between 95 and 100 tons belonging to the temple on the Quirinal and that of Jupiter at Baalbek (fig. 8.20). Had the Pantheon portico been constructed at this magnitude, it would have made a fitting match for the superhuman span of the rotunda.

If weight *per se* was not the critical factor, it is easy to imagine other obstacles. The quarrying and transportation of such shafts must have been a daunting undertaking. Both the Aswan and Mons Claudianus quarries are located in upper Egypt, farther from Rome than even Hadrian's Wall in northern England. The output of these quarries had first to be taken to the Nile, then shipped up to Alexandria on barges, then transferred onto the sea-going *naves lapidariae*. Shipwreck is the most obvious potential disaster, and a consignment lost in this way may have taken a couple of years to replace. The real nature of this risk is highlighted by the number of ancient wrecks known to have had cargoes of columns.[40] Just two 50 ft shafts weigh only a little less than the entire cargo discovered at Mahdia, one that included up to seventy sets of smaller columns.[41] Interestingly enough, underwater investigations have begun near the ancient port of Alexandria, and the first report already mentions hundreds of architectural elements, some colossal granite shafts included.[42] It is also opportune to cite some later

problems related to the supply of monolithic shafts. Michelangelo encountered enormous difficulties in trying to quarry and transport a set of twelve monolithic shafts from Carrara to Florence, a venture that required the construction of custom-made ships.[43] Then there is the late eighteenth-century courthouse in Williamsburg, Virginia, where hovers the curious feature of a cantilevered, column-less pediment. The missing columns were in fact supposed to have come from England, but the ship carrying them sank in mid-ocean.

Before the sea voyage proper, the columns had to be brought down the Nile, which was open to large vessels for only a few months, after which time it was necessary to wait for the next year's inundation. Listen to the tone of urgency in a letter written by one of Diocletian's procurators, Aurelius Isodorus:

10.17 View of the quarries of Mons Claudianus showing the remains of two broken 60 ft column shafts.

10.18 Pentelic marble quarries, Mount Pentelikon, Attica, Greece.

Since the ten state ships being sent to Syene [Aswan] for the transport down river of the columns are insufficient to carry all of them, and since their transportation is most urgent, it has become necessary that other ships should be sent to take the remaining columns on board and bring them down to Alexandria. If these ships do not receive sufficient assistance from the winds . . . they will exceed the time limit by which the columns must be brought to Alexandria, especially as the fall in the level of the water is increasing daily.[44]

Boat voyage was not the only transportational hazard. The Aswan quarries are located close by the Nile, but Mons Claudianus nestles in a range of barren mountains more than 100 km from the river.[45] Dragging 100 ton monsters over such terrain must have been fraught with dangers, including that of fracture. A precious glimpse of the logistical problems happens to concern the transportation of a single 50 ft shaft from Mons Claudianus in AD 118–119, that is to say soon after the Pantheon project was initiated. The document in question is a letter written on papyrus by the contractor in charge of the operation.[46] It called urgently for fresh supplies of food, as those in hand were running out; evidently the journey was taking longer than expected. The shaft must have been one of the first consignments to leave the quarries after Hadrian reopened them following a lull in activity.[47] Even if the connection cannot be proved, it was almost certainly destined for either the Temple of Trajan or the Pantheon.

Nor was transportation the sole obstacle. Quarrying is far from a predictable business. It is one thing to win small blocks of stone, quite another big blocks in matching sets. Pliny states that both Augustus and Tiberius commissioned a hunt for new quarries in the eastern Egyptian desert, but neither met with more than modest success.[48] The quality of Mons Claudianus must have been better than its rivals, but this is not to say that consistency was guaranteed. The geological characteristics of individual quarries varies greatly; in some (for example those at Tivoli, Carrara and Chemtou) good stone could be taken out in vast quantities at a single site. By contrast, planes of weakness in the Pentelic quarries restrict the maximum length of a block to 8 metres or so (fig. 10.18).[49] At other sites suitable outcrops may be small and scattered over a wide area, as is indeed the case for Mons Claudianus and neighbouring Mons Porphyrites. Here the number of separate workfaces, at least 130, illustrates the need to hunt around for good beds of stone.[50] Did Hadrian's engineers expect to extract more large pieces than proved to be feasible? Another danger, breakage due to

structural weakness and mishandling, was probably more common than is generally recognized, since broken pieces were usually cut up for other purposes. A few finished or partly finished abandoned columns survive in the *cipollino* quarries of Euboea (figs 6.35 and 6.38), the *bigio* quarries of Lesbos, the *giallo antico* quarries at Chemtou, the granite quarries of the Troad and in Mons Claudianus itself (fig. 10.17). This last contains a pair of broken shafts 60 ft (18 m) in length, ones that potentially would have matched Pompey's Pillar.

Severe delays could have broken Hadrian's patience. If production was slower than expected or lost at sea, it may not have been possible to complete both Trajan's Temple and the Pantheon on schedule. Assuming that enough 50 ft shafts arrived for only one of them, Hadrian was bound to favour the former. Trajan, *optimus princeps*, was revered like no emperor before him save Augustus; he was, moreover, Hadrian's relation and adopted father. Hadrian's accession was marred by controversy, and he knew that his political duty, if not survival, lay in bolstering his claim to the imperial line and respecting imperial traditions. Building a magnificent temple for his deified 'father' was necessarily a cornerstone of this policy, so this project must have taken priority over the Pantheon.

THE OPTIONS FOR COMPROMISE

Once it was decided, for whatever reason, that the Pantheon could not go ahead as planned, there were three main options available to Hadrian and his architects. The first was simply to wait until a sufficient number of 50 ft granite shafts could be assembled. The second was to build the project to the intended dimensions using shafts made up of multiple pieces, and if necessary of some other stone. The third was to keep to monolithic shafts of the desired material, but to use a smaller size. The last option may seem the least satisfactory, but this was the one chosen. Why was this?

The option of waiting simply must have appeared the most feeble. Roman emperors prided themselves on getting large buildings finished quickly (p. 14), and of all the emperors Hadrian took the most active interest in architecture. Once he reached Rome in AD 118 for the first time since his accession, he initiated a substantial building programme in the part of the Campus Martius centred around the Pantheon (fig. 9.4). All his projects here, as well as other important buildings like the Trajaneum, seem to have been dedicated soon after his return to Rome in 125 after the first of his two protracted 'world' tours.[51] If he wished to preside over an unblemished urban spectacle, an incomplete Pantheon would have presented a serious upset. The portico fiasco may have come to a head at a time when he was still away from Rome. Did his architects write to him for authorization to modify the design, or was the final decision put off until his return?

While the full significance of the Pantheon is not known, it is certain that Hadrian held court there (p. 180). He was doubtless anxious to show off an unprecedentedly ambitious interior. Its inauguration may have been scheduled to coincide with a politically charged event.[52] The specifics need not be of concern here; the point is that Hadrian must have wanted to inaugurate the Pantheon personally, no doubt on some particularly auspicious day. A key deadline may have been a critical factor determining the way the portico crisis was resolved, by ruling out the waiting game.

A PANTHEON OF MARBLES

The other discarded option was to make the shafts out of drums of another material. White marble was one alternative. Carrara (ancient Luni) was by far the nearest source of high quality white, but it seems not to have suited Hadrian's programme. This demanded a pantheon of marbles – the most beautiful and the most exclusive, and ones which contributed to imperial propaganda by virtue of their provenance, symbolizing Rome's dominion over subject lands.[53] The coloured stone used for the interior included porphyry and Mons Claudianus from Egypt; *africano* from Ionia; *giallo antico* from Numidia (Tunisia); *pavonazzetto* from Phrygia; *serpentino* (green porphyry) from the Peloponnese; *verde antico* from Thessaly (figs 5.1, 9.1, 9.28 and 9.29). As for the white marbles, all the cornices, architraves and archivolts come from the Pentelic quarries in Attica, while some of the aedicule pediments came from the island of Proconnesos in the Propontis sea. Only the capitals were made of *marmor lunense*, a choice that derives from its exceptional compactness and freedom from veins and other imperfections, factors that give it the ability to render acanthus foliage with the utmost crispness (fig. 9.2). As for the portico, the pilasters, revetment, door casing, entablature, tympanum, cornices and the majority of the bases are all Pentelic – a veritable mountain of the stuff. Again, *marmor lunense* is conspicuous by its absence, with the probable exception of the capitals.[54]

In general terms, granite was valued for its surface texture and its exceptional durability; it is also effectively stronger than marble (being less prone to imper-

fections), a factor that may have been decisive given the great load imposed by the unusually steep pediment. Another argument for not making the shafts out of drums of white marble, from Carrara or elsewhere, was the question of time. Large enough blocks were probably not routinely available from stockpiles in Rome and Ostia, thus representing a special order. Another time-consuming operation was the fluting of such shafts once they were erected, for fluting was *de rigueur* for columns made up of drums. Alternatively, Hadrian may have insisted on Egyptian granite for the portico for some specific programmatic reason; one might wonder, for example, if Aswan granite shafts had been used in the preceding Pantheon. The Egyptian quarries may have been among the few, at that time, capable of producing very large monoliths. But there was more to it than that: there seems to have been something special about Mons Claudianus. The quarry was the most inhospitable and inaccessible then known, a fact that, paradoxically, was one of the foundations of its appeal, since prestige accrued in direct proportion to the effort expended. This is the logic behind Cicero's belittling reply to the citizens of Chios, when they proudly showed him their city walls made of the attractive local *portasanta* marble: 'I would be more impressed if you had made them of travertine.'[55] His point was not that travertine – a brutish material by comparison – was more beautiful, but that it came from distant Tivoli.

Granites resembling Mons Claudianus were more conveniently available from other sites, principally Kozak Dağ near Pergamon, but no one but the emperors had the power to win, ship and distribute granite from Mons Claudianus itself. It was imported exclusively for major monuments (the traditional Italian name, *granito del foro*, derives from its use in Trajan's Forum). Very few projects outside Rome were granted this privilege.[56] Along with porphyry – the colour of which evoked imperial purple – Mons Claudianus was *the* imperial signature stone in the second century, the Romans' answer to the Pharaohs' Aswan granite.[57] The director of excavations at Mons Claudianus, David Peacock, citing the historian Paul Mantoux, has made a telling parallel with the royal manufactories set up by Louis XIV, and the Gobelins works in particular. First come the words of Mantoux:

'The legions of artists and artisans who were employed there only worked at the King's pleasure, to decorate his palaces and to add to the splendour of his court. Everything here was connected with the person of the King: from him everything came and everything returned. Such an industry was outside the necessities of economic life: it sought no profit and it knew no competition.' [Then Peacock's commentary:] If we substitute *Mons Claudianus* for the Gobelins works and emperors like Trajan or Hadrian for the king, I believe we have a vivid picture of the relationship between Rome and *Mons Claudianus*.[58]

This is the background, then, against which to understand the choice of using 40 ft shafts, as this was the only way of obtaining monoliths of granite from Mons Claudianus, as well, perhaps, as being the fastest available course of action. Once monolithic shafts were delivered to site they could be erected quickly, and there was no need to flute them. 40 ft shafts were certainly a lot more common than 50 ft ones – there are, for example, no fewer than four structures in or around the Forum Romanum that have 40 ft shafts (in order of date the Temple of Vespasian, that of Antoninus and Faustina, that of Saturn and the Column of Phocas), of which two incorporate monoliths. It is interesting to note that when the eastern flank of the Pantheon was repaired in the seventeenth century, three cracked shafts were replaced by the expedient of raiding ancient ruins for ones of the selfsame dimensions (two came from the adjacent Baths of Alexander Severus).[59] Whether or not a fresh order was necessary is an open question. Might a set of 40 footers have been available from Rome's stockpiles and marble yards? Some degree of stockpiling of standard elements no doubt existed, but there is no way of knowing if this practice applied to such costly items as the bigger column shafts (chapter 7, p. 155). Alternatively, Hadrian may have diverted a set of 40 footers from another project about to go on site.[60]

So one is left with the paradox that pagan Rome's most celebrated relic is not a model of perfection but a compromise, a making-do. This feels disconcerting, given that the second century AD was the high point of the Romans' considerable powers, a period when it might be imagined that an emperor could get anything he wanted. But there were limits even for the Romans. Does not the Pantheon itself represent the top limit of spanning capabilities? And was not this the time Rome reached her maximum expansion, when, under Hadrian, she drew back from over-extending her frontiers? The portico compromise is the architectural mirror of such retrenchment.

In recounting these ideas I am aware how many are pure conjecture: this chapter is peppered with 'might', 'may be', 'perhaps', 'could' and 'would'. None the less I cannot resist playing with further speculation. Did Hadrian put Agrippa's name on the portico not only as a gesture of respect to his forebears but also because he did not want to take the credit for a flawed outcome? If, as discussed in the preceding chapter, Apollodorus was possibly the architect of the Pantheon, might disagreement over the revised scheme have provided the real background to his famous quarrel with Hadrian? If the Pantheon was indeed the bone of contention, then clearly it would have been Apollodorus who wanted the portico taller, and Hadrian who insisted on the compromised lower arrangement for the sake of avoiding a protracted and embarrassing delay. The friction between the two men is palpable: on the one hand a stern, abrasive, high-minded professional accustomed to the extraordinary standards of the Forum of Trajan, and on the other an immensely talented dilettante who supposedly was 'deceitful yet straight forward, cruel yet merciful, and always in all things changeable'.

⋆ ⋆ ⋆

On visiting the Pantheon today we have to set our imaginations to work if we wish to re-create its original appearance, mentally reversing the alterations in its context and decoration. Gone is the colonnaded square and the steps leading to the portico, gone the gilded bronze sheathing of the cupola, gone the marble and stucco exterior facing of the rotunda, gone the bronze decoration of the pediment, gone the suspended bronze barrel vaults of the portico, gone the statues and fittings. The arguments presented here suggest that we should also mentally restore a taller portico. Thus emerges a more balanced and spectacular exterior, a match for the magnificent interior. Here is a Pantheon consonant with the thunderous climax of Roman architecture that is Hadrian's legacy.

With hindsight, the Pantheon's enduring appeal is intimately linked with the vicissitudes of its construction. The revised design produced a decidedly more unconventional and enigmatic result than the usual Roman temple. Its idiosyncratic features break down the distance between it and the surrounding urban fabric, fostering an almost picturesque charm. Had it been built as it should be, the Pantheon would have emerged a masterpiece of even surpassing grandeur, but one neither so enchanting nor so intriguing as the one we have grown to love.

10.19 and 20 (*facing page*) Reconstructions of the Pantheon in the form that it was built (*top*), and as initially intended.

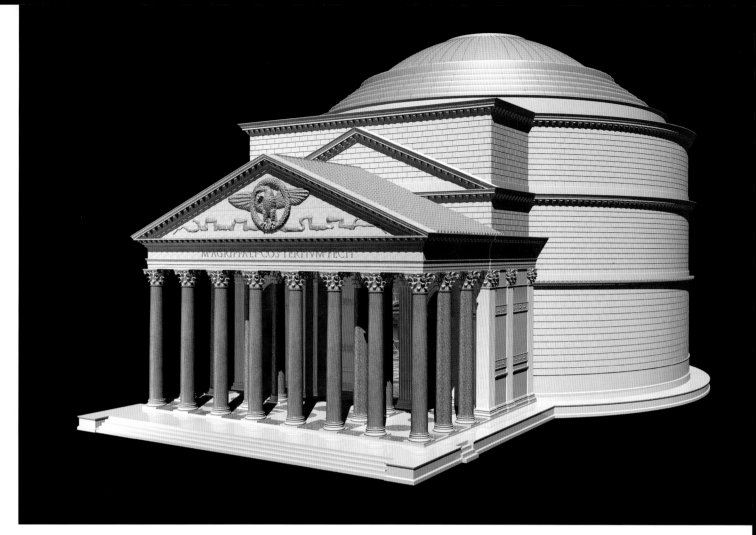

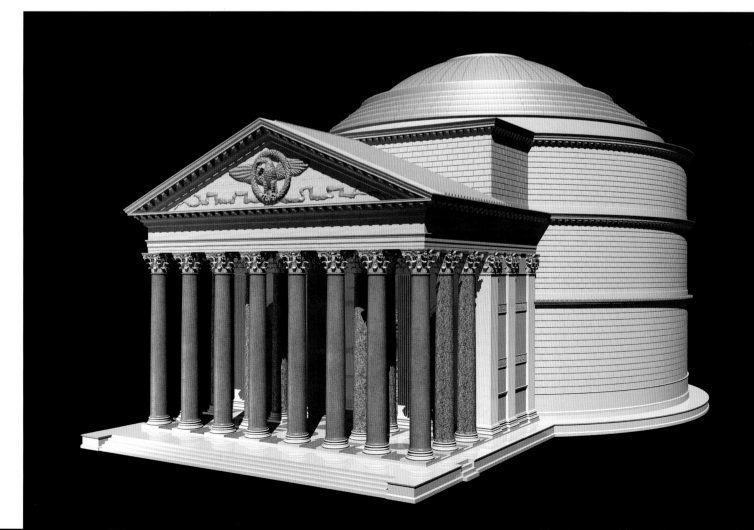

APPENDIX A

TABULATED MEASUREMENTS OF SELECTED BUILDINGS

Surveyed measurements are given in metres and feet, then the percentage difference between these and the hypothetical values on the right. Unless otherwise stated, the foot length is 296mm, although in reality there is likely to have been a spread around this mean. For distances smaller than 3 metres, percentage variations are omitted as they can appear misleadingly great. Where more than one value was available for like measurements (e.g. the widths front and back of a rectangular building), averages are shown.

| | ACTUAL VALUES | | | IDEAL VALUE |
	metres	feet	% diff.	in feet
CHAPTER III				
Maison Carrée, Nîmes, Provence				
(Amy and Gros 1979 [S.7E]): in terms of a foot of 296.7mm				
Overall length of podium	31.816	107.23		
Overall width of podium	15.000	50.56		
Width across the die of the podium	14.210	47.89	−0.22	48
Interaxial length of peristyle	25.230	85.04	+0.04	85
Interaxial width of peristyle	12.340	41.59	+0.22	41½
Height of socle (up to base of columns)	3.337	11.25	0.00	11¼
Height of column	8.966	30.22	+0.73	30
Height of column plus socle	12.303	41.47	−0.08	41½
Height of entablature	2.231	7.52		7½
Height of entablature, exc. cyma	1.993	6.72		6¾
Height of façade, exc. pediment	14.296	48.18	+0.38	48
for measurements relating to the columns see Appendix B.				
CHAPTER IV				
EXTERNALLY ORIENTATED CENTRALIZED BUILDINGS IN OR NEAR ROME LISTED IN TABLE 4.1				
Mausoleum of Augustus				
(G.C. Giglioli, *Capitolium*, VI (1930);				
von Hesberg and Panciera 1994)				
Diameter of structure, excluding facing	≃87.0			
Diameter of drum base	89.310	301.72	+0.57	300
Pyramid tomb of Gaius Cestius (author and H. Bauer)				
Width of base	29.490	99.63	−0.37	100
Length of interior chamber	5.895	19.92	−0.42	20
Width of interior chamber	4.100	13.85	−1.07	14
Height of interior chamber	4.120	13.92	−0.58	14

Tomb of L. Munatius Plancus (author; Fellmann 1957)

Diameter of drum, excluding base	29.550	99.83	−0.17	100
Diameter of interior corridor	23.800	80.40	+0.50	80
Distance between uprights around parapet	2.950	9.97	−0.34	10
Height of drum, including frieze	8.880	30.00	0.00	30
Height of entire façade	11.870	40.10	+0.25	40

Tomb of Caecilia Metella
(author and P. Jacks; Canina 1853, II, tav. XV–XVI)

Width of drum base/die of podium	29.640	100.14	+0.14	100
Diameter of internal chamber	6.640	22.43	+0.31	22½

Torrione di Micara
(author and Dott. C. Micara; McCracken 1942)

Diameter of drum base (and of podium?)	29.430	99.43	−0.57	100

Casal Rotondo
(Fellmann 1957, 73, checked by author;
Canina 1853, II, tav. XXXVI–XXXVIII)

Diameter of drum base	≃29.4			100?

Tomb of the Plautii
(M. Lolli-Ghetti; Canina 1848–[S.GB], VI, tav. CXXI–CXXII)

Diameter of string course/base	≃17.680	≃59.73	−0.45	60
Width of podium platform (and base?)	≃23.710	≃80.10	+0.12	80

Tomb of Lucilius Paetus (Pietrangeli 1940)

Diameter of drum base	35.770	120.84	+0.70	120
Height of socle	≃1.20	≃4.05		4
Height of drum wall	2.370	8.01		8
Height of complete façade	4.470	15.10	+0.67	15

Tomb at Falerii (Gotze 1939)

Diameter of drum	≃10.64	≃35.95		36
Width of (square) podium	≃11.8	≃39.86		40

Tomb at Vicovara
(G. Daltrop, 'Ein Rundgrab bei Vicovara',
RendPontAcc, XLI (1969), 121–36)

Diameter of drum	9.740	32.91	−0.27	33
Estimated diameter of base	10.450			36?

Tomb of the Servilii
(author and M. McCarthy; Bartoli 1727, tav. 30–31)

Width of square podium (including stucco)	≃11.7	≃39.53	−1.17	40
Diameter of drum	≃10.8			36?
Width of cruciform chamber	5.350	18.07	+0.41	18
Width of crossing of chamber	2.965	10.02		10

Il Torrione
(C. Pietrangeli, 'Il Torrione', *Urbe*, VI/5 (1941), 1–7)

Diameter of concrete structure	≃41.0			
Diameter of drum base	43.5–45			150?

Tomb of the Oratii & Curatii (author and C. Simonis)

Width of podium base	≃14.9	≃50.34	+0.68	50

Mausoleum of Hadrian (Pierce 1925)

Width of podium base	≃88.5			300?
Estimated diameter of drum base	≃66.5			225?

INTERNALLY ORIENTATED CENTRALIZED BUILDINGS IN OR NEAR ROME LISTED IN TABLE 4.1

Pantheon: *see* p. 220 below.

Interior diameter (to column centres)	44.520	150.41	+0.27	150

Tomb at Portus
(author and E. Archer; G. Lugli and G. Filibeck,
Il Porto di Roma Imperiale e L'Agro Portuense, Rome 1935, 93–6;
Canina 1848–[S.GB], VI, tav. 186)

Internal diameter	14.770	49.90	−0.21	50
External diameter of cella	≃18.930	≃3.95		64
External circumference	≃59.470	≃200.90	+0.46	200?
Width of niches	3.860	13.04	+0.31	13
Width of wall between niches	1.940	6.55		6½

'Temple of Romulus'
(F.P. Fiore, 'L'Impianto architettonico antico',
QuadIStA, XXVI, 1980, 63–90)

Internal diameter	14.700	49.66	0.67	50

'Pantheon', Ostia
(C.C. Briggs, 'The "Pantheon" of Ostia', *MAAR*, VIII (1930), 161–9).

Internal diameter (structure)	≃18.100	61.15		
Internal diameter (finish)	≃17.8–18.0			60?
External diameter (structure)	≃22.1	≃74.66		75?

Mausoleum of Maxentius (Rasch 1984; author)

Internal diameter	23.650	79.90	−0.12	80
Width of pillar (across corners)	9.350	31.59	−1.28	32?
Width of annular corridor	7.150	24.16	+0.64	24
Width of facets of pillar	3.550	11.99	−0.08	12
Width of window openings	3.570	12.06	+0.50	12
Width of antechamber	8.900	30.07	+0.33	30
External diameter	33.250	112.33	+0.29	112

Tor de' Schiavi (Rasch 1993; author and P. Jacks)

External diameter	19.050	64.36	+0.56	64
External circumference	59.930	202.49	+1.23	200
Internal diameter of upper chamber	13.630	46.05		
Width of niches	2.955	9.98		10
Width of wall between niches	2.230	7.53		7½
Width of apse	3.540	11.96	−0.34	12

Tor Pignattara (F.W. Diechmann, *AA*, IV, 1941, 733–48; Rasch 1998)

Internal diameter	20.180	68.18		
External diameter	27.740	93.72		

CENTRALIZED BUILDINGS IN OR NEAR ROME THAT ARE BIVALENT IN TERMS OF ORIENTATION LISTED IN TABLE 4.1

Santa Costanza (author and P. Davies: Stettler 1943)

Overall internal diameter (structure)	22.280	75.27	+0.36	75
Overall exterior diameter (structure)	≃29.0	≃97.97		
Overall exterior diameter, at base	≃29.6?			100?
External diameter of drum	≃14.4	≃48.65		50?
Internal diameter of drum	11.500	38.85		
Overall width of ambulatory	5.355	18.09	+0.51	18
Height of imposts of arches	5.340	18.04	+0.22	18
Height of column shafts	3.540	11.96	−0.34	12
Internal width of ambulatory	4.010	13.55	+0.35	13½
Column diameter	0.445	1.50		1½

for measurements relating to the columns see Appendix B.

Temple B of the Area Sacra (author and A. Claridge;
F. Coarelli, *L'Area Sacra di Largo Argentina* (Rome 1981),
19–21, tav. 1 and 20–23)

Diameter of podium floor	18.800	63.51	−0.76	64
Diameter of podium base	19.050	64.35	+0.55	64
Diameter of die of podium	17.920	60.54	+0.90	60?
Diameter of cella (structure)	9.540	32.23	+0.72	32

Tholos by the Tiber

(Rakob and Heilmeyer 1973): in terms of a Greek foot of 330.4 mm

Diameter of stylobate (floor)	16.517	49.99	−0.02	50
External diameter of cella	9.906	29.98	−0.06	30
Internal diameter (structure)	8.530	25.82		
Internal diameter (finish/base?)				25?
Width of ambulatory	3.305	10.00		10

for measurements relating to the columns see Appendix B.

Tholos at Tivoli: *see* p. 219 below.

Santo Stefano Rotondo

(Ceschi 1982; Ritz 1980): the foot value used is 294.3 mm.

Internal diameter of inner ring (finish)	≃22.1	75.09	+0.12	75
Internal diameter of middle ring (finish)	42.460	144.27	+0.18	144
External diameter of middle ring (finish)	44.060	149.71	−0.19	150
External diameter of outer ring (finish)	66.060	224.46	−0.23	225
Height of drum	≃22.0			75?
Height of columns	7.060	23.99	−0.04	24

EXTERNALLY ORIENTATED CENTRALIZED BUILDINGS NOT LISTED IN TABLE 4.1

Round tomb on the Via Appia

(W. von Sydow, 'Ein Tumulusgrab an der Via Appia Antica', *AA*, 1978, 433–42)

Internal diameter of cella	2.940	9.93		10
External diameter of cella	4.120	13.92		14
Diameter of platform	4.400	14.86	−0.90	15
Height of pilasters	3.523	11.90	−0.82	12
Height of complete façade	4.415	14.92	−0.53	15

Mausoleum at Glanum, Provence

(Rolland 1969); the foot appears to be about 292 mm long.

Width of plinth	5.875	19.81	−0.94	20?
Width of die of podium	4.385	15.02	+0.10	15
Interaxial width of quadrifrons	3.505	12.09	+0.74	12
Width of tholos platform	4.380	15.00	0.00	15
Interaxial width of tholos	2.920	10.00	0.00	10
Height of podium including socle	4.085	13.99	−0.07	14
Height of quadrifrons columns	4.105	14.06	+0.42	14
Height of tholos order	4.105	14.06	+0.42	14

for measurements relating to the columns see Appendix B.

Le Carcere Vecchie, Capua

(author, P. Chiles and C. Simonis; Pane and De Franciscis 1957, 87–109)

External diameter of drum (including stucco)	20.330	68.68		
External diameter (face of columns/entablature)	20.950	70.78		70?
Interaxial width of normal bay	2.965	10.02		10
Interaxial width of 2 axial bays	3.270	11.05	+0.45	11
Overall width of chamber (stucco)	5.880	19.86	−0.70	20

Tropaeum Traiani, Adamklissi (Florescu 1965)

External diameter	≃30.520	≃103.11		100?

Tomb of L.S. Atratinus, Gaeta (author and M. Jungken)

Estimated diameter of structure	≃34.0			
Diameter including facing/base?	≃35.0–36			120

Le Médracen, Algeria (Christofle 1951, 43)

Diameter of the drum base (plinth)	58.860	198.85	−0.57	200
Diameter of drum	≃56.5	≃190.88		
Circumference of drum	≃197.5	599.67	−0.05	600
Interval of 60 half-columns	≃2.96			10
Height of drum façade	4.430	14.97	−0.23	15

Tomb de la Chrétienne, Algeria
(Christofle 1951, esp. 14–16 and fold-out plan)
Width of plinth, 63.4 × 62.99 ≃63.2 ≃213.50
Diameter of drum 59.8 201.35 +0.67 200

INTERNALLY ORIENTATED CENTRALIZED BUILDINGS NOT LISTED IN TABLE 4.1

Mausoleum of Diocletian, Split ca. AD 400
(R. Adam, *Ruins of the Palace of the Emperor Diocletian at
Spalatro in Dalmatia* (London 1764);
G. Neimann, *Der palast Diokletians in Spalato* (Vienna 1910))
Internal diameter 13.330 44.96 −0.09 45

Temple of Mercury, Baiae
(De Angelis d'Ossat 1982 [S.GA], 148; Rakob 1988, 262)
Internal diameter (structure) ≃21.550 ≃72.80 +1.12 72

Temple of Diana, Baiae
(author and M. Jungken; De Angelis d'Ossat 1982 [S.GA], 148;
Rakob 1988, 274)
Internal diameter (structure) ≃29.620 100.07 +0.07 100?
External width (faces of octagon) ≃35.6 ≃120.27

Herodium, near Jerusalem
(D.M. Jacobson, *Zeitschrift des Deutschen Palästina-Vereins*,
C, 1984, 127–36)
Internal diameter of perimeter wall ≃59.8 202.03 200?

Santa Maria Maggiore, Nocera Superiore (Stettler 1940)
Overall internal diameter 23.600 79.73 −0.34 80
Internal diameter of drum 11.960 40.41 +1.01 40

CENTRALIZED SPACES BELONGING TO LARGER COMPLEXES

Tempio della Tosse, Tivoli
(C.F. Giuliani, *Forma Italiae*, Reg. 1, 7, Rome 1970; Rasch 1998)
Internal diameter 12.32–12.45 ca. 42

Octagonal hall, Domus Aurea, Rome
(author and D. Cavezzali; MacDonald 1982–6 [S.GA], 1, 185)
Circumscribed width (corners) 14.650 49.49 −1.02 50?
Diameter of oculus 5.980 20.10 20

Tepidarium, Baths of Diocletian, Rome
(De Angelis d'Ossat 1982 [S.GA], 234; Rasch 1984, 128)
Internal diameter 19.300 65.20

Exedras, Precinct, Baths of Trajan, Rome
(K. De Fine Licht, *Untersuchungen an der Trajansthermen zu Rom* (1),
AnalRom, supp. 7, 1974, 13, 26)
Exedra D: internal diameter 29.60 100.00 0.00 100
Exedra H: internal diameter 30.60 103.38 100?
Exedra L: internal diameter 28.80 97.30 100?

Exedra, Precinct, Baths of Diocletian, Rome (author)
Internal diameter (structure) 29.75 100.67 +0.67 100
Internal diameter (including finish?) ≃29.65 ≃100.16 +0.16 100

CHAPTER V

Teatro Marittimo, Hadrian's Villa				
(author and M. Jungken; Ueblacker 1985 [S.4C])				
Internal diameter of perimeter (structure)	≃42.70	≃144.25	+0.18	144
Internal diameter of perimeter (finish)	≃42.60	≃143.92	−0.06	144
External diameter of perimeter (structure)	≃44.200	≃149.32		≃150
Internal diameter of canal	24.500	82.77	−0.27	83
External diameter of canal	34.330	115.98	−0.02	116
Annexe, Temple of Venus, Baiae				
(Rakob 1961; Rakob 1988 [S.4c], 272); the foot appears to be about 294.2 mm long				
Diameter to springing of vaults	8.830	30.01	+0.04	30
Internal diameter of corner chambers	4.415	15.01	+0.05	15
Internal diameter of main hall	≃26.300	c89.39	−0.67	90?
Tholos at Tivoli				
(Delbrueck 1907–12 [S.GA], II, 11–22; Cresy and Taylor 1821 [S.GB], II, 66–71; author)				
Diameter of podium (floor)	14.250	48.14	+0.29	48
Axial diameter of colonnnade				
External diameter of cella	8.710	29.42		
Internal diameter of cella (structure)	7.25	24.49		
Internal diameter of cella (finish)	≃7.15	≃24.15	+0.65	24
Width of door opening	2.375	8.02		8
Width of window opening	1.170	3.95		4
Height of columns	7.100	23.98	−0.05	24
Height of podium	2.390	8.07		8
Height of entablature	1.280	4.29		
Height of complete façade	10.770	36.34	+0.94	36
Diameter of columns	0.76	2.57		$2\frac{1}{2}$

for measurements relating to the columns see Appendix B.

CHAPTER VI

Arch of Constantine				
(Cooperativa Modus; author): in terms of a foot of 295 mm				
Overall length (including mouldings)	25.44	86.24	−0.18	$86\frac{2}{5}$
Axial length (*fornices* combined)	22.06	74.78	−0.29	75
Overall width (including mouldings)	10.36	35.11	+0.31	35
Width of central *fornix*	9.48	32.13	+0.41	32
Central intercolumnation	8.59	29.12	+1.01	$28\frac{4}{5}$★
Interaxial width of flank	8.54	28.95	+0.52	$28\frac{4}{5}$★
Height of lateral passages	≃5.93	≃20.10		20
Height of central passage	≃8.51	≃28.85		$28\frac{4}{5}$★
Height of column	8.51	28.85	+0.17	$28\frac{4}{5}$★
Height to bottom of entablature	≃12.64	≃42.85		43
Height to top of entablature	≃14.84	≃50.31		50
Overall height, to top of cornice	≃20.59	≃69.80		70?

for measurements relating to the columns see Appendix B.

★ *$28\frac{4}{5}$ft corresponds to $\frac{6}{5}$ the 24ft shaft height and $\frac{1}{3}$ of $86\frac{2}{5}$; in addition $28\frac{4}{5}$ft is 50ft ÷ $\sqrt{3}$, while $86\frac{2}{5}$ft is 50ft × $\sqrt{3}$.*

CHAPTER VIII

Column of Trajan, Rome

(author, supplementing survey by Cooperative Modus)

Height of base	1.700	5.74		
Height of shaft	26.920	90.94		
Height of capital	1.160	3.92		4
Height of column proper	29.780	100.61	+0.61	100½
Hieght of helical part of stair	29.680	100.27	+0.27	100
Diameter of shaft	3.695	12.48	−0.16	12½
Typical height of drums	1.521	5.14		
Height of pedestal	5.290	17.87		
Height of pedestal, including plinth	6.160	20.81	−0.90	21?
Hieght of column, excluding plinth	28.910	97.67		
Height of top of column above ground	35.07	118.48		

Column of Marcus Aurelius, Rome

(Cooperativa Modus; Cresy and Taylor 1821 [S.GB], II, pl. 107)

Height of base	1.580	5.34		5¼
Height of shaft	26.490	89.49		
Height of capital	1.550	5.24		5¼
Height of column proper	29.620	100.27	+0.27	100
Diameter of shaft	3.780	12.77		
Typical height of drums	1.559	5.27		5¼
Height of pedestal	≈10.1	≈34.1		
Height of top of column above ground	≈39.72	≈134.2		

CHAPTERS IX AND X

Pantheon (author, with, on different occasions, A. Claridge, D. Hemsoll and M. Bruno; Pelletti 1989 [S.9B]; Desgodets 1682 [S.GB]; MacDonald 1982–6 [S.GA], I, 94–121, 203)

Interior:

Interior diameter (wall face)	43.570	147.20		
Interior diameter (column centres)	44.520	150.41	+0.27	150
External diameter (wall face)	≈55.5	≈187.50		
Diameter of oculus	8.920	30.14	+0.45	30
Width of squares of floor	2.955	9.98		10
Height of springing of dome	22.030	74.43	−0.76	75★
Diameter of main interior columns	1.105	3.73		3¾
Height of main interior shafts	8.860	29.93	−0.23	30
Original height of columns	≈10.650	35.98	−0.06	36

Portico:

Interaxial width of portico	32.03	108.21	+0.19	108
Height of transitional block (including cornice)	≈32.23	108.89	+0.82	108
Height of intermediate cornice	≈22.15	74.83	−0.22	75★
Diameter of discs in pavement	4.450	15.03	+0.22	15
Width of door opening	5.980	20.20	+1.00	20
Height of door opening	≈11.8	≈39.86		40
Diameter of columns	1.480	5.00	0.00	5
Shift height	11.800	39.87	−0.32	40
Total height of columns	14.153	47.82	−0.40	48
Typical column spacing (axial, excluding central bay)				15¼

for measurements relating to the columns see Appendix B.

APPENDIX B

MEASUREMENTS AND ANALYSIS RELATING TO THE CORINTHIAN ORDER

Interpretative note: The design of the Corinthian column in the imperial period entailed a set of proportional relationships that, when acting in concert, can be said to constitute orthodox practice. The degree of orthodoxy is assessed in Table 1 on the basis of measurements for fifty relatively well-preserved orders compiled in Table 2. After charting the principal nominal dimensions in feet, and the slenderness ratio (H : D), responses are shown to the following questions:

(i) Do the heights of column and shaft match multiples of 6 ft and 5 ft respectively (i.e. dimensions that suit the 6 : 5 rule)? If so the dimensions are underlined.

(ii) Is the ratio of column height to shaft height ⅚? A tick indicates divergence within ½ per cent, a cross indicates divergence greater than ½ per cent.

(iii) Does the column fit a recognized proportional scheme incorporating the 6 : 5 rule? If so the appropriate letter is shown corresponding to the type of scheme used.

(iv) Does the diameter of the astragal equal the diameter of the shaft (D)?

(v) Does half the diagonal width of the abacus equal D?

(vi) Does half the diagonal width of the plinth equal D?

(vii) Does the height of the kalathos equal D?

(viii) Does the cross-sectional width of the capital equal its height?

(ix) Does the diameter of the flare of the shaft equal the height of the capital?

The responses to questions (iv) to (ix) are standardized as follows:

○   agreement within plus or minus 3 cm

▼   shortfall between 3 and 6 cm

▲   excess between 3 and 6 cm

▼   shortfall greater than 6 cm

▲   excess greater than 6 cm

A consistent set of positive and accurate responses amounts to orthodox practice, the absence of such the contrary. A clear chronological pattern emerges: proportions gradually converge until they come to constitute a coordinated procedure in the Augustan period. Consolidation reaches a peak around the first half of the second century AD, but with the onset of the third century the established orthodoxy starts to weaken.

Entries are listed in chronological order, and for the sake of comparison a couple of Composite orders are included. Dimensions in Table 1 are given in Roman or Attic feet, unless otherwise stated. Dimensions in Table 2 are given in metres.

Abbreviations

D	lower diameter of body of shaft
HB	height of base
HCap	height of capital
h	height of shaft
H	height of column (including base and capital)
HTr	height of trabeation
DA	diameter of astragal at top of shaft
DWAb	diagonal width of abacus of capital
DWP	diagonal width of plinth of base
HKal	height of kalathos of capital
CWAb	cross-sectional width of capital
DF	diameter of flare of shaft
m	monolithic shaft
comp	Composite order

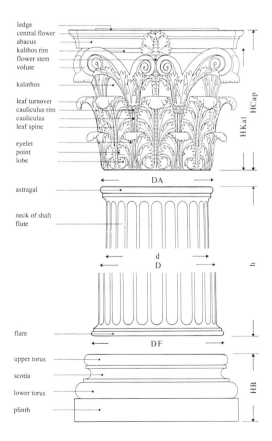

221

TABLE 1

Analysis of Greek and Roman Corinthian columns, showing their principal dimensions, the relative height of the shaft, slenderness and relationships with respect to the column diameter and the capital height.

Question:		(i)			(ii)			(iii)	(iv)	(v)	(vi)	(vii)	(viii)	(ix)
										Do these dimensions = lower diameter (D)?			Dimensions = capital ht?	
					Is H:h 6:5?	% diff.	Slender-ness		DA	½DW Ab	½DW P	H Kal	CW Ab	DF
Building	D	H	h											
Tholos, Epidauros, ca. 360 BC	2	18⅛	15¼		×	−1.22	≃9	×	▼	▼	n/a	▼	○	▲
Monument of Lysicrates, Athens, ca. 330 BC	1⅛	12	10¼		×	−2.32	10⅔	×	○	○	n/a	○	▼	▼
Philippieion, Olympia, 339 BC	1⅓	14	12		×	−3.52	10½	×	—	▼	n/a	▲	▲	—
Mausoleum, Belevi, ?280–250 BC	3⅛	28⅞	23¼		×	+3.42	9¼	×		▼	n/a	○	▼	
Bouleuterion, Miletus, ca. 180 BC	2½	≃23¾	≃20		√?	−0.39	9½	×	▼	▼	n/a	▼	○	▲
Olympieion, Athens, ca. 174 BC	6½	57	47½		√	+0.17	8¾	×	▼	▼	▼	▼	▲	▲
Apsidal building, Palestrina, late 2nd c. BC	2⅝	19½	16¼		?	+0.51	8⅛	×	—	▼	▼	▼	○?	▼
Tholos by the Tiber, Rome, ca. 100 BC	3¼	35¼	30		×	−2.40	10⅞	×		▲	n/a	▲	○	▼
	3¼	36★	30		√	−0.30	11⅛	×						
Tholos, Tivoli, ca. 100 BC	2⅝	24	20⅞		×	−4.07	9⅓	×	○	▼	n/a	▼	○	▲
House of the Faun, Pompeii, ca. 80 BC	1½	14	11⅞		×	−1.86	9¼	×	○	○	n/a	▼	○	▲
Temple of the Dioscuri, Cori, ca. 80 BC	3	30	26		×	−3.80	10	×	○	▼	n/a	▼	○	▲
Temple of Apollo Sosianus, Rome, ca. 20 BC	5	50	42?		×	−1.15	10⅛	×	—	○?	—	○?	▼	
Mausoleum, Glanum	2	14	11⅛		×	+4.23	7⅛	×	○	▲	n/a	▼	▲	▲
Temple of Mars Ultor, Rome, ded. 2 BC	6	60	50		√	+0.16	10	A	○	○	○	▼	▲	○
Sala del Colossos, Forum of Augustus, Rome	3	29	23½		×	+2.36	9⅝	×	○	○	▼	▲	○	▼
Temple of Castor, Rome, 7 BC–AD 6	5	50	42		?	−0.84	10	×	○	○	○	▼	○	▲
Temple of Augustus, Philae, Augustan	2⅜	22	18⅓		×	+0.31	9⅛	F	○	○	▼	▼	▲	
Maison Carrée, Nîmes, ca. AD 5	3	30	25		√	+0.14	10	A	○	▲	▼	○	▲	○
Temple of Aug. & Livia, Vienne	3½	33	27½		√	−0.21	9½	×	○	▼	○	▼	○	▲
Arch, Aosta	3	30	≃25		√	+0.55	10	B?	▲	○	○	▲	○?	○
Temple of Jupiter, Baalbek, 1st half 1st c. AD	7	≃67	≃56		×?	−0.71	9⅗	×	—	—	—	▼	▲	
Temple of Venus, Pompeii, 2nd quarter 1st c. AD	1½	≃14⅜	12		√	+0.28	9⅗	C	○		○	○	○	○

Forum portico, Vienne	$3\frac{1}{2}$	≃36	≃30^m	√	−0.06	$10\frac{1}{8}$	B	○			○	○	▼
Temple of Vespasian, Rome, ca. AD 90	$4\frac{3}{4}$	48	40	√	−0.09	10	B	○	▼	○	▲	○	▼
Forum of Nerva, Rome, ca. AD 97	$3\frac{5}{8}$	36	$29\frac{3}{4}$	×	+1.14	10	×	○	○		▲	▼	
Arch of Trajan, Ancona, ca. AD 110	$2\frac{5}{12}$	24	20	√	+0.08	$9\frac{7}{8}$	B		○	○	○	○	○
Trajaneum, Pergamon	$3\frac{3}{4}$	36?	30?				×	▲	○	▼	○	○	▲
Forum of Trajan, Mactar	$1\frac{2}{3}$	$16\frac{4}{5}$	14^m	√	+0.12	$10\frac{1}{8}$	A	○		○	○	○	○
Altar court, Baalbek	3	$28\frac{7}{8}$	24^m	√	+0.10	$9\frac{5}{8}$	C	○		○	○	○	○
Pantheon portico, Rome, AD 118–126	5	48	40^m	√	−0.06	$9\frac{3}{5}$	C	○	○	○	▼	▲	○
Pantheon interior (restoring full height of plinth)	$3\frac{3}{4}$	36	30^m	√	−0.17	$9\frac{2}{3}$	C	○	○	○	○	○	○
Library of Hadrian Athens, AD ca. 130?	3	$28\frac{2}{3}$	24^m	√	−0.12	$9\frac{3}{4}$	C	○	○	○	○	○	○
Gymnasium, lower order, Pergamon	$2\frac{1}{2}$	$20\frac{3}{4}$	≃$17\frac{1}{2}$	×	−1.88	$8\frac{1}{4}$	×	▼	○	n/a	▼	▲?	▲
Temple of Zeus, Euromos	$2\frac{7}{8}$	$28\frac{1}{4}$	$23\frac{1}{2}$	√	+0.05	$9\frac{2}{3}$	×		○	○	▼	○	
Nymphaeum, Scythopolis	$3\frac{1}{4}$	$29\frac{3}{8}$	$24\frac{1}{2}$^{m}	√	0.00	9	F	○	○	○	▼	▲	▲
Hadrianeum, Rome, AD 140	5	50	$41\frac{2}{3}$	√	+0.02	10	A	○	○	○	○	○	○
Theatre, Byblos	2	$19\frac{1}{5}$	16^m	√	−0.07	$9\frac{3}{5}$	E	○		○	▼	○	▲
Nymphaeum, Byblos	$2\frac{1}{4}$	$21\frac{3}{4}$	18	√	+0.17	$9\frac{3}{5}$	E	○		○		○	
Temple of Ant. & Faustina, Rome, ca. AD 155	5	48	40^m	√	+0.24	$9\frac{3}{5}$	C		○	○	○	○	○
Temple of Bacchus, interior, Baalbek	$4\frac{1}{2}$	≃$41\frac{1}{4}$	≃$34\frac{1}{2}$	√	−0.38	$9\frac{1}{4}$	×		▼	▼			▲?
Agora portico, Perge	2	19	16^m	×	−1.13	$9\frac{1}{2}$	×	○	▼	○		○	
Agora portico, Iassos	$1\frac{7}{8}$	17	14^m	×	+0.93	$9\frac{1}{4}$	×	○			▲	○	○	○
Temple of Artemis, Jerash	5	$44\frac{1}{2}$	$34\frac{3}{4}$	×	+3.74	$8\frac{7}{8}$	×				▲	○	▼	▼
Arch of Marcus Aurelius, Tripoli	2	22	$18\frac{3}{4}$	×	−2.00	$11\frac{1}{4}$	×	▲	▲		○		○
Portico of Octavia, Rome, ca. AD 200	$3\frac{3}{4}$	36	$29\frac{3}{4}$	×	+0.75	$9\frac{2}{3}$	C?		○		○	○	
Arch of Septimius Severus[comp], Rome	3	$28\frac{4}{5}$	24		+0.68	$9\frac{2}{3}$	C/D	○	○	○	○	○	○
Temple of Caelestis, Dougga	$1\frac{3}{4}$	17	14^m	×	+1.11	$9\frac{3}{4}$	×				○	○	
Arch of Constantine, Rome, AD 315	3	$28\frac{4}{5}$	24		+0.07	$9\frac{2}{3}$	C/D	○?	○		○		▲
Santa Costanza[comp], Rome, ca. AD 350	$1\frac{1}{2}$	$14\frac{1}{4}$	12^m	×	−0.57	$9\frac{1}{2}$	C?	○	○	○	○	○	▼
Mausoleum, Taksebt, ca. AD 400	$2\frac{3}{8}$	$24\frac{1}{4}$	21	×	−3.70	$10\frac{1}{2}$	×	▼	▼	n/a	▼	○?	▲

★ the second set of dimensions includes the plinths built into the stylobate.

TABLE 2

Principal measurements of Corinthian columns in metres; those in roman type have been measured directly, while those in italic are the result of indirect measurement and/or calculation. For references see the bibliography to chapter 7.

Building	D	HB	HCap	h	H	HTr	DA	½DW Ab	½DW P	H Kal	CW Ab	DF
Tholos, Epidauros Bauer 1972 [S.7A]	*0.60*	0.20	0.635	4.505	*5.34*	*1.00*	0.565	0.56	n/a	0.52	0.64	0.66
Lysicrates Monument, Athens Bauer 1977 [S.4B]	0.335	0.12	0.405	3.02	3.54	0.82	*0.33*	0.315	n/a	0.33	*0.375*	*0.38*
Philippeion, Olympia *Olympia* [II, 81]	0.425	0.20	0.42	3.93	4.55			0.38	n/a	0.34	0.47	
Mausoleum, Belevi Praschniker 1979 [S.4B]	0.925	*0.54*	1.115	6.865	*8.52*			0.86	n/a	0.91	1.07	
Bouleuterion, Miletus *Milet*, 1.2; author	0.74	0.375	0.765	5.835	6.975	*1.80*	*0.70*	*0.69*	n/a	0.67	0.77	0.82
Olympieion, Athens Penrose 1888 [S.6B]; author[1]	1.925	.875	*1.955*	14.00	16.83		1.85	1.81	1.81	1.60	2.15	2.04
Apsidal building, Palestrina Delbrueck 1912–17 [S.GA], 1	.71	.28	.71	4.80	5.79			.60	.65	.59	.73?	.76
Tholos by the Tiber, Rome including plinth; author	.96	.26★ .49	1.25	8.91	10.43 10.66	1.94	?	1.18	n/a	1.01	1.24	1.05
Tholos at Tivoli Delbrueck 1912–17, 1; Cresy 1821	.76	.19★	.74	6.17	7.10	1.28	.76	.68	n/a	*.60*	0.77	.82
House of the Faun, Pompeii Author	.445	.165	.435	3.49	4.11			.435	.435	n/a	.34	.45	*.50*
Temple of the Dioscuri, Cori von Hesberg [pers. comm.]	.895	*.30*	.90	7.77	8.97			.89	*.84*	n/a	.75	.89	1.00
Temple of Apollo Sosianus, Rome Colini 1940 [S.7E]	1.47	.68	1.65	*12.50*	14.76	3.51			1.45		1.43+	*1.62*	
Mausoleum, Glanum Rolland 1969 [S.4D]	.575	.24	.58	3.27	4.09	1.45	*.60*	.63	n/a	.50	*.67*	*.66*
Temple of Mars Ultor, Rome Author	1.77	.98	2.00	14.76	17.74	*4.06*	1.78	1.77	1.78	1.73	2.07	2.01
Sala del Colosso, Rome Author and H. Bauer	.895	.515	1.08	6.985	8.58			.90	.91	.85	.95	1.06	1.01
Temple of Castor, Rome Author	1.475	.745	1.61	12.40	14.76	3.78	1.46	1.46	1.47	1.41	1.61	1.64
Temple of Augustus, Philae Borchardt 1903 [S.7E]; author	.71	.39	.71	*5.40*	6.50	1.46	.70	.74	.65	.60	.86	
Maison Carrée, Nîmes Amy and Gros 1979 [S.7E]	.89	.49	1.015	7.46	8.965	2.23	*.90*	*.98*	.86	*.87*	1.05	1.00
Temple of Aug. & Livia, Vienne Rey 1821 [S.7E]	1.035	.58	1.05	8.24	9.87	2.045	1.02	0.98	1.055	0.90	1.075	1.19
Arch at Aosta Promis 1862 [S.7E]	.895	.475	1.055	7.40	8.93	1.665	.94	.905	.885	.94	?	1.06
Temple of Jupiter, Baalbek Wiegand 1921 [S.7E], 1	2.08	*1.04*	2.14	16.64	19.82					1.90	2.22	
Temple of Venus, Pompeii Jacobelli and Pensabene 1995–6	.44	.21	.51	3.54	4.26			.43		.44	.45	0.52	0.50
Forum portico, Vienne Rey 1821 [S.7E]	1.035	.525	1.22	8.755	10.50			1.05		1.055	1.04		1.18
Temple of Vespasian, Rome Author	1.405	.705	1.64	11.79	14.135	3.33	1.39	1.36	1.41	1.44	1.65	1.55
Forum of Nerva, Rome Cresy 1821 [S.GB]	1.075	.58	1.30	8.80	10.68			1.075	*1.06*		1.14	1.26	

Arch of Trajan, Ancona Cresy 1821 [S.GB]	.715	.355	.83	5.895	7.08	1.68		.73	.69	.71	.82	.80
Trajaneum, Pergamon Stiller 1888 [S.7E]; author[2]	1.08	.59	1.23	8.21	10.05		1.12	1.09	1.01	1.06	1.25	1.27
Forum of Trajan, Mactar Ferchiou 1975 [S. 6A]; author	.49	.27	.56	4.12	4.95		.49		.52	.495	.555	.55
Altar court, Baalbek Author (cf. Wiegand 1921 [S.7E])	.89	.45	.99	7.15	8.59		.89		.87	.86	1.02	.99
Pantheon portico, Rome Author	1.48	.735	1.64	11.79	14.16	3.33	1.49	1.48	1.46	1.43	1.71	1.63
Pantheon interior Author[3]	1.105	.54	1.26	8.87	10.67	2.57	1.08	1.10	1.10	1.11	1.26	1.25
Library of Hadrian, Athens Author	.87	.43	.98	7.08	8.49		.89	.90	.905	.87	1.01	1.00
Gymnasium, lower order, Pergamon AvP; author	.74	.26	.66	5.185	6.105	1.23	.70	.735	n/a	.56	.77	.78
Temple of Zeus, Euromos Chandler et al. 1769; author[4]	.86	.49	.89	6.92	8.30	1.69		.875	.885	.74	.92	
Nymphaeum, Scythopolis Author	.97	.495	.95	7.225	8.67	1.88?	.96	.985	1.00	.79	1.06	1.12
Hadrianeum, Rome Author	1.475	.81	1.665	12.35	14.83	3.22	1.46	1.47	1.46	1.45	1.67	1.65
Theatre, Byblos Author	.60	.33	.615	4.745	5.69		.59		.59	.54	.62	.65
Nymphaeum, Byblos Author	.67	.365	.72	5.37	6.455		.66					
Temple of Ant. & Faustina, Rome Author (cf. Cresy 1821 [S.GB])	1.48	.735	1.65	11.80	14.18	3.33		1.46	1.46	1.45	1.64	1.66
Temple of Bacchus, interior, Baalbek Wiegand 1921 [S.7E], II; author	1.32	.635	1.36	10.21	12.205			1.28	1.24			
Agora portico, Perge Author	.59	.30	.58	4.72	5.60		.58	.51	.57		.565	
Agora portico, Iassos Author	.53	.29	.58	4.12	4.99	1.18	.51		.565	.52	.59	.58
Temple of Artemis, Jerash Author[5]	1.47	1.28	1.62	10.25	13.15 12.76				1.53	1.475	1.57	1.58
Arch of Marcus Aurelius, Tripoli Aurigemma 1969 [S.7E]	.58	.325	.65	5.54	6.515	1.43	.63	.63	.61	.58		.66
Portico of Octavia, Rome Petrignani 1962; Desgodets 1682 [S.GB]	1.10	.585	1.25	8.78	10.615			1.12		1.09	1.25	
Arch of Septimius Severus, Rome Desgodets 1682; Brilliant 1967	.88	.46	1.01	7.06	8.53	2.04	.89	.895	.875	.87	1.03	.99
Temple of Caelestis, Dougga Ferchiou 1975 [S.6A]; author	.51?	.295	.58	4.10	4.975					.51	.56	
Arch of Constantine, Rome Cresy 1821 [S.GB]; Coop. Modus	.885	.455	.97	7.095	8.52			.87		.85		1.01
Santa Costanza, Rome Author	.445	.225	.535	3.52	4.20	.75	.44	.475	.43	.44	.515	.48
Mausoleum, Taksebt G. Hallier [pers. comm.]	.68	.375	.585	6.17	7.13	1.585	.64	.52		.52	.60?	.73

---

[1] I measured the capital on the ground as 1.98 metres tall, while Penrose gives 1.935 metres.

[2] Stiller reconstructs heights of about 8.21 and 10.05 metres for the shaft and column respectively, but otherwise the measurements of the base and capital suggest a set of 36 ft (about 10.65 metres) tall columns.

[3] The height of the base (and that of the whole column) is reconstructed to take account of the raised floor.

[4] The height of the capitals varies between .86 and .92 metres.

[5] The second line of measurements relates to the floor of the pronaos as opposed to the pavement running around the peristyle. The overall height of the columns is taken from C.H. Kraeling, *Gerasa: City of the Decapolis* (New Haven 1938), 134–5.

ABBREVIATIONS

Note With the exception of Vitruvius, the style of abbreviations used for ancient sources conforms to those published in *The Oxford Classical Dictionary* by N.G.L. Hammond and H.H. Scullard (Oxford 1970, ix–xxii).

General

AA.VV.	*autori varii* (various authors)
ca.	circa
cat.	catalogue of exhibition
con.	congress, conference, colloquium, symposium and other like terms in any language.
DAI	Deutsches Archäologisches Institut
diss.	dissertation/thesis
ed.	edition/editor
et al.	*et alii* (and others)
FU	Fototeca Unione (American Academy at Rome)
supp.	supplement
rev.	revised by
trans.	translation
UA	Collection of Architectural Drawings in the Uffizi Gallery, Florence

Bibliographical

AA	*Archäologischer Anzeiger*
ActaAArtH	*Acta ad archaeologiam et artium historiam pertinentia*
AH	*Architectural History*
AJA	*American Journal of Archaeology*
AM	*Mitteilungen des Deutschen Archäologischen Instituts: Athenische Abteilung*
AnalRom	*Analecta Romana Instituti Danici*
ANRW	*Aufsteig und Niedergang der römischen Welt*
AnnSAAt	*Annuario della scuola archeologica italiana di Atene*
ArchCl	*Archeologia classica*
Architectura	*Architectura: Zeitschrift für Geschichte der Baukunst*

ArchLaz	*Archeologia Laziale*
ArtBull	*Art Bulletin*
AvP	*Altertümer von Pergamon*
BABesch	*Bulletin antieke beschaving*
BAR	*British Archaeological Reports International Series*
BCH	*Bulletin de correspondance hellénique*
BCTH	*Bulletin archéologique du Comité des travaux historiques et scientifiques*
BComm	*Bullettino della Commissione archeologica communale di Roma*
BdA	*Bolletino di archeologia*
BEFAR	*Bibliothèque des Écoles françaises d'Athènes et de Rome*
BollCSStA	*Bolletino del Centro di studi per la storia dell'architettura*
Bolld'A	*Bolletino d'arte*
BSA	*Annual of the British School at Athens*
CIL	*Corpus Inscriptionum Latinarum*
CollEFR	*Collection de l'École française de Rome*
CRAI	*Académie des inscriptions et belles-lettres: Comptes rendues*
DArch	*Dialoghi di archeologia*
DiskAB	*Diskussionen zur archäologischen Bauforschung*
DoA	*The Dictionary of Art*, ed. Jane Turner, 34 vols (London 1996)
DOP	*Dumbarton Oaks Papers*
DossA	*Histoire et archéologie: Les dossiers*
EAA	*Enciclopedia dell'arte antica*
FiE	*Forschungen in Ephesos*
GRBS	*Greek, Rome and Byzantine Studies*
IstMitt	*Istanbuler Mitteilungen (Deutschen Archäologischen Instituts)*
JAT	*Journal of Ancient Topography*
JdI	*Jahrbuch des Deutschen Archäologischen Instituts*
JEA	*Journal of Egyptian Archaeology*
JHS	*Journal of Hellenic Studies*
JRA	*Journal of Roman Archaeology*
JRS	*Journal of Roman Studies*
JSAH	*Journal of the Society of Architectural Historians*

JWCI	Journal of the Warburg and Courtauld Institutes
LSA	Lavori e studi di archeologia
MAAR	Memoires of the American Academy in Rome
MededRom	Mededeelingen van het Nederlands Historisch Instituut te Rome
MEFRA	Mélanges de l'École française de Rome, Antiquité
MemAccLinc	Atti della Accademia nazionale dei Lincei: Memorie
MemNap	Memorie dell'Accademia di archeologia, lettere e belle arti di Napoli
MemPontAcc	Atti della Pontificia accademia romana di archeologia: Memorie
NSc	Atti della Accademia nazionale dei Lincei: Notizie degli scavi di antichità
ÖJh	Jahreshefte des Österreichischen Archäologischen Institutes in Wien
OpusRom	Opuscula Romana: Annual of the Swedish Institute in Rome
PBSR	Papers of the British School at Rome
PEQ	Palestine Exploration Quarterly
ProcBA	Proceedings of the British Academy
QuadIStA	Quaderni dell'Istituto di storia dell'architettura
QuadALibia	Quaderni di archeologia della Libia
RA	Revue archéologique
RE	Paulys Real-Encyclopädie der klassischen Altertumswissenschaft
RendAccLinc	Atti della Accademia nazionale dei Lincei: Rendiconti
RendPontAcc	Atti della Pontificia accademia romana di archeologia: Rendiconti
RIA	Rivista dell'Istituto nazionale d'archeologia e storia dell'arte
RivdA	Rivista di archeologia
RM	Mitteilungen des Deutschen Archäologischen Instituts: Römische Abteilung

NOTES

PREFACE

1 Kidson 1996 [S.5A], 343.

INTRODUCTION

1 See various contributions in *New Literary History*, XVII (1986); D. Carrier, *Principles of Art History Writing* (University Park, Penn., 1994), esp. 3–7; A. Payne, 'Rudolf Wittkower and Architectural Principles in the Age of Modernism', *JSAH*, LIII (1994), 322–42; M. Golden and P. Toohey, ed., *Inventing Ancient Culture: Historicism, Periodization, and the Ancient World* (London 1997), esp. 3–5. In the broader context the critique of Karl Popper remains influential, including his book *The Logic of Scientific Discovery* (1st German ed. 1934; English trans. 1959).

2 S. Giedion, *Space, Time and Architecture* (Cambridge, Mass., 1941), 5.

3 Green 1990 [S.GC], 361.

4 When drawing antiquities Francesco di Giorgio admitted that he would where necessary also use guesswork (*fantasia*); see the Saluzziano codex, f. 82v (C. Maltese, *Francesco di Giorgio Martini: Trattati* (Milan 1967), I, 282, Tav. 152).

5 S. Borsi, *Giuliano da Sangallo: I disegni di architettura e dell' antico* (Rome 1985), 206–8. Cf. Buddensieg 1971 [S.9B], 264–5; Buddensieg, 'Criticism of Ancient Architecture in the Sixteenth and Seventeenth Centuries', *Classical Influences on European Culture AD 1500–1700*, con. Cambridge 1974, ed. R.R. Bolgar (Cambridge 1976), 335–48. B.L. Brown and D.E.E. Kleiner, 'Giuliano da Sangallo's Drawings after Ciriaco d'Ancona: Transformations of Greek and Roman Antiquities in Athens', *JSAH*, XLII (1983), 334.

6 Wittkower 1978 [S.5A]; Borsi 1967 [S.5A]; cf. Payne 1994 (see n. 1).

7 Wittkower 1978 [S.5A], 116. Note for example the use of the irrational ratio √2 in Bramante's Tempietto (Wilson Jones 1990 [S.5A]).

8 Wittkower 1971 [S.5A], 150–53; Wittkower 1978 [S.5A], 117. See also A. Pérez-Gómez, *Architecture and the Crisis of Modern Science* (Cambridge, Mass., 1983).

9 J. Hambidge, *Dynamic Symmetry: The Greek Vase* (New Haven 1920), 142; Hambidge, *The Parthenon and other Greek Temples: Their Dynamic Symmetry* (New Haven 1924). Cf. L.D. Caskey, *Geometry of Greek Vases: Attic Vases in the Museum of Fine Arts Analysed according to the Principles of Proportion Discovered by Jay Hambidge* (Boston 1922).

10 For bibliography see S.5C.

11 Dehio 1895 [S.5A].

12 Brunés 1967. For related approaches, see Lund 1920; Moessel 1926; Wolff 1932; Lesser 1957; Kottmann 1992 and further works cited in S.5A.

13 T.A. Cook, 'A New Disease in Architecture', *The Nineteenth Century*, 1922, 91, 521 ff.

14 Dinsmoor 1975 [S.GC], 161; Dinsmoor, 'How the Parthenon was Planned', *Australian Architecture*, XLVII/6 (1923), 177–80 and XLVIII/1 (1923), 241–4; Hautecoeur 1937 [S.5A], 271.

15 R.W. Gardner, *The Parthenon: its Science of Forms* (New York 1925, reprinted Washington, DC, 1973).

16 *Parthenonkongress*, ed. E. Berger (Mainz 1984).

17 U. Eco, *Il pendolo di Foucault* (Milan 1988), section 48.

18 F. Blondel, *Cours d'architecture* (rev. ed. Paris 1698), V, 4, 8 (p. 744 ff.) and V, 4, 9 (p. 748 ff.) on the Pantheon, of which he writes: 'j'ay trouvé . . . qu'un petit nombre de lignes tirées à propos determinent par leur rencontre tous les grandeurs qui entrent en la composition de cet Ouvrage.'

19 Alberti, VI, 2: 'Many maintain that the forms of buildings are various and changeable according to the taste of each individual and not dependent on any rules of art. This is a common error of ignorance, to maintain that what it does not know does not exist.'

20 A. Blunt, *Artistic Theory in Italy 1450–1660* (Oxford 1962, 1st ed. 1940), 74–5.

21 A. Nesselrath 1984, 'Raffaello e lo studio dell'antico nel Rinascimento', *Raffaello architetto*, ed. C.L. Frommel, S. Ray and M. Tafuri (Rome 1984), 398–9. Cf. H. Günther, 'The Renaissance of Architecture', AA.VV. 1994 [S.3A], 269 ff.; Günther 1988 [S.GA]; F. Hansen, 'Representing the Past: The Concept and Study of Antique Architecture in 15th-century Italy', *AnalRom*, XXIII (1996), 87 ff.

22 H. Burns, 'Baldassarre Peruzzi and Sixteenth Century Architectural Theory', AA.VV. 1988 [S.2B], 211 and 214–18; Wilson Jones 1988 [S.5A], 70; H. Günther, 'Serlio e gli ordini architettonici', *Sebastiano Serlio*, ed. C. Thoenes (Milan 1989), 165–6.

23 Blunt 1962 (see n. 20), esp. 144–6.

24 Desgodets 1682 [S.GB]; W. Herrmann, 'Antoine Desgodets and the Académie royale d'architecture', *ArtBull*, XL (1958), 23–53.

25 But paradoxically Perrault still continued to uphold the law of proportional rules for his own treatise on the orders; see Perrault 1993 [S.6A]; W. Herrmann, *The Theory of Claude Perrault* (London 1973).

26 W. Szambien, *J.-N.-L. Durand: Il metodo e la norma nell'architettura* (Venice 1986, trans. of 1984 French ed.), 83–9.

27 For other comparable schemes, see De Fine Licht 1966 [S.9A], fig. 201, and Brunés 1967 [S.5A], p. 38 ff., fig. 241, 244.

28 Note the mutating proportions of Doric capitals (J.J. Coulton, 'Doric Capitals: A Proportional Analysis', *BSA*, LXXIV (1979), 81–153, or the increase in the relative height of the leaves of the Corinthian capital (Wilson Jones 1991 [S.7C], 142 ff.).

29 Gros 1976 [S.7B], 197; cf. C. Chipiez, 'Le système modulaire et les proportions dans l'architecture grecque', *RA*, XIX (1892), 1–44.

30 MacDonald 1982–6 [S.GA], II, 183.

31 Summerson 1980 [S.6A], 8.

32 H. Günther, 'Die Rekonstruktion des antiken römischen Fussmaßes in der Renaissance', *Kunstgeschichtliche Gesellschaft zu Berlin: Sitzungsberichte*, XXX (1981–2), 8–12; Wilson Jones 1988 [S.5A], 64–5.

33 W.B. Dinsmoor, 'The Sculptured Frieze from Bassae (a Revised Sequence)', *AJA*, LX (1956), 401–52. For later revisions, see F.A. Cooper in B.C. Madigan, *The Temple of Apollo Bassitas, II: The Sculpture* (Athens and Princeton 1993), 38 ff.; I. Jenkins and D. Williams, 'The Sculptured Frieze from the Temple of Apollo Epikourios at Bassae', *Sculpture from Arcadia and Laconia*, ed. O. Palagia and W. Coulson (Oxford 1993), 57–77.

34 H. Bankel, 'Scamilli impares at a Ionic 4th century BC Building at Cnidos', AA.VV. 1999 [S.6B], 127–38.

35 Claridge 1983 [S.3B]. For comparable drawings, see Rockwell 1987–8 [S.3B] and Márquez 1996 [S.3B].

36 Alberti VI, 12 (trans. Rykwert *et. al.*, 188) [S.GA].

37 This method seems to have been inspired in part by that used by Francesco di Giorgio (Magliabechiano codex, f.34v; Saluzziano codex, f.15v). Serlio was also among a number of his contemporaries who advocated rules for column design that mirror ancient practice more closely than current opinion suggests; see Wilson Jones 1989 [S.7A], 48, 65, n. 79; Wilson Jones 1991 [S.7C], 133.

38 Wilson Jones 1988 [S.5A], 69–70. For Peruzzi's drawings after the antique see H. Wurm, *Baldassarre Peruzzi: Architekturzeichnungen* (Tübingen 1984).

39 Plato, *Philebus*, 51c.

40 Quoted in Thulin 1913 (see chapter 4, n. 41), 131, 3–8.

41 As predicted by one of the earliest theorems known to the Greeks (Heath 1921 [S.2B], I, 133–4); cf. Haselberger 1980 [S.3B], 97.

42 However, monoliths of the Numidian marble known as *giallo antico* are commonly fluted (e.g. those of the Pantheon interior).

43 A.W.N. Pugin, *Some Remarks* (London 1850), 11–12.

44 K. Grewe, *Licht am Ende des Tunnels. Planung und Trassierung im antiken Tunnelbau* (Mainz 1998), 135–9.

45 DeLaine 1997 [S.GA], 64–5.

46 Wilson Jones 1993 [S.5B], 434.

47 Wilson Jones 1993 [S.5B], 408.

48 I cannot agree with Amici (1991 [S.7E], 85), who regards this solution as a deliberate transitional device.

49 Suetonius, *Titus*, 7.3; Cassius Dio 66.25.1.

50 *CIL*, 6.1374.

51 Cozza 1982 [S.7E], 7 and 29.

52 DeLaine 1997 [S.GA], 15–16 and 189–90. Cf. Gros 1976 [S.7B], 65–7, and H. Bloch, 'The Serapeum of Ostia and the Brick-Stamps of 123 AD', *AJA*, LXVIII (1959), 225–40 for a construction period little exceeding a year.

CHAPTER I

1 Coulton 1988 [S.GC], 15–29; K. Jeppesen, *Paradeigmata* (Aarhus 1958).

2 The most substantial extant Roman contract, which survives because it was – most unusually – inscribed on three slabs of marble, concerns the building of a wall around the sanctuary of Serapis at Pozzuoli; see T. Wiegand, 'Die puteolanische Bauinschrift', *Jahrbuch für klassische Philologie*, supp. 20 (1894), 660–778; Pearse 1974 [S.GA], 13. For the general background,

see S.D. Martin, *Building Contracts in Classical Roman Law*, diss. Ann Arbor 1982; Anderson 1997 [S.GA], 68–75.

3 For general studies of Roman architects, see S.I, with most recently Donderer 1996 and Anderson 1997, 3–67. On the difficulty of being certain when names belong to architects (as opposed to contractors, for example), see Eck 1997.

4 Thielscher 1961 [S.2A], esp. cols. 420–25; Ruffel and Soubiran 1962 [S.2A], 133–43; G. Tosi, *L'arco dei Gavi* (Rome 1983), 80, 85; Donderer 1996, 270–71; Anderson 1997, 40–41.

5 N. Purcell, 'Atrium Libertatis', *PBSR*, LXI (1993), 125–55; Anderson (1997, 27–8), however, still accepts the traditional attribution.

6 Cicero, *De Or.*, 1,62; Pliny, *HN*, XXXVI,35; Vitruvius III,2,5. Cf. Gros 1973; Gros 1976; Müller 1989, 158–9; Anderson 1997, 17–19.

7 F. Zevi, 'L'identificazione del tempio di Marte in Circo e altre osservazioni', *Mélanges offerts à J. Heurgon: CollEFR*, XXVII (1976), 1047–64. For a capital possibly belonging to the Temple of Neptune, see F. Bianchi and P.L. Tucci, 'Alcuni esempi di riuso dell'antico nell'area del circo Flaminio', *MEFRA*, LXXXVIII (1996), 27–82, esp. 58–62.

8 Gros 1973, 151 ff.; F. Coarelli, *Il Foro Boario* (Rome 1988), 100 ff.; A. Ziolkowski, 'Mummius' Temple of Hercules Victor and the Round Temple on the Tiber', *Phoenix*, XLII (1988), 327.

9 An attribution to Hermodoros arguably conflicts with the identification as the Temple of Hercules Victor (Ziolkowski 1988, see preceding note) which Mummius financed from the spoils of Corinth. Is it likely that Mummius would have used the same architect as did his two arch-rivals, the conquerors of Macedonia (Q. Caecilius Metellus Macedonicus) and of Lusitania (D. Brutus Junius Callaicus), respectively the patrons of Hermodoros' temples of Jupiter and Mars?

10 MacDonald 1982–6, I, 127–9; Müller 1989, 193–200 and 202–4; Anderson 1997, 55–9.

11 For studies of Apollodoros, see Paribeni 1943; Martin 1959; Leon 1961; Gullini 1968; Heilmeyer 1975; MacDonald, 1982–6, I, 129–36; Müller 1989, 134–43; Anderson 1997, 59–64; Scagliarini Corlàita 1993. On the term *praefectus fabrum*, see Anderson 1997, 29–30.

12 Leon 1961; MacDonald 1982–6, I, 129, n. 25, 132, n. 32, 134, n. 40.

13 Heilmeyer 1975; Rasch 1991 [S.4C], 365.

14 MacDonald 1982–6, I, 134. Cf. Leon 1961, 72 ff.; Gullini 1968; Lepper and Frere 1988 [S.8B], 191.

15 R. Meneghini, AA.VV. 1995 [S.8A], I, 143.

16 Giuliani 1987 [S.8A], who supposes the markets were initiated before the forum; but see now L. Lancaster, 'The Date of Trajan's Markets: An Assessment in the Light of some Unpublished Brickstamps', *PBSR*, LXIII (1995), 25–44.

17 Scagliarini Corlàita 1993.

18 Blyth 1992.

19 Procopius of Caesarea, *Aed.*, 4.6.12–13; Lepper and Frere 1988 [S.8B], 190. Cf. 'Apollodoros', *RE*.

20 Dio Cassius, 69.4.

21 Brown 1964 [S.9C], 57.

22 Paribeni 1943, 24; F. Millar, *A Study of Cassius Dio* (Oxford 1964), 60 ff.; Strong 1953 [S.9C], 138; Ridley 1989. On the dubious credibility of Hadrian's treatment of Favorinus, see Birley 1997 [S.9C], 194–5.

23 *SHA. Hadr.*, 19.8–13.

24 Promis 1873, 177; R. MacMullen, 'Roman Imperial Building in the Provinces', *Harvard Studies in Classical Philology*, LXIV (1959), 227, n. 38; Rivoira 1925 [S.GA], 118 ff.; Brown 1964 [S.9C]; Stierlin 1984 [S.9C], 73 ff.

25 *SHA. Hadr.*, 14.8.

26 *SHA. Hadr.*, 19.2–13.

27 Filarete, II, f.7 (J.R. Spencer, *Filarete's Treatise on Architecture*, New Haven 1965, 15–16).

28 MacDonald 1982–6 [S.GA], I, 136.

29 For a reconstruction of the Hadrianic project, see A. Cassatella and S. Panella, 'Restituzione dell'impianto adrianeo del Tempio di Venere e Roma', *ArchLaz*, X/2 (1990), 52–4. On questions of programme see A. Barattolo, 'The Temple of Hadrian-Zeus at Cyzicus', *IstMitt*, XLV (1995), esp. 100 ff.

30 Yourcenar 1988 [S.9C], 157. For further reflections, see A. Barattolo, 'Il Tempio di Venere e Roma: Un tempio greco nell'urbe', *RM*, LXXXV (1978), 387 ff.; and M. Manieri Elia, 'Note sul significato del tempio di Venere e Roma', *Saggi in onore di G. De Angelis d'Ossat* (Rome 1987), 47–54.

31 Coulton 1988 [S.GC], 28–9.

32 Pollitt 1983 [S.GA], 31–3; Green 1990 [S.GC], 338, 566–7.

33 Salies ed. 1994 [S.7F].

34 Schrijvers 1989 [S.2A], 16.

35 *Att.*, xiii, 35; the emphasis is mine (Atticus was of Italian descent).

36 Vitruvius VII, Pref., 15; Rawson 1975, Thompson 1987; Anderson 1997, 19–26; Ward-Perkins 1981 [S.GA], 310.

37 Pliny, *Ep.*, X, 39–40; cf. X, 37 and X, 51–2 with regard to a proposed canal project.

38 N. Purcell, 'The *Apparitores*: A Study in Social Mobility', *PBSR*, LI (1983), esp. 156; Gros 1994 [S.2A], 77–83. Cf. Anderson 1997, 15–50.

39 H. Stuart Jones, *The Sculptures of the Museo Capitolino* (Oxford 1912), 76–7, Pl. 15, II, 8; T. Birt, *Die Buchrolle in der Kunst* (Leipzig 1907), 218, Abb. 143; D.E.E. Kleiner, *Roman Imperial Funerary Altars with Portraits* (Rome 1987), 213–16, Pl. 46.2 and 47.1.

40 Stuart Jones 1912 (see preceding note), 75, Pl. 15,II,6; Adam 1989 [S.GA], fig. 79 and 52 (cf. fig. 48, 50, 51, 52, 78, 79, 224, 228).

41 Plut. *Crass.* 2.4–5; cf. Anderson 1997, 77–8.

42 *Fam.* IX,2,5; Gros 1976 [S.7B], 55 ff.; Schrijvers 1989 [S.2A], 14.

43 Rawson 1975; M. Torelli, 'Industria estrattiva, lavoro artigianale, interessi economici: Qualche appunto', *MAAR*, XXXVI (1980), 319. However, Manolis Korres (*AM*, forthcoming) now argues that the outline of the second-century Olympieion goes back to the fourth century BC.

44 F. Coarelli, 'La costruzione del porto di Terracina in un rilievo storico tardo-repubblicano', Coarelli 1996 [S.GA], 434–54.

45 *Cod. Theod.* XIII,4,1; C. Mango, *The Art of the Byzantine Empire: Sources and Documents* (Englewood Cliffs 1972), 14. Cf. G. Downey, 'Byzantine Architects, their Training and Methods', *Byzantion*, XVIII (1946–8), 96–118.

46 Wilson Jones 1993 [S.5B], 408.

47 *Epitome de Caesaribus*, as quoted by MacMullen 1959 (see n. 24), 215.

48 MacDonald 1982–6, I, 182.

49 Pollitt 1983 [S.GA], 201–2.

50 Susini 1987.

51 Onians 1988 [S.6A], 49–51.

52 Pliny, *Ep.*, X, esp. 37–40, 51–2.

53 Gros 1976 [S.7B], 62.

54 Pensabene 1996 [S.7F], 291.

55 F.S. Kleiner, 'Artists in the Roman World: An Itinerant Workshop in Augustan Gaul', *MEFRA*, LXXXIX/2 (1977), 661–96; P. Pensabene, 'La decorazione architettonica di Cherchel: Cornici, architravi, soffitti, basi e pilastri', *150-Jahr-Feier DAI Rom, RM Ergh.* XXV (1982), 116–69; Pensabene 1996 [S.7F], 305–7; Pensabene, 'Classi dirigenti, programmi decorativi, culto imperiale', *Colonia Patricia Corduba*, ed. P. Léon (Córdoba 1996), 202; N. Ferchiou, 'Un atelier itinérant de marbriers le long des côtes de Proconsulaire', *Antiquités africaines*, XIX (1983), 75–84; A. Roth-Congès, 'L'acanthe dans le décor architectonique protoaugustéen en Provence', *Revue archéologique de Narbonnaise*, XVI (1983), esp. 129; Freyberger 1990 [S.7C].

56 Their presence in a drawing for the refurbishment of a temple at Pergamon follows from the aim to match existing details; see Schwandner 1990 [S.3B].

57 In the Pantheon too the modillion spacing differs substantially on each face, and to either side, of the entablature blocks over the projecting columns flanking the main apse.

CHAPTER II

1 Baldwin 1990; Romano 1987, 18–24; Anderson 1997 [S.GA], 43–4.

2 Fensterbusch 1964, 3 ff.

3 Boëthius 1939, 121. Cf. Romano 1987, 21–5; Fleury ed. 1990, xx–xxiv.

4 Coulton 1979 (see Introduction, n. 28), 81.

5 Wesenberg 1971 [S.6A], 116 ff.; Gros 1990, 150.

6 K.E. Ros, 'Vitruvius and the Design of the Carthage Theater', *Africa romana*, XI (1994), 897–910, esp. 907. For related analyses, see Small 1983; Sear 1990; Amucano 1991 [all S.5B].

7 Gros 1975; Gros 1988; Callebat 1989; Frézouls 1989.

8 Geertman 1989 [S.5B], 157–8; Geertman 1993, 211 [S.5B].

9 Soubiran 1969, esp. xxii–xxxi; xxxviii–xlvii; Bommelaer 1989; A.T. Hodge, ed., *Future Currents in Aqueduct Studies* (Leeds University 1991), 168.

10 Krinsky 1967, 36; Marcucci and Vagnetti 1978, 19–20.

11 Alberti 1988 [S.GA], VI, 1; R. Krautheimer, 'Alberti and Vitruvius', *Studies in Western Art: Acts of the 20th Int. Congress in the History of Art*, II (Princeton 1963), 42–3. Cf. F. Choay, *La règle et le modèle* (Paris 1980), 137 ff.

12 Burns 1988 (see Introduction, n. 22), 216.

13 Gros 1982, 663 ff., 669 ff.; Romano 1987, 7–8. But for more positive comment, see Callebat 1982, 704, 719–20.

14 Plommer 1973, 33.

15 *Sid. Apoll. Epist.*, IV,3,5 (trans. W.B. Anderson, Loeb ed. 1965). Apollinaris was Bishop of Laodicea in Syria around AD 360.

16 *Sid. Apoll. Epist.*, VIII,6,10.

17 Frontinus, 25.1; Callebat 1973, ix–x, xxxviii–xxxix, 165.

18 Boëthius 1939, 115, 129 ff. However, to say 'Vitruvio non è stato mai un costruttore' (Lugli 1957 [S.GA], 373) is going too far.

19 R.A. Tybout, *Aedificiorum figurae: Untersuchungen zu den Architekturdarstellungen des frühen zweiten Stils* (Amsterdam 1989), esp. 55 ff.

20 P. Pensabene, 'Elementi architettonici dalla casa di Augusto sul Palatino', *RM*, CIV (1997), 149–92.

21 Ferri 1960, 4–6, 48, 124; see also Schlikker 1940; Gros 1982, 665 and 673 ff.

22 Over a century later Pliny (*HN*, XXXVI, 65) reminded his readers that *symmetria* had no Latin equivalent.

23 Suet., *Tib.* 71. Ferri 1960, 49; Gros 1990, xliv. Cf. Gros 1982, 685–6; Sallmann 1984; Callebat 1994, 32.

24 Callebat 1994, 32; Gros 1994, esp. 83 ff.

25 Romano 1987, 47–54.

26 E. Fentress *et al.*, 'A Sicilian Villa and its Landscape', *Opus: International Journal for Social and Economic History of Antiquity*, v, 82 ff.

27 G. Rocco, 'Su di un fregio dorico da Villa Adriana: La soluzione vitruviana del conflitto angolare', *Palladio*, xiv (1994), 37–44.

28 F. Lasserre, *Strabon, Géographie III* (Paris 1967), 10 ff.

29 Birnbaum 1914; Schlikker 1940; Gros 1978; Tomlinson 1989.

30 Vitruvius (VII, Pref., 14) also mentions the (lost) architectural writings of Fuficius and Publius Septimius.

31 Xen., *Mem.*, 4,2,8–10; cf. Coulton 1988 [S.GC], 24.

32 Vitruvius, VII, Pref., 12 and x, 2.11; Pliny, *HN*, 36, 21, 96–7; Coulton 1988 [S.GC], 24 and 141–3.

33 Schrijvers 1989, 14.

34 Gros 1975; Knell 1985, esp. 30; Frézouls 1989, 44 ff.; Fleury ed. 1990 (commentary relating to i,2,2–5).

35 Watzinger 1909, esp. 202–3; Ferri 1960, 50–52; Scranton 1974; Pollitt 1974, 165–6; Fleury ed. 1990, 105; Geertman 1994, 15 ff.

36 Geertman 1994, 22 also proposes a three-level scheme, but sees *auctoritas* as the key to the third. Note also the tripartite structure of columns (base, shaft, capital), entablatures (architrave, frieze, cornice) and temple façades (stylobate, column and entablature). Cf. A. Tzonis and L. Lefaivre, *Classical Architecture: The Poetics of Order* (Cambridge, Mass., 1986), 9–23.

37 Schlikker 1940, esp. 72 ff.; Gros 1982, 663.

38 By comparison, *ordinatio* appears five times; *dispositio*, twenty-nine; *eurythmia*, four; *decor*, sixteen; and *distributio*, twenty-two (Callebat and Fleury 1995). Cf. Panofsky 1970, 93–100, esp. n. 19; Pollitt 1974, 14–22; Knell 1985, 30 ff.; Gros 1989; Gros 1990, xiv ff., 56–60; Callebat 1994, 41–3.

39 Pollitt 1974, 15.

40 Pollitt 1974, 257. Scholfield (1958, 20) is representative of many writers who realize that *symmetria* involves proportion and measure, but whose definitions give all the same only part of its meaning.

41 For citations see Callebat and Fleury 1995, col. 91. Cf. Moe 1945, 10 ff.; J.J. Coulton, 'Modules and Measurements in Ancient Design and Modern Scholarship', AA.VV. 1989, 85–9.

42 The connection is made in a passage by Galen (J.E. Raven, 'Polyclitus and Pythagoreanism', *Classical Quarterly*, xlv, 1951, 147–51, esp. 148–9; Pollitt 1974, 14–15). See also R. Tobin, 'The Canon of Polykleitos', *AJA*, lxxix (1975), 307 ff.; E. Berger, 'Zum Kanon des Polyklet', *Polyklet: Der Bildhauer der griechischen Klassik*, ed. P. Bol (Mainz 1990), 156–84; W. Sonntagbauer, 'Ein Spiel zwischen Fünf und Sieben: Zum Kanon des Polyklet', *ÖJh*, lxi (1991–2), 69–123; *Polykleitos, the Doryphoros and Tradition*, ed. W. Moon (Madison 1995).

43 Martines 1989 [S.9B], 4. Cf. Heath 1921, ii, 34–50; and A. Frajese, *Opere di Archimede* (Turin 1974), 23.

44 Heath 1921, ii, 390.

45 Brumbaugh 1968, esp. pl. ii, a and b.

46 Wittkower 1971 [S.5A]; Naredi-Rainier 1989, 13 ff.; R.C.A. Rottländer, 'Untersuchungen am Turm der Winde in Athen', *ÖJh*, lix (1989), 55–92; Heinz 1995, 173 ff.; J. Kappraff, 'Musical Proportions at the Basis of Systems of Architectural Proportion both Ancient and Modern', AA.VV. 1996 [S.5A], 115–33.

47 Vitruvius vi,3,3 (2 : 3); vi,3,4 (3 : 4); vi,3,6 (2 : 3, 3 : 4); vi,3,7 (3 : 4); vi,3,8 (1 : 2, 2 : 3).

48 Xen. *Mem.*, 3.10.10–12, cf. Pollitt 1974, 169–70, 218–28.

49 *De Orat.*, ii, 320.

50 *De Orat.*, iii, 180.

51 Chronometry and engineering might strike the modern reader as curious inclusions, but note also that Pliny the Elder (*HN*, xxxviii, 125) gave Archimedes in a list of seven great architects by virtue of his mastery of siege engineering.

52 Some scholars regard *symmetria*, *eurythmia* and *decor* as subsets of *venustas* (e.g. Germann 1991, 27–9), but *decor* has much to do with *utilitas*. The late antique manual by Faventius confounds the picture further by making *eurythmia* synonymous with both *venustas* and *decor* (i, 287; Plommer 1973, 40–41).

53 Nor is there anything in either chapter to prepare for the main themes of Books iii to vi, the classification of plan types and the orders (*genera*).

54 E. Sackur, 'Die Vitruvius Basilika in Fanum und die neue Ausgabe der decem Libri de Architectura', *Repertorium für Kunstwissenschaft*, xxxvi (Berlin 1913), 1–40; F. Pellati, 'La basilica di Fanum e la formazione del tratto di Vitruvio', *Rend-PontAcc*, xxiii–xxiv (1947–9), 153–74; A. Deli and F. Battistelli, *Immagine di Fano Romana* (Fano 1983), 55–65; W. Alzinger, 'Vitruvs Basilika und der archäologische Befund', AA.VV. 1989, 212–16; K. Ohr, *Die Basilika in Pompeji* (Berlin 1991).

55 Excluding the 'odd man out' 46 ft depth of the tribune, see Gros 1976, 696.

CHAPTER III

1 Suetonius, *Aug.*, 56.2.

2 For a similar complaint, see DeLaine 1997 [S.GA], 9.

3 Benndorf 1902; H. Drerup, *Griechische Baukunst in geometrischer Zeit* (Göttingen 1969), 69 ff.; Staccioli 1968; Manderscheid 1983, 444–7; Horn 1989; Schattner 1990; Haselberger 1997. Cf. E.H. Winlock, *Models of Daily Life in Ancient Egypt* (Cambridge, Mass., 1955). E. Young, 'Sculptors' Models or Votives?', *Bulletin of the Metropolitan Museum*, xxii (1963–4), 246–56.

4 My thanks to Lucos Cozza for sharing his recollections of conversations with John Ward-Perkins.

5 R. Bohn, *Die Theaterterrasse = AvP*, iv (Berlin 1896), Taf. 36; A. Gnirs, *Pola: Ein Führer durch die antiken Baudenkmäler und Sammlungen* (Vienna 1915), fig. 17 (reproduced in Haselberger 1997, fig. 7); De Franciscis 1959.

6 Kalayan 1969 and 1971.

7 Haselberger, 1980, 1983, 1987 and 1991.

8 For Bulla Regia, see Hanoune 1996; for Pergamon, Schwandner 1990. For the drawings at Córdoba, Pompeii and Rome relating to fluting, see pp. 7 and 229n35, and for further masons' marks Hoepfner 1984 [S.2B], 22.

9 J. Harvey, *The Medieval Architect* (1972), 114 ff.; S. Kostof, 'The Architect in the Middle Ages', *The Architect*, ed. Kostof (Oxford 1976), 74–5; F. Claval, 'Les épures de la cathédrale de Clermont-Ferrand', *BCTH*, xx (1984), 185–221; M. Davies, 'La choeur de la cathédrale de Limoges', *Antiquités nationales*, xxii (1989), 77 ff.; for further references, see V. Paul, 'Tracing Floor', *DoA*,xxxi, 274–6.

10 Coulton 1985; Coulton 1988 [S.GC], 53–9; cf. Coulton, 'Greek Architects and the Transmission of Design', AA.VV. 1983 [S.GA], 453–68. For a contrary view, see Petronotis 1972; Adam 1997; W.B. Dinsmoor Jr., 'Preliminary Planning of the Propylaia by Mnesikles', AA.VV. 1985, 135–47.

11 S.P. Springer and G. Deutsch, *Left Brain, Right Brain* (New York 1989, 3rd ed.), esp. 36.

12 Vitruvius referred his reader to ten diagrams, all lost: 1,6,12 (two examples); iii,3,13; iii,4,5; iii,5,8; v,4,1; viii,5,3; ix, Pref.,5; ix, Pref.,8; x,6,4). Cf. Frézouls 1985; Gros 1988 [S.2A], 57–9; Haselberger 1989.

13 Suetonius, *De vita Caesarum*, i,31,1.

14 Cicero, *QFr.*, x,ii,6(5); cf. ii,5,4.

15 Carettoni *et al.*, 1960, 199 ff.; Rodríguez-Almeida 1980 and 1997 (with further references). Of note also is the territorial map which originally lined the walls of a *tabularium* at Orange; see Piganiol 1962.

16 De' Spagnolis 1984.

17 Hülsen 1890, 46 ff.; Carettoni *et al.* 1960, 208; von Hesberg 1984; *id.* 1994 [S.4C], 16; Heisel 1993, 188–91.

18 MacDonald 1982–6 [S.GA], I, 140; von Hesberg 1984, fig. 5; *Invisibilia: Rivedere i capolavori, vedere i progetti* (cat. Rome 1992), 188; Heisel 1993, 191–2.

19 For a house plan on papyrus of Roman date (2nd century AD), see Maehler 1983, 136 ff.; Haselberger 1997, fig. 15.

20 R. Parkinson and S. Quirke, *Papyrus* (London 1995), 16 ff.

21 Petrie 1926, 24; Badawy 1948, 206; H.S. Smith and H.M. Stewart, 'The Gurob Shrine Papyrus', *JEA*, LXX (1984), 54–64; Clarke and Engelbach 1990, 46–59; Heisel 1993, 131–5; Millon 1994, 19.

22 C. Ghisalberti, AA.VV. 1994, 427–9.

23 Aul. Gell., *NA*, XIX,10,2.

24 Adam 1989 [S.GA], fig. 522.

25 Carter and Gardiner 1917. For other Egyptian drawings see Heisel 1993, 76–153.

26 Coarelli 1995, esp. 28 ff., 49–52; cf. Gros 1985, 233. On an elusive series of concentric marks (made by a sculptor?), see E. Bartman, 'Carving the Badmington Sarcophagus', *Metropolitan Museum Journal*, XXVIII (1993), 57–75.

27 Koenigs 1983; Heisel 1993, 158–9.

28 Alberti [S.GA], IX,10, as translated in A. Chastel, *The Studios and Styles of the Renaissance* (London 1965), 28. Full of pertinent comments is Alberti's extended discussion of the value of models in II,1.

29 This is an aspect shared by an Egyptian model of a tomb found at Dashour; see Arnold 1991, 11 and fig. 1.6; Adam 1997, fig. 6.

30 M.F. Squarciapino, *Museo ostiense* (Rome 1962), 18, no. 189; Pensabene 1997.

31 Pensabene 1997; Wilson Jones 1997, 121. A larger scale like 1:48 is theoretically possible but implies improbably wide architraves.

32 Carter and Gardiner 1917, 157.

33 Will 1985, 280.

34 Patrizio Pensabene has kindly pointed out to me an unpublished scale drawing of an arch on such a surface on the Palatine.

35 Perhaps the most astonishing known ancient mock-up is the so-called trial passage made for the construction of the Great Pyramid at Giza (W.M.F. Petrie, *Pyramids and Temples of Gizeh* (London 1883), 50–2). See also Arnold 1991, 47–9; and for the tunnel at Samos, see H.J. Keinast, *Die Wasserleitung des Eupalinos auf Samos* (Bonn 1995), 47, 194.

36 See chapter 1, n. 54.

37 On Agrigento, see B. Wesenberg, *Gnomon*, XLVIII (1976), 800; D. Mertens, *Der Tempel von Segesta* (Mainz 1984), 112–15; Mertens, AA.VV. 1984. For further examples, see F.F. Felten, 'Antike Architekturkopien', *Komos: Festschrift für Thuri Lorenz zum 65. Geburtstag*, ed. G. Erath (Vienna 1997), 61–9.

38 Wilson Jones 1997.

39 This, however, represents only one current of opinion; if anything, relatively heavy entablatures tend to belong to smaller ensembles; cf. Perrault 1993 [S.6A], 72.

40 For a general discussion of this aspect of design in the context of Greek architecture, see Coulton 1988 [S.GC], 74–96.

41 Peterse 1985 [S.5B].

42 DeLaine 1997 [S.GA], 53.

43 A. Hoffman, 'Zum Bauplan des Zeus-Asklepios Tempels im Asklepieion von Pergamon', AA.VV. 1984, 95–103.

44 Wilson Jones 1993 [S.5B].

45 For the Temple of Antoninus and Faustina, see chapter 6, n. 57. This kind of axial emphasis could also affect the planning of circular buildings and amphitheatres.

46 J. Humphrey, *Roman Circuses: Arenas for Chariot Racing* (London 1986), 18 ff., 38, 47 ff., 54, 586 ff.

47 I am grateful to Lynne Lancaster for sharing observations arising from her recent survey.

48 S. De Angeli, *Templum Divi Vespasiani = LSA*, XVIII (Rome 1992), 125.

49 M. Gawlikowski, 'Les *principia* de Dioclétian à Palmyre: Projet et réalisation', AA.VV. 1985, 283–9.

50 M. Euzennat and G. Hallier, 'Les forums de Tingitane: Observations sur l'influence de l'architecture militaire sur les constructions civiles de l'Occident romain', *Antiquités africaines*, XXII (1986), 73–103, esp. 74; Hallier, AA.VV. 1989 [S.2A], 204–5.

51 Coulton 1975 [S.5A], 69 ff.; Gros 1976 [S.7B], 63, n. 79.

52 W.E. Wallace, *Michelangelo at San Lorenzo: The Genius as Entrepreneur* (Cambridge 1994), 3.

53 Clarke and Engelbach 1990, 46–8; E. Iversen, *Canon and Proportions in Egyptian Art* (Warminster 1975); Haselberger 1983, 121–3; Heisel 1993, 46, 81, 85, 131; G. Robbins, *Proportion and Style in Ancient Egyptian Art* (Austin 1994), 92, 170.

54 Notably Kastabos, Labraunda, the Letoon, Magnesia and Teos; see P. Hellström and T. Thieme, *Labraunda, I,3: The Temple of Zeus* (Stockholm 1982); Koenigs 1983; J.J. de Jong, 'The Temple of Athena-Polias at Priene and the Temple of the Hemithea at Kastabos', *BABesch*, LXIII (1988), 129–37; M.D. Uz, 'The Temple of Dionysius at Teos', AA.VV. 1990 [S.GA], 51–61; E. Hansen, 'Le temple de Létô au Létôon de Xanthos', *RA*, 1991, 323–40. On the issue of deviations from the model, see Koenigs 1983, 141–2; de Jong, *supra*, 131.

55 Amy and Gros 1979 [S.7E], I, esp. 175. Selected dimensions are given in Appendix A and Appendix B.

56 For recent studies of the building, see I. Ruggiero, 'Ricerche sul tempio di Portuno nel Foro Boario: Per una rilettura del monumento', *BComm*, XCIV (1991–2), 253–86; J.-P. Adam, *Le Temple de Portunus au Forum Boarium = CollEFR* (Rome 1996).

57 What is more, 48 ft relates simply to the interior dimensions of the cella, 36 × 54 ft, besides being 8/5 the notional column height of 30 ft.

58 To have changed the flanks as well would have upset another series of relationships, for example, the equality of the 8½ ft spacing to the height of the pediment, see Amy and Gros 1979 [S.7E], I, 100 and 102. Their analysis is similar in spirit, although the exact chain of thought differs.

CHAPTER IV

1 M. Korres, 'Der Plan des Parthenon', *AM*, CIX (1994), 59 ff.

2 The sides free of obstacles measure 29.47 and 29.49 m (a difference of 0.07%). A less easy dimension to execute, that from the vertex to the middle of the base, varies by 6 cm or 0.15% (N = 39.62, E = 39.66, S = 39.60, W = 39.63 m, as measured by the author and Heinrich Bauer).

3 For example, in the Pantheon rotunda the ring of columns varies by around 4 cm from a perfect circle, accounting for differences in published measurements; see Pelletti 1989

[S.9B]; Rottländer 1996b, 31 (but note that the value he cites for my own measurement between opposing plinths should read 43.00 m (44.55 m − 1.55 m) and not 43.57 m).

4 Wilson Jones 1993 [S.5B], 408. Note also the marked irregularity of the 'octagonal' envelope of the Temple of Diana at Baiae (Rakob 1988, 274–5).

5 Wesenberg 1976; Dekoulakou-Sideris 1990; Rottländer 1991–2.

6 Rottländer 1996a. A Roman digit of 18.5 mm equals the standard $\frac{1}{28}$ subdivision of a 518 mm cubit.

7 Albertini 1920; Ioppolo 1967; Hallier 1984–5; Barresi 1991. Occasionally two units were used in the same building, either for practical reasons (C.J. Bridges, 'The Pes Monetalis and the Pes Drusianus in Xanten', *Britannia*, xv (1984), 85 ff.; Wilson Jones 1993 [S.5B], 408) or more elevated ones (Wilson Jones 1989 [S.5B], 151; R.C.A. Rottländer, 'Untersuchungen am Turm der Winde in Athen', *ÖJh*, lix (1989), 55–9).

8 Alternatively, some sustain the existence of distinct units: a Punic foot of 294.1 mm, a 'Vindonissa foot' of 292.5 mm and a 'Compromise foot' of 297.7 mm (Rottländer 1996a and b; Heinz 1991). See also chapter 8, n. 23.

9 Bankel 1983; Rottländer 1996b.

10 Rottländer 1966b; Amy and Gros 1979 [S.7E], i, 85.

11 Moneti 1992.

12 Wilson Jones 1989 [S.5B], 106 ff.

13 DeLaine 1997 [S.GA], 63.

14 Colvin 1991; von Hesberg 1994. For background, see Toynbee 1971; S. Walker, *Memorials of the Roman Dead* (London 1985); and I. Morris, *Death-ritual and Social Structure in Classical Antiquity* (Cambridge 1992).

15 See Amand 1987 and the bibliography in S.4B; for the Halikarnassos monument in particular, with a new approach to its reconstruction, see Bury 1998.

16 Holloway 1966; von Hesberg 1994, 13 ff.; 38 ff. Cf. Canina 1853; Fellmann 1957; Pane and De Franciscis 1957; Eisner 1979; Purcell 1987.

17 Von Hesberg 1994, 19. Cf. Neuerburg 1969.

18 Von Hesberg 1994, 50–59.

19 Wilson Jones 1989 [S.5B], 114, n. 16; 117, n. 20.

20 The salient dimensions for the rest of the buildings in this category are again multiples of 10, 12 or 16 units, provided that the tholos by the Tiber was set out using a Greek foot, a hypothesis that is not unreasonable given the almost certain involvement of Greek contractors and craftsmen (Rakob and Heilmeyer 1973, 17). For contrasting analyses, see Geertman 1989 [S.5B], 161–5; De Zwarte 1994, 128 ff.

21 Wilson Jones 1990 [S.5A].

22 The single exception is Tor Pignattara, while the tholos by the Tiber and the Tor de' Schiavi remain open to special pleading.

23 'There is nothing', says Vitruvius, 'to which the architect should devote more thought than to the exact proportions of his building with reference to a certain part selected as the standard' (vi,2,1). This 'standard of *symmetria*' is normally associated with a small module such as the column diameter or triglyph width (i,2,4). But could not large 'critical dimensions' also act as the hub of a network of fractions?

24 'Critical dimensions' corresponding to multiples of 5, 10 or 12 ft are present in seventeen out of twenty-eight Hellenistic and Roman tombs in Cyrenaica (Stucchi 1987); twenty out of twenty-six buildings with concrete domes of diverse location (Rasch 1985); in four out of five structures at Hadrian's Villa (Jacobson 1986 [S.5B], 72 ff.).

25 The circumference took precedence for example at the mausoleum at Taksebt (Algeria), which has a drum articulated by twelve semi-columns at intervals of 10 ft, a scheme that evidently dictated the diameter of $38\frac{1}{5}$ ft. G. Hallier and M. Euzennat, 'Le Mausolée de Taksebt (Algérie)', *CRAI*, 1992, 235–48. I thank Gilbert Hallier for kindly giving me a draft of a more detailed future publication.

26 Chapter 9, n. 47. Cf. M. Ecochard, *Filiation des monuments grecs, byzantins et islamiques. Une question de géométrie* (Paris 1977); J. Wilkinson, 'Architectural Procedures in Byzantine Palestine', *Levant,* xiii (1981), 156–72; Wilson Jones 1990 [S.5A].

27 R. Krautheimer, S. Corbett and A.K. Frazer, *Corpus Basilicarum Christianarum Romae*, v (Rome 1977), 286; cf. G.T. Armstrong, 'Constantine's Churches: Symbol and Structure', *JSAH*, xxxiii (1974), 5–16.

28 L. Luschi, 'Basilicae Centenariae tres', *Studi classici e orientali*, xxxii (1982), 157–78.

29 Frazer 1993 [S.5B]; Wightman 1997 [S.5B]. Cf. Packer 1997 [S.8A], f. 24.

30 A.K. Frazer, 'Hadrian's Teatro Marittimo at Tivoli, and Pantheon', *Architectural Studies in Memory of Richard Krautheimer*, ed. C.L. Striker (Mainz 1996), 77–8. McEwen 1994 [S.9C], esp. fig. 8. See also MacDonald 1976 [S.9A], 85–6, for a link between the Pantheon and the imperial fora.

31 Bauer 1977; Borchardt 1991; Hoepfner 1993; Kaspar 1976.

32 In the *hekatompedon* Parthenon, however, the apparent absence of an element exactly 100 ft long suggests that the term was a legacy from previous temples on the site; see R. Tölle-Kastenbein, 'Das Hekatompedon auf der Athener Akropolis', *JdI*, cviii (1993), 43–75.

33 Then again, the doubling up of the internal diameter of drum to give that of the overall space (as at Santa Costanza) reappears in the seventh-century rotunda of Santa Maria Maggiore at Nocera (see Zettler 1940 and 1943; Wilson Jones 1989 [S.5B], 149, M). Cf. P.A. Underwood, 'Some Principles of Measure in the Architecture of the Period of Justinian', *Cahiers archéologiques,* iii (1948), 64–74. For arguments in favour of a later than mid-fourth century date for Santa Costanza, see D.J. Stanley, *New Discoveries at Santa Costanza, DOP* xlviii (1994), 257–61.

34 H. Bauer, 'Die Cloaca Maxima in Rom', *Leichtweiss-Institut für Wasserbau*, ciii (1989), 43–67.

35 G. Lugli and G. Filibeck, *Il porto di Roma imperiale e l'agro portuense* (Rome 1935), 93–6.

36 L. Cozza, 'I recenti scavi delle Sette Sale', *RendPontAcc,* xlvii (1976), 79–101; K. De Fine Licht, *Sette Sale: Untersuchungen an den Trajansthermen zu Rom = AnalRom*, supp. 19 (1990).

37 Pliny, *HN*, xvi, 201. In xvi, 76 he also mentions a larchwood log (i.e. only part of what must have been a considerably taller tree) 120 ft long. Cf. R. Meiggs, *Trees and Timber in the Ancient Mediterranean World* (Oxford 1982), 191–2; Anderson 1997 [S.GA], 127–39.

38 R.J. Mainstone, *Developments in Structural Form* (London 1975), 115 ff., 194 ff.; Pelliccioni 1986, 44–6; Rasch 1985; Rakob 1988, 289; Rasch 1991; DeLaine 1997 [S.GA], 56–7.

39 See chapter 3, n. 43.

40 L.I. Kahn, 'Measurable, Unmeasurable', *Daidalos*, v (1982), 16–17. Cf. Introduction, n. 8.

41 F. Blume *et al.*, *Die Schriften der römischen Feldmesser: Gromatici Veteres* (Berlin 1848–52); C. Thulin, *Corpus agrimensorum romanorum* (Leipzig 1913); O.A.W. Dilke, *The Roman Land Surveyors: An Introduction to the Agrimensores* (Newton Abbot 1971); the series *Misurare la terra* (1983–); Gros and Torelli 1988 [S.GA]; G. Choquer and F. Favory, *Les arpenteurs romains:*

Théorie et pratique (Paris 1992); B. Campbell, 'Shaping the Rural Environment: Surveyors in Ancient Rome', *JRS*, LXXXVI (1996), 74–99; A. Roth Congès, 'Modalités pratiques d'implantation des cadastres romains: Quelques aspects', *MEFRA*, CVIII (1996), 299–422.

42 G. Castagnoli, *Orthogonal Town Planning in Antiquity* (Cambridge, Mass., 1971); J.R. McCredie, 'Hippodamus of Miletos', *Studies Presented to George M.A. Hanfmann* (Mainz 1971), 95–100; R. Reinders, 'Hellenistic New Towns on the Pagasitic Gulf', *BABesch*, LXI (1986), 34–40; P. Pedersen, 'Town Planning in Halicarnassos and Rhodos', *Archaeology in the Dodecanese*, ed. S. Dietz (Copenhagen 1988), 98–113; R. Bedon et al., *Architecture et urbanisme en Gaule romaine* (Paris 1988).

43 Other inscriptions in the archaeological museum cite plots of 16 × 16 ft, 16 × 20 ft, 16 × 25 ft, 20 × 30 ft, 20 × 40 ft and 45 × 55 ft. For illustrations of further examples, see Adam 1989 [S.GA], 36, 43. Funeral colleges tended to be larger, say 160 × 50 ft (*Camposanto Monumentale di Pisa: Le antichità* (Pisa 1977), 80–81).

44 The stated width of the tomb of the Curii at Aquileia (fig. 4.19), 16 ft, matches that of its enclosure (4.755 m = 16 ft of 0.297 m) measured at the height of the inscription.

45 Petronius, *Satyricon*, 71. For mention of the 1000 × 300 ft family plot of L. Cassius Nomentanus on the Esquiline see Horace, *Sat.* 1,8,10; and Susini 1987 [S.1] for an inscription attesting to a 1000 ft stretch of fortification.

46 R. Stadelmann, *Die große Pyramiden von Giza* (Graz 1990), 112 for the overall dimensions in plan, which vary by just 4½ cm over 230 m. On the precision and possible significance of astronomical alignments, see R. Bauval and A. Gilbert, *The Orion Mystery* (London 1994).

47 J. Vicari and F. Brüschweiler, 'Les ziggurats de Tchogha-Zanbil (Dur-Untash) et de Babylone', AA.VV. 1985 [S.3A], 48–58; H. Schmid, *Der Tempelturm Etemenanki in Babylon* (Mainz 1995).

48 The Holy of Holies measured 20 cubits in length, breadth and height, while other recorded dimensions include 5, 6, 10, 30, 50 and 60 cubits (Kings, I, 6–7). Cf. T. Busink, *Der Tempel von Jerusalem* (Leiden 1970); P. von Naredi-Rainier, *Salomos Tempel und das Abendland* (Cologne 1994).

49 Pliny, *HN*, XXXVI, 19; J.L. Myres, 'The Tomb of Porsena at Clusium', *BSA*, XLVI (1951), 117–21; G.A. Mansuelli, 'Il monumento di Porsina a Chiusi', *CollEFR*, XXVII (1976), 619–26; Wilson Jones 1989 [S.5B], 106.

50 Tacitus, *Ann.* IV, 63–4. Suetonius (*Tib.* 40) cited the hardly much more credible figure of 20,000.

51 *SHA. Sev. Alex.*, 26,7; F. Coarelli, AA.VV. 1987a [S.GA], 440 ff.

52 Strabo, 5.3.7; *Epitome de Caesaribus*, 13.12; G. Saliou, *Les Lois des bâtiments* (Beirut 1992), 212; Campbell 1996 (see n. 41), 84.

53 The interrelations between the chief Roman units of measure may be set out as follows:

	digitus	uncia	pes	cubitus	passus
digit	1				
inch	1⅓	1			
foot	16	12	1		
cubit	24	18	1½	1	
pace	80	60	5	3⅓	1
actus	1920	1440	120	80	24
stadium	10000	7500	625	416⅔	125
mile	80000	60000	5000	3333⅓	1000

CHAPTER V

1 Wilson Jones 1989, 126–8, 131 ff.

2 Better approximations include 17:12 (1.417:1) for $\sqrt{2}$ (1.414), and 26:15 (1.733:1) for $\sqrt{3}$ (1.732).

3 O. Bingöl, 'Vitruvs Volute am Artemis-Tempel von Hermogenes in Magnesia am Mäander', *IstMitt*, XLIII (1983), 399–415; H. Büsing, 'Vitruvs Volutenrahmen und die System-Voluten', *JdI*, CII (1987), 305–38; T. Loertscher, 'Voluta Constructa: Zu einem kaiserzeitlichen Volutenkonstruktions-Modell aus Nordafrika', *Antike Kunst*, XXXII (1989), 82–94; M. Mârgineanu-Cârstoin, 'La composition des chapiteaux ioniques', *BCH* CXXI (1997), 175–233. Cf. M. Losito, 'La ricostruzione della voluta del capitello ionico vitruviano nel Rinascimento italiano', Corso and Romano 1997 [S.2A], 1409–28.

4 Heath 1921 [S.2B], I, 297–8; Brumbaugh 1968 [S.2B], esp. pl. I, b, c and e.

5 P. Frankl, 'The Secret of Medieval Masons', *ArtBull*, XXVII (1945), 46–64; J.S. Ackerman, 'Ars sine Scientia nihil est: Gothic Theory at the Cathedral of Milan', *ArtBull*, XXXI (1949), 84–111; L. Shelby, *Gothic Design Techniques* (Carbondale 1977); K. Hecht, *Mass und Zahl in der gotischen Baukunst* (Hildesheim 1979); R. Recht, '"Théorie" et "traités pratiques" d'architecture au Moyen Age', AA.VV. 1988 [S.2B], 19–30; Kidson 1996; and for further references Hallier 1995, 214, n. 46.

6 On the importance of $\sqrt{2}$ in Egyptian systems of land measurement, see W.M.F. Petrie, *Ancient Weights and Measures* (London 1926); Rottländer 1996a [S.4A], 237. For related observations in the Roman context, see Roth Congès 1996 (see chapter 4, n. 41); Kidson 1996, esp. 349 ff.

7 There are too many studies of Roman buildings highlighting $\sqrt{2}$ to mention more than some of the most recent: Geertman 1989; Hallier 1990 and 1995; Watts and Watts 1996.

8 In support of $\sqrt{3}$ see Kalayan 1971 and 1988; Jacobson 1990–91, 44–7, 55–8; Kidson 1996, 349 ff. On amphitheatres see Golvin 1988; Hallier 1990; Wilson Jones 1993.

9 Wilson Jones 1993, 394–401.

10 Hallier 1995.

11 Vitruvius V,6,1–3; Small 1983; Sear 1990; Gros 1994; Amucano 1991.

12 Kähler 1950 [S.9C]; S. Aurigemma, *Villa Adriana* (Rome 1961); M. De Franceschini, *Villa Adriana: Mosaici, pavimenti, edifici* (Rome 1991); W.L. MacDonald, 'Hadrian's Circles', AA.VV. 1993 [S.GA], 395–408; E. Salza Prina Ricotti, 'Nascita e sviluppo di Villa Adriana', *RendPontAcc*, IV (1992–3), 41–73; W.L. MacDonald and J.A. Pinto, *Hadrian's Villa and its Legacy* (New Haven 1994).

13 Rakob 1984; Jacobson 1986.

14 For slightly differing interpretations, see Ueblacker 1985 [S.4C], 43 ff., Jacobson 1986, 72 ff.

15 The following section summarizes the arguments presented in Jacobson and Wilson Jones 1999. I am most grateful to David Jacobson for many insights and for kindly consenting for this to be published contemporaneously with the main study.

16 The main study of the building is Rakob 1961 [S.4C]. On the context, see F. Yegül, *Baths and Bathing in Classical Antiquity* (Cambridge, Mass., 1992), 93 ff., 108; Yegül, 'The Thermo-Mineral Complex at Baiae and the *De Balneis Puteolanis*', *ArtBull*, LXXVIII (1996), 137–61; F. Zevi and B. Andreae, 'Gli scavi sottomarini di Baia', *La parola del passato*, XXXVII (1982), 114–56; *Archeologia subacquea*, I (1993).

17 MacDonald 1982–6 [S.GA], II, 173. Cf. G. Becatti, ed., *Scavi di Ostia IV: Mosaici e pavimenti marmorei* (Rome 1961), no. 418, p. 221.

18 For the Aquileia example, see H. Kähler, *Die spätantiken Bauten unter dem Dom von Aquileia* (Saarbrücken 1957), 26, Taf. 10–13; for those at Acholla and El Jem, see D. Parrish, *Seasons Mosaics of Roman North Africa* (Rome 1984), nos 3, 31 and 41; for that at Ravenna, F. Berti, ed., *Ravenna I: Mosaici antichi in Italia* (Rome 1976), 71, fig. 15. For further parallels, see Jacobson and Wilson Jones 1999.

19 See chapter 3, n. 53.

20 S. Tebby, 'Geometric Mosaics of Roman Britain', *Proceedings of the Fifth International Colloquium on Ancient Mosaics*, Bath 1987 (1994), 273–94.

21 R. Prudhomme, 'Recherche des principes des construction des mosaïques géométriques romaines', *La mosaïque gréco-romaine 2: Actes du II⁰ Colloque international pour l'étude de la mosaïque antique, Vienne 1971* (Paris 1975); C. Robotti, *Mosaico e architettura: Disegni, sinopie, cartali* (Naples 1983); G. Salies, 'Untersuchungen zu den geometrischen Gliederungs-schemata römischer Mosaiken', *Bonner Jahrbuch*, CLXXIV (1974), 1–178.

22 De Franceschini 1991 (see n. 12), 49–50 (HS 20).

23 F. Guidobaldi, 'Pavimenti in *opus sectile* di Roma e dell' area romana: Proposte per una classificazione e criteri di datazione', AA.VV. 1985 [S.7F], 171–233, esp. 183. For further detail, see Jacobson and Wilson Jones 1999.

24 Geertman 1980 [S.9B]. For other $\sqrt{2}$ geometries, see Williams 1998 [S.9B].

25 V. Scully, *The Earth, the Temple and the Gods: Greek Sacred Architecture* (New York 1969); C.A. Doxiadis, *Architectural Space in Ancient Greece* (Cambridge, Mass., 1972); Coarelli 1995 [S.3B]; W. Hoepfner, 'Hermogenes und Epigonos. Pergamon zur Zeit Attalos I', *JdI*, CXII (1997), 109–48.

26 On view planning in the Roman context, see H. Drerup, 'Bildraum und Realraum im römischen Architektur', *RM*, LXVI (1959), 147–74; Gros 1985 [S.3B]; L. Bek, 'From Eye-sight to View Planning: The Notion of Greek Philosophy and Hellenistic Optics as a Trend in Roman Aesthetics and Building Practice', *Acta hyperborea*, V (1993), 127–50.

27 Zanker 1984 [S.8A]; MacDonald 1976 [S.9A], 78–82.

28 Buddensieg 1976 (see Introduction, n. 5), 340–41. On the importance of vistas in the planning of the Baths of Caracalla, see DeLaine 1997 [S.GA], 63–4.

29 Gros 1976; Geertman 1984; Frey 1990 [all S.2A]; Frey 1994.

30 Kalayan 1988, 21 ff.

31 See also Moessel 1926; Wolff 1932; Lesser 1957; Spremo-Petrovic 1971 and further studies cited in Borsi 1967 and Wittkower 1971. For recent echoes of Brunés work in particular see Wightman 1997; Watts and Watts 1987 and 1992; B. Nicholson, J. Kappraff and S. Hisano, 'The Hidden Pavement Designs of the Laurentian Library', AA.VV. 1998, 87–98.

32 See the bibliography in S.5C, and also Moessel 1926; Wittkower 1978, 118 ff.; Lawlor 1982 [S.2B], 44–64; Esposito and Michetti 1996 [S.9B].

33 Foscari and Volpi Ghiradini 1998. Proposals in favour of the golden section attain a degree of credibility where dimensions involved match terms of the Fibonacci series (1,2,3,5,8,13,21,34...), the pairs of which generate increasingly good approximations to ϕ. See Peterse 1985, 48 for just such an example.

34 Jacobson 1983; Hallier 1995, 204, 218–19.

35 Esposito and Michetti 1996 [S.9B].

36 For further geometrical studies of the Pantheon, see Alvegård 1972 [S.9B] and Sperling 1998 [S.9B].

37 Geertman 1989 and 1993. Geertman's studies represent a suitable challenge because they are so well argued.

38 On the potential importance of measuring to the finish rather than the structure, see Wilson Jones 1989, 114, n. 16.

39 For more detail, see Wilson Jones 1989, 117, n. 20.

40 $(2 - \sqrt{2})/1 \simeq 0.5858$, while $\frac{3}{5} = 0.6$ (the difference is 2.4%).

41

	Overall diam. of podium	Predicted ext. diam. of cella	Actual ext.diam. of cella	Diff. in cm
using $(2 - \sqrt{2})/1$	14.25 m	8.35 m	8.69 m	34
using $\frac{3}{5}$	"	8.55 m	"	14
using $\frac{11}{18}$	"	8.71 m	"	2

42 Wilson Jones 1989 [S.7A], 46, n. 14.

43 The circumference of the ring through the column centres is 40.40 m (the diameter of 12.86 m × π), giving an average arc of 2.244 m between adjacent columns. In theory systyle spacing demands a column diameter of 2.244 m ÷ 3, or 748 mm, just 12 mm less than the actual value of 760 mm.

44 Heath 1921 [S.2B], I, 235–8.

45 Perimeter rhythms in internally orientated circular halls:

	Dimensions in feet		
Building	Width of pier	Width of opening	Ratio
Pantheon	c.29	c.29	1 : 1
Tomb at Portus	6½	13	1 : 2
Tor de' Schiavi	7½	10★	3 : 4
Mausoleum of Maxentius	c.13	20	2 : 3
Santa Costanza	6¾	6¾★★	1 : 1
Asklepieion (Pergamon)	12	18★★★	2 : 3

★ opening on main axis = 12 ft wide
★★ opening on main axis = 13 ft wide (≈ 2 × 6¾ ft)
★★★ opening on main axis = 24 ft wide (= 2 × 12 ft)

46 Geertman (1993) proposes the following proportions: (i) height of portal = height of opening × $(\sqrt{2} + 1)/2$, or 1.2071; (ii) width of opening = height of opening × $(\sqrt{2} - 1)$, or 0.4142; (iii) width of portal = width of opening × $\sqrt{2}$, or 1.4142. But in reality proportion (i) is nearer to 6:5 (7.12 m/5.94 m = 1.1986), while proportion (ii) is nearer to 2:5 (2.40 m/5.94 m = 0.4040). Only proportion (iii) works out convincingly close to $\sqrt{2}$ (3.39 m/2.40 m = 1.4125). However, the principal dimensions relating to this proportion are as follows: width of door opening (w) = 8 ft (96″); width of architraves (a) = $1\frac{2}{3}$ ft (20″); total width (W = w + 2a) = $11\frac{1}{3}$ ft (136″). Exactly the same outcome could also be the result of making the architrave width $\frac{1}{12}$ of the 20 ft tall opening. Vitruvius (IV,6,3), after all, gauged the architrave of his Ionic portal in a similar manner. Moreover, the choice of a 20 inch architrave admirably suits simple arithmetical proportions for the trabeation:

Element of portal	inches	As multiple of 4 inches	feet
height of architrave	20	5	$1\frac{2}{3}$
height of frieze	12	3	1
height of cornice	16	4	$1\frac{1}{3}$
Total	48	12	4

47 Seiler 1986 [S.4B], 40 ff. The only major Roman contribution in terms of composition was the substitution of the stylobate by a high podium.

CHAPTER VI

1 Summerson 1980, 9.

2 *Costume, maniera, modus, sorte* and *specie*; see C. Thoenes, 'Gli ordini architettonici: Rinascita o invenzione?', *Roma e l'antico nell'arte e nella cultura del Cinquecento*, ed. M. Fagiolo (Rome 1985), 266.

3 I. Rowland, 'Raphael, Angelo Colucci, and the Genesis of the Architectural Orders', *ArtBull*, LXXVI (1994), 81–104; Rykwert 1996, 4. For qualification, see C. Thoenes, *Casabella*, no. 642 (January 1997), 78.

4 Pauwels 1989 [S.7D]. Cf. AA.VV. 1992.

5 Alberti [S.GA] VII, 6; Onians 1988, 42–8.

6 R.A. Tomlinson, 'The Doric Order: Hellenistic Critics and Criticism', *JHS*, LXXXIII (1963), 133 ff. See also Roux 1961, 37 ff., 344 ff.; Coulton 1988 [S.GC], 128; Lauter 1986 [S.GC], 237 ff.

7 Onians 1988, 272.

8 Wilson Jones 1993 [S.5B], 432; K. Welch, *The Roman Amphitheatre from its Origins to the Colosseum*, forthcoming.

9 Coarelli 1988 and Ziolkowski 1988 (see chapter 1, n. 8).

10 Lauter 1986 [S.GC], 257 ff.; cf. F.C. Schipper, 'Notes on the Use of the Architectural Orders in Several Atrium Houses in Pompeii', *BABesch*, LXVII (1992), 127–43.

11 Onians 1988, 23–32, 41–8.

12 Onians 1988, 61. This diversity could also reflect difficulties with assembling large sets of homogenous elements; see Panella and Pensabene 1997, 166–74.

13 R.R.R. Smith, 'Myth and Allegory in the Sebasteion', *Aphrodisias Papers I = JRA* supp. (1990), 89–100; Gros 1995, 30.

14 For spiral fluting, see M. Fano Santi, 'La colonna tortile nell'architettura di età romana', *RivdA*, XVII (1993), 71–83. On corkscrew shafts, see Nobiloni 1997, cited in n. 83.

15 On the aesthetics of re-utilization in late antiquity, see F.W. Deichmann, *Die Spolien in der spätantiken Architektur* (Munich 1975); B. Brenk, 'Spolia from Constantine to Charlemagne: Aesthetics versus Ideology', *DOP*, XLI (1987), 103–11; L. de Lachenal, *Spolia: Uso e reimpiego dell'antico dal III al XIV secolo* (Milan 1995); P. Pensabene, 'Riempiego e nuove mode architettoniche nelle basiliche cristiane di Roma', *XII Int. Kongresses für christliche Archäologie*, con. Bonn 1991 (1995), 1076 ff.; Panella and Pensabene 1997.

16 D. Giraud, 'The Greater Propylaia at Eleusis: A Copy of Mneskiles' Propylaia', AA.VV. 1989 [S.GA], 69–76.

17 B.A. Barletta, *Ionic Influence in Archaic Sicily: The Monumental Art*, Studies in Mediterranean Archaeology, XXIII (Gothenburg 1983). For a Doric capital at Amyclae near Sparta with an applied scroll, see Onians 1988, fig. 7.

18 P. Hellström, 'Mixed Orders in Hecatomnid Architecture', *Praktika to XII Diethnous Synedriou klasikiss archaiologias*, IV (Athens 1989), 70–74; Pensabene 1993. Mixed orders are common on numerous smaller-scale artefacts from all around the Mediterranean. Note for example the triglyph frieze and dentil cornice of the sarcophagus belonging to a member of the Cornelii Scipiones family (F. Zevi, 'Considerazione sull'elogio di Scipio Barbato', *Studi miscellanei*, XV (1968–9), 69), and several pedimental stele of the third century BC with Corinthian capitals, Doric friezes and dentil cornices

(P. Pensabene, 'Il tempio ellenistico de S. Leucio a Canosa', *Italici in Magna Grecia = Leucania*, III (1990), 290, n. 150, 151).

19 Cf. A. von Gladiss, 'Der "Arc du Rhône" von Arles', *RM*, LXXIX (1972), 17–87; B. Fornasier, 'Les arcs de triumphe d'Arles', *Histoire de l'art: Monuments*, XXVII (1994), 26 ff.

20 Pensabene 1990 (see n. 18).

21 Fedak 1990 [S.4B], figs 211–12.

22 G.R.H. Wright, 'Architectural Details from the Asklepieion at Belagrae (Beida)', *Libyan Studies*, XXIII (1992), 45–72, fig. 2.

23 G. Pesce, *Palazzo delle Colonne* (Rome 1950).

24 Fedak 1990 [S.4B], fig. 215.

25 *RM*, LXXXIII (1976), fig. 76.

26 Avigad 1954 [S.4D].

27 E. Will and F. Larché, *Iraq al Amir: Le château du Tobiade Hyrcan* (Paris 1991).

28 M. Torelli, 'Monumenti funerari romani con fregio dorico', *DArch*, II (1968), 38, fig. 7.

29 Borchardt 1903 [S.7E].

30 Von Gladiss 1972; Fornasier 1994 (see n. 19).

31 O. Brogan and D.J. Smith, *Ghirza. A Libyan Settlement of the Roman Period* (Tripoli 1984).

32 F. Krauss and R. Herbig, *Der korintisch-dorische Tempel am Forum von Paestum* (Berlin 1939), Taf. 3.

33 Pensabene 1993, 265 ff., Tav. 125.

34 D. Krencker and W. Zscheitzmann, *Römische Tempel in Syrien* (Berlin 1938), fig. 9.

35 Ward-Perkins 1993 [S.7E], 67 ff., esp. 72.

36 Corinthian semi-column capitals of an appropriate size for the third tier of the façade are preserved in some of the storerooms under the *cavea* of the Theatre of Marcellus. For a representative summary of prevailing assumptions, see J.S. Curl, *Classical Architecture: An Introduction to its Vocabulary and Essentials, with a Select Glossary of Terms* (London 1992), 215, with further examples and a subsequent, more judicious analysis in P. Liljenstolpe, 'Surperimposed Orders: The Use of the Architectural Orders in multi-storeyed structures of the Roman imperial era', *OpusRom*, XXIV, forthcoming.

37 As reconstructed on the basis of coins as opposed to actual finds, see Packer 1997 [S.8A], I, 217 ff.

38 Codex Saluzziano, fol. 80, Maltese 1967 (see Introduction, n. 4), I, 280–81; for the translation, see Buddensieg 1971 [S.9B], 264.

39 Loerke 1990 [S.9B], 32.

40 Lauter 1986 [S.GC], Abb. 44a.

41 For further examples involving archways, doors and windows as well as columns, see H. von Hesberg, *Formen privater Repräsentation in der Baukunst des 2. und 1. Jahrhunderts v. Chr.* (Cologne 1994), Abb. 27d, 65a, 86b, 90b and 95a; Colvin 1991 [S.4B], 41.

42 A. Laidlaw, *The First Style in Pompeii: Painting and Architecture* (Rome 1985), pl. 14.

43 H. Kähler, 'Die römischen Torburgen der frühen Kaiserzeit', *JdI*, LVII (1942), 1–104; L. Bacchielli, 'Le porte romane ad ordini sovrapposti e gli antecedenti greci', *RM*, XCI (1984), 79–87.

44 Ward-Perkins 1977 [S.GA], 33; G. Cavalieri-Manasse, 'Porta Leoni: Appunti per la ricostruzione di un monumento', *Scritti in ricordo di Graziella Massari Gaballo e di Umberto Tocchetti Pollini* (Milan 1986), 169.

45 A. Schmidt-Colinet, *Das Tempelgrab Nr. 36 in Palmyra* (Mainz 1992).

46 MacDonald 1982–6 [S.GA], II, 186.

47 Lyttleton 1974, 39; MacDonald 1982–6 [S.GA], II, 184.

48 Lyttleton 1974 (9–16 for the question of definition); MacDonald 1982–6 [S.GA], II, 221–47; McKenzie 1991, 87 ff.; McKenzie, 'Alexandria and the Origins of Baroque Architecture', in *Alexandria and Alexandrianism* (Malibu 1996), 109–25.

49 Coulton 1988 [S.GC], 74. Cf. Vitruvius, III,3,4.

50 Vitruvius associated this scheme with systyle column spacing (III,3,2). Achieving both simultaneously demands a base width of 1½ column diameters, just the ratio he recommends for the Ionic base (III,5,1). In practice, however, such broad proportions were exceptional.

51 U. Tarchi, *L'arte nell'Umbria e nella Sabina* (Milan 1936), I, tav. 171–83.

52 In reality the axial spacing varies, being about 4.43 m or 15 ft on the front and about 10 cm less on the flanks; see Ganzert 1996 [S.7E], Beil. 12.

53 In part due to the poor quality of the local stone, the openings at El Jem are *narrower* than the piers by 4:5; see Wilson Jones 1993 [S.5B], 427–8.

54 The same buildings also use another type of proportion, this time between two measures of height, often equality – as for example, when the height of a pedestal equals that of the entablature over which it stands. See also DeLaine 1997 [S.GA], 59–60, who notes the frequency with which room heights are double either the height of columns or that of a whole order.

55 100 ft was also the likely overall height of the Theatre of Marcellus, see Wilson Jones 1993 [S.5B], fig. 30.

56 Cf. J.-F. Bommelaer, 'Sur la répétition des figures simples dans quelques projets de l'architecture hellénistique', *Akten des XIII. Int. Kongresses für klassische Archäologie* (Mainz 1990), 420–22.

57 Starting from the premise of a hexastyle frontage of columns 5 ft wide and 48 ft tall, the addition of a podium a third as high gave a combined height of about 64 ft (the exact podium height is open to interpretation). Meanwhile a pycnostyle rhythm generated an axial width of 62½ ft, or five times a column bay of 12½ ft. The 64 ft ideal was redeemed by adding 1½ inches to the flanking bays and making the central bay about 1 ft wider still.

58 Krauss and Herbig 1939 (see n. 32); D. Theodorescu, 'Le forum et le temple "Doric-Corinthien" de Paestum: Une experience pré-Vitruvienne', AA.VV. 1989 [S.2A], 114–25.

59 A.L. Frothingham, 'Who built the Arch of Constantine?', *AJA*, XVI (1912), 368–86; *AJA*, XVII (1913), 487–503; *AJA*, XIX (1915), 1–12, 367–84; A. Melucco Vaccaro, *Archeo*, IX/5 (May 1994), 38–43; A. Melucco Vaccaro and A.M. Ferroni, 'Chi costruì l'arco di Costantino: Un interrogativo ancora attuale', *RendPontAcc*, LXXI (1993–4 [1997]), 1–60.

60 H.P. L'Orange, A. von Gerkan, *Der spätantike Bildschmuck des Konstantinsbogens* (Berlin 1939), 4–33; C. Panella, P. Pensabene and M. Milella, 'Scavo nell'area della Meta Sudans e ricerche sull'arco di Costantino', *ArchLaz*, XII/1 (1995), 41–59; Panella and Pensabene 1997.

61 There was a low parapet above the attic cornice; see A. Cassatella and M.L. Conforto, *Arco di Costantino: Il restauro della sommità* (Pesaro 1989), 14 ff., 51, but the cornice could still have been the *conceptual* limit.

62 Some of these 'propositions' were identified in M. Wilson Jones, 'Osservazioni sul progetto dell'arco', *ArchLaz*, XII/1 (1995), 59–61; others are explained in Wilson-Jones 1999 [S.5B].

63 The columns fit Scheme C, as described on p. 148. Ones of this size are quite common, including those of the Library of Hadrian in Athens, the sanctuary at Baalbek, the Severan

temple in Lepcis Magna, and in Rome, both Augustus' and Trajan's Forum.

64 R. Brilliant, 'The Arch of Septimius Severus in the Roman Forum', *MAAR*, XXIX (1967), 35 ff.; S. De Maria, *Gli archi onorari di Roma e dell'Italia romana* (Rome 1988), 58 ff., 197 ff., 316 ff.

65 The precise original ground level is unknown, but it may have been about half a foot to a foot below current grade; see Panella and Pensabene 1997, 259–75.

66 Ward-Perkins 1981 [S.GA], 430.

67 R. Amy *et al.*, *L'arc d'Orange*, xvᵉ supplément, *Gallia* (1962); Traversari 1971 [S.7E], 89–90, tav. 5; Mansuelli 1959 [S.7E], 375–8; E. Ferrero, *L'arc d'Auguste à Suse* (Turin 1901), 11–12. Cf. Dehio 1895 [S.5A], figs 68–77.

68 The $\sqrt{3}$ relationships highlighted by Traversari (see n. 67) are in fact 1.747 and 1.750 respectively, that is to say closer to 7:4 (1.75) than $\sqrt{3}$ (1.732).

69 Thus the complete bay measures 40 ft × 23 ft, yielding a ratio of 1.739 (½% more than $\sqrt{3}$ (1.732)).

70 My thanks to David Jacobson for sharing the last observation. For further arguments, see Wilson Jones 1993 [S.5B], 431–2.

71 Entasis appears first for certain in the Temple of Hera at Paestum (ca. 550 BC), although it has been restored tentatively for Aeolic columns at Old Smyrna of around 600 BC (R.V. Nicholls, 'Early Monumental Religious Architecture at Old Smyrna', *New Perspectives in Greek Art* = *Studies in the History of Art*, XXXII (1991), 162). See Mertens 1988.

72 For various interpretations, see the Vitruvius references in the following note; Thiersch 1873; Pennethorne 1876; Hauck 1879; Penrose 1888; Goodyear 1912; Rankin 1986; Lewis 1994; Rykwert 1996; AA.VV. 1999.

73 Vitruvius, III,3,11 (thickening of corner columns; cf. IV, 4, 2); entasis (III,3,13); III,4,5 (stylobate curvature); III,5,4 (column inclination); III,5,8 (curvature of superstructure).

74 F. Hueber, 'Beobachtungen zu Kurvatur und Scheinperspektive an der Celsiusbibliothek und anderen kaiserzeitlichen Bauten', AA.VV. 1984 [S.3A], 175–200; Hueber 1999. On the other hand, it is well to take a sceptical view of some further possible occurrences; the pediment of the Temple of Hercules at Cori may now display concavity in plan (Goodyear 1912, 42 ff.), but this is surely a deformation due to the collapse of the roof; see A. von Gerkan, 'Die Krümmungen im Gebälk des dorischen Tempels in Cori', *RM*, XL (1925), 167.

75 P. Davies and D. Hemsoll, 'Entasis and Diminution in the Design of Renaissance Pilasters', AA.VV. 1992, 339–53.

76 F. Blondel, *Resolution des quatre principaux problèmes d'architecture* (Paris 1673).

77 See n. 72; for recent confirmation of the extreme subtlety of refinements on the Acropolis, see Korres 1999.

78 Penrose 1888, 85; cf. A. Choisy, *Vitruve* (Paris 1909), I, 154 ff.; Dinsmoor 1975 [S.GC], 167–8. For the mathematical background, see Heath 1921 [S.2B] and Seybold 1999.

79 Stevens 1924. He also endorsed Vignola's second and more complicated solution, one corresponding to another curve known in antiquity, the conchoid of Nicomedes of Gerasa. (See P. Tannery, 'Pour l'histoire des lignes et des surfaces courbes dans l'antiquité: Les concoïdes de Nichomède', *Mémoires scientifiques*, II/2 (1912), 40–42; Heath 1921 [S.2B], I, 238–40; Stevens 1924, 134 ff.; cf. G. Hallier, 'Le premier forum de Rougga', *BCTH*, XVIIb (1984), 108.) In technical terms, the particular trouble with Stevens's work was his tendency to smooth out what he supposed were imperfections, as well as the extreme scale exaggeration he used to describe the results.

Combined together, this has the effect of making a negligible deviation from a straight line look like a curve.

80 For the theatre at Aphrodisias, see Hueber 1999; Wilson Jones 1999; cf. N. de Chaisemartin and D. Theodorescu, 'Recherches préliminaires sur la *frons scaenae* du théâtre', *Aphrodisias Papers*, II (1991). On Pergamon, see R. Bohn, *Die Theaterterrasse = AvP*, IV (Berlin 1896), Taf. 36; Heisel 1993 [S.3A], 208 ff.

81 The same applies to the Erechtheion, where the method may have originated. Compare Penrose 1888, pl. 14; L.D. Caskey *et al.*, *The Erechtheion* (Cambridge, Mass., 1927), 82; Wilson Jones 1999.

82 Wilson Jones 1999. But note, however, the case of a shaft left behind in the Proconnesos quarries where a fairly common type of profile seems to have been applied incorrectly, with the top and bottom sections inverted.

83 B. Nobiloni, 'Le colonne vitinee della basilica di San Pietro a Roma', *Xenia antiqua*, VI (1997), 81–142.

84 Wilson Jones 1999.

85 On constructional constraints relating to Greek refinements see J.J. Coulton, 'Coping with Curvature: The Practical Aspects', AA.VV. 1999.

86 On fabrication see Pensabene 1996 [S.7F], 294 ff.; Pensabene, 'Sulla tecnica di lavorazione delle colonne del tempio tetrastilo di *Thignica* (Aïn Tougga)', *Africa romana*, XI (1994), 1103–23; Wilson Jones 1999.

CHAPTER VII

1 K. Lange, 'Die Athena Parthenos', *AM*, VI (1881), 72; N. Leipen, *Athena Parthenos: A Reconstruction* (Ontario 1971), 38; Pedersen 1989.

2 Now lost, it was measured and drawn by Haller von Haller-stein and others in the early nineteenth century. For recon-structions, see Gütschow 1921, 44 ff.; G. Roux, 'Le chapiteau corinthien de Bassae', *BCH*, LXXVII (1953), 124–38; Bauer 1972, 14–65; Cooper 1996, 305 ff. It is a matter of debate whether there were originally three Corinthian capitals, or just the central one.

3 Bauer 1977 [S.4B]. Third-century examples include Ptolemy II's propylon at Samothrace, the mausoleum at Belevi, the adyton of the Didymaion and the Doric-Corinthian temple at Paestum (fig. 6.22). See Boysal 1957; Roux 1961 [S.6A]; Lauter 1986 [S.GC], 257 ff.; Pensabene 1993 [S.6A], 115 ff.

4 R. Tölle-Kastenbein, 'Sur l'Olympieion comme premier temple périptère d'ordre corinthien', *Actes des XIII. Int. Kongress für klassische Archäologie* (Berlin 1990), 426 ff.; Tölle-Kastenbein 1994. The date of the Diocaesarea temple is dis-puted, see Williams 1974; Wesenberg 1983 [S.GC], 174; Gros 1993, 30. It is also possible that a set of capitals at Hermoupolis Magna in Egypt datable to around 200 BC belonged to the exterior of a temple (Pensabene 1993 [S.6A], 251). For further Hellenistic examples, see M. Waelkens, 'Hellenistic and Roman Influence in the Imperial Architecture of Asia Minor', AA.VV. 1989 [S.GA], 80, n. 34.

5 Gros 1982 [S.2A], 679 ff.

6 Euripides, *Iphigenia in Tauris*, 47.

7 But it must be emphasized that caryatids typically support capitals on top of the head.

8 This argument is developed in a forthcoming publication of mine.

9 Wesenberg 1971 [S. 6A]; Rykwert 1996 [S. 6A].

10 Hersey 1988 [S.6A], 30; cf. Vitruvius, IV, 1,7.

11 Riegl 1992, 191, 205. Cf. Ferri 1960 [S.2A], 144 ff.; Roux 1961 [S.6A], 359 ff.; Heilmeyer 1970, 13; Onians 1988 [S.6A], 35; Gros 1993, 29 and works cited in Rykwert 1996 [S.6A], 495, n. 7.

12 Homolle 1916; Roux 1961 [S.6A], 190; Rykwert 1980; Rykwert 1996 [S.6A], 320–27; Pensabene, *ArchCl*, XXXIV (1982), 58, n. 83; Onians 1988 [S.6A], 19.

13 For a rendered elevation, see F.K. Yegül, *Gentlemen of Instinct and Breeding: Architecture at the American Academy in Rome* (Oxford 1991), pl. 82.

14 Diod. Sic. XVIII, 26–28; Giuliani 1995.

15 Gros 1995 [S.6A], 27.

16 Ziolkowski 1988 (see chapter 1, n. 8). This pulls the date much earlier than is generally given, but such would be consistent with its precocious and incompletely resolved character, and in particular the oddities of the columns, the shafts of which are so thin as to evoke some sort of misunderstanding.

17 Lauter 1986 [S.GC], 237 ff.; Mallwitz 1981, 345 ff.

18 See the bibliography in S.7C. Cf. E.D. Maguire, 'Range and Repertory in Capital Design', *DOP*, XLI (1987), 351–61.

19 See Zanker 1988, and other works cited in S.7B.

20 Cf. Onians 1988 [S.6A], esp. p. 20.

21 H.P. L'Orange, 'L'Ara Pacis Augustae: La zona floreale', *ActaAArtH*, I (1962), 7–16; Zanker 1988, 172 ff.; G. Sauron, 'Le message esthétique des rinceaux de l'*Ara Pacis Augustae*', *CRAI*, 1982, 80–101; P. Pollini, 'The Acanthus of the Ara Pacis as an Apolline and Dionysiac Symbol of Anamorphosis, Anakyklosis and Numen Mixtum', *Festschrift für Alois Machatschek* (Vienna 1993), 181–217; Castriota 1995. For a purely decorative interpretation, see B. Andreae, *The Art of Rome* (New York 1977), 116.

22 Sauron 1993, 90 ff.

23 Zanker 1988, 48 ff., 85 ff., 201 ff.; Evans 1992, 93 ff.

24 Walker and Burnett 1981; Zanker 1988, 98–100, 301–2; D. Boschung, *Die Bildnisse des Augustus: Das römische Herrscherbild* (Berlin 1993); Galinsky 1996, 164 ff.; R.R.R. Smith, 'Typology and Diversity in the Portraits of Augustus', *JRA*, IX (1996), 31–47.

25 See the bibliography in S.7C; on the Italic type in particular, see Cocco 1977; De Maria 1981; Rizzo 1984 [S.7A]; Lauter-Bufe 1987; Villa 1988 [S.7A].

26 Strong and Ward-Perkins 1960, 7; Abramson 1974.

27 Heilmeyer 1970, 42–8; Gros 1976, esp. 211 ff., 229 ff.

28 Hesberg 1981, 23 ff.; Viscogliosi 1996.

29 Heilmeyer 1970, 25–32; Amy and Gros 1979, 133–4.

30 Strong 1963; Hesberg 1980 and 1981, 27 ff.; Pensabene 1993, 99 ff.

31 Hesberg 1980, 100–141.

32 It is unclear whether a key pair of monuments in Rome with modillions, the Temple of Deified Caesar and the Temple of Saturn (both 42–29 BC) had Corinthian as opposed to Ionic columns. See Ward-Perkins 1967, 24 ff.; Gros 1976, 207 ff.; P. Pensabene, *Tempio di Saturno = LSA*, V (Rome 1984), 75–7.

33 Strong 1963, 83 ff.

34 Strong 1953 [S.9C]; P. Liljenstolpe, '*De Ornamentis Templi Urbis*: Reconstructing the Main Order of the Temple of Venus and Roma in Rome', *OpusRom*, XX (1996), 47–67.

35 Amy and Gros 1979, 142–5; Pensabene 1982; Pensabene 1982 (cited chapter 1 above, n. 55, esp. 119 and 164). On Augustus' forum, see Zanker 1984; Ward-Perkins 1981 [S.GA], 28–33; Ganzert 1996.

36 With regard to columnar proportions, compare the measure-ments given in Appendix B for the mausoleum at Glanum,

the tholos by the Tiber, the Temple of Artemis at Jerash and the Arch of Marcus Aurelius at Tripoli.

37 Gros 1993, 29, 33. Among those that it most closely resembles in terms of proportion are capitals from the House of the Faun in Pompeii and the Olympieion in Athens, but both represent something of a dead end in this respect; see Wilson Jones 1991, 91, 115, 145.

38 Wilson Jones 1991.

39 Wilson Jones 1991, 150. Cf. Tomasello 1983 and Pagello 1992 (the square 'a' coincides with the cross-sectional width); Dolci 1994, 110.

40 Wilson Jones 1991, 117, 145.

41 Wilson Jones 1991. Cf. Pensabene 1986, 288 ff.

42 A minority trend was for the axial width of the abacus to be about 5–10 per cent greater than the height. Examples include Vitruvius' capital, those from the Olympieion in Athens and the Odeon of Agrippa in Athens, the Temple of Mars Ultor and the Pantheon (portico) in Rome, and the Asklepieion in Pergamon. It is, however, conceivably possible that a variant of the cross-section rule applied, for in these cases the capital height roughly matches the upper diameter of the kalathos.

43 The 36 ft height makes allowance for the part of the plinth of the base now obscured by a rise in floor level.

44 Vignola [S.6A], pl. 21; Wilson Jones 1989, 65.

45 V. Mortet, 'La mesure des colonnes à la fin de l'époque romaine, d'après un très ancien formulaire', *Bibliotèque de l'École des chartes*, LVII (1896), 277–324. One formula makes the column height two-and-a-half times the lower circumference, yielding almost 8:1 ($2\frac{1}{2} \times 22/7 = 7\frac{6}{7}$). Another states that the width of the bottom flare and the astragal should be respectively one-seventh and one-eighth of the shaft height. The latter ratio must also apply to the body of the shaft (measured above the flare), since this normally matched the astragal.

46 Scheme D repeats Scheme C, with a sub-plinth under the base so as to achieve a 10:1 slenderness for the entire ensemble (Pantheon aedicules; Arch of Septimius Severus); see Wilson Jones 1989, 44–6.
Scheme E has an 8:1 shaft like Scheme C, but like Scheme A it has a capital twice as tall as the base (Byblos, theatre and nymphaeum).
Scheme F repeats the last relation, but with a capital height equal to the shaft diameter, and an overall slenderness of 9:1 (Philae, temple; Scythopolis, nymphaeum).

47 Schemes E and F, see the preceding note.

48 All these relationships were proposed by Renaissance commentators who advocated systems based on the lower diameter. For example, Serlio gives D = DA and $\frac{1}{2}$DWP = $\frac{1}{2}$DWAb = D, while Palladio gives LWAb = $1\frac{1}{2}$D and HKal = $\frac{1}{2}$DWAb = D.

49 Vertical correspondance seems to be a long-standing principle; note the following instances in which the *lateral* width of the torus/plinth equals the *lateral* width of the abacus:

Building	diameter of torus (DT)	width of cap. LWAb	diff. in cm
Tholos of Epidauros	0.79	0.79	0
Olympieion, Athens	2.56	2.57	1
Bouleuterion, Miletos	1.03	1.04	1
Tholos at Tivoli	1.04	1.02	2
Apsidal Building, Palestrina	0.92	0.92	0
Temple of the Dioscuri, Cori	1.285	1.30	$1\frac{1}{2}$
House of the Faun, Pompeii	0.625	0.65	$2\frac{1}{2}$

50 Ferchiou 1975 [S.6A], 47 ff.; Wesenberg 1983 [S.GC], 26 ff., 101 ff., 110 ff. For objections, see Gros 1990 [S.2A], Appendix, 203–7; B.F. Weber, 'Columnae Crassitudo: Zur Bemessung des unteren Säuledurchmessers (UD)', *IstMitt*, XLI (1991), 423–38.

51 Wilson Jones 1991, 91, 115 (n. 28), 119, 145.

52 Analogous considerations affected the flare of the shaft, which respond both to such schemes and the general rule that it be about $\frac{9}{8}$ or $\frac{8}{7}$ the diameter of the body of the shaft.

53 The diameter is $4\frac{3}{4}$ ft (4.75 ft) as opposed to the theoretical value of $4\frac{4}{5}$ ft (4.8 ft = one-tenth the column height).

54 At the 'Sala del Colosssos' in the Forum of Augustus the floor slopes towards the boundary wall, perhaps due to settlement during construction. The shafts follow the slope, but the architrave was made level, so again the capitals absorb the difference (9 cm).

55 Pliny, *HN*, XXXVI, 6.45. Although it is widely thought that the columns in question came from the exterior of the Olympieion, they could have come from the interior instead, see Abramson 1974, while Richardson 1992 [S.GA], 222–3, suggests that the columns may have been Doric ones from the original Pisistratid temple. Cf. Wycherley 1964; Rawson 1975 [S.1].

56 On the ambiguities of the columns from the tholos by the Tiber, see Wilson Jones 1989, 38 and 57.

57 Without plinths the 6:5 rule is bound not to apply; see for example Dupré i Raventos 1994, 206–7.

58 For similar observations regarding the column size used at the Arch of Constantine, see chapter 6, p. 124.

59 For the Baths of Caracalla, see DeLaine 1997 [S.GA], 258.

60 Ward-Perkins 1993, 45, 57 and 67 ff.

61 L. Cozza, 'Le tegole marmoree del Pantheon', *Città e architettura nella Roma imperiale = AnalRom*, supp. 10 (1983), 109–18.

62 Asgari 1988 and 1990.

63 AA.VV., *I marmi di Lasinio* (cat. Pisa 1993), 190–91.

64 Patrich 1996; McKenzie 1991 [S.6A]. For other Egyptian capitals not unlike those at Philae, see G. Castel, *et al.*, *Les fontaines de la porte nord, Dendera* (Cairo 1984), 26 ff.

65 Cf. Fischer 1989. On the link between the Troad and Proconnesos quarries, see Ward-Perkins 1992, 65, 81; Ponti 1995, 292.

66 Asgari 1988; Wilson Jones 1991, 133–4; Dolci 1994.

67 For the marble trade in general see S.7F; and in particular Ward-Perkins 1951, 95; Ward-Perkins 1992, esp. 81; Gnoli 1988; Dodge 1991; Fant 1993; and Salies ed. 1994.

68 See Table 1 in Appendix B. Note also the 20, 25, 30 and 40 ft shafts of the Baths of Caracalla (DeLaine 1997 [S.GA], 259 ff.); the 20, 25 and 30 ft (recycled) ones of Old St Peter's and St Paul's. Since 30 ft shafts remain at the *giallo antico* quarries (Rakob 1993), 40 ft ones at the *cipollino* quarries (Hankey 1965), 20, 30 and 60 ft ones at Mons Claudianus, the 38 ft examples in the Troad quarries (Ponti 1995, 313 ff.) hardly dent the general trend. But for reservations, see H. Dodge in Ward-Perkins 1992, 25, n. 18 (who cites wrongly 39 ft rather than 40 ft for the shafts of the Temple of Antoninus and Faustina; cf. Fant 1993, 156).

69 For example in Trajan's Forum there are sets of 12, 16 and 24 ft shafts along with 30 and 50 ft ones (Packer 1997 [S.8A], 385 ff.). At Mons Claudianus the shafts group into the following lengths: multiples of 10 ft (60, 50, 30, 20, 10 ft), multiples of 8 ft (24, 16, 8 ft) and one of 14 ft; see Peacock and Maxfield 1997 [S.9D].

70 Note how the three non-standard shaft heights at the Baths of Caracalla were selected to fit total column heights of 20,

71 25 and 50 ft; see DeLaine 1997 [S.GA], 178 (Table 17), 259 ff.

71 Cicero, *Att.*, 12, 19.

72 Ward-Perkins 1992, 109–10 (but see the editor's comments, 110, n. 19). The main argument for stockpiling is simply the sheer quantity of standardized elements. 15 ft shafts and 2 ft capitals, for example, are so common that it is difficult to believe that quarry managers did not run up surpluses during lulls between specific orders on the assumption they would be absorbed by future demand.

73 *Peripl. M. Rubr.* 1–2, as translated in Ward-Perkins 1992, 29.

74 Wilson Jones 1989, 48.

CHAPTER VIII

1 The scenes do not however present a strictly chronological report. See Hannestad 1986 [S.GA], 158; T. Hölscher, *Monumenti statali e pubblico* (Rome 1994), 111 ff. On architectural representations, see Coulston 1990a.

2 AA.VV. 1988; J.E. Moore, 'The Monument, or, Christopher Wren's Roman Accent', *ArtBull*, LXXX (1998), 498–533.

3 Amm. Marc., XVI,10,15.

4 P. von Blanckenhagen, 'The Imperial Fora', *JSAH*, XIII (1954), 25; Packer 1994, 172 ff.; Frazer 1993; Wightman 1997; Packer 1997, I, 260–68.

5 G. Rodenwalt, *Gnomon*, II (1926), 338 ff.; Zanker 1970, 505 ff.; Boatwright 1987 [S.9C], 83 ff.; Packer 1997, I, 259–60.

6 AA.VV. 1985 [S.GB], 181, 206; Amici 1982, 17 ff.; Packer 1997, I, 139–215.

7 Meneghini 1998. However, excavations have not turned up a temple at this end either.

8 Amici 1982, 76; Boatwright 1987 [S.9C], 88 ff.; Claridge 1993, 20 ff.

9 Zanker 1970, 538 ff.; Ward-Perkins 1992 [S.7F], 111; Settis *et al.* 1988, 75–82; Packer 1994, 171; Packer 1997, I, 261.

10 Dio Cass., LXVIII,16,3; Eutropius, *Breviarium ab urbe condita*, VIII, 5, 3. Cf. Settis *et al.* 1988, 60–75; Davies 1997. For the date of dedication, see Anderson 1984, 148, 151; Boatwright 1987 [S.9C], 88.

11 For an affirmative view, see Zanker 1970; Settis *et al.* 1988, 49–56; Packer 1994, 171.

12 Lepper and Frere 1988, 22, 191, 223; Claridge 1993, 11.

13 *CIL*, VI. 960; E.M. Smallwood, *Documents Illustrating the Principates of Nerva, Trajan and Hadrian* (Cambridge 1966), no. 378; Lepper and Frere 1988, 21. Cf. Claridge 1993, 9.

14 Dio Cass., LXVIII,16,3.

15 The total depth, including the section beyond the last plaque, is 128 ft; see Canina 1853 [S.4A], I, 25; Wurm 1984 (see Introduction, n. 38], 48; *Il Lazio di Thomas Ashby = British School at Rome Archive*, IV (1994), 190–91.

16 Boni 1907; Tummarello 1989; Claridge 1993, 9, n. 9.

17 Claridge 1993, 9–10.

18 XVI,10.14: *elatosque vertices qui scansili suggestu consurgunt, priorum principum imitamenta portantes.*

19 Lanciani 1894 [S.GA], 97.

20 My thanks to Amanda Claridge for this information.

21 N. Asgari, 'Zwei Werstücke für Konstantinopel aus den prokonnesischen Steinbrüchen', *IstMitt*, XXXIX (1989), 60.

22 Aurès 1863; H. Bauer, 'Porticus Absidata', *RM*, XC (1983), 136, n. 33.

23 Rottländer 1996b [S.4A], 16–30. The usual Roman foot was used for the forum as a whole (Packer 1997, I, 471 proposes a value of around 294 mm).

24 On the plan, see Packer 1997, I, 260–68; for the shafts, see Packer 1997, I, 385–91; Amici, 1982, 18, 25, 37; Ward-Perkins 1992 [S.7F], 112.

25 Frazer 1993; Wightman 1997.

26 I thank Lynne Lancaster for showing me the results of her recent survey.

27 *CIL*, VI. 1585; Martines 1992, 1040.

28 Rockwell 1985; Lepper and Frere 1988, 30 ff.

29 Settis *et al.* 1988, 49–56.

30 Lepper and Frere 1988, 19–26.

31 Claridge 1993.

32 Martines 1983; Martines 1992, 1042. Cf. Rockwell 1985.

33 Lepper and Frere 1988, 191; Packer 1994.

34 *Pace* R. Bianchi Bandinelli, 'Un problema di arte romana: Il "maestro dell imprese di Traiano"', *Le arti*, I (1938–9), 325–34; reprinted in *Storicità dell'arte classica* (Florence 1943), 193–216.

35 Typically risers in this region measure between 17 and 21 cm, a range that corresponds roughly both with the value used in Trajan's Column (19 cm) and with modern norms. By contrast, taller risers were traditionally more typical in Rome (sometimes as much as 29–30 cm or 1 ft). For other oriental connections, see Gullini 1968 [S.1].

36 Martines 1983, 61; Martines 1989 [S.9B], 6.

37 In elevation the soffit would have occurred at the level where the shaft began to rise straight, just above the flare; the problem arises because in plan the landing falls outside the compass of the shaft.

38 This problem did not occur to me until I began to draw the cut-away perspective illustrated in fig. 8.8, a view taken from the diagonal.

39 Martines 1983 and 1992; Martines 1989 [S.9B]; Lancaster 1999.

40 Wilson Jones 1993, 31.

41 Fontana 1978; Dibner 1970; cf. Santillo 1996.

42 P. Hodges and J. Keable, *How the Pyramids were Built* (Longmead 1989); Arnold 1991 [S.3B], 57 ff.

43 Adam 1977, esp. 52.

44 Coulton 1974, 16 and 19 cites 108 tonnes, but I estimate 99–102.

45 Coulton 1974; Adam 1977, 31 ff.; Adam 1989 [S.GA], 30, 44–9; Fleury 1995, 95 ff.

46 Rough calculations made using my own measurements (which agree well with those of Desgodets 1682 [S.GB], 68, and F. Toebelmann, *Römische Gebälke* (Heidelberg 1923), Taf. XII), yield around 95 tons. Cf. Santangeli Valenzani, 'ΝΕΩΣ ΥΠΕΡΓΕΘΗΣ: Osservazioni sul tempio di Piazza del Quirinale', *BComm*, XCIV (1991–2), 7–16; G. Scaglia, *Bolld'A*, LXXII (1992), 1–10; Liljenstolpe (see chapter 7, n. 34), 55.

47 Asgari 1989 (*supra* n. 21), 54 ff.

48 Adam 1977, 40, fig. 4; Giuliani 1990 [S.GA], 199 ff.; Kozelj and Kozelj 1993, 127–9. Fleury 1995 [S.2A], 107, cites 15 tons 'théoriques', while C. O'Connor (*Roman Bridges*, Cambridge 1993, 49) calculates 6.2 tons for a crane of the type represented on the Haterii relief. Lancaster (1999) converges on 7 tons or so, following consideration of the likely limits of stress associated with hemp ropes and the Lewis irons by which force was transferred to individual blocks.

49 Fontana 1978.

50 Happily my intuitions now find substantiation in Lynne Lancaster's detailed study (1999), which she kindly sent me before this went to press.

51 Canina 1853 [S.4A], 19.

52 Notable fractions of 100 ft include:

(a) height of the capital, 4 ft, = 100 ft/25;

(b) diameter of the shaft, 12½ ft, = 100 ft/8;

(c) width of the capital, 14⅜ ft, = 100 ft/7;

(d) width of the torus, 16⅔ ft, = 100 ft/6.

Notable multiples of 7 feet (cf Bauer 1983, cited in n. 22), include:

(a) diameter of the core at the start of the helical stair, 3½ ft, = 7 ft/2;

(b) diameter of the flare at the bottom of the shaft, 14 ft, = 7 ft × 2;

(c) height of the relief band on the pedestal, 10½ ft, = 7 ft × 3/2;

(d) height and width of pedestal, 21 ft, = 7 ft × 3.

53 Martines 1992, 1046.

CHAPTER IX

1 Ziolkowski 1994; Macrobius' mention, for example, makes it clear that *Pantheion* was just the name by which the building was generally known (*Sat.*, 3.17.18).

2 Dio Cassius, 59.27.2–4.

3 Ziolkowski 1994, 261, 272.

4 *SHA. Hadr.* 19.10: 'Romae instauravit Pantheum, Saepta, Basilica Neptuni, sacras aedes plurimas, Forum Augusti, Lavacrum Agrippae.'

5 Godfrey and Hemsoll 1986; cf. J.E. Stambaugh, 'The Functions of Roman Temples', *ANRW*, II. 16.1 (1978), 557 ff.

6 Gros 1996 [S.GA], 175 ff.

7 But according to Ziolkowski (1994), Mars is less apt from this point of view.

8 O. Gilbert, *Geschichte und Topographie der Stadt Rom im Altertum* (Leipzig 1883–90), III, 115–16; Zeigler 1949, 741–2; Will 1951; MacDonald 1976, 77; Coarelli 1983, 42, 44; Godfrey and Hemsoll 1986, 197.

9 A further connection is suggested by Pliny the Elder's statement that the Athenian artist Diogenes made caryatids for Agrippa's Pantheon (*HN*, XXXVI. 38); caryatids modelled on those of the Erechtheion in Athens were also prominent in Augustus' forum.

10 Coarelli 1983. For bibliography on Augustan architecture and propaganda, see S.7B.

11 Dio Cassius, 69.7.1; Godfrey and Hemsoll 1986, esp. 202.

12 Loerke 1982, 51; Thomas 1997, 174. Oudet (1992, 38) gives the Pantheon axis as about 3½° off meridian, a value I have roughly checked by observing the position of the light pool of the oculus at midday. Maps indicate that the axis joining the Pantheon and the mausoleum is between 3 and 3¼° off meridian.

13 Ziolkowski 1994. In my view this thesis hangs on the form of Agrippa's building (see p. 182). If it was T-shaped, then the subsequent change of typology might be explained by the change of use. Conversely, an Agrippan rotunda would rule out a temple of Mars, since a great round hall was so antithetical to normal cult practices.

14 Lanciani 1897, 479 ff.; Beltrami 1898, 33; Guey 1936; De Fine Licht 1968, 186–90, 285–91. Due to a minority of Trajanic brickstamps, Heilmeyer (1975) dates inception to just before Hadrian's accession. But it is not unusual for masonry to contain bricks of mixed vintage, since production was not necessarily consumed immediately (A.C.G. Smith, 'The Date of the "Grandi Terme" of Hadrian's Villa at Tivoli', PBSR, XLVI

(1978), 73–93, esp. 73–8; Boatwright 1987, 43; Loerke 1990, 22; Haselberger 1994, 296–303).

15 Lanciani 1897, 483; Platner and Ashby 1929 [S.GA], 384 ff., Kähler 1965, fig. 9; Shipley 1933, 62; Will 1951; Gros 1976 [S.7B], pl. 26; MacDonald 1976, 12; Geertman 1980, Appendix, fig. 12; Coarelli 1983, 41; Zanker 1988 [S.7B], 140; Richardson 1992 [S.GA], 183; Gros 1996 [S.GA], 175.

16 Richter 1893; Lugli 1971, 15; Loerke 1982, 50 ff.; Tortorici 1990, 30–42; Simpson 1997; Thomas 1997.

17 The republican Temple B (probably that of Fortuna Huiusce Diei) in the Area Sacra of the Largo Argentina echoes the same shape, with its circular peristyle and frontal flight of steps, but it is unclear if it ever included a full-blooded porch.

18 References cited in n. 16. For a summary of opinion, see also Gruben and Gruben 1997, 72–3.

19 Apparently Hadrian customarily showed respect to his predecessors in this way. See *SHA. Hadr.* 19.10; D.R. Stuart, 'Imperial Methods of Inscription on Restored Buildings: Augustus and Hadrian', *AJA*, IX (1905), 427–49; Boatwright 1987, 43.

20 Boatwright 1987, 46, 52, 72.

21 Beltrami 1898, fig. 34; Lugli 1971, 15; De Fine Licht 1968, 173. In the Forum of Augustus the interior coloured marble slabs are similarly 5–7 cm thick, while the exterior paving is 13–16 cm thick.

22 Loerke 1982, 50; Thomas 1997, esp. 169.

23 *HN*, XVI, 201.

24 Lanciani 1897, 482–3; Beltrami 1898, fig. xxv; Tortorici 1990, 38.

25 Cf. E.B. Smith, *The Dome: A Study in the History of Ideas* (Princeton 1950); for the Domus Aurea, see H.P. L'Orange, *Studies in the Iconography of the Cosmic Kingship in the Ancient World* (Oslo 1953), esp. 30–31.

26 McEwen 1993, 62; Sperling 1998, 129.

27 Cicero, *De Div.*, II, 18 (cf. 1,2); Vitruvius, 1,6; S. Weinstock, 'Martianus Capella and the Cosmic System of the Etruscans', *JRS*, XXXVI (1946), 101–29; De Fine Licht 1968, 197; Loerke 1990, 36; McEwen 1993, 57, 61. Cf. J. Rykwert, *The Idea of a Town* (Cambridge, Mass., 1988).

28 This excludes the respondent pilasters concealed behind the apse columns; see Alvegård 1972, 16, n. 47; Martines 1989, 8.

29 1 + 2 + 4 + 7 + 14 add up to 28, and each divide into it. Only three other such numbers were known in antiquity, 6, 496 and 8128; see Heath 1921 [S.2B], 1, 74; Martines 1989, 7; Loerke 1990, 37; Sperling 1998, 130–32.

30 De Fine Licht 1968, 200; MacDonald 1976; Loerke 1990, 38. But twenty-nine days is a better approximation still.

31 T. Mommsen, *Archäologische Zeitung*, XXV (1867), 55; De Angelis d'Ossat 1982 [S.GA], tav. 19; Alvegård 1972, 6, 15, 19.

32 But the proposals of Oudet (1992, 30 and 41) are not so convincing as the phenomena noted for the Domus Aurea (J.-L. Voisin, '*Exoriente sole* (Suétone, *Ner.* 6): D'Alexandrie à la Domus Aurea', AA.VV. 1987a [S.GA], 509–43, esp. fig. 3). Nor does the Pantheon align exactly north-south, as might be expected if it performed as an astronomical device; see H. Nissen, *Das Templum* (Berlin 1869), 223–5; Nissen, *Orientation: Studien zur Geschichte der Religionen*, III (Berlin 1940), 340; Alvegård 1972, 14.

33 Donelly 1986.

34 Beltrami 1898, 74; cf. R. Bergh, 'En studia avgolvet i Pantheon', *Konshistorisk tidskrift*, XXIII (1954), 11–17; De Fine Licht 1968, 100 ff. and 263, n. 8.

35 Lanciani 1897, 482.

36 For early appreciation of the curve by Peruzzi and the author of the Codex Coner, see H. Burns, 'A Peruzzi Drawing in Ferrara', *Mitteilungen des Kunsthistorischen Instituts in Florenz*, XII (1966), 248; see also Pelletti 1989, fig. 2.

37 Loerke 1990, 43; cf. MacDonald 1982–6. [S.GA], I, 118–21; McEwen 1993, 62–3.

38 Pantagruel V: 'Et n'est à passer en silence que l'ouvrage d'icelle chapelle rond estoit en telle symmetrie compassé que le diamètre du projet estoit la hauteur de la voûte.' For measurements, see Pelletti 1989.

39 Wilson Jones 1989 [S.5B], 140. Vitruvius, V,5,9, recommended 1 : 1 for the *laconium* in bath buildings, excluding the vault; cf. DeLaine 1997 [S.GA], 57–8.

40 Cicero, *Tusculanae disputationes*, V, 23; Plutarch, *Lives, Marcellus*, XVII, 7. Cf. Heath 1921 [S.2B], II, 34–50; Martines, 1989, 3–4; D.L. Simms, 'The Trail for Archimedes' Tomb', *JWCI*, LIII (1990), 281–6.

41 There are signs that the floor level is slightly raised with respect to the original, explaining why the plinths of the columns are extraordinarily thin, and partly obscured by the flooring.

42 Not only is there no column screen in this position, but there is the door opening as opposed to a portion of concentric wall.

43 Note, however, the contrary arguments of Esposito and Michetti 1996.

44 MacDonald 1976, 62; Wilson Jones 1989 [S.5B], 127. As executed, the drum is $74\frac{1}{2}$ ft tall rather than 75. This may represent a compromise between half of 150 ft and half of 147 ft, or perhaps an $8\frac{1}{2}$ ft entablature was thought visually superior to one of 9 ft. On the other hand Gruben and Gruben (1997, 69) reconcile the 75 ft datum courtesy of a relatively short foot of 294 mm.

45 Terenzio 1932. De Angelis d'Ossat 1982 [S.GA], 68 ff.; MacDonald 1982 [S.GA], 104 ff.

46 Buddensieg 1971, 260; Buddensieg 1976, 336 (see Introduction, n. 5).

47 E. Battisti, *Filippo Brunelleschi* (Milan 1976), 114 ff.

48 Flavio Biondo, *Roma instaurata* (Rome 1446), III, 62; Henry James, *Letters*, ed. Leon Edel (London 1975), I, 164. James also made his fictive character Count Valerio say that the Pantheon 'is the best place in Rome – worth fifty St. Peter's'; see W.L. Vance, *America's Rome* (New Haven 1989), I, 157.

49 E.E. Viollet-le-Duc, *Entretiens sur l'architecture* (Paris 1863–72), translated as *Discourses on Architecture* by B. Bucknall (New York, 2nd ed., 1959), esp. 113.

50 See chapter 6, n. 38.

51 Buddensieg 1971.

52 UA 874v (Bartoli 1914–22 [S.GA], III, pl. 237, fig. 414, with text, VI, 76).

53 Serlio [S.GA], III, 52 and 54v; Buddensieg 1971, 264 ff.; Marder 1989, esp. 637. Cf. J. Dell, *Zeitschrift für bildende Kunst*, new series, IV (1893), 277 ff.

54 MacDonald 1976, 94 ff.

55 Buddensieg 1971, 266; J. Shearman, 'Raffaello e lo studio dell'antico', *Raffaello architetto* (Rome 1984), 402–3; Scaglia 1995, esp. 23 ff. on the question of the prototype. In an otherwise quite detailed section Peruzzi simply avoided the problem, by leaving them off altogether; see Burns 1966 (cited in n. 36), 248.

56 Marder 1989, esp. 634–40.

57 See F. Arisi, *Gian Paolo Panini e i fasti di Roma del Settecento* (Rome 1986), nos. 220 and 236; Pasquali 1996, 39, fig. 22 (and fig. 13 for Demesmay's elaboration of a radial plan).

58 Procopius, *De aedificiis libri VI*, I, 1, 29.

59 E. Kieven, in *Exploring Rome: Piranesi and his Contemporaries*, ed. C.D. Denison, M. Nan Rosenfeld and S. Wiles (Cambridge, Mass., 1993), xxi. Cf. Pasquali 1996, 82–9.

60 Adapted from *The Lives of the Painters, Sculptors and Architects*, as translated by A.B. Hinds (London and New York 1963), 275–6. A seventeenth-century source (Cod.Barb.Lat. 4309, f.11v) also attributed to Michelangelo the judgement that the first of the three phases was so good as to be 'the product of angels' (*un disegno angelico e non umano*), implicitly condemning the two others by exclusion. Cf. Buddensieg 1971, 265.

61 Desgodets 1682 [S.GB], 20–21; Loerke 1990, 26.

62 Fontana 1694, 454 ff. and fig. on p. 467. For his reliance on Demontiosus' proposal of 1585, see Pasquali 1996, 12–14.

63 Pliny, *HN*, XXXVI, 38. Friedrich Adler (1871, Bl. II) returned to similar ideas, this time reinstating columns and adding caryatid-faced piers in front of exposed vaults at attic level. See Hirt 1791 for another variation.

64 It is impossible now to date the attic facing (Terenzio's reconstructed portion does not incorporate authentic material), so a later date remains conceivable (Guey 1936). However, the original capitals appear to be Hadrianic; see Strong 1953, 119, n. 5; De Fine Licht 1968, 270, n. 10.

65 Cozzo 1929; Terenzio 1932.

66 Mainstone 1975 (cited chapter 4, n. 38), 116–17; Mark and Hutchinson 1986; Mark 1990, 60 ff.

67 These were begun later than the rotunda (since at low level they butt up against it), yet by the top they had caught up, and are bonded integrally.

68 Given their untidy resolution, the radial relieving arches in the vaults over the exedrae on the diagonal axes may be afterthoughts (fig. 9.14), but the fabric round about shows no sign of successive phases. They have the function of discharging load from the apex of the barrel vaults, and as such they are integral parts of the original project. Similar arches were superfluous in the semi-domes on the cross-axes because these distribute load evenly as opposed towards either end, as in the case of barrel vaults.

69 MacDonald 1976, 70; Marder 1989; Loerke 1990, esp. 30 ff.

70 Kähler 1942 (see chapter 6, n. 43). A later parallel can be found in Santa Sofia, where the second level of arcades in the lobes of the nave do not stand over the supports below.

71 For a comparable arrangement, see Maxentius' reconstruction of the Temple of Venus and Rome.

72 Heilmeyer 1975.

73 Strong 1953, 120.

74 Martines 1989, 4.

75 The rule is not quite hard and fast: the elevation of the semi-domed apse at the end of the so-called Canopus is a case in point.

76 That the scansion of the coffering was conceived in tandem with the main order is confirmed by the exact equivalence between the axial width of the exedrae and two coffer intervals; see Pelletti 1989, 15, fig. 3.

77 Saalman 1988, 122; cf. Loerke 1982, 35, n. 41.

78 See Williams 1997 for an appreciation of other aspects of the floor design.

79 The red porphyry shafts were paired with pilasters of *rosso antico* which are still in place. My thanks to Mario Lolli-Ghetti and Alessandro Bonanno for sharing observations made during the recent conservation programme. Cf. De Fine Licht 1968, fig. 133; Heilmeyer 1975, 332 ff.; Onians 1988 [S.6A], 53.

80 See Davies, Hemsoll and Wilson Jones 1987, Addendum (but I now find our overall argument less convincing).

CHAPTER X

1 The newcomer 'sera ravi en proportion de la sensibilité que le ciel lui a donnée pour les beaux-arts' (*Promenades dans Rome*, Paris 1873 (1st ed. 1829), 254).

2 Buddensieg 1971, pl. 2; D. Cole Ahl, *Benozzo Gozzoli* (New Haven 1996), fig. 205.

3 Serlio [S.GA], f.50r. For summaries of criticism of the Pantheon, see Venuti 1803; De Fine Licht 1968, 186 ff.; Buddensieg 1971; Davies, Hemsoll and Wilson Jones 1987, 133–4. My warmest thanks go to co-authors Paul Davies and David Hemsoll from whom I learnt much; in effect, this chapter goes on to extend and amplify the results of our collaboration.

4 Palladio [S.GA], IV, cap. 20; Fontana 1694, 454 ff., fig. on p. 457. For Demesmay's corroboration of Fontana's façade, see Pasquali 1996, fig. 12.

5 Desgodets 1682, 1; his attribution of the portico to the emperors 'Severus and M. Aurelius' is a misreading of the text (*IMP CAES L SEPTIMIVS SEVERV . . . ET IMP CAES M AVRELIVS ANTONINVS . . . PANTHEVM VETVSTATE CORRVPTVM CVM OMNI CVLTV RESTITVERVNT*), since the second name is really Caracalla's.

6 F. Milizia, *Roma delle belle arti del disegno*, I (Bassano 1787), 48. According to another theory, Agrippa originally intended to build the rotunda alone, but later added the portico; see Venuti 1803, 115–16.

7 Durm 1905 [S.GA], 556 ff.

8 Lanciani 1897, 483.

9 Cozzo 1928 [S.GA], esp. figs 115–16; Cozzo 1929.

10 Colini and Gismondi 1927; Beltrami 1929. For further references, see chapter 9, n. 14.

11 MacDonald 1982 [S.GA], 113; cf. MacDonald 1976, 62–70.

12 Even Bernini has been criticized for the way he resolved comparable junctions in the churches of Santa Maria at Albano and Sant'Andrea on the Quirinal – although here there is the danger of a circular argument, since these designs were in part inspired by the Pantheon. See M. Morresi, 'Assimilazione e interpretazione barocca del Pantheon: La chiesa e il pronao di S. Andrea al Quirinale', *Rivista storica del Lazio*, IV (1996), 99–123; cf. MacDonald 1982 [S.GA], 111.

13 Vighi 1959, 11–12; cf. Rivoira 1925 [S.GA], 118 ff.; Stierlin 1984, 73 ff.

14 Ward-Perkins 1981 [S.GA], 112.

15 This occurs on the west side only; its absence on the east side is explained by modern restorations.

16 There are two aspects to the bonding: firstly the interdigitation of individual bricks, secondly continuity in the bonding courses of *bipedales*. I thank Lynne Lancaster for kindly drawing my attention to this second issue.

17 Davies, Hemsoll and Wilson Jones 1987, 135 ff.

18 The lower cornice of the rotunda could have continued along the flanks of the transitional block without conflicting with the capitals; alternatively it could have aligned with reliefs analogous to those now at a lower level.

19 However Haselberger (1994, 303–7) regards the systyle arrangement as a deliberate feature of the design.

20 In effect ⅝ ft splits the difference between the intended column width of 6¼ ft and the executed 5 ft.

21 I have assumed that the existing portal is the same as that originally intended, i.e. one four-fifths as tall as the original columns. Indeed, the great majority of Roman portals are lower than the columns in front (although in the tholos at Tivoli, the Temple of Hadrian at Ephesos and the Capitolium

at Dougga the relationship is comparable with the Pantheon as built).

22 R. Turcan, *Religion Romaine, II: Le culte* (Leiden 1988), 32–3, no. 72, tav. 38 (my thanks to Licia Luschi for this reference). One of Pirro Ligorio's drawings (Naples, Biblioteca Nazionale, MS. XIII. B4) shows a lost Pantheon-like tomb façade, but again with a single pediment.

23 On Pantheon-inspired architecture generally, see MacDonald 1976, 94–132.

24 The vaulted chambers in the upper part may well exist for no other reason than to reduce the weight of the extra brickwork. Likewise, one of the reasons for narrowing the entrance passage could have been to support the barrel vault needed to carry the now more substantial mass of masonry above.

25 In the hypothetical portico the stairs could have emerged near its apex, near enough to the rotunda for access to have been resolved in a discreet manner.

26 Bagnani 1929, xvii–xviii.

27 Haselberger 1994, 279–93.

28 According to Tacitus (*Ann.*, 3.9), Calpurnius Piso disembarked by the Mausoleum of Augustus on his return from Syria in AD 20. See C. D'Onofrio, *Il Tevere* (Rome 1980), 279 ff.; Maischberger 1997 [S.7F], 106.

29 Wilson Jones 1991 [S.7C], 134.

30 Haselberger 1994, 299. Measurements of the stump in the Vicolo del Orlando Spada made by Matthias Bruno and me yield a diameter of 1.4–1.45 metres, consistent with a maximum of 1.46–1.49 metres, or 5 Roman feet. The Temple of Venus and Rome is another candidate for the capital, but its location argues against a connection with the Campus Martius yards.

31 In Davies, Hemsoll and Wilson Jones 1987, we gave 74¼ ft on the assumption that the exterior cornice aligned with its internal counterpart. In fact the former is about half a foot higher (Pelletti 1989, fig. 7), yielding 74¾ ft.

32 The slope, at around 24°, is relatively steep for such a large pediment; those of the Temple of Mars Ultor and the major temples at Baalbek are around 15–16°. For further data, see Haselberger 1994, 281, n. 9.

33 A lone shaft from the Basilica of Maxentius now stands in front of Santa Maria Maggiore (see Stevens 1924 [S.6B], 142); for the Quirinal temple, see chapter 8, n. 46; for that at Cyzicus, see chapter 1, n. 29.

34 Pensabene 1993 [S.6A], 200, 323 ff.

35 Wilson Jones 1989 [S.7A], 59.

36 Cicero, *Att.*, 12, 19.

37 Of the larger shafts mentioned earlier, only those of the Basilica of Maxentius and Pompey's Pillar were single pieces. Examples as large as the latter (60 ft) are unknown outside Egypt save for a broken one abandoned at the *cipollino* quarries (see M. Bruno, 'Su un fusto colossale di cipollino sopra le cave di Kylindroi nel distretto di Myloi', AA.VV. 1998 [S.7F], 327–32).

38 This shaft was extracted in AD 105–6 (Ward-Perkins 1992 [S.7F], 109); the set for Trajan's Baths was roughly contemporary, since the building was dedicated in 109 (J.C. Anderson, 'The Date of the Thermae Trajani and the Topography of the *Oppius Mons*', *AJA*, LXXXIX (1985), 499–509). The Traianeum was finished around 126–8, like the Pantheon, but its form and commencement date is disputed (see chapter 8, p. 162).

39 See, for example, Aelius Aristides, *Or.*, 27.18–21.

40 For summaries of diverse shipwrecks and cargoes, see A.J. Parker, *Ancient Shipwrecks of the Mediterranean and the Roman*

Provinces – *BAR*, DLXXX (1992), nos. 163, 222, 566, 621, 672, 695, 1082, 1153 and 1157. See also G. Di Stefano, 'La nave delle colonne', *Archeo* (March 1991), 115 ff.; Salies ed. 1994 [S.7F].

41 Salies ed. 1994 [S.7F], 175–94 (the height of the shafts varies between 3 and 5 metres).

42 J.-Y. Empereur, *BCH*, XIX (1995), 757.

43 Wallace 1994 (see chapter 3, n. 52), 47 ff.

44 Ward-Perkins 1992 [S.7F], 72. For a Pharaonic representation with two columns (7–11 metres long?) on a boat bound north from Aswan, see Stadelmann 1990 (cited in chapter 4, n. 46), 249, Abb. 165.

45 Sidebotham *et al.* 1991, 574 (fig. 2); Brown and Harrell 1996 [S.9D].

46 Peña 1989 [S.7F].

47 My thanks to Adam Bülow-Jacobsen for this information.

48 Pliny, *NH*, XXXVI, 55; Fant 1993 [S.7F], 150.

49 M. Korres, *From Pentelicon to the Parthenon: The Ancient Quarries and the Story of a Half-worked Column Capital of the First Marble Parthenon* (Athens 1995, 1st German ed. 1992), 82–3; Korres, AA.VV. 1996 [S.7F].

50 Peacock and Maxfield 1997, 177.

51 Birley 1997, 189–91.

52 The occasion could perhaps have coincided with Hadrian's assumption of the title *pater patriae* (AD 127?); see L. Perret, *La titulature impériale d'Hadrien* (Paris 1929), 62–73; Birley 1997,

200–201. Marguerite Yourcenar (1988, 159) pictured him inaugurating the Temple of Venus and Rome on the same day, but this gives it an improbably early date.

53 Fant 1993 [S.7F], 163 ff.

54 The insistence on this marble evidently overrode practical considerations, for a surprising amount of it is second rate, with pronounced micaceous veining. Better quality stone was surely available from Carrara. The marble of the capitals remains to be identified; MacDonald (1982 [S.GA], 98) and De Fine Licht (1968, 39) cite Pentelic, but Pensabene (1996 [S.7F], 284) judges them Carrara; pending detailed analysis, I too would opt for the latter.

55 Pliny, *NH*, XXXVI, 46.

56 Peacock 1993, 62 ff.; Peacock and Maxfield 1997, 333.

57 Fant 1993 [S.7F], 150. With time it lost potency; at the time of Diocletian's edict it was only the seventh mostly costly decorative stone; see Gnoli 1988 [S.7F], 14.

58 Peacock 1993, 65.

59 MacDonald 1982–6 [S.GA], I, 98; De Fine Licht 1968, 241.

60 More than any other emperor, Hadrian is known for directing the traffic of monolithic shafts. His largest recorded donations are 100 *giallo antico* shafts for his library in Athens, 100 *pavonazetto* shafts again for Athens, and 96 assorted ones for Smyrna (Pausanius, I, 18, 8–9; Fant 1993 [S.7F], 155–6). See also Golvin 1988 [S.5B], 204 ff. on columns for the amphitheatre at Capua.

BIBLIOGRAPHY

General

S. GA GENERAL WORKS AND COLLECTED ESSAYS

AA.VV. 1976 *Hellenismus in Mittelitalien*, ed. P. Zanker (con. Göttingen 1974).

AA.VV. 1983 *Architecture et société de l'archaïsme grec à la fin de la République romaine* = *CollEFR*, LXVI (con. Rome 1980).

AA.VV. 1987a *L'urbs: Espace urbain et histoire (Ier siècle av. J.-C. – IIIe siècle ap. J.-C.)* = *CollEFR*, XCVIII (con. Rome 1985).

AA.VV. 1987b *Roman Architecture in the Greek World*, ed. S. Macready and F.H. Thompson, London.

AA.VV. 1989 *The Greek Renaissance in the Roman Empire: Papers from the Xth British Museum Classical Colloquium* = *Bulletin of the Institute of Classical Studies*, supp. 55.

AA.VV. 1990 *Architecture and Architectural Sculpture in the Roman Empire*, ed. M. Henig, Oxford.

AA.VV. 1993 *Eius Virtutis Studiosi: Classical and Post-classical Studies in Memory of Frank Edward Brown*, ed. R.T. Scott and A.R. Scott, Hanover and London.

Adam, J.-P. 1989 *L'arte di costruire presso i Romani*, Milan (1st French ed. 1984).

Alberti, L.B. 1988 *De re aedificatoria* (1st ed. 1486, 1st English trans. 1726); ed. and trans. as *On the Art of Building in Ten Books*, with commentary by J. Rykwert, N. Leach, R. Tavernor, Cambridge, Mass.

Anderson, J.C. 1997 *Roman Architecture and Society*, Baltimore.

Bartoli, A. 1914–22 *I monumenti antichi di Roma nei disegni degli Uffizi di Firenze*, Rome, 6 vols.

Bianchi-Bandinelli, R. 1970 *Rome, the Centre of Power: Roman Art to AD 200*, London.

Blagg, T. 1983 'Architecture' (chapter 1), *A Handbook of Roman Art*, ed. M. Henig, London, 26–65.

Boëthius, A. 1978 *Etruscan and Early Roman Architecture*, Harmondsworth (1st ed. 1970).

Brown, F.E. 1961 *Roman Architecture*, New York.

Choisy, A. 1873 *L'art de bâtir chez les romains*, Paris.

Coarelli, F. 1996 *Revixit ars: Arte e ideologia in Roma dai modelli ellenistici alla tradizione repubblicana*, Rome.

Cozzo, L. 1970 *Ingegneria romana*, Rome (1st ed. 1929).

Crema, L. 1959 *L'architettura Romana* = *Enciclopedia classica*, XII, Turin.

De Angelis d'Ossat, G. 1982 *Realtà dell'architettura: Apporti alla sua storia, 1933–78*, Rome.

Delbrueck, R. 1907–12 *Hellenistische Bauten im Latium*, Strassbourg, 2 vols.

DeLaine, J. 1997 *The Baths of Caracalla: A Study in the Design, Construction, and Economics of Large-scale Building Projects in Imperial Rome* = *JRA*, supp. 25, Portsmouth, Rhode Island.

Durm, J. 1905 *Die Baukunst der Etrusker. Die Baukunst der Römer*, Stuttgart.

Giuliani, C.F. 1990 *L'edilizia nell'antichità*, Rome.

Grenier, A. 1960 *Manuel d'archéologie gallo-romaine, 1: Architecture et urbanisme* (2 vols.), *2: Les monuments des eaux* (2 vols.), Paris.

Gros, P. 1996 *L'architecture romaine, 1: Les monuments publics*, Paris.

Gros, P. and Torelli, M. 1988 *Storia dell'urbanistica: Il mondo romano*, Bari.

Günther, H. 1988 *Das Studium der antiken Architektur in den Zeichnungen der Hochrenaissance*, Tübingen.

Hannestad, N. 1986 *Roman Art and Imperial Policy*, Aarhus.

Lanciani, R. 1894 *Ancient Rome in the Light of Recent Discoveries*, Boston.

Lanciani 1897 *The Ruins and Excavations of Ancient Rome*, London.

Lugli, G. 1952–60 *Fontes ad topographiam veteris urbis Romae pertinentes*, 8 vols.

Lugli 1957 *La tecnica edilizia romana*, Rome.

MacDonald, W.L. 1982–6 *The Architecture of the Roman Empire*, New Haven, 2 vols. (1st ed. of vol. 1 1965).

Nash, E. 1968 *Pictorial Dictionary of Ancient Rome*, London and New York.

Palladio, A. 1997 *I quattro libri dell'architettura* (1st ed. Venice 1570); trans. as *Andrea Palladio: The Four Books on Architecture* by R. Tavernor and R. Schofield, Cambridge, Mass.

Pearse, J.L.D. 1974 *The Organization of Roman Building during the Late Republic and Early Empire*, diss. Cambridge University.

Picard, G. 1964 *The Roman Empire* (Living Architecture series), London.

Platner, S.B. and Ashby, T. 1929 *A Topographical Dictionary of Ancient Rome*, Oxford.

Plommer, W.H. 1956 *Ancient and Classical Architecture*, London.

Pollitt, J.J. 1983   *The Art of Rome c.753* BC *−337 A.D.: Sources and Documents*, Cambridge (1st ed. 1966).

Rakob, F. 1967   *Römische Architektur*, Berlin.

Richardson, L. 1992   *A New Topographical Dictionary of Ancient Rome*, Baltimore and London.

Rivoira, G.T. 1925   *Roman Architecture and its Principles of Construction under the Empire*, Oxford (1st Italian ed. 1921).

Robertson, D.S. 1943   *A Handbook of Greek and Roman Architecture*, Cambridge (1st ed. 1929).

Sear, F. 1982   *Roman Architecture*, London.

Serlio, S. 1996   *Tutte l'opere d'architettura et prospettiva* (1st complete ed. Venice 1584); Book III published separately in 1540, Book IV in 1537; 1st English trans. 1611); ed. and trans. as *Sebastiano Serlio on Architecture*, with commentary by V. Hart and P. Hicks, New Haven.

Steinby, M. ed. 1993–   *Lexicon topographicum urbis Romae*, Rome.

Tomlinson, R.A. 1995   *Greek and Roman Architecture*, London.

Ward-Perkins, J.B. 1977   *Roman Architecture*, New York (1st Italian ed. 1974).

Ward-Perkins 1981   *Roman Imperial Architecture*, Harmondsworth (1st ed. 1970).

Watkin, D. 1992   Architecture, *The Legacy of Rome*, ed. R. Jenkyns, Oxford, 329–65.

S. GB   COLLECTED SURVEYS

AA.VV. 1985   *Roma antiqua: 'Envois' degli architetti francesi (1788–1924): L'area archeologica centrale*, cat. Rome and Paris.

AA.VV. 1992   *Roma antiqua: 'Envois' degli architetti francesi (1786–1901): Grandi edifici publici*, cat. Rome.

Canina, L. 1848–56   *Gli edifizii di Roma antica e contorni*, Rome, 6 vols.

Chandler, R., Revett, N. and Pars, W. 1769–97   *Antiquities of Ionia*, The Society of Dilettanti, London, 2 vols.

Cresy, E. and Taylor, G.L. 1821   *The Architectural Antiquities of Rome*, London, 2 vols.

Desgodets, A. 1682   *Les édifices antiques de Rome*, Paris.

D'Espouy, H. 1905   *Fragments d'architecture antique*, Paris; ed. and trans. as *Fragments from Greek and Roman Architecture: The Classical America Edition of Hector d'Espouy's Plates*, with introduction by J. Blatteau and C. Sears, New York 1981.

Stuart, J. and Revett, N. 1761–1816   *The Antiquities of Athens Measured and Delineated*, London, 4 vols.

S.GC   SELECTED WORKS ON GREEK ARCHITECTURE

AA.VV. 1990   *Hermogenes und die hochhellenistische Architektur*, ed. W. Hoepfner and E.-L. Schwandner, Mainz (con. Berlin 1988).

Coulton, J.J. 1988   *Ancient Greek Architects at Work*, Oxford (1st ed. 1977).

Dinsmoor, W.B. 1975   *The Architecture of Ancient Greece*, New York and London (1st ed. 1950).

Fyfe, T. 1936   *Hellenistic Architecture: An Introductory Study*, Cambridge.

Green, P. 1990   *Alexander to Actium: The Historical Evolution of the Hellenistic Age*, Berkeley.

Knell, H. 1980   *Grundzüge der griechische Architektur*, Darmstadt.

Lauter, H. 1986   *Die Architektur des Hellenismus*, Darmstadt.

Lawrence, A.W. 1983   *Greek Architecture*, rev. R.A. Tomlinson (1st ed. 1957).

Pollitt, J.J. 1974   *The Ancient View of Greek Art: Criticism, History and Terminology*, New Haven.

Pollitt 1986   *Art in the Hellenistic Age*, Cambridge.

Steele, J. 1992   *Hellenistic Architecture in Asia Minor*, London.

Wesenberg, B. 1983   *Beiträge zur Rekonstruktion griechischer Architektur nach literarischen Quellen*, Berlin.

Chapter I

S.I   ARCHITECTS AND THEIR TRADE

AA.VV. 1999   *L'arte dell'assedio di Apollodoro di Damasco*, ed. A. La Regina, Rome (not consulted at time of writing).

Anderson 1997   S.GA.

Blyth, P.H. 1992   'Apollodorus of Damascus and the *"Poliorcetica"* ', *GRBS*, XXXIII, 127–58.

Briggs, M.S. 1927   *The Architect in History*, Oxford, 28–52.

Clarke, M.L. 1963   'The Architects of Greece and Rome', *AH*, VI, 9–22.

Coarelli, F. 1980   *Artisti e artigiani in Grecia*, Rome and Bari.

Coulton 1988   S.GC.

Donderer, M. 1996   *Die Architekten der späten römischen Republik und der Kaizerzeit: Epigraphische Zeugnisse*, Erlangen.

Eck, W. 1997   'Auf der Suche nach Architekten in der römischen Welt', *JRA*, X, 399–404.

Frothingham, A.L. 1909   'Roman Architects', *Architectural Record*, XXV, 179–92.

Giuliani 1987   S.8A.

Gros, P. 1973   'Hermodore et Vitruve', *MEFRA*, LXXXV, 137–61.

Gros 1976   'Les premières générations d'architectes hellénistiques à Rome', *Mélanges offerts à J. Heurgon = CollEFR*, XXVII, 387–410.

Gros 1983   'Statut social et rôle culturel des architectes: Période hellénistique et augustéenne', AA.VV. 1983 [S.GA], 425–50.

Gullini, G. 1968   'Apollodoro e Adriano: Ellenismo e Classicismo nell'architettura romana', *Bolld'A*, LIII, 63–80.

Heilmeyer, W.-D. 1975   'Apollodorus von Damascus, der Architekt des Pantheon', *JdI*, XC, 317–47.

Leon, C. 1961   *Apollodorus von Damascus und die Trajanische Architektur*, diss. Innsbruck University.

MacDonald, W.L. 1977   'Roman Architects', *The Architect: Chapters in the History of the Profession*, ed. S. Kostoff, New York.

MacDonald 1982–6   S.GA, I, 122–42.

Martin, R. 1959 'Apollodorus of Damascus', *Encyclopedia of World Art*, ed. B.S. Myers, New York, I, 511–14.

Müller, W. 1989 *Architekten in der Welt der Antike*, Zurich and Munich.

Paribeni, R. 1943 'Apollodoro di Damasco', *Atti della reale accademia d'Italia: Rendiconti*, VII/4, 124–30.

Pearse 1974 S.GA.

Promis, C. 1873 'Gli architetti e l'architettura presso i romani', *Reale accademia delle scienze di Torino: Memorie*, XXVII, 1–187.

Rawson, E. 1975 'The Activities of the Cossutii', *PBSR*, XLIII, 36–47.

Ridley, R. 1989 'The Fate of an Architect: Apollodoros of Damascus', *Athenaeum*, LXVII, 551–65.

Scagliarini Corlàita, D. 1993 'Per un catalogo delle opere di Apollodoro di Damasco, architetto di Traiano', *Ocnus: Quaderni della scuola di specializzazione in archeologia, Università di Bologna*, I, 185–93.

Susini, G. 1987 'L'architectus Sarsinate: Un assetto urbano e la sua scrittura', *Saggi in onore di G. De Angelis d'Ossat*, Rome, 67–8.

Thompson, H.A. 1987 'The Impact of Roman Architects and Architecture on Athens', AA.VV. 1987b [S.GA], 1–17.

Toynbee, J.M.C. 1951 *Some Notes on Artists in the Roman World = Collection Latomus*, VI, Brussels.

Chapter II

S.2A VITRUVIUS

AA.VV. 1978 *2000 anni di Vitruvius: Studi e documenti di architettura*, VIII, ed. L. Vagnetti, Florence.

AA.VV. 1984 *Vitruv Kolloquium: Schriften des Deutschen Archäologen-Verbandes*, VIII, ed. H. Knell and B. Wesenberg, Darmstadt.

AA.VV. 1989 *Munus non ingratum: Proceedings of the International Symposium on Vitruvius' De architectura and Hellenistic and Republican Architecture = BABesch*, supp. 2, Leiden.

AA.VV. 1994 *Le projet de Vitruve: Objet, destinataires et réception du 'De architectura'*, CollEFR, CXCII.

Baldwin, B. 1990 'The Date, Identity and Career of Vitruvius', *Latomus*, XCIV, 425–34.

Birnbaum, A. 1914 *Vitruvius und die griechische Architektur*, Vienna.

Boëthius, A. 1939 'Vitruvius and the Roman Architecture of his Age', *Dragma: Essays in Honour of M.P. Nilsson*, Lund and Leipzig, 114–43.

Bommelaer, J.-F. 1989 'Sur les rapports de Vitruve avec le science de son temps: Questions de topographie et de géographie', AA.VV. 1989, 22–30.

Callebat, L. 1973 *Vitruve: De l'architecture, Livre VIII*, trans. with commentary, Paris.

Callebat 1982 'La prose du "De architectura" de Vitruve', *ANRW*, XXX/1, 696–722.

Callebat 1989 'Organization et structures du *De architectura* de Vitruve', AA.VV. 1989, 34–8.

Callebat 1994 'Rhétorique et architecture dans le *De architectura* de Vitruve', AA.VV. 1994, 31–46.

Callebat et al. 1984 *De architectura concordance: Documentation bibliographique, lexicale et grammaticale*, Hildesheim.

Callebat, L. and Fleury, P. 1995 *Dictionnaire des termes techniques du 'De architectura' de Vitruve*, Hildesheim.

Choisy, A. 1909 *Vitruve*, Paris.

Corso, A. and Romano, E. 1997 *Vitruvio: De architectura*, trans. with commentary, ed. P. Gros, Turin.

Dwyer, E. 1996 'Vitruvius', *DoA*, XXXII, 632–6.

Fensterbusch, C. 1964 *Vitruv: Zehn Bücher über Architektur*, Darmstadt.

Ferri, S. 1960 *Vitruvio: Architettura dai libri I–VII*, Rome.

Fleury, P. ed. 1990 *Vitruve: De l'architecture, Livre I*, trans. with commentary, Paris.

Fleury 1995 *La mécanique de Vitruve*, Caen.

Frey, L. 1990 'Médiétès et approximations chez Vitruve', *RA*, 285–330.

Frézouls, E. 1985 'Vitruve et le dessin d'architecture', AA.VV. 1985 [S.3], 213–29.

Frézouls 1989 'Fondements scientifique, armature conceptuelle et *praxis* dans le *De architectura*', AA.VV. 1989, 39–48.

Geertman, H. 1984 'Vitruvio e i rapporti numerici', *BABesch*, LIX, 53–62.

Geertman 1994 'Teoria e attualità della progettistica architettonica di Vitruvio', AA.VV. 1994, 7–30.

Germann, G. 1991 *Vitruve et le Vitruvianisme*, Lausanne.

Granger, F. 1931–4 *Vitruvius on Architecture*, trans., New York, 2 vols.

Gros, P. 1973 'Hermodore et Vitruve', *MEFRA*, LXXXV, 137–61.

Gros 1975 'Structures et limites de la compilation vitruvienne dans les livres III et IV du *De architectura*', *Latomus*, XXXIV/2, 986–1009.

Gros 1976 'Nombres irrationels et nombres parfaits chez Vitruve', *MEFRA*, LXXXVIII, 669–704.

Gros 1978 'Le dossier vitruvien d'Hermogénès', *MEFRA*, XC, 687–703.

Gros 1982 'Vitruve: L'architecture et sa theorie, à la lumière des études récentes', *ANRW*, XXX/1, 659–95.

Gros 1988 'Vitruve et les ordres', AA.VV. 1988 [S.2B], 49–59.

Gros 1989 'Les fondements philosophiques de l'harmonie architecturale selon Vitruve', *Aesthetics: Journal of the Faculty of Letters, Tokyo University*, XIV, 13–22.

Gros 1990 *Vitruve: De l'architecture, livre III*, trans. with commentary, Paris.

Gros 1992 *Vitruve: De l'architecture, livre IV*, trans. with commentary, Paris.

Gros 1993 'Situation stylistique et chronologique du chapiteau de Vitruve', AA.VV. 1993 [S.7A], 27–37.

Gros 1994 'Munus non ingratum: Le traité vitruvien et le notion de service', AA.VV. 1994, 75–90.

Hallier, G. 1989 'Entre les règles de Vitruve et la réalité archéologique: l'atrium tosan', AA.VV. 1989, 194–211.

Knell, H. 1985 Vitruvs Architekturtheorie: Versuch einer Interpretation, Darmstadt.

Krinsky, A. 1967 'Seventy-eight Vitruvius Manuscripts', JWCI, XXX, 36–70.

Marcucci, L. and Vagnetti, M. 1978 'Per una coscienza Vitruviana: Regesto cronologico e critico', AA.VV. 1978, 11–184.

Moe, C.J. 1945 Numeri di Vitruvio, Milan.

Morgan, W.H. 1914 Vitruvius: The Ten Books of Architecture, trans., Cambridge, Mass.

Plommer, H. 1973 Vitruvius and Later Roman Building Manuals, Cambridge.

Pollitt 1974 S.GC.

Romano, E. 1987 La capanna e il tempio, Rome.

Ruffel, M. and Soubiran, J. 1962 'Vitruve ou Mamurra?', Pallas, XI, 123–79.

Sallmann, K. 1984 'Bildungsvorgaben des Fachschriftstellers: Bemerkungen zur Pädagogik Vitruvs', AA.VV. 1984, 11–26.

Schlikker, F.W. 1940 Hellenistische Vorstellungen von der Schönheit des Bauwerks nach Vitruv, Würzburg.

Schrijvers, P.H. 1989 'Vitruve et la vie intellectuelle de son temps', AA.VV. 1989, 13–21.

Scranton, R.L. 1974 'Vitruvius' Arts of Architecture', Hesperia, XLIII, 494–9.

Soubiran, J. 1969 Vitruve: De l'architecture, livre IX, trans. with commentary, Paris.

Thielscher, P. 1961 'Vitruvius', RE, IX A 1, cols. 419–89.

Tomlinson, R.A. 1989 'Vitruvius and Hermogenes', AA.VV. 1989, 71–5.

Watzinger, C. 1909 'Vitruvstudien', Rheinisches Museum für Philologie, LXIV, 202–23.

S.2B   MATHEMATICS AND DESIGN THEORY

AA.VV. 1988 Les traités d'architecture de la Renaissance, ed. J. Guillaume (con. Tours 1982), Paris.

AA.VV. 1992 Mathématiques dans l'Antiquité = Mémoires du Centre Jean-Palerne, XI, Saint-Étienne.

Barbera, A. ed. 1990 Music Theory and its Sources: Antiquity and the Middle Ages, Notre Dame, Indiana.

Brumbaugh, R.S. 1968 'Symbolism in the Plato Scholia III: A Final Summary', JWCI, XXXI, 1–11.

Fowler, D. 1987 The Mathematics of Plato's Academy: A New Reconstruction, Oxford.

Heath, T.L. 1921 A History of Greek Mathematics, Oxford, 2 vols.

Heidel, W.A. 1940 'The Pythagoreans and Greek Mathematics', AJP, LXI, 1–33.

Heinz, W. 1995 'Antike Bautheorie: Vorüberlegungen zu einer Systematik römischer Architektur', Ordo et mensura, III, ed. D. Ahrens and R.C.A. Rottländer (con. Trier 1993), 161–79.

Hersey, G.L. 1976 Pythagorean Palaces: Magic and Architecture in the Italian Renaissance, Ithaca and London.

Hoepfner, W. 1984 'Maße-Proportionen-Zeichnungen', AA.VV. 1984 [S.3A], 13–23.

Jong, J. de 1989 'Greek Mathematics, Hellenistic Architecture and Vitruvius', AA.VV. 1989 [S.2A], 100–113.

Koenigs, W. 1990 'Maße und Proportionen in der griechischen Baukunst', Polyklet: Der Bildhauer der griechischen Klassik (cat. Frankfurt), Mainz, 119–74.

Kruft, H.W. 1994 A History of Architectural Theory from Vitruvius to the Present, London and Princeton.

Laroche, R.A. 1995 'Popular Symbolic/Mystical Numbers in Antiquity', Latomus, LIV, 568–76.

Lawlor, R. 1982 Sacred Geometry: Philosophy and Practice, London.

Naredi-Rainier 1982 S.5A.

Nicomache de Gérase 1978 Introduction arithmétique, trans. J. Berthier, Paris.

Panofsky, E. 1970 'History of the Theory of Human Proportions' (chapter 2), Meaning in the Visual Arts, London, 82–138.

Pesce, D. 1961 Idea, numero e anima: Primi contributi a una storia del platonismo nell'antichità, Padua.

Pollitt 1974 S.GC.

Scholfield 1958 S.5A.

Théon de Smyrne 1982 Des connaissances mathématiques utiles pour la lecture de Platon, trans. J. Dupuis, Paris.

Thomas, I. 1957 Selections Illustrating the History of Greek Mathematics, Cambridge, Mass., 2 vols.

Wittkower 1971 S.5A.

Chapter III

S.3A   DRAWINGS AND MODELS: GENERAL STUDIES

AA.VV. 1984 Bauplanung und Bautheorie der Antike = DiskAB, IV, Darmstadt.

AA.VV. 1985 Le dessin d'architecture dans les sociétés antiques (con. Strassbourg 1984).

AA.VV. 1994 The Renaissance from Brunelleschi to Michelangelo: The Representation of Architecture, ed. H.A. Millon, V.M. Lampugnani (cat. Venice), Milan.

AA.VV. 1997 Las casas del Alma: Maquetas arquitectónicas de la antigüedad, cat. Barcelona.

Adam, J.-P. 1997 'Dibujos y maquetas: La concepción arquitectónica antigua', AA.VV. 1997, 25–33.

Badawy, A. 1948 Le dessin architectural chez les anciens egyptiens, Cairo.

Benndorf, O. 1902 'Antike Baumodelle', ÖJh, V, 175–95.

Haselberger, L. 1997 'Architectural Likenesses: Models and Plans of Architecture in Classical Antiquity', *JRA*, X, 77–94.

Heisel, J. 1993 *Antike Bauzeichnungen*, Darmstadt.

S.3B DRAWINGS AND MODELS: DETAILED THEMES OR STUDIES

Arnold, D. 1991 *Building in Egypt: Pharaonic Stone Masonry*, Oxford.

Carettoni, G., Colini, A.M., Cozza, L. and Gatti, G. 1960 *La pianta marmorea di Roma antica: Forma urbis Romae*, Rome.

Carter, H. and Gardiner, A.H. 1917 'The Tomb of Ramesses IV and the Turin Plan of a Royal Tomb', *JEA*, IV, 130–58.

Claridge, A. 1983 'Roman Methods of Fluting Corinthian Columns and Pilasters', *Città e architettura nella Roma imperiale = AnalRom*, supp. 10, 119–28.

Clarke, S. and Engelbach, R. 1990 *Ancient Egyptian Construction and Architecture*, New York (1st ed. 1930).

Coarelli, F. 1995 *Da Pergamo a Roma: I Galati nella città degli Attalidi*, with Appendix by M. Fincker, 'Il diagramma inciso sul plinto del Galata morente', cat. Rome.

Coulton, J.J. 1985 'Incomplete Preliminary Planning in Greek Architecture: Some New Evidence', AA.VV. 1985 [S.3A], 103–21.

De Franciscis, A. 1959 'Osservazione sul disegno d'arco dell'anfiteatro campano di S. Maria Capua Vetere', *RendAccLinc*, XIV, 399–402.

De' Spagnolis, M.C. 1984 *Il Tempio dei Dioscuri nel Circo Flaminio*, LSA 4, Roma.

Frézouls, E. 1985 'Vitruve et le dessin d'architecture', AA.VV. 1985 [S.3A], 213–29.

Gros, P. 1985 'Le rôle de *scaenographia* dans le projets architecturaux du début de l'Empire romain', AA.VV. 1985 [S.3A], 231–53.

Hanoune, R. 1996 'Un dessin d'architecture au théâtre de *Bulla Regia* (Tunisie)', *Africa romana*, XI, 911–14.

Haselberger, L. 1980 'Werkziechnungen am Jüngeren Didymeion: Vorbericht', *IstMitt*, XXX, 191–215.

Haselberger 1983 'Bericht über die Arbeit am Jüngeren Apollontempel von Didyma', *IstMitt*, XXXIII, 90–123.

Haselberger 1987 'The Construction Plans for the Temple of Apollo at Didyma', *Scientific American*, December, 126–32.

Haselberger 1989 'Die Zeichnungen in Vitruvs *De architectura*', AA.VV. 1989 [S.2A], 69–70.

Haselberger 1991 'Aspekte der Bauzeichnungen von Didyma', *RA*, 99–113.

Haselberger 1994 S.9B.

Hesberg, H. von 1984 'Römische Grundrisspläne auf Marmor', AA.VV. 1984 [S.3A], 120–33.

Horn, H.G. 1989 '*Si per me misit, nil nisi vota feret*: Ein römischer Spielturm aus Froitzheim', *Bonner Jahrbücher*, CLXXXIX, 139–60.

Hueber, F. 1998 'Werkrisse, Vorzeichnungen und Meßmarken am Bühnengebäude des Theaters von Aphrodisias', *Antike Welt*, XXIX, 439–45.

Hülsen, C. 1890 'Piante iconografiche incise in marmo', *RM*, V, 46–63.

Kalayan, H. 1969 'The Engraved Drawing on the Trilithon and the Related Problems about the Constructional History of Baalbek Temples', *Bulletin du Musée de Beyrouth*, XXII, 151–5.

Kalayan 1971 'Notes on Assembly Marks, Drawings and Models concerning the Roman Period Monuments in Lebanon', *Annales archéologiques arabes Syriennes*, XXI, 269–73.

Koenigs, W. 1983 'Der Athenatempel von Priene', *IstMitt*, XXXIII, 134–75, esp. 165–8.

Maehler, H. 1983 Anhang III: Der Hausgrundriss aus Oxyrhynchos', *Das römisch-byzantinische Ägypten*, ed. G. Grimm et al., Mainz.

Manderscheid, H. 1983 'Ein Gebäudemodell in Bonn', *Bonner Jahrbücher*, CLXXXIII, 429–47.

Márquez, C. 1996 'Técnicas de talla en la decoracíon arquitectónica de *Colonia Patricia Cordoba*', *Africa romana*, XI, 1123–30.

Millon, H.A. 1994 'Models in Renaissance Architecture', AA.VV. 1994 [S.3A], 19–72.

Pensabene, P. 1997 'Maqueta di templo en mármol de Luna', AA.VV. 1997 [S.3A], 129–32.

Petrie, W.M.F. 1926 'Egyptian Working Drawings', *Ancient Egypt*, III, 237–41.

Petronotis, A. 1972 *Zum Problem der Bauzeichnungen bei den Griechen*, Athens.

Piganiol, A. 1962 *Les documents cadastraux de la colonie romaine d'Orange = Gallia*, supp. 16.

Rockwell, P. 1987–8 'Carving Instructions on the Temple of Vespasian', *RendPontAcc*, LX, 53–69.

Rodríguez-Almeida, E. 1980 *Forma urbis marmorea: Aggiornamenti generale 1980*, Rome.

Rodríguez-Almeida 1997 'El mapa de Roma en mármol de la época severiana (*Forma urbis marmorea*)', AA.VV. 1997 [S.3A], 133–8.

Schattner, T. 1990 *Griechische Hausmodelle: Untersuchungen zur frühgriechischen Architektur*, Berlin.

Schwandner, E.L. 1990 'Beobachtungen zur hellenistischen Tempelarchitektur von Pergamon', AA.VV. 1990 [S.GC], 85–102.

Staccioli, R.A. 1968 *Modelli di edifici Etrusco-Italici: I modelli votivi*, Florence.

Will, E. 1985 'La maquette de l'adyton du Temple A de Niha', AA.VV. 1985 [S.3A], 277–82.

Wilson Jones, M. 1997 'Los procesos del diseño arquitectónico: Comprender Vitruvio a partir del los dibujos y maqutas romanas', AA.VV. 1997 [S.3A], 119–28.

Chapter IV

S.4A METROLOGY

AA.VV. 1998 *Ordo et mensura*, IV (con. Tübingen 1995), V (con. Munich 1997), ed. D. Ahrens and R.C.A. Rottländer, St Katharinen.

Albertini, E. 1920 'Table de mesures de Djemila', *CRAI*, 315–19.

Bankel, H. 1983 'Zum Fussmaß attischer Bauten des 5. Jahrhunderts v. Chr.', *AM*, XCVIII, 65–99.

Barresi, P. 1991 'Sopravvivenze dell'unità di misura punica e suoi rapporti con il piede romano nell'Africa di età imperiale', *Africa romana*, VIII, 479–502.

Berriman, A.E. 1953 *Historical Metrology*, London and New York.

Büsing, H. 1982 'Metrologische Beiträge', *JdI*, XCVII, 1–45.

Canina, L. 1853 *Ricerche sul preciso valore delle antiche misure romane*, Rome.

Dekoulakou-Sideris, I. 1990 'A Metrological Relief from Salamis', *AJA*, XCIV, 445–51.

De Zwarte, R. 1994 'Der ionische Fuß und das Verhältnis der römischen, ionischen und attischen Fußmaße zueinander', *BABesch*, LXIX, 115–43.

Fernie, E. 1978 'Historical Metrology and Architectural History', *Art History*, I, 383–99.

Hallier 1992 'Coudée', *Encyclopédie berbère*, ed. G. Camps, Aix-en-Provence, XIV, 2111–2121.

Hecht, K. 1979 'Zum römischen Fuß', *Abhandlungen der Braunschweigerischen Wissenschaftlichen Gesellschaft*, XXX, 107–37.

Heinz, W. 1991 'Der Vindonissa-Fuß', *Gesellschaft pro Vindonissa Jahresbericht*, 65–79.

Hultsch, F. 1882 *Griechische und römische Metrologie*, Berlin.

Ioppolo, G. 1967 'La tavola delle unità di misura sul mercato augusteo di Leptis Magna', *QuadALib*, V, 89–98.

Rottländer, R.C.A. 1991–2 'Eine neu aufgefundene antike Masseinheit auf dem metrologischen Relief von Salamis', *ÖJh*, LXI, 63–8.

Rottländer 1996a 'New Ideas about Old Units of Length', *Interdisciplinary Science Reviews*, XXI/3, 235–41.

Rottländer 1996b 'Studien zur Verwendung des Rasters in der Antike II', *ÖJh*, LXV, 1–86.

Wesenberg, B. 1976 'Zum metrologischen Relief in Oxford', *Marburger Winckelmann Programm*, VI, 15–22.

Zimmer, G. 1983 'Maßstäbe römischer Architekten', AA.VV. 1984 [S.3A], 265–76.

S.4B   CENTRALIZED MONUMENTS: PRE-ROMAN

Bauer, H. 1977 'Lysikratesdenkmal, Baubestand und Rekonstruktion', *AM*, XCII, 197–227.

Borchardt, J. 1991 'Ein Ptolemaion in Limyra', *RA*, 309–22.

Bury, J. 1998 'Chapter III of the *Hypnerotomachia Poliphili* and the Tomb of Mausolus', *Word and Image*, XIV, 40–60.

Camps, G. 1973 'Nouvelles observations sur l'architecture et l'âge du Medracen, mausolée de Numidie', *CRAI*, 470–516.

Coarelli, F. and Thèbert, Y. 1988 'Architecture funéraire et pouvoir: Réflexions sur l'hellénisme numide', *MEFRA*, C, 761–818.

Colvin, H. 1991 *Architecture and the After-life*, New Haven (esp. chapter 3).

De Angelis d'Ossat 1982 S.GA.

Di Vita, A. 1976 'Il mausoleo punico-ellenistico B di Sabratha', *RM*, LXXXIII, 273–85.

Fedak, J. 1990 *Monumental Tombs of the Hellenistic Age = Phoenix*, supp. 37.

Hammond, N.G.L. 1967 'Tumulus-burial in Albania, the Grave Circles of Mycenae and the Indo-Europeans', *BSA*, LXII, 77–105.

Hoepfner, W. 1993 'Zum Mausoleum von Belevi', *AA*, 111–23.

Jeppesen, K. 1981–6 'The Mausolleion at Halikarnassos, Aarhus', 2 vols.

Kaspar, S. 1976 'Der Tumulus von Belevi (Grabungsbericht)', *ÖJh*, LI, 127–79.

Koenigs, W. *et al.* 1980 *Rundbauten in Kerameikos = Kerameikos*, XII, Berlin.

Naso, A. 1996 'Osservazioni sull'origine dei tumuli monumentali nell'Italia centrale', *OpusRom*, XX, 69–85.

Pelon, O. 1976 *Tholos, tumuli et cercles funéraires (IIIe e IIe millénaires av. J.-C.) = BEFAR*, CCXXIX.

Praschniker, C. and Theuer, M. 1979 *Das Mausoleum von Belevi = FiE*, VI, Vienna.

Richard, J.-C., 1970 'Mausoleum: d'Halicarnasse à Rome, puis à Alexandrie', *Latomus*, XXIX, 370–88.

Seiler, F. 1986 *Die griechische Tholos*, Mainz.

Waywell, G. 1988 'The Mausoleum at Halicarnassus', *The Seven Wonders of the World*, ed. P.A. Clayton and M.J. Price, 100–23.

S.4C   ROMAN CENTRALIZED MONUMENTS IN ITALY

Amand, M. 1987 'La reápparation de la sépulture sous tumulus dans l'Empire romain', *L'antiquité classique*, LVI, 161–82.

Aurigemma, S. 1963 *I monumenti funerari di Sarsinia-BollCSStA*, XIX.

Bartoli, P.S. 1727 *Gli antichi sepolcri ovvero mausolei romani ed etruschi*, Rome (1st ed. 1697).

Canina, L. 1848–61 S.GB.

Canina 1853 *Via Appia dalla Porta Capena a Boville*, Rome 2 vols.

Ceschi, C. 1982 *S. Stefano Rotondo = MemPontAcc*, XV, Rome.

Colvin 1991 S.4B.

Cordingley, R.A. and Richmond, I.A. 1927 'The Mausoleum of Augustus', *PBSR*, X, 23–35.

Eisner, M. 1979 'Zur Typologie der Mausoleen des Augustus und Hadrian', *RM*, LXXXVI, 143–58.

Eisner 1986 *Zur Typologie der Grabbauten im Suburbium Roms*, Mainz.

Fellmann, R. 1957 *Das Grab des Lucius Munatius Plancus bei Gaeta*, Basle.

Frazer, A.K. 1966 'The Iconography of the Emperor Maxentius' Buildings on the Via Appia', *ArtBull*, XLVIII, 385–92.

Gabelmann, H. 1979 *Römische Grabbauten*, Stuttgart.

Götze, B. 1939 *Der Rundgrab in Falerii*, Stuttgart.

Hesberg, H. von, 1994 *Monumenta: I sepolcri romani e la loro architettura*, Milan (1st German ed. 1992).

Hesberg, H. von and Panciera, S. 1994 *Das Mausoleum des Augustus: Der Bau und seine Inschriften*, Munich.

Holloway, R.R. 1966 'The Tomb of Augustus and the Princes of Troy', *AJA*, LXX, 171–3.

Isabelle, E. 1855 *Les édifices circulaires*, Paris.

Johnson, J.M. 1986 *Late Antique Imperial Mausolea*, diss. Ann Arbor.

Lugli, G. 1953 'Edifici rotondi del tardo impero in Roma e suburbio', *Studies Presented to D.M. Robinson*, St Louis, II, 1211–23.

McCracken, G. 1942 'The Villa and Tomb of Lucullus at Tusculum', *AJA*, XLVI, 325–40.

Moneti, A. 1992 'Nuovi sostegni all'ipotesi di una grande sala cupolata alla Piazza d'Oro di Villa Adriana', *AnalRom*, XX, 67–92.

Neuerburg, N. 1969 'Greek and Roman Pyramids', *Archaeology*, XXII, 106–15.

Pane, R. and De Franciscis, A. 1957 *Mausolei romani in Campania*, Naples.

Pelliccioni, G. 1986 *Le cupole romane: La stabilità*, Rome.

Pierce, S.R. 1925 'The Mausoleum of Hadrian', *JRS*, XV, 75–103.

Pietrangeli, C. 1940 'Il monumento dei Lucili sulla Via Salaria', *Urbe*, V/11, 20–28.

Purcell, N. 1987 'Tomb and Suburb', *Römischen Gräberstrassen*, ed. H. von Hesberg and P. Zanker, Munich.

Rakob, F. 1961 '"Litus beatae Veneris aureum": Untersuchungen am "Venustempel" in Baiae', *RM*, LXVIII, 1961, 114–19.

Rakob 1988 'Romische Kuppelbauten in Baiae', *RM*, XCV, 257–301.

Rakob, F. and Heilmeyer, W.D. 1973 *Der Rundtempel am Tiber in Rom*, Mainz.

Rasch, J.J. 1984 *Das Maxentius-Mausoleum an der Via Appia in Rom*, Mainz.

Rasch 1985 'Die Kuppel in der römischen Architektur: Entwicklung, Formbildung, Konstruktion', *Architectura*, XV, 117–39.

Rasch 1991 'Zur Konstruktion spätantiker Kuppeln vom 3. bis 6. Jahrhundert', *JdI*, CVI, 311–83.

Rasch 1993 *Das Mausoleum bei Tòr de' Schiavi in Rom*, Mainz.

Rasch 1998 *Das Mausoleum der Kaiserin Helena in Rom und der 'Tempio della Tosse' in Tivoli*, Mainz.

Stettler, M. 1940 'Das Baptisterum zu Nocera Superiore', *Rivista di archeologia cristiana*, XVII, 83–142.

Stettler 1943 'Zur Rekonstruktion von S. Costanza', *RM*, LVIII, 76–86.

Toynbee, J.M.C. 1971 *Death and Burial in the Roman World*, London.

Ueblacker, M. 1985 *Das Teatro Marittimo in der Villa Hadriana*, Mainz.

Wilson Jones 1989 S.5B.

S.4D CENTRALIZED TOMBS AND CELEBRATIVE MONUMENTS OUTSIDE ITALY

Avigad, N. 1954 *Ancient Monuments in the Kidron Valley*, Jerusalem.

Borchardt, J. 1974 'Ein Kenotaph für Gaius Caesar', *JdI*, LXXXIX, 217–41.

Christofle, M. 1951 *Le tombeau de la Chrétienne*, Paris.

Cid Priego, C. 1949 'El sepulcro de mediterráneo y sus relaciones con la tipología monumental', *Ampurias*, XI, 91–126.

Cormack, S. 1990 'A Mausoleum at Ariassos, Pisidia', *Anatolian Studies*, XXXIX, 31–40.

Florescu, F.B. 1965 *Das Siegesdenkmal von Adamklissi*, Bonn and Bucharest.

Formigé, J. 1949 'La trophée des Alpes (la Turbie)', *Gallia*, supp. 2.

Ganzert, J. 1984 *Das Kenotaph für Gaius Caesar in Limyra*, Tübingen.

Hallier, G. 1993 'Étude architecturale', *Les Flavii de Cillium: Étude du Mausolée de Kasserine = CollEFR*, CLXIX, 37–56.

Lauffray, J. 1990 *La tour de Vésone à Périgueux = Gallia*, supp. 49.

Rakob, F. 1983 'Architecture royale numide', AA.VV. 1983 [S.GA], 325–48.

Rolland, H. 1969 *Le mausolée de Glanum = Gallia*, supp. 21.

Stucchi, S. 1987 'L'architettura funeraria suburbana cirenaica', *QuadALibia*, XII, 249–378.

Stupperich, R. 1991 'Das Grabmal eines Konsolaren in Attaleia, *IstMitt*, XLI, 417–22.

Chapter V

S.5A PROPORTION: GENERAL AND INTERPRETATIVE STUDIES NOT CONFINED TO THE ROMAN PERIOD

AA.VV. 1996 *Nexus: Architecture and Mathematics*, I, ed. K. Williams, Florence.

AA.VV. 1998 *Nexus: Architecture and Mathematics*, II, ed. K. Williams, Florence.

Borsi, F. 1967 *Per una storia della teoria delle proporzioni = Quaderni della cattedra di disegno della facoltà di architettura*, II, Florence.

Brunés, T. 1967 *The Secrets of Ancient Geometry and their Use*, Copenhagen.

Coulton, J.J. 1975 'Towards Understanding Greek Temple Design: General Considerations', *BSA*, LXX, 59–99.

Dehio, G. 1895 *Ein Proportiongesetz der antiken Baukunst*, Strassbourg.

Fonseca, R. 1996 'Geometry, Number and Symmetry: The Persistence of Ad Quadratum', *Architectura*, XXVI, 89–104.

Hautecoeur, L. 1937 'Les proportions mathematiques et l'architecture', *Gazette des beaux-arts*, LXXIX, 263–74.

Hersey, G.L. 1976 S.2B.

Kidson, P. 1996 'Architectural Proportion, I (Before circa 1450)', *DoA*, II, 343–51.

Kottmann, A. 1992 *Die Kultur vor der Sintflut: Das gleiche Zahlendenken in Ägypten, Amerika, Asien und Polynesien*, Heiligkreutzal.

Lesser, G. 1957 *Gothic Cathedrals and Sacred Geometry*, London.

Lorenzen, E. 1966 *Technological Studies in Ancient Metrology*, Copenhagen.

Lorenzen 1975 *Along the Line where Columns are Set* (Technological Studies in Ancient Metrology, II), Copenhagen.

Lund, F.M. 1920 *Ad quadratum*, Paris.

Moessel, E. 1926 *Die Proportion in der Antike und Mittelalter*, Munich.

March, L. 1998 *Architectonics of Humanism: Essays on Number in Architecture*, London (not consulted at time of writing).

Naredi-Rainier, P.V. 1982 *Architektur und Harmonie*, Cologne.

Padovan, R. 1999 *Proportion: science, philosophy, architecture*, London and New York (not consulted at time of writing).

Scholfield, P.H. 1958 *The Theory of Proportion in Architecture*, Cambridge.

Texier, A. 1934 *Géométrie de l'architecte*, Paris.

Ungers, O.M. 1994 '*Ordo, fondo et mensura*: The Criteria of Architecture', AA.VV. 1994 [S.3A], 307–17.

Wilson Jones, M. 1988 'Palazzo Massimo and Baldassare Peruzzi's Approach to Architectural Design', *AH*, XXXI, 59–87.

Wilson Jones 1990 'The Tempietto and the Roots of Coincidence', *AH*, XXXIII, 1–28.

Wittkower, R. 1971 *Architectural Principles in the Age of Humanism*, New York (1st ed. London 1949).

Wittkower 1978 'The Changing Concept of Proportion', *Idea and Image*, London, 109–23 (1st ed. *Architects' Year Book*, 1953).

Wolff, O. 1932 *Tempelmasse: Das Gesetz der Proportion in den antiken und altchristlichen Sakralbauten*, Vienna.

S.5B   SELECTED PROPORTIONAL AND METRICAL STUDIES

AA.VV. 1984 S.3A.

AA.VV. 1985 S.3A.

AA.VV. 1989 S.2A.

Almaro-Gorbea, M. and Jiménez, J.L. 1982 'Metrología y modulación del templo de Juno Gabina', *Italica*, XVI, 59–86.

Amucano, M.A. 1991 'Criteri progettuali nel teatro romano: Ipotesi per un nuovo metodo interpretativo', *JAT*, I, 37–56.

Frazer, A. 1993 'The Imperial Fora: Their Dimensional Link', AA.VV. 1993 [S.GA], 411–19.

Frey, L. 1994 'Le transmission d'un canon: Les temples ioniques', AA.VV. 1994 [S.2A], 139–70.

Geertman, H. 1984 'Geometria e aritmetica in alcune case ad atrio pompeiane', *BABesch*, LIX, 31–52.

Geertman 1989 'La progettazione architettonica in templi tardo-repubblicana e nel *De architectura*', AA.VV. 1989, 154–77.

Geertman 1993 'Vitruvio, la realtà architettonica e la progettazione de porte templari', *BABesch*, LXVIII, 209–45.

Golvin, J.-C. 1988 *L'amphithéâtre romain*, Paris.

Gros, P. 1994 'La schéma vitruvienne du théâtre latin et sa signification dans le système normative du *De architectura*, *RA*, 57–80.

Hallier, G. 1989 S.2A.

Hallier 1990 'La géométrie des amphithéâtres militaires sur les limes du Rhin et du Danube', *Akten des 14. Internationalen Limeskongresses in Carnuntum* (con. Vienna 1986), 71–82.

Hallier 1995 'Le monument circulaire du plateau de l'odeon à Carthage: Précisions sur la conception et la géométrie d'un parti original', *Antiquités africaines*, XXXI, 201–30.

Hoepfner, W. 1984 S.2B.

Jacobson, D.M. 1981 'The Plan of the Ancient Haram El-Khalil in Hebron', *PEQ*, CXIII, 73–80.

Jacobson 1984 'The Design of the Fortress of Herodium', *Zeitschrift des deutschen Palästina Vereins*, C, 127–36.

Jacobson 1986 'Hadrianic Architecture and Geometry', *AJA*, XC, 69–85.

Jacobson 1990–91 'The Plan of Herod's Temple', *Bulletin of the Anglo-Israel Archaeological Society*, X, 36–66.

Jacobson, D.M. and Wilson Jones, M. 1999 An Exercise in Hadrianic Geometry: The "Annexe" of the Temple of Venus at Baiae', *JRA*, 12 (forthcoming).

Kalayan, H. 1971 'The Temple of Bacchus and its Geometry of Proportion and Symmetry', *Bulletin du Musée de Beyrouth*, XXIV, 57–60.

Kalayan 1972 'The Geometry of Proportioning in Plan and Elevation of the Temple of Baalshamin in Palmyra', *Annales archéologiques arabes syriennes*, XXII, 157–65.

Kalayan 1988 *Architectural Information through Symmetry*, Amman.

Kurrent, T. 1977 'Vitruvius on Module', *Archeoloski vestnik*, XXVIII, 209–32.

Peterse 1985 'Notes on the Design of the House of Pansa (VI,6,1) in Pompeii', *MededRom*, XLVI, 35–55.

Rakob, F. 1984 'Metrologie und Planfiguren einer kaiserlichen Bauhütte', AA.VV. 1984 [S.3A], 220–37.

Sear, F. 1990 'Vitruvius and Roman Theater Design', *AJA*, XCIV, 249–58.

Small, D.B. 1983 'Studies in Roman Theater Design', *AJA*, LXXXVII, 55–68.

Spremo-Petrovic, N. 1971 *Proportions architecturales dans les plans des basiliques de la préfecture de l'Ilyricum*, Belgrade.

Thieme, T. 1989 'Metrology and Planning in Hekatomnid Labraunda', *Architecture and Society in Hecatomnid Caria = Boreas*, XVII, 77–90.

Watts, C.M. and Watts, D.J. 1987 'Geometrical Ordering of the Garden Houses at Ostia', *JSAH*, XLVI, 265–76.

Watts and Watts 1992 'The Role of the Monuments in the Geometrical Ordering of the Roman Master Plan of Gerasa', *JSAH*, LI, 306–14.

Watts and Watts 1996 'The Square and the Roman House: Architecture and Decoration at Pompeii and Herculaneum', AA.VV. 1996 [S.5A], 167–81.

Wightman, G. 1997 'The Imperial Fora at Rome: Some Design Considerations', *JSAH*, LVI, 64–88.

Wilson Jones, M. 1989 'Principles of Design in Roman Architecture: The Setting Out of Centralised Buildings', *PBSR*, LVII, 106–51.

Wilson Jones 1993 'Designing Amphitheatres', *RM*, C, 391–442.

Wilson Jones 1999 'Note sulla progettazione architettonica', *Arco di Costantivio tra archeologia e archeometria*, ed. C. Panella, P. Pensabene, Rome, 75–100.

S.5C GOLDEN SECTION

Borissaviliévitch, M. 1958 *The Golden Number and the Scientific Aesthetics of Architecture*, London (1st French ed. 1952).

Chen, D. 1985 'Sir Archibald Creswell's Setting Out of the Plan of the Dome of the Rock Reconsidered', *PEQ*, CXVII, 128–32.

Clayet-Michaud, M. 1973 *Le nombre d'or*, Paris.

Coxeter, H.S.M. 1953 'The Golden Section, Phyllotaxis and Whytoff's Game', *Scripta mathematica*, XIX, 135–43.

Foscari, M. and Volpi Ghiradini, L. 1998 'Contra Divinam Proportionem', AA.VV. 1998 [S.5A], 65–74.

Funke-Hellet, C. 1951 *De la proportion: L'équerre des maîtres d'oeuvre*, Paris.

Ghyka, M. 1931 *Le nombre d'or*, Paris.

Huntley, H.E. 1970 *The Divine Proportion: A Study in Mathematical Beauty*, New York.

Jacobson, D. 1983 'The Golden Section and the Design of the Dome of the Rock', *PEQ*, CXV, 145–7.

Neveux, M. 1995 'Le mythe du nombre d'or', *La recherche*, XXVI/278, 810–16.

Zeising, A. 1854 *Neue Lehre von den Proportionen des menschlichen Körpers*, Leipzig.

Chapter VI

S.6A THE ORDERS IN GENERAL

AA.VV. 1992 *L'emploi des ordres dans l'architecture de la Renaissance*, ed. J. Guillaume (con. Tours 1986), Paris.

AA.VV. 1996 *Säule und Gebälk: Zu Struktur und Wandlungsprozeß griechisch-römischer Architektur*, ed. E.-L. Schwandner, *DiskAB*, VI, Mainz.

Chipiez, C. 1876 *Histoire critique des ordres grecs*, Paris.

Deichmann, F.W. 1940 'Säule und Ordnung in der frühchristlichen Architektur', *RM*, LV, 114–30.

Ferchiou, N. 1975 *Architecture romaine de Tunisie: L'ordre, rhythmes et proportions dans le Tell*, Tunis.

Gros, P. 1995 'La sémantique des ordres à la fin de l'époque hellénistique et au début de l'Empire: Remarques préliminaires', *Studi archeologicia in onore di Antonio Frova: Studi e ricerche sulla Galla Cisalpina*, VIII, Rome, 23–32.

Hersey, G.L. 1988 *The Lost Meaning of Classical Architecture*, Cambridge, Mass.

Lyttleton, M. 1974 *Baroque Architecture in Classical Antiquity*, London.

Mauch, J.M. 1845 *Neue systematische Darstellung der architektonischen Ordnungen*, Potsdam.

McKenzie, J. 1991 *The Architecture of Petra*, Oxford.

Panella, C. and Pensabene, P. 1997 'Riempiego e progettazione architettonica nei monumenti tardo-antichi di Roma', *RendPontAcc*, LIX (1993–4), 111–283.

Pensabene, P. 1993 *Elementi architettonici da Alessandria e di altri siti egiziani*, Rome.

Perrault, C. 1993 *Ordonnance for the Five Kinds of Columns after the Method of the Ancients*, trans. I.K. McEwen of 1683 ed., with commentary by A. Pérez-Gómez, Santa Monica, Calif.

Onians, J.B. 1988 *Bearers of Meaning: The Classical Orders in Antiquity, the Middle Ages, and the Renaissance*, Princeton.

Roux, G. 1961 *L'architecture de l'Argolide aux IVe e IIIe siècles*, Paris.

Rykwert, J. 1996 *The Dancing Column*, Cambridge, Mass.

Stratton, A. 1931 *The Orders of Architecture*, London.

Summerson, J. 1980 *The Classical Language of Architecture*, London (1st ed. 1963).

Vignola, G.B. 1562 *Regola delli cinque ordini d'architettura*, Rome; trans. as *Giacomo Barozzi da Vignola: Canon of the Five Orders of Architecture* by B. Mitrovic (New York 1999).

Wesenberg, B. 1971 *Kapitelle und Basen = Bonner Jahrbücher*, Beiheft 32.

Wesenberg 1983 S.GC.

Wesenberg 1996 'Die Entstehung der griechischen Säulen- und Gebälkformen in der literarischen Überlieferung der Antike', AA.VV. 1996, 1–15.

Wilson Jones, M. 1996 'Orders, Architectural', *DoA*, XXIII, 477–84.

S.6B REFINEMENTS

AA.VV. 1999 *Appearance and Essence: Refinements in Classical Architecture – Curvature* (con. Philadelphia 1993), ed. L. Haselberger.

Coulton 1988 S.GC, 108–13.

Goodyear, W.H. 1912 *Greek Refinements*, New Haven.

Haselberger, L. 1999 'Curvature: The Evidence of Didyma', AA.VV. 1999, 173–84.

Hauck, G. 1879 *Die subjektive Perspektive und die horizontalen Curvaturen des dorischen Styls*, Stuttgart.

Hueber, F. 1999 'Ephesos: Optical Refinements in Imperial Roman Architecture', AA.VV. 1999, 211–23

Korres, M. *et al.* 1989 *Study for the Restoration of the Parthenon*, Athens.

Korres 1999 'Refinements of Refinements', AA.VV. 1999, 79–104.

Lawrence 1983 S.GC, 222–7.

Lewis, D.C. 1994 *Revealing the Parthenon's 'Logos optikos'. A historical, optical and perceptual investigation of twelve Classical adjustments of form, position and proportion*. Diss. Ann Arbor.

Mertens, D. 1988 'Zur Enstehung der Entasis griechischer Säulen', *Bathron. Festschrift für H. Drerup*, Saarbrücken, 307–18.

Pennethorne, J. 1876 *The Geometry and Optics of Ancient Architecture*, London.

Penrose, F.C. 1888 *Principles of Athenian Architecture*, London (1st ed. 1851).

Rankin, E. 1986 'Geometry Enlivened: Interpreting the Refinements of the Greek Doric Temple', *Acta classica: Proceedings of the Classical Association of South Africa*, XXIX, 29–41.

Rykwert 1996 S.6A, 220–29.

Seybold, H. 1999 'The Mathematical Basis for the Evaluation of Curvatures', AA.VV. 1999, 105–12.

Stevens, G.P. 1924 'Entasis of Roman Columns', *MAAR*, IV, 121–52.

Thiersch, A. 1873 'Optische Täuschungen auf dem Gebiete der Architektur', *Zeitschrift für Bauwesen*, XXIII, 10–38.

Wilson Jones, M. 1999 'The Practicalities of Roman Entasis', AA.VV. 1999, 225–49.

Homolle, T. 1916 'L'origine du chapiteau corinthien', *RA*, 17–60.

Mallwitz, A. 1981 'Ein Kapitell aus gebranntem Ton: Oder zur Genesis des korinthischen Kapitells', *Bericht über die Ausgrabungen in Olympia*, X, Berlin.

Pedersen, P. 1989 *The Parthenon and the Origin of the Corinthian Capital*, Odense.

Pensabene 1993 S.6A.

Riegl, A. 1992 *Problems of Style: Foundations for a History of Ornament* (German ed. 1893); trans. E. Kain, with commentary by D. Castriota, Princeton.

Rizzo, M.A. 1984 'Capitelli corinzio-italici da Creta', *AnnSAAt*, XLVI, 151–75.'

Rykwert, J. 1980 'The Corinthian Order', *The Necessity of Artefice*, Cambridge.

Rykwert 1996 S.6A.

Strong, D. 1963 'Some Observations on Early Roman Corinthian', *JRS*, LIII, 73–84.

Theodorescu, D. 1989 'Le forum et le temple "doric-corinthien" de Paestum: Une experience pré-Vitruvienne', AA.VV. 1989 [S.2A], 114–25.

Villa, A. 1988 *I capitelli di Solunto*, Rome.

Williams, C. 1974 'The Corinthian Temple of Zeus Olbios at Uzuncaburc: A Reconsideration of the Date', *AJA*, LXXVIII, 405–14.

Wilson Jones, M. 1989 'Designing the Roman Corinthian Order', *JRA*, II, 35–69.

Wycherley, R.E. 1964 'The Olympieion at Athens', *GRBS*, V, 161–79.

Chapter VII

S.7A DEVELOPMENT AND THEMATIC ISSUES

AA. VV. 1993 *L'acanthe dans la sculpture monumentale de l'antiquité à la Renaissance = Mémoires de la section d'archéologie et d'histoire de l'art*, IV, Paris.

Abramson, H. 1974 'The Olympieion in Athens and its Connections with Rome', *California Studies in Classical Antiquity*, VII, 1–25.

Bauer, H. 1972 *Korinthische Kapitele des 4. und 3. Jahrhunderts v. Chr. = AM*, Beiheft 3.

Boysal, Y. 1957 'Die korinthische Kapitele der hellenistischen zeit anatoliens', *Anatolia*, II, 124–32.

Cooper, F.A. 1996 *The Temple of Apollo Bassitas, I: The Architecture*, Athens and Princeton (with folio drawings in vol. IV).

Giuliano, A. 1995 'Vitruvio e l'acanto', *Palladio*, XVI, 29–36.

Gros 1993 'Situation stylistique et chronologique du chapiteau de Vitruve', AA.VV. 1993, 27–37.

Hesberg, H. von, 1980 *Konsolengeisa des Hellenismus und der frühen Kaiserzeit = RM*, Esheft. 24, Mainz.

Hesberg 1981 'Lo sviluppo del ordine corinzio in età tardo-repubblicana', *L'art décoratif à Rome à la fin de la República et au debut du Principat*, Rome.

S.7B AUGUSTAN ARCHITECTURE AND PROPAGANDA

AA. VV. 1988 *Kaiser Augustus und die verlorene Republik* (cat. Berlin), Mainz.

Bonnefond, M. 1987 'Transfers de fonctions et mutation idéologique: Le capitole et le forum d'Auguste', AA.VV. 1988, 251–78.

Castriota, D. 1995 *The Ara Pacis Augustae and the Imagery of Abundance in Later Greek and Early Imperial Art*, Princeton.

Evans, J.D. 1992 *The Art of Persuasion: Political Propaganda from Aeneas to Brutus*, Ann Arbor.

Galinsky, K. 1996 *Augustan Culture: An Interpretative Introduction*, Princeton.

Gros, P. 1976 *Aurea Templa: Recherches sur l'architecture religieuse de Rome à l'époque d'Auguste*, Rome.

Holmes, T.R. 1928–31 *The Architect of the Roman Empire*, Oxford, 2 vols.

Pollini, J. 1992 'The Augustus from Prima Porta and the Transformation of the Polykleitan Heroic Ideal', *Polykleitos, the Doryphoros and its influence*, ed. W. Moon, Madison.

Sauron, G. 1993 'La promotion apollonienne de l'acanthe et la définition d'une esthétique classique à l'époque d'Auguste', AA.VV. 1993 [S.7A], 75–97.

Sauron 1995 *Quis deum?: L'expression plastique des idéologies politiques et religieuses à Rome à la fin de la République et au début du Principat = BEFAR*, CCLXXXV.

Simon, E. 1986 *Augustus: Kunst und Leben in Rom um die Zeitenwende*, Munich.

Walker, S. and Burnett, A. 1981 *The Image of Augustus*, London.

Wallace-Hadrill, A. 1993 *Augustan Rome*, Bristol.

Zanker, P. 1988 *The Power of Images in the Age of Augustus*, Ann Arbor (1st German ed. 1987).

S.7C THE ROMAN CORINTHIAN CAPITAL

Barrera Anton, J.L. 1984 *Los capiteles romanos de la península ibérica*, Badajoz.

Bauer, H. 1974 'Das Kapitell des Apollo Palatinus-Tempels', *RM*, LXXVI, 183–204.

Cocco, M. 1977 'Due tipi di capitelli a Pompei: "Corinzio-italici" e "a sofà"', *Cronache pompeiane*, III, 57–148.

Deichmann, F.W. and Tschira, A. 1936 'Die frühchristlichen Basen und Kapitelle von S. Paolo fuori le mura', *RM*, LIV, 99–111.

De Maria, S. 1981 'Il problema del corinzio-italico in Italia settentrionale: A proposito di un capitello non finito di Rimini', *MEFRA*, XCIII, 565–616.

Diaz Martos, A. 1985 *Capiteles corintios de España: Estudio-catálogo*, Madrid.

Fischer, M. 1990 *Das korinthische Kapitell im alten Israel in der hellenistischen und römischen Periode*, Mainz.

Freyberger, K. 1990 *Stadtrömische Kapitelle aus der Zeit von Domitian bis Alexander Severus: Zur Arbeitsweise und Organisation stadtrömischer Werkstätten der Kaiserzeit*, Mainz (DAI).

Gutíerrez Behemerid, M. 1992 *Capitelos romanos de la península ibérica*, Valladolid.

Gütschow, M. 1921 'Untersuchungen zum korinthischen Kapitell', *JdI*, XXXVI, 44–84.

Heilmeyer, W.D. 1970 *Korinthische Normalkapitelle*, Heidelberg.

Kahler, H. 1939 *Römische Kapitelle des Rheingebietes*, Berlin.

Kautzsch, R. 1936 *Kapitellstudien*, Berlin.

Kramer, J. 1994 *Korinthische Pilasterkapitelle in Kleinasien und Konstantinopel*, Tübingen.

Lauter-Bufe, H. 1987 *Die Geschichte des sikeliotisch-korinthischen Kapitells*, Mainz.

Margineanu-Cârstoiu, M. 1988 'Römische korinthische Kapitelle von Histria', *Dacia*, XXXII, 37–52.

Pagello, E. 1992 'Un capitello non finito da Leptis Magna', *QuadALibia*, XV, 235–52.

Pensabene, P. 1973 *Scavi di Ostia, VII: I capitelli*, Rome.

Pensabene 1982 *Les chapiteaux de Cherchel = Bulletin d'archéologie algerienne*, supp. 3.

Schlumberger, D. 1933 'Les forms anciennes du chapiteau corinthien en Syrie, en Palestine et en Arabe', *Syria*, XIV, 283–317.

Tomasello, F. 1983 'Un prototipo di capitello corinzio in Sabratha', *QuadALibia*, XIII, 87–103.

Ward-Perkins, J.B. 1967 'An Augustan Capital in the Forum Romanum', *PBSR*, XXXV, 23–8.

Wilson Jones, M. 1991 'Designing the Roman Corinthian Capital', *PBSR*, LIX, 89–150.

S.7D COMPOSITE AND 'CORINTHIANIZING' CAPITALS

Fischer, M.L. 1989 'Figured Capitals in Roman Palestine: Marble Imports and Local Stone: Some Aspects of "Imperial" and "Provincial" Art', *PEQ*, CXXI, 112–32.

Gans, U.-W. 1992 *Korinthisierende Kapitelle der römischen Kaiserzeit: Smuckkapitelle in Italien und nordwestlichen Provinzen*, Cologne.

Herrmann, J.J. 1974 *The Schematic Composite Capital: A Study of Architectural Decoration at Rome in the Later Empire*, diss. Ann Arbor.

Hesberg, H. von 1981–2 'Elemente der frühkaiserzeitlichen Aedikulaarchitektur', *ÖJh*, LVI, 43–86.

Ismail, Z. 1980 'Les chapiteaux de Petra', *Le monde de la Bible*, XIV, 27–9.

McKenzie 1991 S.6A.

Mercklin, E. von 1962 *Antike Figuralkapitelle*, Berlin.

Patrich, J. 1996 'The Formation of the Nabataean Capital', *Judaea and the Greco-Roman World in the Time of Herod in the Light of Archaeological Evidence* (con. Jerusalem 1988), Göttingen.

Pauwels, Y. 1989 'Les origines de l'ordre composite', *Annali di Architettura*, I, 29–46.

Ronczewski, K. 1923 'Variantes des chapiteaux romains', *Acta Universitatis Lataviensis*, VIII, 115–74.

Ronczewski 1927 'Les chapiteaux corinthiens et variés du Musée greco-romain d'Alexandrie', *Bulletin de la Societé archeologique d'Alexandrie*, supp. 22, 3–36.

Strong, D.E. 1960 'Some Early Examples of the Composite Capital', *JRS*, L, 119–28.

S.7E MONUMENTS WITH CORINTHIAN ORDERS

Amici, C. 1991 *Il foro di Cesare*, Rome.

Amy, R. and Gros, P. 1979 *La Maison Carrée de Nîmes*, Paris, 2 vols.

Amy, R., Seyrig, H. and Will, E. 1975 *Le temple du Bel a Palmyre*, Paris.

Apolloni, B.M. 1936 *Il foro e la basilica severiana di Leptis Magna = Monumenti italiani*, VIII–IX, Rome.

Aurigemma, S. 1938 *L'arco di Marco Aurelio e di Lucio Vero in Tripoli = Monumenti italiani*, XIII, Rome.

Aurigemma 1969 *L'arco quadrifronte di Marco Aurelio e Lucius Vero a Tripoli = Libya antiqua*, supp. 3.

Borchardt, J. 1903 'Der Augustustempel auf Philae', *JdI*, XVIII, 73–90.

Cagnat, R. and Gauckler, P. 1898 *Monuments historiques de Tunisie, I: Les temples païens*, Paris.

Carettoni, G. 1980 'Capitelli ellenistici della Casa di Augusto', *RM*, LXXXVII, 131–6.

Caristie, A. 1856 *Monuments antiques à Orange: Arc de triomphe et théâtre*, Paris.

Colini, A.M. 1940 'Il Tempio di Apollo', *BComm*, LXVIII, 5–40.

Collart, P. and Vicari, J. 1969 *Le sanctuaire de Baalmashin à Palmyre*, Rome.

Cozza, L. ed. 1982 *Tempio di Adriano = LSA*, I, Rome.

Cunliffe, B. and Davenport, P. 1985 *The Temple of Sulis Minerva at Bath*, Oxford.

Dupré i Raventos, X. 1994 *L'arc romà de Berà*, Rome.

Duval, N. 1978 *Les basiliques de Sbeitla = BEFAR*, CCXVIII.

Ganzert, J. 1996 *Der Mars-Ultor Tempel auf dem Augustusforum in Rom*, Mainz.

Gaspari, C. 1979 *Aedes Concordiae Augustae*, Rome.

Jacobelli, L. and Pensabene, P. 1995–6 'La decorazione architettonica del Tempio di Venere a Pompei, contributo allo studio e al ricostruzione del santuario', *Rivista di studi pompeiani*, VII, 44–75.

Joly, E. and Tomasello, F. 1984 *Il tempio a divinità ignota di Sabratha*, Rome.

Krencker, D. *et al*. 1932 *Palmyra: Ergebnisse der Expeditionen von 1902 und 1917*, Berlin.

Krencker, D. and Schede, M. 1938 *Der Tempel in Ankara*, Berlin.

Lanckoronski, K. 1890–92 *Städte Pamphyliens und Pisidiens*, Vienna, 2 vols.

Mansuelli, G.A. 1960 *Il monumento augusteo del 27 a.c.: Nuove ricerche sull'arco di Rimini*, Bologna.

Merlin, A. 1912 *Forum et églises de Sufetula = Notes et documents de la Direction des antiquités et arts de la Tunisie*, V, Paris.

Paton, S. 1991 'A Roman Corinthian Building at Knossos', *BSA*, LXXXVI, 297–318.

Pensabene, P. 1992 'Il tempio della Gens Septimia a Cuicul', *Africa romana*, IX, 771–802.

Petrignani, M. 1960 'Il portico d'Ottavia', *BollCSStA*, XVI, 37–74.

Promis, C. 1862 *Augusta Praetoria Salassorum*, Turin.

Rakob and Heilmeyer 1973 S.4C.

Rega, G. 1890 *La vestigia del tempio di Castore e Polluce e del teatro di Nerone*, Naples.

Rey, E. Vietty 1831 *Monuments romains et gothiques de Vienne en France*, Paris.

Stiller, H. 1888 *Das Traianeum*, *AvP*, V/2, Berlin.

Strocka, V.M. 1991 *Casa del Labirinto*, *Haüser in Pompeji*, IV, Munich.

Strong, D.E. and Ward-Perkins, J.B. 1960 'The Round Temple in the Forum Boarium', *PBSR*, XXVIII, 7–32.

Strong and Ward-Perkins 1962 'The Temple of Castor in the Forum Romanum', *PBSR*, XXX, 1–30.

Tölle-Kastenbein, R. 1994 *Das Olympieion in Athen*, Cologne.

Traversari, G. 1971 *L'arco dei Sergi a Pola*, Padua.

Viscogliosi, A. 1996 *Il tempio di Apollo in circo e la formazione del linguaggio architettonico augusteo*, Rome.

Ward-Perkins, J.B. 1993 *The Severan Buildings of Lepcis Magna: An Architectural Survey = Society for Libyan Studies Monograph*, II, London.

Wiegand, T. *et al*. 1921–5 *Baalbek: Die Ergebnisse der Ausgrabungen und Untersuchungen in den Jahren 1898–1905*, Berlin and Leipzig, 3 vols.

Zanker, P. 1984 *Il Foro di Augusto*, Rome (1st German ed. 1968).

S.7F   ASPECTS RELATED TO MARBLE AND ITS PRODUCTION

AA.VV. 1985 *Marmi antichi = Studi miscellanei*, XXVI (1981–3), ed. P. Pensabene.

AA.VV. 1988 *Classical Marble: Geochemistry, Technology, Trade*, ed. N. Herz, M. Waelkens, Dordrecht.

AA.VV. 1990 *Pierre eternelle: Du Nil au Rhin: Carrieres et prefabrication/Eeuwige steen: Van Nijl tot Rijn: Groeven en prefabricatie*, ed. M. Waelkens, Brussels.

AA.VV. 1993 *Archeologia delle attività estrattive e metallurgiche*, ed. R. Francovich (con. Campiglia Marittima), Florence.

AA.VV. 1996 *The Study of Marble and other Stones used in Antiquity* (con. Athens 1993), ed. Y. Maniatis *et al.*, Dorchester.

AA.VV. 1998 *Cave e tecnica di lavorazione, provienze e distribuzione = Studi miscellanei*, XXXI (1993–5), ed. P. Pensabene.

Asgari, N. 1988 'The Stages of Workmanship of the Corinthian Capital in Proconnesus and its Export Form', AA.VV. 1988, 115–21.

Asgari 1990 'Objets de marbre finis, semi-finis et inachevés du Proconnèse', AA.VV. 1990, 106–26.

Dodge, H. 1991 'Ancient Marble Studies: Recent Research', *JRA*, IV, 28–50.

Dolci, E. 1994 'Nuovi ritrovamenti nelle cave lunense di Carrara', *Archeologia nei territori Apuo-Versiliese e Modense-Reggiano: Atti della giornata di studio, Massa, Oct. 1993*, Modena.

Fant, J.C. 1993 'Ideology, Gift and Trade: A Distribution Model for the Roman Imperial Marbles', *The Inscribed Economy = JRA*, supp. 6, 145–70.

Gnoli, R. 1988 *Marmora Romana* (1st ed. 1971), Rome.

Hankey, V. 1965 'A Marble Quarry at Karystos', *Bulletin du Musée de Beyrouth*, XVIII, 53–61.

Lauter-Bufe, H. 1972 'Zur Kapitellfabrikation in spätrepublikanischer Zeit', *RM*, LXXIX, 323–9.

Maischberger, M. 1997 *Marmor in Rom: Anlieferung, Lagerund Werkplätze in der Kaiserzeit = Palilia*, I, Wiesbaden.

Peña, J.T. 1989 'P. Giss 96: Evidence for the Supplying of Stone Transport Operations in Roman Egypt and the Production of Fifty-Foot Monolithic Column Shafts', *JRA*, II, 126–32.

Pensabene, P. 1986 'La decorazione architettonica: L'impiego del marmo e l'importazione di manufatti orientali a Roma, in

Italia e in Africa (II–VI) DC', *Società romana in impero tardoantico: Le merci, gli insediamenti*, III, Rome.

Pensabene 1996   *Le vie del marmo: I blocchi di cava di Roma e di Ostia: Il fenomeno del marmo nella Roma antica*, Rome.

Ponti, G. 1995   *Marmor troadense*: Granite Quarries in the Troad: A Preliminary Survey, *Studia troica*, V, 291–320.

Rakob, F. ed. 1993   *Simitthus, I: Die Steinbrüche und die antike Stadt*, Mainz.

Salies, G.H. ed. 1994   *Das Wrack: Der antike Schiffsfund von Mahdia*, Bonn.

Ward-Perkins, J.B. 1951   'Tripolitania and the Marble Trade', *JRS*, XLI, 89–104.

Ward-Perkins 1992   *Marble in Antiquity: Collected Papers of J.B. Ward-Perkins = Archaeological Monographs of the British School at Rome*, VI, ed. H. Dodge and B. Ward-Perkins, Rome.

Chapter VIII

S.8A   TRAJAN'S FORUM AND RELATED MONUMENTS

AA.VV. 1985   S.GB.

AA.VV. 1995   *I luoghi del consenso imperiale: Il Foro di Augusto: Il Foro di Traiano*, ed. E. La Rocca, R. Meneghini, L. Ungaro, Rome, 2 vols.

Amici, C.M. 1982   *Foro di Traiano: Basilica Ulpia e biblioteche*, Rome.

Anderson, J.C. 1984   *The Historical Topography of the Imperial Fora = Coll. Latomus*, CLXXXII.

Bauer, H. 1977   'Il foro transitorio e il tempio di Giano', *RendPontAcc*, XLIX, 117–48.

Boni, G. 1907   'Esplorazione del Forum Ulpium', *NSc*, 361–427.

Frazer 1993   S.5B.

Ganzert 1996   S.7E.

Giuliani, C.F. 1987   'Mercati e Foro Traiano: Un fatto di attribuzione', *Saggi in onore di Guglielmo de Angelis d'Ossat*, Rome, 25–8.

Meneghini, R. 1995   'Preesistenze, cronologia e significato architettonico dei Fori Imperiali', AA.VV. 1995, I, 15–18.

Meneghini 1996   'Nuovi dati sulle biblioteche e il templum Divi Traiani nel Foro di Traiano', *BdA*, XIX–XXI, 13–21.

Meneghini 1998   'L'architettura del Foro di Traiano attraverso i ritrovamenti archeologici più recenti', *RM*, CV, 127–47.

Meneghini, R., Messa, L. and Ungaro, L. 1990   *Il Foro di Traiano*, Rome.

Milella, M. 1995   'Il Foro di Traiano', AA.VV. 1995, I, 91–101.

Packer, J.E. 1992   'The Forum of Trajan 1989', *AJA*, XCVI, 151–62.

Packer 1994   'Trajan's Forum Again: The Column and the Temple of Trajan in the Master Plan Attributed to Apollodorus(?)', *JRA*, VII, 163–82.

Packer 1997   *The Forum of Trajan in Rome: A Study of the Monuments*, with architectural reconstructions by K.L. Sarrinen, Berkeley, 3 vols.

Pensabene, P. and Milella, M. 1989   'Foro di Traiano: Introduzione storico e quadro architettonico', *ArchCl*, XLI, 33–54.

Piazzesi, G. 1989   'Foro di Traiano: Gli edifici – Ipotesi ricostruttive', *ArchCl*, XLI, 125–98.

Plommer, H. 1974   'Trajan's Forum', *Antiquity*, XLVIII, 126–30.

Tummarello, B.M. 1989   'Foro di Traiano: Preesistenze – Il problema del *Mons*', *ArchCl*, XLI, 121–4.

Ungaro, L. and Messa, L. 1989   'Foro di Traiano: Rilievi moderni e ricostruzioni 1926–1986', *ArchCl*, XLI, 199–214.

Wightman 1997   S.5B.

Zanker, P. 1970   'Das Trajansforum in Rom', *AA*, LXXXV, 499–544.

Zanker 1984   *Il Foro di Augusto*, Rome (1st German ed. 1968).

S.8B   TRAJAN'S COLUMN AND RELATED MONUMENTS

AA.VV. 1988   *La Colonna Traiana e gli artisti francesi da Luigi XIV a Napoleone I*, cat. Rome.

Aurès, M. 1863   'Etude des dimensions de la Colonne Trajane, au seul point du vue de la métrologie', *Mémoires de l'Académie du Gard*, Nîmes.

Beccati, G. 1960   'La colonna coclide istoriata: Problemi storici, iconografici, stilistici', *Museo dell'impero romano: Studi e materiali*, VI, Rome.

Bellori, G.P. 1673   *Colonna Traiana: Nouvamente desegnata, et intagliata da Pietro Santi Bartoli*, Rome.

Brilliant, R. 1984   *Visual Narratives: Storytelling in Etruscan and Roman Art* (Ithaca and London, 1984), chapter 3, 'The Column of Trajan and Its Heirs: Helical Tales, Ambiguous Trails', 90–123.

Calderini, L., Petersen, E. and Domaszewski, A. 1896   *Die Marcus-Säule*, Munich.

Claridge, A. 1993   'Hadrian's Column of Trajan', *JRA*, VI, 5–22.

Coulston, J.N.C. 1990a   'The Architecture and Construction Scenes on Trajan's Column', AA.VV. 1990 [S.GA], 39–50.

Coulston 1990b   'Three New Books on Trajan's Column', *JRA*, III, 290–309.

Davies, P.J.E. 1997   'The Politics of Perpetuation: Trajan's Column and the Art of Commemoration', *AJA*, CI, 41–65.

Hamberg, P.G. 1945   'The Columns of Trajan and Marcus Aurelius and their Narrative Treatment', *Studies in Roman Art*, Uppsala, 104–61.

Jordan-Ruwe, M. 1990   'Zur Rekonstruktion und Datierung der Marcussäule', *Boreas*, XIII, 30–31.

Lancaster, L. 1999   'Building Trajan's Column', *AJA* CIII, 419–39.

Lepper, F. and Frere, S. 1988   'Trajan's Column: A New Addition of the Cichorius Plates: Introduction, Commentary and Notes', Gloucester.

Kuttner, A. 1996   'Trajan's Column', *DoA*, XXVI, 791–2.

Maffei, S. 1993   'Forum Traiani: Columna', in Steinby ed. 1993– [S.GA].

Martines, G. 1983 'La struttura della Colonna Traiana: Un'esercitazione di meccanica alessandrina', *Prospettiva*, XXXII, 60–71.

Martines 1992 'L'ordine architettonico della Colonna Traiana', *Saggi in onore de Renato Bonelli = QuadIStA*, XV–XX, 1039–1048.

Pomponi, M. 1991–2 'La Colonna Traiana nelle incisioni de P.S. Bartoli: Contributi allo studio del monumento nel XVII secolo', *RIA*, XIV–XV, 347–78.

Rockwell, P. 1985 'Preliminary Study of the Carving Techniques of the Column of Trajan', AA. VV. 1985 [S.7F], 101–12.

Rottländer 1996b S.4A, 16–31.

Settis, S. *et al.* 1988 *La Colonna Traiana*, Turin.

Stucchi, S. 1989 '*Tantis Viribus*, L'area della Colonna nella concezione generale del Foro di Traiano', *ArchCl*, XLI, 125–98.

Vogel, L. 1973 *The Column of Antoninus Pius*, Cambridge, Mass.

Wilson Jones, M. 1993 '100 Feet and a Spiral Stair: The Problem of Designing Trajan's Column', *JRA*, VI, 23–38.

S.8C   LIFTING AND TRANSPORTATION

Adam, J.P. 1977 'À propos du Trilithon de Baalbek: La transport et la mise en oeuvre des mégalithes', *Syria*, LIV, 31–63.

Adam 1989 S.GA.

Burford, A.M. 1960 'Heavy Transport in Classical Antiquity', *Economic History Review*, XIII, 1–18.

Coulton, J.J. 1974 'Lifting in Early Greek Architecture', *JHS*, XCIV, 1–19.

Dibner, B. 1970 *Moving the Obelisks*, Cambridge, Mass. (1st ed. 1950).

Fleury 1995 S.2A.

Fontana, D. 1978 *Della trasportatione dell'Obelisco Vaticano*, reprint of 1590 ed. with commentary by A. Carugo, Milan.

Giuliani, F.C. 1990 S.GA.

Korres, M. 1997 'Wie kam der Kuppelstein auf dem Mauerring? Die einzigartige Bauweise des Grabmals Theoderichs des Großen zu Ravenna und das Bewegen schwerer Lasten', *RM*, CIV, 219–58.

Kozelj, T. and Kozelj, M.W. 1993 'Les transports dans l'antiquité', AA. VV. 1993 [S.7F], 97–142.

Santillo, R. 1996 'Il *Saxum ingentum* a Ravenna a copertura del Mausoleo di Teodorico', *OpusRom*, XX, 105–33.

Chapters IX and X

S.9A   GENERAL STUDIES OF THE PANTHEON

Bagnani, G. 1929 *The Pantheon*, New York.

De Fine Licht, K. 1968 *The Rotunda in Rome*, Copenhagen.

Kähler, H. 1965 *Das Pantheon in Rom*, Munich.

Lucchini, F. 1996 *Pantheon*, Rome.

Lugli, G. 1971 *The Pantheon and Adjacent Monuments*, Rome.

MacDonald, W.L. 1976 *The Pantheon: Design, Meaning and Progeny*, London.

Vighi, R. 1959 *The Pantheon*, Rome.

S.9B   PARTICULAR ASPECTS

Adler, F. 1871 *Das Pantheon zu Rom = Winckelmanns-Programme*, XXXI, Berlin.

Alvegård, L. 1972 *The Pantheon Metrological System*, diss. Chalmers University of Technology.

Beltrami, L. 1898 *Il Pantheon, coi rilievi e disegni dell'architetto Pier Olinto Armanini*, Milan.

Beltrami 1929 *Il Pantheon rivendicato ad Adriano*, Rome.

Buddensieg, T. 1971 'Criticism and Praise of the Pantheon in the Middle Ages and the Renaissance', *Classical Influences on European Culture AD 500–1500*, con. Cambridge 1969, ed. R.R. Bolgar, Cambridge, 259–67.

Coarelli, F. 1983 'Il Pantheon, l'apoteosi di Augusto e l'apoteosi di Romolo', *AnalRom*, X, 41–6.

Colini, A.M. and Gismondi, I. 1927 'Contributi allo studio del Pantheon', *BComm*, LIV, 67–92.

Cozzo, G. 1929 'Un primitivo atrio meridionale del Pantheon ed una crisi statica dell'edifici rivelata da nuove indagini', *BolldA*, VII, 291–309.

Cozzo 1970 S.GA.

Cresy and Taylor 1821 S.GB.

Davies, P., Hemsoll, D. and Wilson Jones, M. 1987 'The Pantheon, Triumph of Rome or Triumph of Compromise?', *Art History*, X, 133–53.

De Angelis d'Ossat, G. 1930 'Roccie adoperate nella cupola del Pantheon', *Atti della Pontificia accademia della scienze dei nuovi lincei*, LXXXIII, 211–15.

De Angelis d'Ossat 1982 S.GA.

De Blaauw, S. 1994 'Das Pantheon als christlicher Tempel', *Boreas*, XVII, 13–26.

Desgodets 1682 S.GB, chapter 1.

Donelly, J.P. 1986 'To Close a Giant's Eye: The Pantheon 1591', *Archivium historiae pontificiae*, XXIV, 377–84.

Esposito, F. and Michetti, A. 1996 'Il Pantheon: Teoria e tecnica della *commodulatio*', *Disegnare: Rivista semestrale del Dipartimento di rappresentazione e rilievo, Università degli studi di Roma La Sapienza*, XIII, 69–80.

Fontana, C. 1694 *Il Tempio Vaticano e sua origine*, VII, 451–74.

Geertman, H. 1980 'Aedificium Celeberrimum: Studio sulla geometria del Pantheon', *BABesch*, XL, 203–29.

Godfrey, P. and Hemsoll, D. 1986 'The Pantheon: Temple or Rotunda?', *Pagan Gods and Shrines of the Roman Empire*, ed. M. Henig and A. King, 195–209.

Gruben, D. and Gruben, T. 1997 'Die Tür des Pantheon', *RM*, CIV, 3–74.

Guey, I. 1936 'Devrait-on dire: Le Pantheon de Septime Sévère?', *MEFRA*, LIII, 198–249.

Haselberger, L. 1994 'Ein Giebelriss der Vorhalle des Pantheon: Die Werkrisse vor dem Augustusmausoleum', *RM*, CI, 279–308.

Heilmeyer 1975 S.1.

Hirt, A. 1791 *Osservazioni istorico-architettoniche sopra il Pantheon*, Rome.

Lanciani, R. 1897 S.GA, 476–88.

Loerke, W.C. 1982 'Georges Chédanne and the Pantheon: A Beaux-Arts Contribution to the History of Roman Architecture', *Modulus: University of Virginia School of Architecture Review*, 40–55.

Loerke 1990 'A Rereading of the Interior Elevation of Hadrian's Rotunda', *JSAH*, XLIX, 22–43.

MacDonald 1982–6 S.GA, esp. I, chapter 5, 94–121.

McEwen, I.K. 1993 'Hadrian's Rhetoric, I: The Pantheon', *Res: Anthropology and Aesthetics*, XXIV, 55–66.

Marder, T.A. 1989 'Bernini and Alexander VII: Criticism and Praise of the Pantheon in the Seventeenth Century', *ArtBull*, LXXI, 628–45.

Marder 1991 'Alexander VII, Bernini and the Urban Setting of the Pantheon in the Seventeenth Century', *JSAH*, L, 273–92.

Mark, R. 1990 *Light, Wind, and Structure*, Cambridge, Mass., 59–67.

Mark, R. and Hutchinson, P. 1986 'On the Structure of the Roman Pantheon', *ArtBull*, LXVIII, 22–34.

Martines, G. 1989 'Argomenti di geometria antica a proposito della cupola del Pantheon', *QuadIStA*, XIII, 3–10.

Oudet, J.-F. 1992 'Le Panthéon de Rome à la lumière de l'equinoxe', *Readings in Archeoastronomy* (con. Warsaw 1990), 25–52.

Pasquali, S. 1996 *Il Pantheon: Architettura e antiquaria nel Settecento a Roma*, Modena.

Pelletti, M. 1989 'Note al rilievo del Pantheon', *QuadIStA*, XIII, 10–18.

Pelliccioni 1986 S.4C, 15–22.

Richter, O. 1893 'Das Pantheon', *AA*, 1–5.

Rottländer 1996b S.4A, 31–60.

Saalman, H. 1988 'The Pantheon Coffers: Pattern and Number', *Architectura*, XVIII, 121–2.

Sanpaolesi, P. 1971 'Strutture a cupola autoportanti', *Palladio*, XXI, 3–64, esp. 11–14.

Scaglia, G. 1995 'Eleven Facsimile Drawings of the Pantheon's Vestibule and the Interior in Relation to the Codex Escurialensis and Giuliano da Sangallo's Libro Drawings', *Architectura*, XXV, 9–28.

Scaife, S.H.O. 1953 'The Origin of some Pantheon Columns', *JRS*, XLIII, 37.

Simpson, C.J. 1997 'The Northern Orientation of Agrippa's Pantheon: Additional Considerations', *L'antiquité classique*, LXVI, 169–76.

Sperling, G. 1998 'The "Quadrivium" in the Pantheon of Rome', AA.VV. 1998 [S.5A], 127–42.

Terenzio, A. 1932 'La restauration du Panthéon de Rome', *Museion*, VI, 52–7.

Thomas, E. 1997 'The Architectural History of the Pantheon in Rome from Agrippa to Septimius Severus via Hadrian', *Hephaistos*, XV, 163–86.

Venuti, R. 1803 *Accurata e succinta descrizione topografica delle antichità di Roma* (1st ed. 1763), part II, 114–53.

Will, E. 1951 'Dodekathéon et Panthéon', *BCH*, LXXV/2, 233–46.

Williams, K. 1997 'Il Pantheon e la creazione dell'universo', *Lettera matematica pristem*, XXIV, 4–9.

Zeigler, K. 1949 'Pantheion', *RE*, XVIII, 697–727.

Ziolkowski, A. 1994 'Was Agrippa's Pantheon the Temple of Mars *in campo*?', *PBSR*, LXII, 261–77.

Ziolkowski 1998 'Pantheon', in Steinby ed. 1993– [S.GA], IV, 54–61.

S.9C   PROGRAMME AND PATRONAGE

Birley, A.R. 1997 *Hadrian: The Restless Emperor*, New York and London.

Boatwright, M.T. 1987 *Hadrian and the City of Rome*, Princeton.

Brown, F.E. 1964 'Hadrianic Architecture', *Essays in Memory of Karl Lehmann*, New York, 55–8.

Henderson, B.W. 1923 *The Life and Principate of the Emperor Hadrian*, London.

Kähler, H. 1950 *Hadrian und seine Villa bei Tivoli*, Berlin.

Roddaz, J.-M. 1984 *Marcus Agrippa = BEFAR*, CCLIII.

Shipley, F.W. 1933 *Agrippa's Building Activities in Rome*, St Louis.

Stambaugh, J.E. 1978 'The Functions of Roman Temples', *ANRW*, II 16.2, 544–608.

Stierlin, H. 1984 *Hadrien et l'architecture romaine*, Paris.

Strong, D.E. 1953 'Late Hadrianic Architectural Ornament in Rome', *PBSR*, XXI, 118–51.

Tortorici, E. 1990 'L'attività edilizia de Agrippa a Roma', *Il bimillenario di Agrippa*, Genoa, 19–55.

Yourcenar, M. 1988 *Memorie di Adriano*, with commentary by L.S. Mazzolani (1st French ed. 1951).

S.9D   MONS CLAUDIANUS QUARRIES

Brown, V.M. and Harrell, J.A. 1996 'Topographical and Petrological Survey of Roman Quarries in the Eastern Desert of Egypt', AA.VV. 1996 [S.7F], 221–34.

Bülow-Jacobsen, A. 1988 'Mons Claudianus: Roman Granite Quarry and Station on the Road to the Red Sea', *Acta Hyperborea*, I, 159–65.

Klein, M.J. 1988 *Untersuchungen zu den kaiserlichen Steinbrüchen an Mons Porphyrites und Mons Claudianus in der östlichen Wüste Ägyptens*, Bonn.

Klemm, R. and Klemm, D. 1993 *Steine und Steinbrüche im Alten Ägypten*, Berlin, 305–53 for Aswan, 395–408 for Mons Claudianus.

Kraus, T. and Röder, J. 1961 'Voruntersuchungen am Mons Claudianus im März 1961', *JdI*, LXXVII, 693–745.

Meredith, D. 1952–3 'Roman Remains in the Eastern Desert of Egypt', *JEA*, XXXVIII, 94–111.

Peacock, D.P.S. 1993 '*Mons Claudianus* and the Problem of the "Granito del foro"', AA.VV. 1993 [S.7F], 49–69.

Peacock *et al.* 1994 '*Mons Claudianus* and the Problem of the "granito del foro": A Geological and Geochemical Approach', *Antiquity*, LXVIII, 209–30.

Peacock, D.P.S. and Maxfield, V.A. 1997 *Mons Claudianus 1987–1993, I: Topography and Quarries*, Cairo.

Peña 1989 S.7F.

Röder, J., Kraus, T. and Muller-Wiener, W. 1967 '*Mons Claudianus – Mons Porphyrites*, Bericht über dei zweite Forschungsreise 1964', *Mitteilungen des Deutschen Archäologischen Instituts, Abteilung Kairo*, XXII, 108–205.

Sidebotham, S., Zitterkopf, R.E. and Riley, J.A. 1991 'Survey of the 'Abu Sha'ar-Nile Road', *AJA*, XCV, 571–622.

INDEX

Maison Carrée   29, 55, 61, 65–8, 71–3, 120, 122, 139, 214, 222, **3.28–31**
Noah's Ark   83
Nocera Superiore (NUCERA ALFATERNA), S. Maria Maggiore 218, 233 n. 33
Nonius Datus   11
numerology   41–3, 82–3, 183

obelisk, lifting   172
   Vatican   172, **p. 158**
Octavian   34–5; *cf.* Augustus
Olympia, Philippieion   222
Olympieion *see* Athens
Onians, John   110
optical alignments   100–01
optical refinements   43, 58–9, 127, 184
opus sectile   90, 96–8, **5.1, 5.9, 5.22**
Orange (ARAUSIO) arch   122, **6.27**
orders   5–6, 109–12, 114–21, 146
   the canonic five   5, 109–10
   choice of   44, 109–11
   distribution *see* column design, rhythm
   giant   46, 117
   lack of vertical alignment   116–19, 191–4
   mixed   44, 111–14, **2.8, 4.17, 6.2–7**; *cf.* **3.14**
   proportion   5–6, 120–21, 143–8
   superimposition   114–19
   see also Corinthian; Composite; Doric; Ionic; Tuscan
orientation (vis-à-vis exterior/interior)   74
Ostia
   Arch of Caracalla, capital   **7.19**
   College of the Augustales   55
   Forum Baths   60, **3.18**
   Forum of the Corporations, shaft   **6.36**
   'House of Cupid and Psyche'   **5.1**
   temple model   61–2, **3.9**
   'Pantheon'   79, 216

Packer, James   162
Paestum (POSIDONIA)
   Doric-Corinthian temple   112, 122
   Temple of Hera   13–14, **0.22**
Palestrina (PRAENESTE), Apsidal building   222
Palladio, Andrea   189, 200, 203, 239 n. 48
Palmyra
   Diocletian's principia   62, **3.22**
   temple-tomb   117
Pannini, Gian Paolo   190
Pantheon   5, 22, 177–95, 199–212, 219, 223, **9.1–5, 9.7–21, 9.23–9, 10.1–12, 10.14–16, 10.19–20**
   Agrippa's building   36, 180–82, 201
   antae of the portico   203–4, 206, **10.7–9**
   attribution   22, 192–3, 202, 206, 212
   background to commission   177–82, 210–11
   base (column)   **7.26**
   brickstamps   180, 201, **9.5**
   colour   194–5, 208
   criticism   187–8, 191–2, 199–203
   design of exterior   199–206
   design of interior   193–5
   Domitian's building   182
   excavations of 1890s   180, 201
   excavations of 1990s   182
   geometry   5, 93, 100, 102–3, 184–5, **9.11–12**

illumination   183
initial design   204–9, 211–12, **10.12**
inscriptions   177, 200
interior elevation   186, **9.25**
junction of rotunda and portico   203, **10.1, 10.5**
marble display   195, 211
metrology   72, 219, 223
modified design (exterior)   203–5, **10.12**
monolithic construction   209
name   178–80, 190
oculus   183, 187
order   204, 208, **7.24, 9.2**
proportions   5, 76, 100, 102–3, 184–6, 208–9, 223, **0.10, 5.27, 9.16**
purpose   178–80, 182–3, 190, 210–11
roof tiles, recycled   152
site   178–82, 190, **9.4**
structure   184, 186–7, 191, 201, 203
supply of columns   208–9, 212
symbolism   182–5, 209, 211
template drawing for portico   206–7, **10.14–15**
'transitional block'   203–4
weight of blocks   209
papyrus   50, 52, 210
parchment   50, 52
Pappus   43, **2.14**
Parthenon *see* Athens
Paulin, Edmond   **1.1**
pediment, setting out   29–30, 206–7, **3.16, 10.14**
Penrose, Francis   127–8
Penteli, quarries (Greece)   210–11, **10.18**
Pergamon   153
   Asklepieion   60, **3.19**
   Gymnasium   223
   Stoa of Athena   112
   Temple of Trajan   223
   Temple of Zeus–Asklepios   82
Pergamon environs, Kozak Dag quarries   211
Perge   155
   Agora portico   223
Perrault, Claude   6, **0.5**
Perugia, marble plan   51, **3.5**
Peruzzi, Baldassare   6, 9, 242 nn. 36, 55, **0.16**
Petra   111, 153
   'El Deir'   111, **6.2**
   'Kasr el Bint'   116
   'Khasneh' (El)   **6.1**
   'Palace Tomb'   112, 117–19, **6.15**
Petra environs, Khirbet et-Tannur   111
Petronius   83
Philae, Augustan temple   112, 222, **6.7**
Piranesi, Giovanbattista   190
Pisa, capital from cathedral   152, **7.23**
Plato   10, 41, 43, 90; *cf.* 58
Platonic solids   41, **2.13**
Pliny the Elder   20, 35, 82–3, 182, 190, 210, 241 n. 9
Pliny the Younger   25
polychromy   124, 194–5, 208, **5.1**
polygons, contigous   43, **2.14**
Polykleitos   41
Pompeii
   basilica   111, 114, **2.18**
   Central Baths, column shaft
   'Garland Tomb'   112

ILLUSTRATION CREDITS

FREQUENTLY USED SOURCES

Author: All illustrations other than those listed below.
J. Burge: **9.28**, **9.29**, **10.18**, **10.19**.

DAI, Rome: **3.8**: neg. 70.1341; **4.8**: neg. 76.2817; **4.12a**: neg. 57.1201; **4.13**: neg. 59.128; **4.15**: neg. 64.1472; **4.16**: neg. 64.225; **5.14**: neg. 67.643; **5.15**: neg. 59.1405; **5.21**: 63.342 (Musée du Bardo inv. no. 2751); **6.4**: neg. 72.3501; **6.5**: neg. 69.1204; **6.18**: transparency; **6.23**: neg. 61.2297; **7.9**: neg. 72.655; **7.10**: neg. 58.45; **7.13a**: neg. 63.1556; **7.13b**: neg. 63.1564; **7.21**: neg. 41.2416; **8.16**: neg. 81.2857.

De Fine Licht 1968 [S.9A]: **9.3**: figs 98 and 105; **9.5**: fig. 198; **9.7**: fig. 193; **9.15**: fig. 99.

DeLaine 1997 [S.GA]: **0.19**: fig. 38; **5.5**: figs 32, 34; **6.16**: fig. 39.

École Nationale Supérieure des Beaux Arts, Paris: **0.1**; **1.1**; **1.2**.

American Academy in Rome, Fototecca Unione: **2.9**: neg. 5585; **7.14**: 3596F; **9.17**; **10.3**.

MacDonald 1982 [S.GA]: **1.4**: fig. 40; **1.7**: fig. 59; **3.6**: fig. 128; **9.14**: fig. 103; **9.16**: fig. 106.

Serlio [S.GA]: **0.4**: IV, f. 3; **0.15b**: IV, f. 4; **6.12**: III, fol. 63; **7.27a**: IV, f. 45; **10.6a**: III, f. 3.

Ward Perkins 1981 [S.GA]: **0.18**: fig. 65; **1.8a**: fig. 59; **2.4**: fig. 8 (drg by Sheila Gibson); **3.11**: fig. 209 (drg by Sheila Gibson).

REMAINING ILLUSTRATIONS, SEQUENTIALLY

Fig. on p. vi: Author with P. Siwek.

0.3a: Kähler 1942 [cited ch. VI, n. 43], Abb. 48; **0.3b**: C. Hülsen, *Il libro di Giuliano da Sangallo: Codice Vaticano Barberiniano Latino 4424* (Leipzig 1910), f. 41r.; **0.5**: Perrault 1683 [S.6A], pl. 1; **0.6**: Desgodets 1682 [S.GB], 123; **0.7**: Hambidge 1924 [cited Intro., n. 9], fig. b; **0.8**: Gardner 1925 [cited Intro., n. 15], pl. 1; **0.9**: F. Blondel 1698 [cited Intro., n. 18], v, 4, 9, fig. on p. 752; **0.10a**: Texier 1934 [S.5A], fig. 71; **0.10b**: Geertman 1980 [S.9B], fig.6; **0.12**: Claridge 1983 [S.3B]; **0.14**: Claridge 1983 [S.3B], fig. 12; **0.15a**: Alberti 1988 [S.GA], 187; **fig. on p. 16a**: Author with K. Hankins; **fig. on p. 16b**: Author with G. Midgett.

1.3: Codex Magliabechiano, II, 1. 141, f. 27v, detail; **1.6**: James Packer; **1.8b**: Sear 1989 [S.GA], fig. 109 (drg by J. DeLaine); **1.9**: Louvre, museum neg.; **1.10**: Louvre, museum neg.; **1.11**: Capitoline Museums, inv. 212, museum neg.; **1.12**: Capitoline Museums, inv. 208, museum neg.; **1.13**: Adam 1989 [S.GA], fig. 52; **1.14**: Adam 1989 [S.GA], fig. 90; **1.16**: Texier 1934 [S.5A], fig. 66.

2.1: *Dipinti murali di Pompei*, cat., Naples, 1888, pl. IX (Fouilles de 1828, drg by V. Loria); **2.6**: G. Carettoni, *Das Haus des Augustus auf dem Palatin* (Mainz 1983), Abb. 10; **2.7**: DAI, Athens, neg. 80.4198; **2.8**: Sear 1989 [S.GA], fig. 118 (drg by J. DeLaine); **2.10**: Author after Hansen 1991 [cited ch. III, n. 54], fig. 11; **2.11**: Tölle-Kastenbein 1994 [S.7E], pl. 17; **2.13**: Author, after R. Lawlor, *Sacred Geometry: Philosophy and Practice* (London 1982), fig. on p. 97; **2.15**: G.P. Bellori, *Descrizzione delle quattro immagini dipinte da Raffaele d'Urbino nelle camere del Palazzo Apostolico Vaticano* (Rome 1695); **2.16**: R. Fréart de Chambray, *Parallèle de l'architecture antique avec la moderne* (Paris 1650), 63; **2.17a**: K. Ohr, 'Die Form der Basilika bei Vitruv', *BJb* 175 (1975), 113–27, fig. 4; **2.17b**: Morgan 1914 [S.2A], 135; **2.18**: Ohr 1991 [cited ch. II, n. 54], Taf. 61.

3.2: Petrie Museum, University College, London; **3.3**: De Spagnolis 1984 [S.3B], fold-out; **3.4a**: MacDonald 1986 [S.GA], fig. 119; **3.4b**: von Hesberg [S.3B], fig. 6; **3.5**: Von Hesberg 1984 [S.3B], fig.3; **3.7**: after Coarelli 1995 [S.3B]; **3.9**: after Pensabene 1997 [S.3B], fig. 1; **3.10**: Will 1985 [S.3B], fig. 4; **3.12**: Koenigs 1984 [S.3B], Abb.1; **3.13**: Haselberger 1991 [S.3B], fig. 6; **3.16**: Kalayan 1969 [S.3B], fig. 1; **3.17**: Author after Kalayan 1971 [S.3B], fig. 6; **3.18**: Sear 1989, fig. 75 (drg by J. DeLaine); **3.19**: adapted from Hoffman 1984 [cited ch. III, n. 43], Abb. 3; **3.21**: Humphrey 1986 [cited ch. III, n. 46], fig. 54; **3.22**: Gawlikowski 1985 [cited ch. III, n. 49], figs 2 and 3; **3.23**: Hallier 1989 [S.2A], fig. 18; **3.24**: MacDonald 1986 [S.GA], fig. 57; **3.25**: D. Mertens; **3.26**: Author after Adam 1996 [cited ch. III, n. 56], figs 30 and 65; **3.27**: Adam 1996 [cited ch. III, n. 56], figs 42 and 66; **3.28**: Amy and Gros 1979 [S.7E], pl. 18; **3.29**: adapted from Amy and Gros 1979 [S.7E], figs 32, 35; **3.30**: adapted from Amy and Gros 1979 [S.7E], figs 36, 39; **3.31**: Musée Archeologique, Nimes.

4.3: Ioppolo 1967 [S.4A]; **4.4**: Colvin 1991 [S.4B], fig. 44; **4.5**: Colvin 1991 [S.4B], fig. 44; **4.6**: Colvin 1991 [S.4B], figs 38 and 40; **4.9**: Rasch 1984 [S.4C], Taf. 84 and 85; **4.10**: Rasch 1993 [S.4C], Taf. 88b and 87b; **4.11**: Author and S. Lardonis; **4.12b**: amended version of Colvin 1991 [S.4B], fig. 106 (drg E. Impey); **4.14**: F. Rakob; **4.18**: adapted from Rolland 1969 [S.4D], figs. 7, 9, 12 and 19.

5.7: British Museum inv. nos 15285 and 100041, museum neg.; **5.9**: Guidobaldi 1985 [cited ch. V, n. 23], fig. 5; **5.12a**: Author, after De Fine Licht 1990, Abb. 33 and 34; **5.12b**: Author, after plan supplied by Lucos Cozza; **5.16**: F. Rakob [cf. E. Hansen, *La Piazza d'Oro e la sua cupola. AnalRom*, supp. 1 (Copenhagen, 1960), 51–9, folding plate]; **5.17**: F. Rakob; **5.18**: Jacobson 1986 [S.5B], figs 11 and 12; **5.19a**: Ueblacker 1985 [S.4C], Beil. 19; **5.20**: adapted from Gullini 1968, figs 38 and 39; **5.22**: Guidobaldi 1985 [cited ch. V, n. 23], fig. 8; **5.23**: Author with G. Rottinghaus; **5.27**: Esposito and Michetti 1996 [S.9B], fig. 19; **5.29**: Author (adapted from Geertman 1989 and 1993 [S.5B]).

6.6: Will and Larché 1991 [cited ch. VI, n. 27], fig. 100; **6.7**: Borchardt 1903 [S.7E], Taf. 5; **6.10**: F. Zevi, *Pompei* (Naples 1992), fig.

on p. 57; **6.11**: adapted from A. Barbet, *La Peinture murale romaine: les styles décoratifs pompéiens* (Paris 1985), fig. 2 (drawn by T. Adam); **6.13**: Kähler 1942 [cited ch. VI, n. 43], Abb.50; **6.14**: Kähler 1942 [cited ch. VI, n. 43], Abb. 64; **6.15**: Viscogliosi 1996 [S.7E], fig. 190; **6.21**: Rasch 1984 [S.4C], Taf. 78; **6.22**: Author with J. Ying; **6.25**: Author and T. Semeraro on base by Cooperativa Modus; **6.26b**: Brilliant 1967 [cited ch. VI, n. 64], pl. II; **6.27**: Amy *et al.* 1962 [cited ch. VI, n. 67], pl. 4 and 42; **6.28**: Stevens 1921 [S.6B], fig. 15; **6.29**: Haselberger 1991 [S.3], fig. 5; **6.31**: Hueber 1998 [S.3B], fig. 9; **6.33**: Nobiloni 1997 [cited ch. VI, n. 83], fig. 72 (from A. Ronca, *Modo e regola di fare le colonne a Spira* (Rome, 1630).

7.3a: Lawrence 1993 [S.GC], fig. 203; **7.3b**: A. Mallwitz 1962, 'Cella und Adyton des Apollontempels in Bassai', *AM*, LXXVII (1962): 140–71, Abb. 2; **7.4**: Cooper 1996 [S.7A], IV, pl. 49; **7.5**: Codex *Magliabechiano* f. 33v; **7.6**: Homolle 1916, fig. 9; **7.7**: P. Orsi and F.S. Cavallari, 'Megara Hyblaea, Storia, Topografia, Necropoli e Anathemata', *Monumenti antichi* 1 (1890), 689–950, Tav. II bis; **7.8**: Viscogliosi 1996, fig. 188; **7.12**: Soprintendenza Archeologica di Roma negs 4099 and 4100; **7.15**: Gros 1976 [S.7A], pl. 58; **7.19a**: Bauer 1972 [S.7A]; **7.19b**: Villa 1988 [S.7A]; **7.19d**: Tomasello 1983 [S.7C]; **7.19e**: Pensabene 1973 [S.7C]; **7.19f**: C. Strube, *Baudekoration in Nordsyrischen Kalksteinmassiv* (Mainz 1993), Taf. 80; **7.22a**: Capitoline Museums inv. no. 2900, neg. A/4541; **7.22b**: Capitoline Museums inv. no. 1241, neg. d/9627; **7.22c**: Capitoline Museums inv. no. 2215, neg. Author; **7.22d**: Capitoline Museums inv. no. 2854, neg. Author; **7.23**: Museo dell'Opera del Duomo, Pisa; neg. Soprintendenza 136193; **7.24**: Author and C. Simonis; **7.29**: Cun-

cliffe & Davenport 1985 [S.7E], I, fig. 11; **7.30**: A. Machatschek, 'Die Grabtempel von Dösene im Rauhen Kilikien', *Mélanges Mansel* (Ankara, 1974), 251–264, fig. 53; **7.31**: A. Claridge; **fig. on p. 158**: coloured print after Giovanni Guerra and Natale Bonifacio da Sebenico (Fontana 1978, Introduction, Tav. 4).

8.2: Packer 1997 [S.8A], frontispiece; **8.4**: Author, after base supplied by James Packer; **8.5**: Packer 1997 [S.8A], folio 54; **8.12**: Author and J. Uresti after survey by Cooperativa Modus; **8.13**: Author and P. Musty after survey by Cooperativa Modus; **8.18**: P. Collart, J. Coupel, *L'Autel monumental de Baalbek* (Beirut 1951), pl. 62; **8.19**: Martines 1992 [S.9B], fig. 9 (drg by Cooperativa Modus).

9.1: National Gallery of Art, Washington, Samuel H. Kress Collection 1939.1.24; **9.4**: Coarelli 1983 [S.9B]; **9.6a**: Lauter 1986 [S.GC], Abb. 59a; **9.6b**: H.A. Thompson, *The Tholos of Athens and its Predecessors*, *Hesperia*, supp. 4 (Athens 1940), fig. 63; **9.8**: Beltrami 1898 [S.9B], figs XXV and XXXV; **9.10**: P. True; **9.12**: Pelletti 1989 [S.9B]; **9.18**: Codex *Saluzziano*, f. 80 (C. Maltese, *Francesco di Giorgio Martini. Trattati* (Milan 1967), I, Tav. 147); **9.19**: UA 874v (Bartoli 1914–1922 [S.GA], III, fig. 414); **9.20**: UA 164r (Bartoli 1914–1922 [S.GA], I, fig. 99; **9.21**: Fontana 1694 [S.9B], p. 467; **9.21b**: I. d'Ayala Valva; **9.22**: De Fine Licht 1990 [cited ch. V, n. 36], Abb. 57; **9.23**: Pelletti 1989 [S.9B], fig. 1.

10.4; Bibliotecca Hertziana, Rome, UPl. D34074; **10.6b**: Fontana 1694 [S.9B]; **10.6c**: Durm 1905 [S.GA], fig. 631; **10.14**: Haselberger 1994 [S.9B], Abb. 1; **10.15**: Haselberger 1994 [S.9B], Abb. 5 (after Leclére, 1813).